Ideas in Unexpected Places

Ideas in Unexpected Places

Reimagining Black Intellectual History

✦

Edited by Brandon R. Byrd,
Leslie M. Alexander,
and Russell Rickford

NORTHWESTERN UNIVERSITY PRESS
EVANSTON, ILLINOIS

Northwestern University Press
www.nupress.northwestern.edu

Printed in the United States of America

10 9 8 7 6 5 4 3 2 1

Library of Congress Cataloging-in-Publication Data

Names: Byrd, Brandon R., editor. | Alexander, Leslie M., editor. | Rickford, Russell John, editor.
Title: Ideas in unexpected places : reimagining Black intellectual history / edited by Brandon R. Byrd, Leslie M Alexander, and Russell Rickford.
Other titles: Reimagining Black intellectual history
Description: Evanston, Illinois : Northwestern University Press, 2022. | Includes index.
Identifiers: LCCN 2021061183 | ISBN 9780810144736 (paperback) | ISBN 9780810144743 (cloth) | ISBN 9780810144750 (ebook)
Subjects: LCSH: African Americans—Intellectual life. | Blacks—West Indies—Intellectual life.
Classification: LCC E185.89.I56 I34 2022 | DDC 305.896073—dc23/eng/20211215
LC record available at https://lccn.loc.gov/2021061183

To all the unrecognized Black thinkers whose ideas have helped construct a collective vision of liberation

CONTENTS

FOREWORD

Davarian L. Baldwin

Expanding the Boundaries of Intellectual History

Around 2001, I was doing what many young scholars just out of graduate school do: I was trying to convert an unwieldy dissertation into a book that someone besides my committee might want to read. In what became *Chicago's New Negroes* I was pushing hard to conceptualize the notion of a "marketplace intellectual life." I wanted to explore how and why Black migrants turned to the realm of urban consumer culture as a viable space for producing ideas and fostering political debate. But intellectual history remains generally committed to focusing on those who reserve a significant part of their "professional" life to the production of ideas and culture. So it was quite audacious to follow the path of actual migrants into the unexpected commercial realm to see how they both crafted and contested ideas about racial identity, class-consciousness, and national belonging. But because *Chicago's New Negroes* did not feature professionally trained academics or clergy, visual/literary artists, or at least concert musicians, how could it ever be considered an intellectual history?

I continued to push forward, despite the clear academic "side-eye," because I was guided by the standard historical axiom to "follow the sources." With a focus on Chicago's historic Black community, I peered into the four commercial areas of beauty culture, gospel music, filmmaking, and sport in the 1920s and 1930s. Pouring through the dynamic ephemera of pictures, advertisements, correspondence, films, song sheets, and editorials, I saw a powerful intersection between Black knowledge making and consumer culture. Everything I had been taught about traditional understandings or the legitimate study of intellectual history warned me to focus on the documented ideas and actions of academics, writers, clergy, political figures, and perhaps classically trained visual and performing artists. But a vibrant marketplace intellectual life jumped out at me that orbited around beauty culturist Madam C. J. Walker, independent filmmaker Oscar Micheaux, gospel blues musician Thomas Dorsey, and the sporting exploits of boxer Jack Johnson and baseball entrepreneur Andrew "Rube" Foster. Moreover, I couldn't deny a network of what I ultimately called "consumer patrons" that sponsored, challenged, and even reinterpreted the ideas and products of the above leading lights.[1]

For migrants that largely served as consumer patrons, the creation, circulation, and debate over hairstyles and moviegoing etiquette did not confirm the "freedom" of the so-called free market. My growing concern was to reconstruct a critical moment when Black migrants used the consumer marketplace to build collective identities, challenge community tradition, rally against racial injustice, and yes, even contest the dehumanizing effects of capitalism. I was fully inspired by examining how these subjects of history etched out spaces of leisure that could help them think through the possibilities of a better or at least different world. In order to fully capture this Chicago experience, I was unwittingly pushing at the boundaries of intellectual history.

This discovery of a Black marketplace intellectual life was exciting. So I sent my manuscript to the logical presses given the subject matter on Chicago. A well-known book series on the historical studies of urban America offered me a contract. However, in their comments the main series editor expressed serious reservations about my notion of a marketplace intellectual life:

> I don't see what differentiates an "intellectual" from anyone else who has ideas. . . . I think the issue really involves the concept of intellectual history . . . yes we must consider all the realms in which ideas are created. . . . But that doesn't mean that the people who develop these ideas are intellectuals. . . . I think Baldwin faces a difficult challenge in finding evidence that consumers really are intellectuals.

To be sure, I could have made some revisions and pulled back on the claim that everyday consumers can produce an intellectual life. I certainly agree with this editor that the simple act of creating an idea does not make one an intellectual. Perhaps the approach in *Chicago's New Negroes* calls for a shift away from the more rarefied concept of "intellectual history" to think about a "history of ideas." But I think this collection of essays, edited by Leslie M. Alexander, Brandon R. Byrd, and Russell Rickford, powerfully begs the question, What gets lost, or more importantly gets preserved, when we don't push at the boundaries of what constitutes intellectual history in its most formal sense?

The essays assembled here capture the underexamined lives of traditional Black intellectuals while also challenging the very limiting understandings of intellectuals as professionally trained and professionally focused individuals. These scholars allow us to consider the more dynamic realms in which ideas are produced. This collection shows us the fruits of expanding the boundaries of intellectual history to include marginal ideas or to even rethink the identity of an "intellectual" as provisional, as a concentrated moment in time instead of as a job, especially for the slave, domestic, dockworker, activist, or auntie without access to or interest in any sustained occupation of the classroom, the editorial page, or the pulpit. These authors remind me that to define an intellectual by training, employment, or even the vaunted idea of vocation also leaves unexamined the gatekeeping elitism and capitalist blind spot that the very notion of "professionally trained" leaves intact.

Importantly, *Ideas in Unexpected Places* points us toward reconstructing all of the amazing lifeworlds of knowledge production and knowledge producers that could never be constrained or even seen within traditional understandings of intellectual history. Although I remain less invested in naming who is or is not an intellectual, writing *Chicago's New Negroes* confirmed for me that we cannot leave the boundaries unchallenged. We must use these unconventional archives and modes of analysis to break open the academic boundaries around what gets captured under a limiting notion of "intellectual history." In doing so, we both democratize the field and recover the range of ways in which knowledge is produced.

Therefore, the concept of a marketplace intellectual life was more than an exercise in academic reinterpretation. For me it was personal. Where the series editor who reviewed my work saw a "difficult challenge in finding evidence" of intellectuals, I saw an abundance of everyday brilliance. Here I offer my own intellectual history to demonstrate how the very ideas I grappled with on the page were produced by witnessing a vibrant world of everyday people continually expanding the boundaries of intellectual life all around me in ways that speak directly to the aims of this collection.

A "Difficult Challenge"?

I grew up in Beloit, Wisconsin, a hardscrabble, small industrial town that included a tight core of Black factory workers, hustlers, Holy Ghost saints, and housekeepers, sitting right on the Illinois-Wisconsin border.

Within this Black community, driven primarily by heavy industry, one's class position or orientation toward life was not solely determined by occupation but largely shaped by the factory in which one worked. General Motors or Chrysler offered higher wages and status, while Frito-Lay and Hormel furnished more modest opportunities. In purely economic terms, these jobs represented a relatively similar class position. Yet an extremely diverse and contested world of local Blackness and belonging could be found in the cultural world of religion, civic associations, and nightlife. Underneath the smoke and soot, this factory life powered a vibrant Black public sphere of churches, jukes, associations, and taverns. Migrants cultivated social ties and clubs that sponsored fish fries, dances, and scholarships. At Juneteenth celebrations, for example, every stripe of Prince Hall Mason, Eastern Star, military veteran, pop-up barrel barbeque business, dance troupe, and church choir served in prideful attendance.

This Black public sphere was always more than an escape toward frivolity because it cultivated an undeniable "world away" from the dictates of factory life, a place to shake off the coveralls and stand upright no longer as anonymous industrial cogs but as deacons, church mothers, big timers, auxiliary secretaries, and stars of the show. Dusty work clothes transformed into elegant sequined gowns and mirror shined nob toes at Socialite Club fashion shows where the runway spilled out into the audience and onto the street.[2]

But I also saw in this Black public sphere deep thinking about the seemingly most visceral, everyday, fine-grain details of this local world. Were these the thoughts of "intellectuals"? I didn't really care. But I was committed to the idea that Black working-class people's collective and provisional thoughts about everyday life and struggles over the meanings of their consumer practices constitute the archive for an intellectual history. I witnessed vigorous intentionality and anxiousness over worship practices, clothing and hair styles, processional formation, drink etiquette, policy gambling "dream books," that were all . . . thoughtful.

All this is to say that I faced no "difficult challenge" finding ideas in these unexpected places.

The Marketplace of Ideas

The irony is that while scholars remain loath to acknowledge that consumers produce an intellectual life, capitalists continue to see profit in the "marketplace of ideas," with entrepreneurs being knighted "thought leaders" simply because they have achieved financial success. In *Chicago's New Negroes* I witnessed an equivalent convergence between ideas and industry, but not one overdetermined by the profit values of capital. In the

Chicago archive I saw migrants use the marketplace and the networks of commercial culture to make money, but to also think "somewhere else," and even to build the infrastructure for a world without capitalism. Will we let the mainstream thought leaders control our imagination about the possible ways ideas and industry can converge?

When I think back to the gauntlet thrown down by that series editor who challenged the idea of consumers producing an intellectual life, I am reminded that my personal Black intellectual history tells a different story. Those Black migrants from Mississippi who made lives in Beloit weren't just blank slates. No! They were the thought leaders that brought along their fight against Jim Crow, their designs on social life beyond the shop floor, their desires for both intimate and collective pleasure. They brought preexisting systems of meaning to their marketplace.

In expanding the boundaries of intellectual history, I am not suggesting that free markets equal freedom nor am I naïve about the dehumanizing impacts of mass consumer culture. But in the same way that we denounce the lie that the Internet radicalized Tahir Square or Ferguson or Baltimore or Flint, we testify today that digital and commercial tools are only as good as the people who were present. We can't forget the people who do unexpected things in unexpected places. We can't forget the people who saw Mike Brown's body languish in a Ferguson, Missouri, street in 2014. We can't forget the people who bore witness to the life and death of countless unarmed youth guilty of "noncompliance." We can't forget the people who said, "No more," picked up the Molotov and the smartphone and thought through a way to take the materials of received knowledge and reworked them into a new framework and new pathways to liberation. Because thinking through the possibility of another world is always within reach.

There is no question that the history of a marketplace intellectual life is confirmed in the present. Although my more senior colleagues couldn't make sense of this praxis, history has exposed their blindness. By contrast I find affirmation in the essays collected here. Not every writer in these pages eschews traditional understandings of intellectual history. But we all know that expanding the boundaries by lifting up suppressed voices, interrogating new archives, embracing new approaches, and instigating new conversations about Black intellectual history will collectively build the infrastructure for new possibilities.

For younger scholars, expanding our vision of how and where ideas are produced may seem like common sense. But sometimes it is important, as historians of ideas, to consider "the world before," the world in which, to paraphrase the great Michel-Rolph Trouillot, such notions like a marketplace intellectual life were "unthinkable." I remember when traditional, let alone alternative, visions of Black intellectual history were not embraced by the society of intellectual historians. The marketplace is certainly not a panacea for rethinking the parameters of intellectual history. But at the same time my engagement with a marketplace intellectual life can remind us that producing ideas differently or about different futures is always within reach, even for those without access or the desire to enter the ivory tower, church pulpit, labor meeting, writing workshop, or TEDx forum.

The following essays demonstrate that brilliance, intellect, and the profundity and blueprints of possibility grow within the living archives of our full range of everyday experiences, no matter where these wellsprings are found . . . even in unexpected places.

Notes

1. This notion of a "marketplace intellectual life" was guided by a core group of thinkers. C. L. R. James's 1950s notion of the "popular arts" in his *American Civilization* set the table for his explosive consideration of cricket as a fulcrum for an anticolonial consciousness in his landmark work *Beyond a Boundary*. In *Crisis of the Negro Intellectual*, Harold Cruse astutely confirmed my impulses when he suggested that the Harlem Renaissance offered a limited impact because it failed to build on the consumer interests of the masses. In short he argued that a "dull fusion of black bourgeois sentiments and leftwing ideology" got in the way of seeing the mass consumer marketplace as the site for a much broader intellectual and political model (64–65). Finally, Lawrence W. Levine's *Black Culture and Black Consciousness: Afro-American Folk Thought from Slavery to Freedom* (1978; New York: Oxford, 2007) offered arguably the most crystalized account for my thinking about the existence of ideas in unexpected places. In it, Levine observed, "Those who would restrict intellectual history to the educated, the intelligentsia, the elite, would do well to look carefully at the richness of expression, the sharpness of perception, the uninhibited imagination, the complex imagery that form . . . the mind of the black folk" (x).

2. My mother serves as a perfect embodiment of this thoughtful "world away." By day she toiled as one of few African Americans and even fewer women at a state-line factory where she endured racist slurs and gendered double standards and even dealt with dangerously sabotaged machines while still finding ways to take pride in her work rate. But when she threw off her work uniform, I witnessed an amazing storyteller. Her beautiful mathematical mind could anticipate all of the numerical options during intense rounds of spades. She read Ntozake Shange and Toni Morrison, went to Bob Marley concerts and Louis Farrakhan rallies adorned in Norma Kamali dresses and Paloma Picasso fragrances, before the easy reach of the Internet. All around me I witnessed Black people insert meaning into their consumption to make sense of their lives and to push forward firm political positions in ways that many times went directly against the branding intentions of advertisers.

As a member of the hip-hop generation, I can also remember supporting the record industry with my hard-earned cash, but at the same time I received a complex political education that ran counter to the intentions of the music labels. The album jackets of Public Enemy, KRS-One, X-Clan, and so on introduced me to organizations and social movements around the globe that may have never come to my attention in Beloit, Wisconsin.

ACKNOWLEDGMENTS

The volume editors would like to give warm thanks to the extraordinary group of scholars who contributed their work to this volume. Our dynamic intellectual engagement has not only enhanced this collection; it has also enriched our lives. We are grateful for the opportunity to be in community with you.

We would also like to thank the leadership and the members of the African American Intellectual History Society (AAIHS) for shedding light on Black intellectual history, a subject that has been neglected for far too long, and for providing the inspiration for this volume.

Along with the AAIHS community, we are grateful for the team at Northwestern University Press. In particular, we owe special thanks to Gianna Mosser and Trevor Perri for their faith in this volume and their hard work in ensuring its publication.

Last, but certainly not least, we would like to thank our friends, families, and loved ones for providing each of us with the support, encouragement, and love that we needed to bring this collection into fruition. We could not have done it without you!

Ideas in Unexpected Places

INTRODUCTION

Brandon R. Byrd, Leslie M. Alexander, and Russell Rickford

What does it mean and what has it meant to "do" Black intellectual history? How should we define "intellectual"? These questions among many others animated the second annual conference of the African American Intellectual History Society (AAIHS), a gathering that brought together hundreds of scholars from the United States, the Caribbean, and Europe in the spring of 2017. The richly varied answers generated by the conference left the editors of this volume convinced that the conference's animating questions deserved even more exploration. Building upon Davarian Baldwin's stimulating keynote address, we were determined to reconsider existing definitions of and assumptions about intellectual history by foregrounding Black actors and unearthing ideas and thinkers in what Baldwin called "unexpected places."

The resulting collection, *Ideas in Unexpected Places*, seeks to push the study of intellectual history, and especially Black intellectual history, in new directions by interrogating five themes: slavery and sexuality; abolitionism; Black internationalism; Black protest, politics, and power; and the intersections of the digital humanities and Black intellectual history.[1] The works addressing those themes draw from diverse methodologies and fields, including history, Africana studies, feminist theory, and literature. They examine the ideas and actions of self-defined and organic Black intellectuals across the world, from the eighteenth century to the present, providing critical new insights into the complexities and contours of Black thought.

As Baldwin's foreword suggests, this volume employs an expansive definition of "Black intellectual." While the volume does not neglect well-known, literate, and self-defined intellectuals such as Olaudah Equiano and W. E. B. Du Bois, its chapters also mine new and traditional archives for the voices of Black people who never escaped slavery, who lacked formal education, or who developed their ideas outside of the written text. Those organic intellectuals include enslaved people in the antebellum

US South, the settlers of Jonestown, Guyana, and the foot soldiers (and sometime theorists) of the civil rights and Black Power revolutions. They are men, women, and even children whose knowledge production has typically been placed beyond the conceptual and disciplinary boundaries of intellectual, even Black intellectual, history.[2]

Since the beginnings of the transatlantic trade in humans, enslaved Africans and their descendants played key roles in shaping all aspects of thought in the Americas, the Atlantic world, and beyond. They produced and transformed ideas about slavery, freedom, resistance, rights, and self-determination as they struggled to carve out spaces of survival, joy, belonging, and dignity within and across national and imperial boundaries. Creative methodologies can recover the voices of the people who left scant archival records, thus demonstrating the central place of Black thought and Black thinkers in the global histories that forged the modern world. In highlighting the histories of such people, *Ideas in Unexpected Places* encourages readers to reconsider sites of intellectual production and sources of inquiry into intellectual history.

Sources often associated with traditional intellectual history—books produced by professional publishers and US-based newspapers, for example—remain critical texts in this volume. But so are the first constitutions of Haiti, speeches delivered at Emancipation Day celebrations, testimonies given to the Freedmen's Bureau, lessons learned and taught at the Communiversity of Chicago, and the digital spaces claimed and crafted by Black people in the twenty-first century. Practices and activities matter, too. In fact, they matter just as much as words because, as this volume attests, distinctions between "activist" and "intellectual" or "thinker" and "doer" were often blurred by Black people who necessarily occupied both roles. Recognizing that truth, *Ideas in Unexpected Places* connects the everyday experiences of Black people to the production of their ideas. It shows the links between social movements and ideology and highlights how ideas shape political change. It reimagines Black intellectual history while encouraging scholars to do the same.

In part 1, "Intellectual Histories of Slavery's Sexualities," introduced by Thavolia Glymph, Shannon C. Eaves, Alexis Broderick, and Deirdre Cooper Owens show the centrality of sex and sexuality to the study of slavery and emancipation through their exploration of free and enslaved Black women's experiences, actions, and thought in the nineteenth-century US South. Slavery was not only a ruthless system of forced labor but also one of systematic sexual violence in which enslaved women experienced acutely the harm of medical experimentation, rape, incest, and familial separation. Building on recent work in Black women's intellectual history, the authors of this part not only affirm that the relationship among slavery, gender, and sexuality demands even more scholarly attention but also offer remarkable new insights into how enslaved Black women understood, experienced, and contested their enslavement.[3]

Together, the chapters by Eaves, Broderick, and Cooper Owens explore how Black women expressed their own understandings of femininity, womanhood, and sexuality while contesting their individual and collective, physical and affective, experiences of sexual violence, especially at the hands of white men, including enslavers, overseers, and physicians. During slavery and in its immediate aftermath, Black women insisted that freedom entailed an unequivocal right to bodily integrity, and they sought to repair the violence inflicted upon them during slavery. Such subversive ideas, which persisted well into the next century, are found in diverse sources ranging from narratives and interviews written by or conducted with formerly enslaved people to sworn statements about their children's paternity that Black women made to agents of the Freedmen's Bureau. As Cooper Owens argues, the recovery of Black women's experiences and intellectual histories demands greater attention to archival practice—to how scholars experience, think, and write about the documents that not only reveal the routine, nonconsensual handling of Black women's bodies but also give insights into their more intimate, interior lives.

Following Kellie Carter-Jackson's introduction to part 2, "Abolitionism and Black Intellectual History," Vincent Carretta, Marlene L. Daut, and Jeffrey R. Kerr-Ritchie explore the long intellectual history of abolitionism in the Americas. During the era of the American and French Revolutions, Black people's demands for freedom and the recognition of human equality came in the form of freedom petitions submitted to colonial, state, and national political bodies, freedom suits presented to local courts, and daring acts of escape, rebellion, and military service on behalf of nations and empires that promised them emancipation. Numerous Black writers, including Olaudah Equiano, the subject of Carretta's chapter, demonstrated their intellectual capacities while highlighting the pain and suffering that slavery and the slave trade produced.

In the same era that Equiano and other Black writers pioneered the genre of the slave narrative, enslaved people in Saint Domingue launched a monumental challenge to slavery and colonialism: the Haitian Revolution. As Daut demonstrates in her chapter, that revolution not only resulted in Haitian independence but also led to a historic national constitution that articulated a revolutionary anticolonial politics foundational to radical Black thought. In fact, the Haitian Revolution would provide a powerful example of Black self-liberation and self-determination for free and enslaved Black people throughout the Atlantic world. Black abolitionists and activists in North America were prominent among foreign observers who identified the Haitian Revolution as the first chapter in a hemispheric struggle for freedom. That struggle, initiated by the thought and actions of Haitians, included the 1833 passage of the British Abolition of Slavery Bill, an event whose enactment on August 1, 1834, became the cause of annual celebrations across Black North America. Kerr-Ritchie brings renewed attention to those celebrations and the international consciousness of Black thinkers in his chapter in this volume.

Introduced by Michael O. West, part 3, "Black Internationalism," further explores how Black internationalism served as an insurgent response to slavery, colonialism, and imperialism across time and place.[4] Soon after gaining its independence, Haiti became central to early Black nationalism, an intellectual tradition that prioritized Black political and economic self-determination, racial separatism, Black pride, and emigration.[5] The deep consideration of Haitian independence was a formative aspect of early nineteenth-century Black political thought, as Leslie M. Alexander demonstrates in her chapter. Across the nineteenth century, thousands of Black North Americans would also identify Haiti as a desirable site for resettlement. Others looked to Liberia as a refuge from slavery and oppression. As Jessica Millward shows, the project of Black nation building in the nineteenth-century Atlantic world was a political and intimate process. The idea and longing for family was inextricable from the era's various emigration and colonization movements as well as the internationalist thought on which they were built.

For Black activists and intellectuals, Haitian, Liberian, and Ethiopian independence assumed particular importance as models of Black self-determination and modernity amid the resurgence of white world supremacy in the late nineteenth and early twentieth centuries. Accordingly, the beginning of the US occupation of Haiti in 1915 caused great consternation for Black internationalists, including W. E. B. Du Bois. In his contribution to part 3, Brandon R. Byrd explores how Du Bois derived significant albeit overlooked lessons from the occupation and history of Haiti and applied those lessons to his monumental study of the United States' Reconstruction era, *Black Reconstruction in America: An Essay toward a History of the Part Which Black Folk Played in the Attempt to Reconstruct Democracy in America, 1860–1880.*

While Du Bois worked on that transformative and internationalist work of Black history, he also advanced Black thought and political culture through a series of Pan-African congresses that coincided with and encouraged major shifts in global Black politics and intellectual life.[6] During the first three decades of the twentieth century, hundreds of thousands of refugees fled from racial violence and poverty in the Jim Crow South with the hope of building better lives in the major cities of the US Northeast and Midwest. Thousands of migrants from the Caribbean, impacted by the economic dislocations of World War I, joined them. Together, these Black men, women, and children laid the foundations of the Harlem Renaissance or "New Negro Movement," a flowering of Black artistic expression, cultural production, and radical political thought. As African Americans such as Du Bois and Alain Locke provided platforms for Black political and cultural expression, Afro-Caribbean intellectuals, including Marcus Garvey, Amy Jacques Garvey, and Hubert Harrison, stimulated a resurgence of Pan-Africanism, the belief that people of African descent, wherever they live, share a common past, struggle, and destiny.[7]

These developments had an enduring effect explored by Russell Rickford in the final chapter of part 3. The Pan-African congresses brought US-based New Negro radicalism into conversation with African anticolonialism, Haitian *indiginisme*, and *négritude*, a philosophy of Black cultural pride and anticolonialism espoused by numerous Francophone intellectuals, including Martinican poet Aimé Cesaire, Senegalese theorist Leopold Senghor, and Martinican writer Paulette Nardal.[8] These political, intellectual, and cultural currents informed subsequent social movements throughout the African diaspora, including an effort by African American dissidents to forge radical ties with postcolonial Guyana. As Rickford demonstrates, that crusade helped provide ideological context for the notorious Jonestown tragedy, an incident that brought the small Caribbean country to the world's attention in 1978.

In part 4, "Black Protest, Politics, and Power," introduced by N. D. B. Connolly, William Sturkey, Richard D. Benson II, Quito Swan, and Charisse Burden-Stelly elaborate on the proliferation of Black protest thought in the late twentieth-century United States. In the years and decades after World War II, Black men and women drew on a language of citizenship and universal human rights and used various forms of media, from television to newspapers, in their struggle to dismantle white supremacy in the United States. Sturkey draws new attention to the pivotal role of youth—of ordinary schoolchildren in Mississippi—in that struggle for rights and freedom. As Burden-Stelly argues, the Black liberation struggle also remained internationalist in scope, particularly in the leftist tradition of what she theorizes as "radical Blackness." By the late 1960s and 1970s, the various strands of radical Black thought coalesced into the call and politics of Black Power. This intellectual and political expression of

Black pride, self-determination, and self-defense took form in a diverse range of institutional and organizational sites, from Pan-Africanist primary and secondary schools to the Black Panther Party for Self-Defense to the Communiversity of Chicago.[9] In his novel examination of the latter "training ground," Benson reexamines the praxis of Black educational self-determination and encourages further exploration of the many overlooked sites of intellectual production from which Black thinkers crafted Black Power into a global metalanguage of Black liberation. Offering remarkable new insights into those global dynamics of Black Power, Swan explores the unfamiliar history of the Niugini Black Power Group at the University of Papua New Guinea. His chapter reorients our view of Black intellectual history, turning from the Black Atlantic to the Black Pacific, which he theorizes as "an understudied region of historical migration, exchange and struggle on the part of African-descended people."

In many respects, Black Power advocates evinced the creativity that has been a central and enduring aspect of Black intellectual history.[10] To support the twin goals of study and struggle, those intellectuals created new institutions and demanded the recreation of existing ones, including US colleges and universities. They formed extracurricular reading groups and other critical sites of intellectual exchange while testing and expressing ideas from the pages of independent newspapers and political pamphlets or even the walls of buildings dotting city landscapes. In an era after the ostensible end of legal segregation in the United States and the collapse of formal European colonialism in Africa, Asia, and the Caribbean, Black thinkers inside and outside of the academy have continued to offer new sites and methods of intellectual production. Some Black intellectuals and media creators have been among the most creative and introspective digital humanists, using blogs, Twitter, listservs, Facebook, and Tumblr to explore and reflect on Black life in the past and the present or even imagine new worlds and possible Black futures.[11]

In part 5, "The Digital as Intellectual: Poetics and Possibilities," the final part of this volume, introduced by Marisa Parham, Alexis Pauline Gumbs, Christy Hyman, and Jessica Marie Johnson examine the possibilities and potential impacts of Black intellectual practice and production in the digital age. Reflecting on her story map of Moses Grandy's enslavement in the Great Dismal Swamp, Hyman demonstrates how modern geospatial technologies can help us conceptualize the mental and physical geographies of enslaved people and, in some ways, recreate their world as they knew it. Her chapter speaks to what Johnson identifies as insurgent possibilities of Black digital practice, which "curates narrative history, disrupts political claims of legitimacy, and witnesses multiple registers of violence." Along with Johnson, who writes not just as an observer of "insurgent digital humanistic thought" but as the creator of African Diaspora, Ph.D.,[12] Gumbs considers the implications of our current digital practices. Reflecting on their own scholarly practice as well as building on the work of queer Black feminists, Gumbs offers a "speculative documentary"—an Afrofuturist call for us to consider our present from the archive and perspective of the future made possible by our current thinking.

Together, these chapters affirm the persistent need to think creatively about intellectual history. While intellectual history is often associated with written publications and institutional structures such as universities, Black thought—particularly the subversive ideas emerging from the subaltern experiences and expressions of global Blackness—has and will continue to take many different forms. Its recovery and elucidation will require a multitude of methods. *Ideas in Unexpected Places* highlights the critical interventions of a range of established and emerging scholars who are offering fresh approaches to Black intellectual history and more expansive understandings of "intellectual," reconsidering the lives and thought of well-known thinkers, and exploring future areas of scholarly inquiry. It is not intended as the final or definitive comment on the diverse expressions and geographies of Black thought. Instead, it is designed to stimulate further scholarship on and, ultimately, new imaginings of Black intellectual history.

Notes

1. This volume also draws inspiration from the volume of essays produced from the first AAIHS conference. See Keisha N. Blain, Christopher Cameron, and Ashley D. Farmer, eds., *New Perspectives on the Black Intellectual Tradition* (Evanston, IL: Northwestern University Press, 2018). Other recent or forthcoming edited works on African American intellectual history include Jonathan Holloway and Ben Keppel, eds., *Black Scholars on the Line: Race, Social Science, and American Thought in the Twentieth Century* (Notre Dame, IN: University of Notre Dame Press, 2007); Mia Bay, Farah J. Griffin, Martha S. Jones, and Barbara D. Savage, eds., *Toward an Intellectual History of Black Women* (Chapel Hill: University of North Carolina Press, 2015); Adolph Reed Jr. and Kenneth W. Warren, eds., *Renewing African American Intellectual History: The Ideological and Material Foundations of African American Thought* (New York: Routledge, 2016); Brian D. Behnken, Gregory D. Smithers, and Simon Wendt, *Black Intellectual Thought in Modern America: A Historical Perspective* (Jackson: University Press of Mississippi, 2017); Sherrow O. Pinder, ed., *Black Political Thought: From David Walker to the Present* (New York: Cambridge University Press, 2020); Melvin L. Rogers and Jack Turner, eds., *African American Political Thought: A Collected History* (Chicago: University of Chicago Press, 2020); and Derrick Alridge and Cornelius Bynum, eds., *The Black Intellectual Tradition:*

African American Thought in the Twentieth Century (Urbana: University of Illinois Press, forthcoming).

2. For a recent reflection on the history and historiography of African American intellectual history as a field of academic inquiry, see Brandon R. Byrd, "The Rise of African American Intellectual History," *Modern Intellectual History* 18, no. 3 (September 2021): 833–64.

3. On Black women's intellectual history, see especially Bay et al., *Toward an Intellectual History of Black Women.*

4. On Black internationalism, see especially Michael O. West, William G. Martin, and Fanon Che Wilkins, eds., *From Toussaint to Tupac: The Black International since the Age of Revolution* (Chapel Hill: University of North Carolina Press, 2009); and Keisha N. Blain and Tiffany M. Gill, eds., *To Turn the Whole World Over: Black Women and Internationalism* (Urbana: University of Illinois Press, 2019).

5. This definition of Black nationalism is influenced by a number of works including Sterling Stuckey, *The Ideological Origins of Black Nationalism* (Boston: Beacon Press, 1972); E. U. Essien-Udom, *Black Nationalism: A Search for Identity in America* (Chicago: University of Chicago Press, 1962); John H. Bracey Jr., August Meier, and Elliott Rudwick, eds., *Free Blacks in America, 1800–1860* (Belmont, CA: Wadsworth, 1971); Wilson Jeremiah Moses, *The Golden Age of Black Nationalism* (New York: Oxford University Press, 1978); Leslie M. Alexander, *African or American? Black Identity and Political Activism in New York City, 1784–1861* (Urbana: University of Illinois Press, 2008); and Keisha N. Blain, *Set the World on Fire: Black Nationalist Women and the Global Struggle for Freedom* (Philadelphia: University of Pennsylvania Press, 2018).

6. Recent and forthcoming work on Du Bois includes Charisse Burden-Stelly and Gerald Horne, *W. E. B. Du Bois: A Life in American History* (Santa Barbara, CA: ABC-CLIO, 2019); and Chad L. Williams, *The Wounded World: W. E. B. Du Bois and World War I* (New York: Farrar, Straus and Giroux, forthcoming).

7. This definition of Pan-Africanism is particularly informed by Hakim Adi, *Pan-Africanism: A History* (London: Bloomsbury, 2018).

8. Foundational scholarship on this formative moment in global Black intellectual history includes T. Denean Sharpley-Whiting, *Negritude Women* (Minneapolis: University of Minnesota Press, 2002); and Davarian L. Baldwin and Minkah Makalani, eds., *Escape from New York: The New Negro Renaissance beyond Harlem* (Minneapolis: University of Minnesota Press, 2013).

9. Russell Rickford, *We Are an African People: Independent Education, Black Power, and the Radical Imagination* (New York: Oxford University Press, 2016).

10. For recent perspectives on the United States and global histories of Black Power, see especially Peniel E. Joseph, *Rethinking the Civil Rights–Black Power Era* (New York: Routledge, 2006); Peniel E. Joseph, *Waiting 'til the Midnight Hour: A Narrative History of Black Power in America* (New York: Henry Holt, 2006); Nico Slate, ed., *Black Power beyond Borders: The Global Dimensions of the Black Power Movement* (London: Palgrave Macmillan, 2012); Ashley D. Farmer, *Remaking Black Power: How Black Women Transformed an Era* (Chapel Hill: University of North Carolina Press, 2017); and Quito J. Swan, *Pauulu's Diaspora: Black Internationalism and Environmental Justice* (Gainesville: University Press of Florida, 2020).

11. Kim Gallon, "Making a Case for the Black Digital Humanities," in *Debates in the Digital Humanities*, ed. Lauren F. Klein and Matthew K. Gold (Minneapolis: University of Minnesota Press, 2016), 42–49; Jessica Marie Johnson and Mark Anthony Neal, eds., "Black Code Studies," special issue, *Black Scholar: Journal of Black Studies and Research* 47, no. 3 (Fall 2017); Jessica Marie Johnson, "Markup Bodies: Black [Life] Studies Slavery [Death] Studies at the Digital Crossroads," *Social Text* 36, no. 4 (137): 57–79; and Marlene L. Daut, "Haiti @ the Digital Crossroads: Archiving Black Sovereignty," *Sx/archipelagos*, July 11, 2019, http://smallaxe.net/sxarchipelagos/issue03/daut.html.

12. https://africandiasporaphd.com.

Part 1

✦

Intellectual Histories of Slavery's Sexualities

INTRODUCTION

Thavolia Glymph

During slavery, women resisted sexual violence, but they could not take white or black rapists to court; neither could their husbands or fathers. They could, however, be prosecuted for resisting their rapists as the well-known case of Celia in Missouri demonstrates. They could also be prosecuted for infanticide, the fate of a fourteen-year-old child in Missouri and twenty-eight-year-old Letty in Virginia. Under examination, Letty offered this justification for infanticide: "If the child had been one of her own colour, she would not have done *as she did*."[1] Enslaved women resisted sexual violence; they fought, hid, ran, sometimes murdered their assailants, and committed infanticide, and tried to protect themselves from painful medical interventions, but no legal path to justice was available to them until after emancipation.[2]

What would an intellectual history of this story look like? How might it contribute to our understanding of the sexual violence of slavery? How might it help us to better see the work enslaved and free black women engaged in to make sense of a world structured by law and custom to crush their ability and right to critique it? These are, if not the animating questions of the essays by Shannon C. Eaves, Alexis Broderick, and Deirdre Cooper Owens, their critical subtext. The methodological and analytical approaches these essays take differ, but each probes the questions above from the ground of intellectual history. Building on revisionist scholarship in slavery studies, they remind us of the ways in which the history of slavery is a history of the gross and profane exploitation of enslaved people and black women in particular. The essays also contribute to a growing body of scholarship that interrogates the archive of slavery—how it was constructed and might be reconstructed—and related questions of objectivity and subjectivity, white supremacy, and black rebellion.[3] They serve as a reminder of the barrenness of a field that neglects or discards the thoughts and ideas of people not typically seen as part of the intelligentsia.

The fact that sexual violence in the South was rife, an "open secret," meant that confrontation could not be avoided either by black or white Southerners. In "'The Greater Part of Slaveholders Are Licentious Men': Articulating a Culture of Rape and Exploitation in the Slave South," Shannon C. Eaves explores this confrontation and its "communal impact." It led, she writes, to the articulation of "shared cultural understandings of the South's rape culture" and a shared understanding of the instrumental role systemic rape and sexual exploitations played in "shaping the hierarchal framework of southern society." In response, Eaves argues, enslaved people developed a collective consciousness that helped them navigate the terrain of sexual violence.

Eaves focuses largely on the impact sexual violation of enslaved women had on enslaved men. To tell this story, she turns to ex-slave narratives published before or during the Civil War and oral testimony from the 1930s. Sexual violence is a prominent topic in these narratives.[4] The sexual violation of enslaved women was also one of the major themes invoked by abolitionists in support of emancipation and much of it echoed patriarchal notions even among black abolitionists. For example, as Eaves writes, Frederick Douglass, Henry Box Brown, and James Pennington, who had all experienced slavery, processed the sexual abuse of black women as a violation of their patriarchal duties and rights. It "attacked their sense of themselves as respectable, viral, protective, and authoritative leaders within the enslaved family and community," denying them "the same authority" as white men. Henry Bibb declared that he had "a right to his own wife and children." Henry Box Brown committed "to resist intimate relationships altogether." (This option, of course, was rarely available to enslaved men who typically had no more power than enslaved women to resist a slaveholder's power to decide with whom they lived and procreated.)

By contrast, Eaves argues, enslaved women developed "a mental survival guide on how to traverse the plantation" communicated "between mothers and daughters, fathers and sons, and the old and the young" across generations. It was such a guide communicated by her grandmother, Harriet Jacobs recalled, that gave her the tools to navigate the rape culture of the South. Black women used these tools as weapons in the struggle to ensure their safety and survival and that of future generations. They were the culmination of the intellectual work of enslaved people as they processed the South's rape culture. In the Works Progress Administration narratives, Eaves points out, formerly enslaved people recalled the struggle to navigate the violence of slavery's sexual terrain and their resistance. Many, like Fanny Berry famously, had fought back with physical force. Others recalled the physical and emotional toil sexual violence had on their lives. In the end, Eaves concludes that despite pervasive sexual exploitation of black women, enslaved men and women found sustenance in marriage and children. Family, she writes, prevented their "crumbling in the wake of sexual exploitation."

For Alexis Broderick, conversely, the crumbling of black families is the historical problem. "'If I Had My Justice': Freedwomen, the Freedmen's Bureau, and Paternity in the Postemancipation South" opens with the story of Peggy, tried for murdering her master for attempting to rape her; he was also her father. Like Celia, Peggy could make no claims to protection from rape under the law. During slavery, as Broderick writes, black women had "to be charged with murder in order to publicly expose the abuse of white men in positions of power." Even when they were tried for murdering their rapists or for infanticide, they could not testify on their own behalf. Instead, their voices were filtered through lawyers, judges, and physicians called to testify as to their sanity. No more. As free women, they made claims for child support, publicly exposing the men who had owned and raped them. In the process, they testified to the sexual violence they had experienced: the rapes, the incest, the violence that came with resistance, the intimidation.

In freedom enslaved women did more than speak up.[5] Broderick shows them mobilizing on their own behalf the logic of paternalism that had been used to justify their enslavement and sexual abuse against white men who had fathered their children. Slaveholders had maintained that slavery created one family, black and white. They were now called to account differently for the black members of these families. Framing their paternity cases in the language of justice, equity, and equal rights as well as material need, black women invoked legal concepts derived from civil codes pertaining to custody and bastardy law. They called on the state for justice, to do for them what it did for white women—to make children deemed illegitimate legitimate under the law. They thus "reimagined their relationship with law and American society." Turning to the law, they exposed the slaveholders' "fantasy" plantation family that had covered and disguised "the antagonistic relations of labor, torture, rape and incest," and posited them "instead as bonds of attachment, mutual responsibility, and familial love."[6] All knew the cover story was a sham never allowed to be adjudicated at law. The open secret was now visible not just to the eyes of the wives and children of former slaveholders but to the prying eyes of poor white Southerners and the Northern men of the Freedmen's Bureau called to adjudicate the claims of black women for child support.[7] The result, Broderick writes, was a postemancipation world that to ex-slaveholders appeared as a nightmarish "vision of a wrecked plantation family."

Assaults on the bodies of enslaved women, as Deirdre Cooper Owens reminds us in her essay "Hapticity and 'Soul Care': A Praxis for Understanding Bondwomen's History" also came in other forms and practices. Adapting the field of haptic studies to the study of slavery, sexuality, and medicine, Cooper Owens explores the meaning of touch, the haptic, in the sensory lives of enslaved women and in the emotional lives of scholars.[8] Within the field of the history of the senses, the history of slavery and tactility remains largely unexplored.[9] Cooper Owens's essay makes an important contribution to the literature and takes it in new directions. Cooper Owens understands touch as political, but her concern here is not so much what makes touch political or to explore particular cases of gynecological experimentation on enslaved women or their medical care more broadly, work she undertakes in her recent book.[10] While particular cases like that of Rhody and Nanny are important to her argument, her principal concern as indicated in the title "Hapticity and 'Soul Care'" is twofold: to think about how historians frame and study such cases and the emotional labor involved.

A haptic-centric framework of analysis, Cooper Owens argues, offers a useful methodological tool for understanding the power dynamics of slavery especially as they are imbedded in the history of medicine. She also sees haptic studies as a way to navigate the "hapticity of the archives," that is, a "praxis for assuming the emotional labor involved in rescuing forgotten narratives." "Haptic visuality" (generally understood as a kind of embodied spectatorship), she argues, permits the use of the "eye like an organ of touch" or a methodological tool for giving "voice" to the tactile experiences of enslaved women.

As Cooper Owens acknowledges, getting at the sensory lives of enslaved people is a difficult, if not nearly impossible, proposition. The archive does not provide answers to the questions that trouble her; indeed, it is terribly unhelpful. It is silent on how an enslaved woman who carried a dead fetus in her body for years felt, or her thoughts as the hands of white doctors examined her, pressing on and in her body. How then can historians "give voice to tactile experiences" of enslaved women? Cooper Owens sees the answer in the notion of "soul care." She proposes "soul care" as a new methodological approach for understanding the emotional and tactile lives of enslaved women. "Soul care," she writes, allows historians equipped with "cultural knowledge" to access resistant archives filled with "the violence of the archives" and their own "haptic dimensions."[11]

Collectively these essays advance our understanding of slavery and sexuality. Each in its own way draws upon and responds to Nell Painter's call for a cost accounting of slavery that recognizes that the "beating and raping of enslaved people was neither secret nor metaphorical" and had consequences for "an entire society." Each documents the impact sexual violence had on enslaved and formerly enslaved people, how they articulated its cost, and the intellectual work they did to save themselves—whether by the creation of a collective consciousness that served to educate black women on their vulnerability to sexual assault, insisting as "citizens" that justice be served on white men who violated black girls and women, suing for child support, or coming to the aid of women who could not protect themselves. In exploring the ways in which black women articulated their experience of sexual violence, the essays aim to penetrate what some scholars call "archival silences" in order to document the intellectual labor of enslaved and formerly enslaved women. They document the ways in which black women's testimony unraveled the "beautiful tableaux" of paternalism and one family black and white.[12] They show how that testimony, as it circulated within the slave community and was remembered decades later, formed the architecture of an archive of slavery's psychological damage.

The intellectual work of enslaved and formerly enslaved people was not indexed in the papers slaveholders left behind in archives or in the records of federal agencies such as those studied by the Freedmen and Southern Society Project. But the story of what enslaved people thought about sexual violence and how they fought it resides nonetheless in all such archives. The essays by Broderick, Cooper Owens, and Eaves plumb these sources to convey the depths of slavery's injuries. They make an important contribution to the growing field of black women's intellectual history.[13] If intellectual history is the history of "the ideas and symbols that people use to make sense of the world," these essays situate the intellectual labor of enslaved and formerly enslaved black women and the larger slave community squarely within the field.[14]

These essays also raise difficult questions that remain to be answered and which gesture toward different kinds of reckonings. Can existing analytical frameworks account for women like Lucy Bibb, who claimed that she "loved" her master with whom she had two children and seemed to believe that her white skin counted for something in the relationship. Was she also part of the wreckage? Were white men who sexually assaulted enslaved women more likely to be sexually violent with white women? What part of the "training" on black women did they carry back to their own hearths? Finally, near the beginning of this introduction I used the word "intelligentsia." I used it intentionally to raise a sticky question. The word has a long and difficult history and pedigree. Recognizing, as Raymond Williams noted many decades ago, that the "social tensions around the word [intellectual] are significant and complicated," how do these tensions affect the work of black intellectual history? How does the work of black intellectual history, its challenge to include the work of "ordinary" people, reflect or reorder these tensions?[15]

Notes

1. As quoted in Wilma King, "'Mad' Enough to Kill: Enslaved Women, Murder, and Southern Courts, *Journal of African American History* 92 (Winter 2007): 43. The italics are from King and not the original source. The court commuted Letty's sentence of death by hanging to sale outside the state of Virginia. Nelly was indicted for infanticide but spared the death sentence.

2. In the United States, the exceptions were in cases where the assailant was an enslaved man. For a perspective from the Caribbean, see Sasha Turner, *Contested Bodies: Pregnancy, Childrearing, and Slavery in Jamaica* (Philadelphia: University of Pennsylvania Press, 2017), 214–17.

3. Darlene Clark Hine, "Rape and the Inner Lives of Black Women in the Middle West," *Signs* 14 (Summer 1989): 912–20; and Deborah Gray White, *Ar'n't I a Woman? Female Slaves in the Plantation South* (New York: Oxford University Press, 1985). In addition to the field-defining work of Hine and White, see, e.g., Deirdre Cooper Owens, *Medical Bondage: Race, Gender and the Origins of American Gynecology* (Athens: University of Georgia Press, 2017); Daina Ramey Berry, *The Price for Their Pound of Flesh: The Value of the Enslaved from Womb to Grave, in the Building of a Nation* (New York: Beacon Press, 2016); and Stephanie M. H. Camp, *Closer to Freedom: Enslaved Women and Everyday Resistance in the Plantation South* (Chapel Hill: University of North Carolina Press, 2004). On the question of the archive as subject, see, e.g., Thavolia Glymph, "Black Women and Children in the Civil War: Archive Notes," in *Beyond Freedom: Disrupting the History of Emancipation*, ed. David W. Blight and Jim Downs (Athens: University of Georgia Press, 2017), 121–35; Nell Irvin Painter, *Southern History across the Color Line* (Chapel Hill: University of North Carolina Press, 2002), 6; and Marisa Fuentes, *Dispossessed Lives: Enslaved Women, Violence, and the Archive* (Philadelphia: University of Pennsylvania Press, 2016). For a recent statement on historians and objectivity, see Chris Cameron, "Black Intellectual History and the Long Struggle for Freedom," *Black Perspectives*, June 10, 2019.

4. See also Gregory D. Smithers, *Slave Breeding: Sex, Violence, and Memory in African-American History* (Gainesville: University Press of Florida), 108–10.

5. On this point, see also Hannah Rosen, *Terror in the Heart of Freedom: Citizenship, Sexual Violence, and the Meaning if Race in the Postemancipation South* (Chapel Hill: University of North Carolina Press, 2009).

6. Nell Irvin Painter describes this as "slavery's family romance." See "Soul Murder and Slavery: Toward a Fully Loaded Cost Accounting," in *U.S. History as Women's History: New Feminist Essays*, ed. Linda K. Kerber, Alice Kessler Harris, and Kathryn Kish Sklar (Chapel Hill: University of North Carolina Press, 1995), 146.

7. Diane Miller Sommerville, *Rape and Race in the Nineteenth Century* (Chapel Hill: University of North Carolina Press, 2004), 147–75. For an important exploration of the impact on white households, see King, "'Mad' Enough to Kill."

8. Haptic studies cover a broad field united by an interest in understanding the meaning of touch, or what is called the system of touch. Haptic scholars are interested, for example, in understanding how "affective" or loving touch differs from threatening or clinical touch; Adam Gopnik, "Feel Me: What the New Science of Touch Says about Ourselves," *New Yorker*, May 16, 2016, https://www.newyorker.com/magazine/2016/05/16/what-the-science-of-touch-says-about-us.

9. For an exception, see Mark M. Smith, "Getting in Touch with Slavery and Freedom," *Journal of American History* 95 (September 2008): 381–91. On sensory history and slavery more broadly, see Mark. M. Smith, *How Race Was Made: Slavery, Segregation, and the Senses* (Chapel Hill: University of North Carolina Press, 2008); and Mark M. Smith, *Listening to Nineteenth-Century America* (Chapel Hill: University of North Carolina Press, 2001).

10. Cooper Owens, *Medical Bondage*; see also Marie Jenkins Schwartz, *Birthing a Slave: Motherhood and Medicine in the Antebellum South* (Cambridge, MA: Harvard University Press, 2006).

11. On the violence of the archive, see Saidiya Hartman, "Venus in Two Acts," *Small Axe* 26 (June 2008): 1–14.

12. Painter, "Soul Murder and Slavery," quotes at 141, 146; Thavolia Glymph, *Out of the House of Bondage: The Transformation of the Plantation Household* (Cambridge: Cambridge University Press, 2008); and White, *Ar'n't I a Woman?*, 9, 90–118.

13. A recent important work is Mia E. Bay et al., eds., *Toward an Intellectual History of Black Women* (Chapel Hill: University of North Carolina Press, 2005). This collection, however, does not directly address black women and slavery. To date, there exists no major work focusing on slavery and the black intellectual tradition or the intellectual history of slavery and sexuality.

14. Quote at Chris Cameron, "Five Approaches to Intellectual History," *Black Perspectives*, April 5, 2016, https://www.aaihs.org/approaches-to-black-intellectual-history/.

15. Raymond Williams, *Keywords: A Vocabulary of Culture and Society*, rev. ed. (1976; New York: Oxford University Press, 1983), 169–71.

Chapter 1

"The Greater Part of Slaveholders Are Licentious Men"

Articulating a Culture of Rape and Exploitation in the Slave South

Shannon C. Eaves

When asked about her experiences as a formerly enslaved woman, Fannie Berry described an incident when a white man tried to throw her to the ground and rape her. Though he failed in knocking her down, she said, "we tusseled an' knocked over chairs an' when I got a grip I scratched his face all to pieces." Berry revealed that attacks like these were not out of the ordinary. Rather, rape and sexual exploitation of enslaved women was infused into Southern culture.[1] "Dese here ol' white men said, 'what I can't do by fair means I'll do by foul,'" said Berry. She proclaimed herself to be "one slave dat de poor white man had his match," yet, she knew the heaviness of the burden placed on enslaved women as a whole. "Us Colored women had to go through a plenty, I tell you."[2]

These sentiments were not unique to Berry. White and black Southerners shared a common understanding of white men's propensity to engage in sexual relations with enslaved women. "Dat was a ginerel thing 'mong de slaves owners," said formerly enslaved Jacob Mason of North Carolina. Rose Maddox likened the enslaved woman's body to a training ground on which white men looked to gain sexual experience at an early age. At the very least, "they wanted to start themselves out" on enslaved women, she said. Even the most elite of the South's slave-owning class could not deny that rape and sexual exploitation of enslaved women had become woven into the very fabric of Southern life. Mary Boykin Chesnut, the wife of US Senator James Chesnut of South Carolina and member of one of South Carolina's most elite slave-owning families, wrote, "Our men live all in one house with their wives & their concubines, & the mulattoes one sees in every family exactly resemble the white children." For Chesnut and many others—white, black, enslaved, and free—this was one of the vilest aspects of antebellum chattel slavery.[3]

Taken together, these sentiments illustrate that white men's "illicit" intercourse with enslaved women resonated within the Southern consciousness, making it the biggest open secret in the antebellum South.[4] More importantly, they expose how instrumental the systemic rape and sexual exploitation of enslaved women were in shaping the hierarchal framework of Southern society.[5] Through a close reading of sources, I argue that for Southerners, such as Berry, Maddox, and Chesnut, shared cultural understandings of the South's rape culture informed them of their ascribed positions of power and powerlessness within the plantation paradigm. Although the historical archive of enslaved people's voices has been wrought by violence and contains many silences, their articulations of rape and sexual exploitation reveal the depths of their sadness and insecurities and their sense of responsibility to protect their families, communities, and future generations of girls and women.[6] Articulations of the South's rape culture reveal the process by which enslaved people formed cultural understandings of rape and sexual exploitation and transferred them across generational lines. Factors such as gender and access to public platforms shaped the tenor of enslaved people's expressions, but together they created a collective consciousness that aided survival and navigation across a terrain marred by sexualized violence and exploitation.

Communications between mothers and daughters, fathers and sons, and the old and the young were crucial in developing a mental survival guide on how to traverse the plantation. Harriet Jacobs, in her widely circulated memoir, testified most clearly to how a young enslaved girl would come of age in this era of violence and exploitation. Whether through word of mouth or shrewd advice, a little girl "will become prematurely knowing in evil things" and eventually be "compelled to realize that she is no longer a child," said Jacobs. A mistress exhibiting hate and "violent outbreaks of jealous passion" for a particular woman she felt garnered too much of her husband's attention was one such sign of "evil things," according to Jacobs. Even before she reached the age of twelve, the enslaved girl could not help but understand the cause of the conflict, Jacobs said. And a time will come when the enslaved girl "will learn to tremble when she hears her master's footfall."[7]

As Jacobs approached the threshold of womanhood she said, "I now entered on my fifteenth year—a sad epoch in the life of a slave girl." What Jacobs was describing here—this sad epoch—equated to a state of mind.

An enslaved woman needed to be wary of those men in her household and surrounding community who had reputations for sexually harassing enslaved women. She had to understand that being beckoned to a poorly lit barn, an empty bedroom, or the edge of the woods could be a ruse and rather an opportunity for a power-wielding man to assault her outside of the earshot of those in and around the plantation household. There was hope that one could avoid unwanted attention by being cognizant of mannerisms that might be misconstrued as seductive. Although this was an unearned burden, Jacobs and other enslaved women understood that *how* they navigated these spaces of containment mattered, and these lessons were articulated from one generation to the next.[8] Teaching and maintaining a hypervigilance regarding sexualized violence were part of enslaved communities' efforts to establish and maintain basic safety. For Jacobs, it was around the time she turned fifteen that being alone in the same room with her owner, James Norcom, made for a dangerous situation. "My master began to whisper foul words in my ear," Jacobs said. "Young as I was, I could not remain ignorant to their import."[9]

The trauma of sexualized violence had a communal impact, and within the bounds of the slave quarters many enslaved men perceived white men's sexual exploitation of enslaved women as an intrusion and assault not only on the enslaved woman's body but also on themselves. It attacked their sense of themselves as respectable, viral, protective, and authoritative leaders within the enslaved family and community. White men claimed themselves to be the appointed guardians of white women and children and their slaves, but many enslaved men desired the same authority.[10] In their testimonies, enslaved men laid bare the ways in which they engaged with and embodied the patriarchal sentiments of the time. As Henry Bibb saw it, "Licentious white men, can and do, enter at night or day the lodging places of slaves; break up the bonds of affection in families; destroy all their domestic and social union for life; and the laws of the country afford them no protection." Many enslaved men expressed a desire for the law also to codify their right to protect their families and communities. Henry Bibb charged that all men were "free, moral, intelligent, and accountable human beings." Undoubtedly inspired by Thomas Jefferson's impassioned claims in the Declaration of Independence over seventy years prior that all men are created equal and endowed by their creator with certain unalienable rights, Bibb argued that a man had a right to wages for his labor and the pursuit of liberty and happiness and "a right to his own wife and children."[11]

Despite these convictions, enslaved men learned from generations of experience that white men's dominance rested on their subjugation.

Through violence, they received constant reminders of their prescribed position within Southern white men's patriarchal framework. When interviewed, William Ward shared the moment when he came face-to-face with the undeniable reality of his owner's power and his wife's vulnerability to sexual exploitation. "One day he tol' me dat if my wife had been good lookin', I never would slep wid her again 'cause he'd kill me an' take her an' raise chillums off'n her," said Ward. This was a stark reminder that his owner intended for him to feel no sense of entitlement to his wife or the right to protect her; sexualized violence rendered them both powerless. To best reconcile these realities, Henry Box Brown suggested that it was best for enslaved men to avoid marriage and having children altogether. Brown declared, "And here let me state, what is well known by many people, that no such thing as real marriage is allowed to exist among the slaves. Talk of marriage under such a system!" According to Brown, "The slave's wife is his, only at the will of her master, who may violate her chastity with impunity."[12]

In his autobiography, Henry Box Brown, who was also a noted antislavery activist, said, "The greater part of slaveholders are licentious men." Beginning in the 1830s, formerly enslaved antislavery activists like Brown utilized the genre of autobiography to create a consciousness among Northern whites and Europeans of what Southern slaves and enslavers already knew.[13] "Who does not know, that in three-fourths of the colored race, there runs the blood of the white master—the breeder of his own chattels," said James Pennington. Pennington, another formerly enslaved autobiographer, averred that only willful ignorance could blind any Northerner or Southerner to white men's voracious exploitation of enslaved women's sexuality and sexual reproduction across the entire South. Yet too often they encountered a white population that accommodated, ignored, denied, or outright defended these atrocities, especially in the face of burgeoning abolitionist movements on both sides of the Atlantic.[14]

These slave narratives, as they traditionally have been called, were published and disseminated widely from the 1830s to the turn of the century as part of larger bodies of antislavery literature and postbellum reflections of antebellum plantation life. Most touched on very similar themes, including labor, family life, and violence. They also told tales of slave owners, overseers, and slave patrollers waging sexual assaults on enslaved women. Although scholars have argued that these publications were largely propagandist in nature, shaped by white abolitionists and their agenda, they recounted real lived experiences, and their enslaved authors were also invested in the antislavery agenda. Stated more simply, these formerly enslaved writers knew of which they spoke.[15] Henry

Bibb, another proclaimer of Southern white men's sexual depravity, was himself the progeny of a white slave owner, James Bibb. The same was true of Frederick Douglass and William Wells Brown, two other prolific autobiographers.[16] Elizabeth Keckley informed readers that in addition to having a white slave-owning father herself, her son, George, was fathered by a white man named Alexander Kirkland who sexually assaulted her over the course of four years. Keckley and George were the physical embodiment of the systemic rape of enslaved women.[17] As experience is foundational to knowledge that then informs people's consciousness, it is no surprise that sexualized violence was prominently placed within this genre of antislavery literature.[18]

So devoted to stirring the imaginations of whites and having a keen understanding of the power of the written word, William Wells Brown moved from autobiography into the genre of fiction to bring attention to the prevalence of interracial sex between white men and enslaved women. His novel *Clotel*, hailed as the first novel published by an African American, tells the story of a young enslaved woman named Clotel who was fathered by Thomas Jefferson, third president of the United States. In writing *Clotel*, ostensibly a work of fiction, Brown intended to rouse memories of Jefferson, who over fifty years prior was publicly shamed with allegations that he was engaged in a sexual relationship with his female slave Sally Hemings and had fathered several of her children. For some, the idea of Jefferson, an eloquent and ardent advocate for freedom, engaging in sexual relations with an enslaved woman belied his character as a dignified and moral leader. For Brown, however, evoking Jefferson and his real-life sexual liaison with Sally Hemings was the perfect fodder for exposing the inconsistencies between Southerners' verbal rebuffs of interracial sex and their actual behavior.[19]

The novel tells of the demise of Clotel, her mother, and sister, allowing Brown to illuminate the generational consequences of interracial sex for enslaved people. Having a white father himself, Brown could speak with authority on the subject. Scholar Robert Levine writes, "*Clotel* can be read, in part, as a meditation on the history of such violations—one that is informed by a complex mix of Brown's guilt and anger at the violation that brought about his existence."[20] Brown found solace in the written word and raising awareness of slavery's many atrocities. Having published *Clotel*, numerous autobiographies, and collections of songs and speeches, Brown established himself as arguably the most accomplished African American writer of the nineteenth century.

When Works Progress Administration interviewers, mostly young white men and women, knocked on doors across the South in the 1930s, they found unsuspecting men and women on the other side who, unlike the abovementioned autobiographers, never imagined that their names and experiences would be preserved for generations to come. After being granted entrance into these homes, interviewers solicited these men and women to talk at length about their experiences, ranging from the intimate to the mundane. As many were children and adolescents when the Thirteenth Amendment was passed, they remembered things that were certainly a combination of events they witnessed, stories they heard, and lessons they were told never to forget from the days of slavery. Even seventy years after emancipation, interviewees easily recalled owners, overseers, or neighboring men engaging in sexual relations with female slaves. These memories signal the efforts previous generations made to educate their youth on how best to navigate the violent trappings of slavery and cope with the inescapable injuries of violence and oppression. Shane Harris of Georgia said, "Dat mixed-up color in niggers come from slav'ey times. Some de marsters beat de slave women to make 'em give up to 'em." Markers of interracial parentage, such as light-colored skin, allowed even those born after slavery to partake in the body of knowledge generated by these events.

While Harris was quite forthcoming, other interviewees exhibited more caution. When asked, Minnie Davis talked about her mother, Aggie Crawford, and her four siblings, including a brother named Ned whom she identified as a "mulatto." Soon after, she stated her desire not to expound further on the topic. She said, "I know who his father was, but of course you won't ask me that. I wouldn't want to expose my mother or the man who was Ned's father." She clearly wanted a modicum of control over the telling of her family's history. Her choice is understandable in the context of the Jim Crow South when engaging in sex across the color could be a matter of life or death for black people. In addition, white men continued to employ sexualized violence against black women long after slavery ended. Abuses against domestic workers and politically and economically engaged black men and women continued as a strategy of white supremacy. The memories of the formerly enslaved were more than reflections of the past; they also reflected their present-day consciousness, providing a road map for navigating a new, though all too familiar, landscape.[21]

After escaping slavery, Mary Walker, who was owned by the prominent Cameron Family of Raleigh, North Carolina, immediately sought the emancipation of her two children, Agnes and Bryant. She solicited the help of J. P. Lesley, a noted geologist and antislavery advocate, who wrote numerous correspondences to her former owner Mildred Cameron. In a letter written in 1859, Lesley said that Walker suffered exquisite pain, "fearing night and day some terrible calamity befalling either or both of her children." Yet, according to Lesley, Walker was especially fearful for her daughter, whose "blooming womanhood exposes her more terribly than the worst adventures happening to a young man." Though desperate to free them both, Walker feared nothing more intensely than the potential rape of her teenaged daughter. For Walker, the only way to protect her daughter from sexual assault was to purchase her freedom and remove her from the slaveholding South.[22]

Knowing how enslaved and formerly enslaved people like Mary Walker processed as well as articulated enslaved women's vulnerability to rape and sexual exploitation is essential because it can further our understanding of how enslaved people defined and constructed relationships within and outside of enslaved communities. The unfathomable nature of sexualized violence and exploitation unsurprisingly led enslaved people to make choices that defied conventional expectations. In the case of Mary Walker, she looked to J. P. Lesley to appeal to her former owner Mildred Cameron. Her desperation to free her children bound Walker to the entire Lesley family, and for a decade they and others advocated on her behalf, writing a multitude of letters. Though J. P. Lesley and Mildred Cameron fell on opposite sides of the slavery divide, Lesley and Walker desperately hoped that Cameron would be willing to save at least one enslaved girl from the threat of sexual assault. Yet Cameron never relented. Walker was eventually reunited with her children, then young adults, in 1865 only after Union general William Tecumseh Sherman's army swept through the Carolinas.[23]

Instead of crumbling in the wake of rape and sexual exploitation, the enslaved found means to navigate the various aspects of their lives, including relationships and childrearing. At times, this meant challenging prescribed gender roles and race relations. Some attempted to resist intimate relationships altogether to deny slave owners the opportunity to break up these unions for their own sexual gratification or economic gain. Some chose to lash out against sexual abusers, stepping way outside the bounds set for them. Yet, before strategies were devised and decisions were made, there was a consciousness of these threats and the limitations that enslavement posed. This consciousness was simultaneously a consequence of and a weapon against a widely lamented and reprehensible rape culture in the antebellum South.

Notes

The author would like to thank Steven Miller, Leslie Rowland, and the staff at the Freedmen and Southern Society Project at the University of Maryland, College Park, for their generous assistance with facilitating the research that led to this essay. She is also extremely grateful to Leslie M. Alexander, Brandon R. Byrd, Russell Rickford, and the participants in the African American Intellectual History Society Workshop for their invaluable insights.

1. Deborah Gray White, *Ar'n't I a Woman: Female Slaves in the Plantation South*, 2nd ed. (New York: W. W. Norton, 1999); Thelma Jennings, "'Us Colored Women Had to Go through a Plenty': Sexual Exploitation of African-American Slave Women," *Journal of Women's History* 1, no. 3 (1990): 45–74; Nell Irvin Painter, "Soul Murder and Slavery: Toward a Full Loaded Cost Accounting," in *Southern History across the Color Line* (Chapel Hill: University of North Carolina, 2002), 15–39; and Jennifer Morgan, *Laboring Women: Reproduction and Gender in New World Slavery* (Philadelphia: University of Pennsylvania Press, 2004). For information on enslaved men and boys and sexual exploitation, see Thomas A. Foster, "The Sexual Abuse of Black Men under American Slavery," *Journal of the History of Sexuality* 20, no. 3 (2011): 445–64.

2. Fannie Berry interview in George Rawick, ed., *The American Slave: A Composite Autobiography* (Westport, CT: Greenwood Press, 1979), 16.5 (Virginia).

3. Jacob Manson interview in Rawick, *The American Slave*, 15.2 (North Carolina), 97–99; Jack and Rosa Maddox interview in Rawick, *The American Slave*, suppl. ser. 2, 7.6 (Texas), 2531; and Mary Boykin Miller Chesnut, *The Private Mary Chesnut: The Unpublished Civil War Diaries* (New York: Oxford University Press, 1984), 21, 42.

4. Southerners frequently used words like "illicit" or "licentious" to describe interracial sex.

5. For further discussion regarding coercive and consensual sex across the color line in the nineteenth century, see Martha E. Hodes, *White Women, Black Men: Illicit Sex in the Nineteenth-Century South* (New Haven, CT: Yale University Press, 1997); and Joshua Rothman, *Notorious in the Neighborhood: Sex and Families across the Color Line in Virginia, 1787–1861* (Chapel Hill: University of North Carolina Press, 2003).

6. Norrece T. Jones, "Rape in Black and White: Sexual Violence in the Testimony of Enslaved and Free Americans," *Slavery and the American South*, ed. Winthrop Jordan (Jackson: University Press of Mississippi, 2003). For more on violence and the archive, see Marisa Fuentes, *Dispossessed Lives: Enslaved Women, Violence, and the Archive* (Philadelphia: University of Pennsylvania Press, 2016).

7. Harriet Jacobs, *Incidents in the Life of a Slave Girl*, ed. Jean Fagan Yellin (Cambridge, MA: Harvard University Press, 2000), 28.

8. Stephanie M. H. Camp, *Closer to Freedom: Enslaved Women and Everyday Resistance in the Plantation South* (Chapel Hill: University of North Carolina Press, 2004), 16, 38; and Katherine McKittrick, *Demonic Grounds: Black Women and the Cartographies of Struggle* (Minneapolis: University of Minnesota Press, 2006), 7. Camp argues that enslaved people's "social" place was affirmed by white control over their literal place, creating geographies of containment.

9. Jacobs, *Incidents in the Life of a Slave Girl*, 27.

10. Edward Baptist, "The Absent Subject: African American Masculinity and Forced Migration to the Antebellum Plantation Frontier," in *Southern Manhood: Perspectives on Masculinity in the Old South*, ed. Craig Thompson Friend and Lorri Glover (Athens: University of Georgia Press, 2004), 136–38.

11. Henry Bibb, *Life and Adventures of Henry Bibb: An American Slave* in *African American Slave Narratives: An Anthology*, ed. Sterling Lecater Bland Jr. (Westport, CT: Greenwood Press, 2001), 2:365.

12. William Ward interview in Rawick, *The American Slave*, 13.4 (Georgia), 133. Henry Box Brown, *Narrative of Henry Box Brown, Who Escaped from Slavery Enclosed in a Box 3 Feet Long and 2 Wide. Written from a Statement of Facts Made by Himself. With Remarks upon the Remedy for Slavery by Charles Stearns* in Bland, *African American Slave Narratives*, 2:457–58.

13. See William Andrews, *To Tell a Free Story: The First Century of Afro-American Autobiography, 1760–1865* (Urbana: University of Illinois Press, 1986); Marion Wilson Starling, *The Slave Narrative: Its Place in American History* (Washington, DC: Howard University Press, 1988); Robert B. Stepto, *From behind the Veil: A Study of Afro-American Narrative* (Urbana: University of Illinois Press, 1991); and Frances Smith Foster, *Witnessing Slavery: The Development of Ante-Bellum Slave Narratives* (Madison: University of Wisconsin Press, 1994) for discussion on the genre of slave narratives within abolitionist literature.

14. Brown, *Narrative of Henry Box Brown*, 2:457–58; and James Pennington, *The Fugitive Blacksmith; or Events in the History of James W.C. Pennington, Pastor of a Presbyterian Church, New York, Formerly a Slave in the State of Maryland, United States* in Bland, *African American Slave Narratives*, 2:546.

15. Frances Foster argues that most slave narratives were written by men, and in their efforts to gain support for the abolitionist movement they, at times, overemphasized slave women's sexual vulnerability to appeal to white sympathetic audiences. See Frances Foster, "Ultimate Victims: Black Women in Slave Narratives," *Journal of American Culture* 1, no. 4 (Winter 1978): 845–54.

16. For more on the lives of Henry Bibb, Frederick Douglass, and William Wells Brown, see Bibb, *Life and Adventures of Henry Bibb*; William Wells Brown, *Narrative of William Wells Brown: A Fugitive Slave* in Bland, *African American Slave Narratives*, vol. 2; and Frederick Douglass, *Narrative of the Life of Frederick Douglass, an American Slave* in *Douglass Autobiographies* (New York: Library of America, 1996).

17. Elizabeth Keckley, *Behind the Scenes, or Thirty Years a Slave, and Four Years in the White House*, ed. Frances Smith Foster (Urbana: University of Illinois Press, 2001), 24; and Jennifer Fleischner, *Mrs. Lincoln and Mrs. Keckly: The Remarkable Story of the Friendship between a First Lady and a Former Slave* (New York: Broadway Books, 2003), 84.

18. David K. Jordan and Mark J. Swartz, *Culture: The Anthropological Perspective* (New York: Wiley, 1980), 49–51.

19. See Annette Gordon-Reed, *Thomas Jefferson and Sally Hemings: An American Controversy* (Charlottesville: University of Virginia Press, 1997).

20. William Wells Brown, *Clotel; or, The President's Daughter: A Narrative of Slave Life in the United States*, ed. Robert Levine (Boston: Bedford/St. Martin's, 2001), introduction.

21. Shang Harris interview in Rawick, *The American Slave*, 12.2 (Georgia), 117–25; Minnie Davis interview in Rawick, *The American Slave*, 12.1 (Georgia), 252–64. Historian Darlene Clark Hine argues that black women's systematic rape and sexual abuse generated a culture of dissemblance—an appearance of openness and disclosure that actually shielded the truth of their inner lives and selves from their oppressors. Hine, "Rape and the Inner Lives of Black Women: Thoughts on the Culture of Dissemblance," in *Hine Sight: Black Women and the Re-Construction of American History* (New York: Carlson Publishing, 1994).

22. J. P. Lesley to Mildred Cameron, September 4, 1859, folder 1197, Cameron Family Papers, 1757–1978 #00113, Southern Historical Collection, Louis Round Wilson Special Collections Library, University of North Carolina at Chapel Hill.

23. For a biographical sketch of Walker, see Sydney Nathans, *To Free a Family: The Journey of Mary Walker* (Cambridge, MA: Harvard University Press, 2012).

Chapter 2

"If I Had My Justice"

Freedwomen, the Freedmen's Bureau, and Paternity in the Postemancipation South

Alexis Broderick

In the fall of 1830, in New Kent County, Virginia, an enslaved woman named Hannah testified in open court to the attempted sexual assault of her sister Peggy. Peggy had repeatedly refused to have sex with her enslaver, a man named John Francis. When Peggy refused to consent, Francis threatened to beat Peggy "almost to death," vowed to sell her, and "declared he would have her held [down] if she did not consent." This was not, however, a trial against the would-be rapist John Francis. Instead, it was Peggy who was on trial. She was accused of murdering Francis, who had been beaten to death and then set on fire. During the trial, enslaved people testified that John Francis had kept Peggy chained to a block in his meat house because she would not "consent to intercourse with him." The reason why she could not do that was "because the deceased was her father, and she could not do that sort of thing with her father."[1]

Being an enslaved woman, Peggy could not easily appeal to the state of Virginia for relief. Indeed, it was the state that pursued Peggy, charging her with murder. Because she was accused of killing her father/enslaver/abuser, Peggy's experiences of attempted rape and incest entered into the historical record. Peggy and Hannah's testimony perseveres only by dint of a criminal investigation into Francis's death, not because their experiences were thought to be of intrinsic social, legal, or historical value. The legal and social system of slavery rarely documented the voices of enslaved women, nor did it offer enslaved women many options for legal relief. After emancipation, however, the possibilities for documentation—and remediation—changed dramatically. Women no longer had to be charged with murder in order to publicly expose the abuse of white men in positions of power; they could bring their own cases against the men who had abused and enslaved them. As this chapter describes, freedwomen brought complaints to the Freedmen's Bureau, demanding child support from the former enslavers who had fathered their children and, in doing so, described the sexual assaults they had suffered and resisted under slavery. In their sworn statements, these women articulated experiences of sexual violence through the intellectual frameworks of equal rights and justice.[2]

As W. E. B. Du Bois argued, "Sexual chaos was always the possibility of slavery."[3] Yet slavery, as an institution, was also bolstered by the theory that "slaves were part of the family," as Du Bois himself reminds us.[4] Even as sexual assault, incest,[5] and other forms of abuse were a constant threat to enslaved people, enslavers defended their regime of violence and sexual abuse in paternalistic language. The metaphor of the plantation family helped to obscure the rape and sexual assault that were actually happening; one "big happy plantation family" could not possibly include rape and sexual assault. After emancipation, former enslavers continued to marshal paternalistic ideology and familial language when referring to freedpeople. Former enslavers who wrote to the Freedmen's Bureau routinely deployed the rhetoric of family in order to perpetuate slavery's property and power dynamics. In cases involving the apprenticeship of freed children, for example, former owners might write of their feelings of fatherly attachment and obligation.[6] Such an appeal might raise the likelihood that the former owner would be successful in having his former slaves bound and apprenticed to him, thereby continuing the exploitation of freedpeople's bodies and labor.[7] Thus, one Alabama planter referred to "family negroes [who] have always lived in the family" when petitioning the bureau for financial assistance in 1866.[8] As the Freedmen's Bureau records reveal, the same men who had coerced sexual relations with and impregnated their slaves might later refer to these women as their family members when it was expedient.

But freedwomen were quick to adopt and adapt slaveholder's professed ideology of family for their own purposes. Specifically, I have found more than a dozen cases in which freedwomen authored complaints to the Freedmen's Bureau alleging their former enslavers fathered their children and were refusing to support them.[9] These women seized on the revolutionary potential of Reconstruction policy to engage the state in the adjudication of slavery's evils. But they also sought to hold former owners to the same code of family that they had professed (when it was expedient) during and after slavery. The result was a vernacular jurisprudence of justice that drew on the logics of both slavery and emancipation.

Margarite Hood, for example, made a powerful claim for her own rights as a mother and a citizen while at the same time exposing the ways in which her former enslaver had utilized the tenets of paternalism for his own material gain. Margarite Hood told the Bureau that her former owner, Govy Hood, had unfairly exploited his status as the former enslaver and biological father of her two daughters. As Margarite Hood explained, Govy Hood was the "former master and self-reported father" of her children. Govy Hood "claimed to exercise the privilege and prerogatives of a supervision of some description over them," but he used that authority to illegally bind the girls to him for life. Margarite Hood asserted that her former enslaver had misused his position as a father and self-professed protector of her daughters, effectively "render[ing] their condition no better than slaves."[10] In doing so, he had also broken the laws established in Louisiana's Civil Code pertaining to custody, which amounted to a "manifest and palpable injustice" for Margarite and her daughters.[11] Margarite's complaint thus mixed slaveholder ideology, formal law, and a vernacular sense of justice to renegotiate the terms of emancipation, both for her and her daughters.

Such complaints brought by freedwomen regarding the paternity and paternalism of their former enslavers illuminate the intellectual labor of emancipation in several ways. First, they demonstrate that the language of paternalism lingered after emancipation, and that this rhetoric of fictive family (my former slave is a member of my family) could be coupled, perversely, with a denial of biological paternity (I will not pay to support my biological children whose mother I used to own). Former enslavers continued to refer to their former slaves as members of their families whether or not they sought to dodge the financial responsibilities of fatherhood. Second, the paternity cases show us that freedwomen used the language and logic of paternalism for their own ends, attempting to hold their former owners to the framework that the men themselves had espoused. Third, the cases indicate that freedwomen understood their attempts to win child support from their former owners as more than material necessity; they often framed their complaints in terms of justice and equal rights. By invoking these potent legal concepts against their former masters, freedwomen reimagined their relationship with law and American society.

The paternalistic logic and language that the women adopted in their complaints emerged directly out of slaveholder ideology. Charles Smith, a former slaveholder in Knoxville, Tennessee, for example, gave his slave Julia his last name and impregnated her about six months before Tennessee ratified the Thirteenth Amendment. Smith refused to acknowledge his paternity but nevertheless persisted in his use of paternalistic language to refer to Julia. On September 5, 1865, Julia Smith swore in an affidavit to the Freedmen's Bureau that her eight-week-old infant, who was born about three months after legal emancipation in Tennessee, was the offspring of Charles. Julia Smith approached the Freedmen's Bureau for assistance in recouping child support after her former "mistress," Charles's wife, drove her away from their plantation, threatening to "cow hide" the nine months pregnant Julia and "throw hot water on her" if she did not leave immediately.[12]

Despite these threats of bodily harm, Julia took her case to the state. As Captain David Boyd, the bureau's agent in Knoxville, wrote in his enclosure on the case, "[Charles Smith] denied being the father of this child but would not make an affidavit that he had no sexual intercourse with her." Ultimately, Charles agreed to pay Julia the "amounts required by the laws of the state of Tennessee to be paid by father of bastards for their support."[13] However, the official agreement did not recognize or reveal the real reason why Charles Smith was paying Julia. In the agreement, Charles Smith wrote that the payments were for "the support of a col'd woman 'Julia' formerly a slave belonging to me she being unable to support herself and young child. I do not wish to have so disagreeable [a] person in my family."[14]

Why did Charles Smith use the rhetoric of family in the very document that was designed to obfuscate the fact that he was the biological father of Julia's child?[15] There is a dual process occurring in Smith's agreement, a denial of paternity and a perverted profession of paternalism, a disowning and owning occurring simultaneously. Smith cannot acknowledge his paternity of his former slave's child, but he still includes Julia in his vision of a wrecked plantation family. He does not want *her* in his family any longer, but the child, who is actually his biological offspring, was born free and was therefore never included in Smith's plantation family to begin with.

The behavior of former owners like Smith reveals how thin, how limited, and how self-serving the metaphor of the plantation family had always been. Paternalism was based on the fact that the paternal figure could extract his slaves' labor, and his children's labor, and was bolstered by the fact that those two conditions often overlapped: their children were often their slaves. After the legal binds of slavery were broken, after fathering children by one's slave no longer added to an enslavers' material wealth, the obligation to provide for these children and play the part of the "great white father" was no longer self-serving. Still, in many cases former owners clung to the rhetoric of the plantation family, a fact that is further demonstrated in their petitions to have former slave children apprenticed to them and in their refusals to recognize the familial claims of freedpeople more generally. Former enslavers resisted the profound realignment of emancipation; it was a loss not only of property but also of a system of domestic relations.[16] Theirs was a slaveholder fantasy of a plantation family, black and white, that had seen the antagonistic relations of labor, torture, rape, and incest not for what they were, but instead as bonds of attachment, mutual responsibility, and familial love.

David Chenault was another planter who mixed the language of paternalism with the practice of sexual assault of enslaved women. His behavior was laid bare through the case brought before the bureau by his former slaves Mary and Rachel Malone. Chenault was a white planter with "good property" in Sumner County, Tennessee, who owned twenty slaves in 1860. According to the testimony of Mary, Rachel, and their mother Rebecca, Chenault had admitted to fathering children by both sisters. Lieutenant Robert McMillan, a subassistant commissioner for the bureau, explained in his enclosure to General Clinton Fisk, the assistant commissioner for Tennessee and Kentucky, that in addition to fathering children with his former slaves, Mary and Rachel, Chenault had a lawful white wife who had three children. "His wife and each Mary and Rachel Malone have children, their youngest that are within less than (2) two months of the same age. I send you this case as one wanting special attention. As the citizens want some example in such cases."[17] McMillan was clearly disturbed by Chenault's actions, the secretive sexual predation of a man in violation of two sisters whom he owned and who were living in his house. That the citizens of Sumner County wanted an example of how "such cases" would be handled by the bureau suggests that interracial and incestuous sex within the domestic spaces of slavery was not uncommon. But who were these "citizens" McMillian was referring to? The new citizens as outlined in the Fourteenth Amendment or white citizens?

The mere act of bringing their cases before the Freedmen's Bureau testified to the formerly enslaved women's desire to collect what they deserved, to exercise their rights as free women. Rebecca Malone, the mother of Rachel and Mary, said that when she "reviled [Chenault] about such conduct, having two sisters and a wife in the same yard, he said, "Well, Aunt 'Becca' I can't help it."[18] Chenault's choice to address Rebecca Malone as "Aunt Becca" could reflect a paternalistic former planter's condescension to an older black woman. But Rebecca Malone was, in fact, the grandmother of six of his children. He had fathered children by two women who were related to one another, and who lived in the same house as the mother of his lawful wife and children. Chenault had impregnated all three within the span of a few months, and all three lived and worked in the "same yard." Rebecca Malone *was* something like family to Chenault: she was his children's grandmother.

Despite (or perhaps because of) her complex relationship to Chenault, Rebecca not only confronted Chenault privately, but she also testified publicly to the bureau about his conduct. Rebecca said that Chenault had told her to keep the matter secret, which she did until his abusive treatment began, at which point, Rebecca said, "I could not keep it any longer." Freedwomen like Rebecca and Mary Malone delivered sworn statements that exposed the imbrication of kinship, sex, and property that constituted the systemic abuses of slavery. These women may not have invoked the language of justice or equal rights explicitly, but the Malones took powerful actions against the man who months earlier had legally owned them and their children.

Lucy Ann Bibb, a freedwoman living in Louisa County, Virginia, wrote to General Brown at the Freedmen's Bureau office in Richmond on June 29, 1867. In her appeal, which was not transcribed by a bureau agent but written with emphatic underlines, strikethroughs, and signed not with an *X* but with her full name, Bibb outlined a powerful case. In the letter, which seems to be written in Bibb's own hand, she explained that a man named Samuel Parsons, an assistant clerk of the county court, had lived with her for several years and fathered her two children but had since deserted her. In fact, Bibb writes that Parsons "lived with me," underlining the word that inscribes her personhood as if to highlight the dehumanizing nature of Parson's subsequent desertion and dissolution of his responsibilities. Parsons had legally owned Bibb, but he had "always promised to be a husband" to her, and Bibb explained that she "loved him and trusted him as such for nearly six years." Bibb continued, "We could not be married because I was a slave although I am as white as most white people and have been as well bred in most respects. I have been true to him as I think no one will deny." Despite her fidelity, wifeliness, whiteness, and his own promise, Parsons had deserted Bibb and her children and was now refusing to provide sufficient support.[19]

Bibb was navigating a delicate path with her appeal. She wrote to the bureau as a former slave but presented herself as a well-bred white woman. She invoked concepts of wifeliness, loyalty, and love that would have meant something to the Northern bureau agents reading her letter, yet she wrote as someone devoid of the legal benefits (such as they were) of marriage. Through her letter she had to not only construct a narrative representing her side of the case but create a counternarrative to ideas about the promiscuity, color, "breeding," and respectability of slaves. Bibb was powerfully self-aware, and the letter reveals her in the act of crafting her own image on the page, an image that would appeal to the men she needed to have on her side. She wrote, "Can not something be done to compel him to ~~support~~ help me support my children?" Bibb crossed out "support" and added "help me" to literally underline her own ability and responsibility in the matter. She was not asking the federal government for a handout; she was simply asking for assistance in pursuit of the same kind of justice that any respectable woman should expect.

As Bibb explained in her letter, one of her children was born in June 1865, while the other was born a slave. Parsons offered to give Bibb bond for twenty-five dollars per year (the word "year is underlined in Bibb's letter, as if to highlight the absurdity of such a low figure) to support the freeborn child if she agreed not to go to a magistrate about her case. Bibb asked the reasonable and logical question: "Why should he not help support both?" Indeed, there is nothing in her own letter or the bureau agent's enclosures on the case to indicate why Parsons felt he was bound to support a child conceived during slavery but not one born in slavery. Bibb closes her letter with a final, pained appeal, a profound distillation of the condition many freedpeople found themselves in at the war's end: "Is this the best I can do?"[20]

Women like Bibb found themselves in impossible positions, confronted by a set of laws that were not designed to accommodate the particularities bred by slavery, face to face with a brigade of bureau agents who often seemed completely mystified by the disordered family situations left in slavery's wake. Not only was the bureau plagued by a profound lack of resources and personnel—at its height the agency employed only nine hundred men to cover the entire South—the agents who were there often proved ill equipped at disentangling the familial, sexual, and property dynamics brought before them.[21]

Many freedwomen couched their complaints in intellectual frameworks of equity and law, whereas some formerly enslaved women, such as Flora Murphy, framed their appeals in the more totalizing terms of "justice." Murphy could hardly have been more clear, writing, "I wish the assistance of the Bureau to obtain justice for myself and children." As Murphy outlined in her May 23, 1866, complaint to the subassistant commissioner for the Freedmen's Bureau in Mount Pleasant, South Carolina, "The facts of my case are as follows: I was born and raised a slave and have always been a house servant in the family of John Holbeck." Murphy continues, "While the property of said John Holbeck and subject to his authority I became the mother of two children by him. . . . Since I have been made free John Holbeck neglects and refuses to render me any assistance to support myself or my children. I am poor, and I ask that he may be compelled to contribute something toward the support of his and my children" (underline in original).[22] Murphy is clear about what she wants: justice for her and her children in the form of monetary child support. She deftly manages to communicate the reality of the sexual assault she was subjected to as an enslaved woman while nodding to the politics of respectability and femininity that would have appealed to a man like the commissioner. She was "subject to [her master's] authority," and that is why she became pregnant with his children, not because she was promiscuous or lacked morals. Murphy skillfully maneuvered through white legal and moral strictures to her own advantage. The bureau agent was somewhat sympathetic to Murphy's situation, forwarding her complaint up the chain of command to the assistant commissioner in Charleston, writing, "This petition seems most just but I am in doubt whether the Bureau can afford relief, even if the facts are as stated." There is another notation by the commissioner made the day after Murphy gave her testimony, "P.S. Held back at request of complainant." There is no further information in her file, no indication of why she retracted her complaint. Perhaps Murphy's threats were enough to make her former owner pay.

One of the clearest illustrations of freedwomen's contributions to the discourse of equal rights and sexual justice came from Eliza Cook of Wake County, North Carolina. Cook did not initially approach the bureau to bring a paternity suit against her former master, Dr. James Cook. Instead, James Cook sought out the bureau agents himself, requesting their help in evicting Eliza and her seven children (who were also his children) from his property in 1866. At first the bureau agent, A. G. Brady, accepted Dr. Cook's version of events, that Eliza had become "insulting and abusive" to Cook's white family. Brady wrote a patronizing and condescending letter to Eliza, informing her that Dr. Cook had allowed her to live in his house since the surrender and had charged her nothing for the privilege. Brady continued, "Now that you have become very insulting and abusive to him he has applied to the Bureau to have you removed from his house and premises. Eliza the Bureau does not approve of such conduct on the part of the freed people. They are required to be respectful of their former masters also whites and blacks generally."[23] Brady told Eliza to appear at his office on the following Thursday at nine o'clock to answer for the charges, which she did. Eliza Cook told Brady that the charges of her being insulting and abusive to her former master were untrue. She had never had any difficulty with Dr. Cook. It was Cook's wife who had a problem with *her*. Dr. Cook had married since the surrender, and as Eliza put it, this woman was "trying to make trouble and have me driven off the plantation" because Dr. Cook was cohabitating with his new wife "in the same way he did with me."

Eliza testified that she had been owned by Dr. Cook's father and that at the age of sixteen she was "seduced" (in her words) by Dr. Cook. Eliza testified that he had "cohabitated" with her ever since the year "1844 till 1865 or thereabouts" and gave birth to nine children by him, seven of whom were still living. It is Eliza Cook's recounting of the behavior of her new "mistress" that gives rise to her most powerful appeal to equal rights. Eliza Cook testified in her deposition to Brady: "[Dr. Cook] has never told me to leave the plantation. . . . His wife told me one day when I went to get some apples to go away. I told her I would not that master (Dr. Cook) always let me have whatever I wanted in his plantation for myself and children and *if I had my justice I had as much right there as she had*" (emphasis added). For Eliza Cook to tell a white government agent that she had as much a right to be somewhere as a white woman was a powerful act. The actions she took next further reinforce her commitment to articulating her understanding of justice and of equal rights.

After defending herself against Dr. Cook's accusations and recounting her side of the story to bureau agent Brady, Eliza asked for assistance, appealing to the agency to "take some measures to secure for me and my children (and his) a home and support." Brady then wrote to Dr. Cook informing him that Eliza, under oath, "has made the matter appear in a very different light from what you did." Indeed. Eliza Cook first asked that Dr. Cook support all seven of her children in accordance with North Carolina's bastardy laws. As in the case of Julia Smith, however, the state bastardy laws proved ineffective at winning justice for freedwomen. According to North Carolina's law, mothers of illegitimate children had to name the father within three years of the child's birth. Since Eliza Cook's children were born while she was enslaved, she was obviously unable to appeal to the government and name the father of her children, who was also her/their owner. The relations of power, money, and sex that fueled slavery relied precisely on her inability to make such an official appeal.

Eliza Cook went still further in her appeal for justice for herself and her children, invoking the Civil Rights Act of 1866. She argued that the bastardy laws of North Carolina should apply to her and her children "as if they were white persons." Since the laws failed to provide for them, and she had been "deprived of her rights," she argued that jurisdiction should be transferred to the federal government to ensure equal treatment under the law. As the agent reported, "She respectfully submits that by and under the Civil Rights Bill passed by the Congress of the United States in its last session, she on behalf of her children is fully entitled to relief through the military authority."[24] The case was brought to Judge James Brooks, of the US District Court, but Judge Brooks found that the federal Civil Rights Act did not apply in this case and that Eliza Cook could find no redress from the federal government. She was evicted from Dr. Cook's plantation and had to rely on the bureau for support.

As the testimony of women like Margarite Hood, Julia Smith, and Flora Murphy demonstrates, enslavers had created environments across the South that engendered what Annette Gordon-Reed called "bizarre" or "weird family situations." Situations like the one that Sally Hemings found herself in, where "husbands [were] having children with their wives and then their wives' enslaved half sisters."[25] Gordon-Reed notes that "these weird family situations actually violated emerging norms for the family in the eighteenth and nineteenth centuries, which is why Southern whites of that time worked so assiduously to hide this aspect of Southern life."[26] After emancipation, freedwomen employed their knowledge both of the "weird situations" and the norms being violated to expose this aspect of Southern life—to unmask this corner of the world the slaveholders made. Not only did these women keenly articulate the dynamics behind the sexual and familial violence of slavery, their testimony demonstrates that they knew how to deploy this knowledge against their former owners. By weaponizing the concept of paternalism, they sought and at times achieved financial restitution and justice. Through their testimony, freedwomen exposed how the lines between sex, family, and rape were blended to the point of erasure under slavery. Their intellectual labor—articulated in their exposure and indictment of the sexual dynamics of slavery—contributed to the still ongoing discourse of equal rights and sexual justice in American society. The testimony of these freedwomen gives us a glimpse into the intellectual and legal possibilities they opened up at the moment of emancipation—a moment in which formerly enslaved women deployed the concept of justice against a system that had been so radically unjust.

Notes

1. Case of Peggy, Patrick, and Franky, Executive Papers—Pardon Papers, box 316, May–September 1830, Library of Virginia, Richmond.

2. As Kidada Williams argues, when freedpeople testified about experiences of racial violence "they were not merely giving statements; they were resisting violence discursively." Williams, *They Left Great Marks on Me: African American Testimonies of Racial Violence from Emancipation to World War I* (New York: New York University Press, 2012), 6.

3. W. E. B. Du Bois, *Black Reconstruction in America: 1860–1880* (1935; repr., New York: Free Press, 1998), 35.

4. Du Bois, *Black Reconstruction in America*, 43.

5. Du Bois addressed the presence of incest directly, writing, "Southerners who had suckled food from black breasts vied with each other in fornication with black women, and even in beastly incest. They took the name of their fathers in vain to seduce their own sisters." Du Bois, *Black Reconstruction in America*, 125. In my dissertation, "American Incest: Kinship, Sex and Commerce in Slavery and Reconstruction" (University of Pennsylvania, 2018), I explore the way that incest, defined both literally and conceptually, was integral to the perverted dynamics of sex, property, and kinship that characterized slavery and the system of race relations constructed in its aftermath.

6. On apprenticeship, see Rebecca J. Scott, "The Battle over the Child: Child Apprenticeship and the Freedmen's Bureau in North Carolina," in *Growing Up in American: Children in Historical Perspective*, ed. N. Ray Hiner and Joseph M. Hawes (Urbana: University of Illinois Press, 1985), 193–207; Laura F. Edwards, "'The Marriage Covenant Is at the Foundation of All Our Rights': The Politics of Slave Marriages in North Carolina after Emancipation," *Law and History Review* 14, no. 1 (Spring 1996): 81–124; Karin L. Zipf, "Reconstructing 'Free Woman': African-American Women, Apprenticeship, and Custody Rights during Reconstruction," *Journal of Women's History* 12 (Spring 2000): 8–3; Mary Farmer-Kaiser, *Freedwomen and the Freedmen's Bureau: Race, Gender and Public Policy in the Age of Emancipation* (New York: Fordham, 2010); Eric Foner, *Reconstruction: America's Unfinished Revolution, 1863–1877* (New York: HarperCollins, 1988) 201–2; and Barbara Jeanne Fields, *Slavery and Freedom on the Middle Ground: Maryland in the Nineteenth Century* (New Haven, CT: Yale University Press, 1985).

7. See, e.g., the case of John Long of Pleasureville, Kentucky. Long petitioned the Freedmen's Bureau to apprentice two children to him, siblings whom he had "raised as his slaves." Long wrote that he felt "a great anxiety to see them do well." Long to Frederick; Louisville, KY; April 3, 1867, Superintendent and Subassistant Commissioner, Letters Received, G 105 (Records of the Bureau of Refugees, Freedmen, and Abandoned Lands), FSSP A-4508, National Archives. Freedmen and Southern Society Project, University of Maryland, College Park, hereafter cited as FSSP.

8. C. W. Duetan to BG W. Swayne, January 26, 1866, Unregistered Letters Received, ser. 9, box 3, FSSP A-2809, National Archives.

9. These cases were all drawn from the FSSP, part of the History Department of the University of Maryland at College Park. The FSSP collection consists of facsimiles of fifty thousand documents, selected by editors from among millions of similar sources held at the National Archives of the United States. It is therefore important to acknowledge that in all likelihood there are far more than a dozen extant cases. On freedwomen and the Freedmen's Bureau generally, see Farmer-Kaiser, *Freedwomen and the Freedmen's Bureau*.

10. Petition of Margarite Hood, January 2, 1867, Unregistered Letters Received, ser. 2363, box 54A, Warren co, MS & Carroll par, 1A, VBG, RG 105 (Records of the Bureau of Refugees, Freedmen, and Abandoned Lands), FSSP A-9275, National Archives.

11. Petition of Margarite Hood.

12. Affidavit of Julia Smith, September 5, 1865, filed with Miscellaneous Records, Affidavits and Other Papers Relating to Freedmen's Complaints, ser. 3510, box 58, Knoxville, TN, Subasst. Comr., RG 105 (Bureau of Refugees, Freedmen, and Abandoned Lands), FSSP A-6445, National Archives. On slave-owning women's violence, see Thavolia Glymph, *Out of the House of Bondage: The Transformation of the Plantation Household* (New York: Cambridge University Press, 2008).

13. Enclosure written by Capt. David Boyd, Miscellaneous Records.

14. Agreement of M. F. Smith, September 8, 1865, filed with Miscellaneous Records, Affidavits and Other Papers Relating to Freedmen's Complaints, ser. 3510, box 58, Knoxville, TN, Subasst. Comr., RG 105 (Bureau of Refugees, Freedmen and Abandoned Lands), FSSP A-6445, National Archives.

15. These are all cases that center on children, although the experiences of the children themselves are beyond the scope of this paper. On children's experience of slavery, Reconstruction, and how they shaped contests over rights, citizenship, and families, see Catherine Jones, *Intimate Reconstructions: Children in Postemancipation Virginia* (Charlottesville: University of Virginia Press, 2015); Wilma King, *Stolen Childhood: Slave Youth in Nineteenth-Century America* (Bloomington: Indiana University Press, 1997); Mary Jenkins Schwartz, *Born in Bondage, Growing Up Enslaved in the Antebellum South* (Cambridge, MA: Harvard University Press, 2000); and Mary Niall Mitchell, *Raising Freedom's Child: Black Children and Visions of the Future after Slavery* (New York: New York University Press, 2010). Monographs with significant material regarding the lives of enslaved and free children include Herbert Gutman, *The Black Family in Slavery and Freedom, 1750–1925* (New York: Vintage, 1977); and Deborah Gray White, *Ar'n't I a Woman? Female Slaves in the Plantation South* (New York: Norton, 1985).

16. On the reordering of the plantation households and the transformation of domestic work, see Thavolia Glymph, *Out of the House of Bondage*; Tera W. Hunter, *To 'Joy My Freedom: Southern Black Women's Lives and Labors after the Civil War* (repr.; Cambridge, MA: Harvard University Press, 1998).

17. Lieutenant Robert McMillan (Pro Marshal) to Fisk, July 18, 1865, M-23 1865, Letters Received, ser. 3379, box 3, Gallatin, TN, RG 105 (Bureau of Refugees, Freedmen, and Abandoned Lands), FSSP A-6169, National Archives.

18. Deposition of Rebecca Malone, July 18, 1865, M, M-23, Gallatin, TN, Letter Received, FSSP A- 6169.

19. In her work on the relationship between sexual violence and sexual labor in the antebellum South, Emily Owens examines cases in which black women used the term "wife" to describe their relationships with men who had once owned them. In her discussion of the case of Ann Maria Barcley, Owens illuminates the ways in which the "wife claim" was strategic and was used to establish something close to claim of freedom. "'As His Wife': Redefining Wifeliness in the Face of Unfreedom," paper presented at the African American Intellectual History Society Conference, Nashville, March 2017.

20. Lucy Ann Bibb to OB, Louisa CH, Gordonvil, VA, June 29, 1867, Letters Received, ser. 4056, box 29, RG 105 (Bureau of Refugees, Freedmen, and Abandoned Lands), FSSP A-8177, National Archives.

21. Eric Foner, *Reconstruction: America's Unfinished Revolution, 1863–1877* (New York: HarperCollins, 1988), 143. On the bureau and its navigation of

domestic disputes, see Mary Farmer-Kaiser, *Freedwomen and the Freedmen's Bureau*. The bureau relied heavily on Northern philanthropists, charitable organizations, and capitalists to aid in their relief efforts. See Emma Teitelman, "Governing the Peripheries: The Social Reconstruction of the South and West after the American Civil War" (PhD diss., University of Pennsylvania, 2018), chap. 1. The bureau was reliant on private capital for many aspects of their operations. See Drew Gilpin Faust, *This Republic of Suffering: Death and the American Civil War* (New York: Alfred A. Knopf, 2008); Robert Hamlett Bremner, *The Public Good: Philanthropy and Welfare in the Civil War Era* (New York: Knopf, 1980); Willie Rose, *Rehearsal for Reconstruction: The Port Royal Experiment* (New York: Oxford University Press, 1976); Jacqueline Jones, *Soldiers of Light and Love: Northern Teachers and Georgia Blacks, 1865–1873* (Chapel Hill: University of North Carolina Press, 1980); Robert Charles Morris, *Reading, 'Riting, and Reconstruction: The Education of Freedmen in the South, 1861–1870* (Chicago: University of Chicago Press, 1981); and Joe Martin Richardson, *Christian Reconstruction: The American Missionary Association and Southern Blacks, 1861–1890* (Athens: University of Georgia Press, 1986).

22. Flora Murphy to D. T. Cordin, May 23, 1866, Letters Received, ser. 3201, Charleston Dist, SC, RG 105 (Bureau of Refugees, Freedmen, and Abandoned Lands), FSSP A-7174, National Archives.

23. Brady to Eliza Cook, July 9, 1866, BB-094 1866, Letters Received, ser. 15, box 25, RG 105 (Records of the Bureau of Refugees, Freedmen, and Abandoned Lands), FSSP A-2946, National Archives.

24. North Carolina Assistant Commissioner Bomford to General O. O. Howard, 13 December 1866, vol. 3, Register of Letters Received, RG 105 (Records of the Bureau of Refugees, Freedmen, and Abandoned Lands), FSSP A-2946, National Archives.

25. Annette Gordon-Reed, *The Hemingses of Monticello: An American Family* (New York: W. W. Norton, 2008), 559.

26. Gordon-Reed, *The Hemingses of Monticello*, 559.

Chapter 3

Hapticity and "Soul Care"

A Praxis for Understanding Bondwomen's History

Deirdre Cooper Owens

Rhody, a thirty-four-year-old North Carolina enslaved woman, was "distressed" about her health and shared her worry with her owner Thomas Robinson. Waiting one year after Rhody had not given birth, Robinson finally called for local doctor W. P. L. Jennings to examine his slave. Rhody informed Jennings, according to his medical journal article, "that she had gone over twelve months with her child, then in utero." The physician described Rhody, a mother of five children, as "a woman of unusual good sense for a negro" but also determined in the end that she had lied to him about the true nature of her condition. He did not believe that she was carrying a fetus. From his initial visit to Robinson's slave farm to examine Rhody, it is not hard to imagine that Dr. Jennings had probably not imagined that his medical relationship with the enslaved woman would last six years. From 1843 to 1849, Dr. Jennings and the colleagues he invited to team up with him worked on Rhody to restore her reproductive health. In the beginning phase, he and his peers determined two possible causes for Rhody's mysterious condition: either she had experienced an extrauterine pregnancy or was infested with tapeworms. By April 1849, Rhody's health had begun to deteriorate quickly. Most prominent among her symptoms was diarrhea and tenesmus, a cramping rectal pain. In the course of one visit, Dr. Jennings and his medical team examined Rhody's fecal matter and found in it two bones from an infant. One bone was from the baby's spine and the other from its foot.[1] Not so amazingly, Rhody, a mother of five children, seemed to know her body and its functions better than Dr. Jennings and all of his "most respected" colleagues who puzzled over her ailment for six years.

As a historian of both antebellum-era slavery and medicine, I am aware of how much touch and the handling of black women's bodies was a normative practice embedded within the institution of slavery and US early gynecological development. Black slave women's bodies were prodded, pawed, and examined like meat in slave markets and were treated in nearly identical ways in hospitals and slave cabins by the white men charged to heal them. There was no space, either public or private, to which enslaved women could escape to exercise autonomy over their bodies. The handling and mishandling of black women's bodies must be investigated as a condition of both slavery and medicine.

Besides the calls for scholars to integrate psychological ideations into slavery studies, historical scholarship on hapticity or tactile research and slavery does not exist and should be included in our research methodological and theoretical framing of the slave past. In her pamphlet "Soul Murder and Slavery," historian Nell Irvin Painter urged historians of slavery to carefully probe the archives to construct more nuanced narratives about the psychological injuries that slavery inflicted on black people's bodies, their interior lives, and their anima or souls. Taking the provocative questions Painter raised in her writing about the need to find even more precise language and concepts that articulate better the sociopsychic dimensions of slavery, I am proposing that we apply haptic studies in our analyses of slavery to locate new ways of understanding the sensory lives of slaves related to touch and medical practices. Undertaking this methodological and theoretical work will allow scholars to craft a better defined and formulated praxis for assuming the emotional labor involved in rescuing forgotten narratives in the archival and writing work that we do.

Haptics researcher and engineer Katherine J. Kuchenbecker argues, "Haptic intelligence is vital to human intelligence."[2] In the age of slavery in both colonial America and the United States, the politics of touch was political and ultimately about power. Who was able to touch other people with freedom and impunity was linked to the respect they garnered and the cultural capital they possessed. As gynecology began to progress as a legitimate medical field that was built on the wombs of the dispossessed, it is important to not only note but also analyze the practice of white medical men who began to examine, experiment, and operate on black women's bodies with more frequency. Buoyed by scientific and cultural beliefs that stated black women were immodest, white men could open their vaginas with pewter spoons to examine their cervixes and perform surgeries on them while they were naked.[3] Quite literally, like the auction block, both the examination and operating tables allowed for the legal touching of black women's bodies by white men; it was intimate public interracial touching that did not need to be hidden. In some instances, the events were public ones. To be clear, only elite white men were allowed open access to black women's bodies because the financial gains earned from slavery garnered them a social mobility and freedom to make taboo behavior, black women's public nudity, permissible. Thus what I am insisting in this essay is that scholars of slavery, women's history, and the history of medicine challenge how we approach the archives and even "objectivity" because the researcher knows what touch feels like because she cannot escape her skin. The somatic is then embedded in slavery and haptic studies.

Returning to Rhody's medical case, the enslaved woman whose gynecological experiences opened this essay, allows us to understand the inherent power white men had and wielded as slave owners and doctors over black women. How much physical and emotional pain was the bondwoman in to make her reveal her yearlong suffering to her owner? Most slaves did not desire white people's intrusion into their intimate lives, especially their medical ones. Yet Rhody made public her private pain, and it left her even more vulnerable as a woman, a mother, and a sick slave. I wonder whether she was fearful about what would happen to her medically, especially if there were black women healers in her community who were trained to be noninvasive in their patient care. Would she be able to trust that Dr. Jennings's handling of her body would be gentle, affirming, and even humane? Human relations are first formed through touch, and when touch is not reciprocal, human beings learn quickly that the ability to touch others freely is hierarchical and rooted in power, especially in a nineteenth-century white supremacist, capitalist, and patriarchal slaveholding society.

Asking questions from a haptic-centric framing allows us to think more broadly about the power dynamics that existed between various people: patient and doctor, slave owner and slave, and white man and black woman. Although Dr. Jennings and his colleagues deemed Rhody as exceptionally bright despite her "negro-ness" and "femaleness," they erased her knowledge as the mother five living children and also denied that she knew how a pregnancy felt, even an aborted one. Rhody, however, knew how a baby's kick in her belly felt; after multiple pregnancies, she was familiar with the itching associated with a stretching stomach that was growing to accommodate her fetus. For these reasons alone, these medical professionals, who literally took six years to determine that Rhody's dead fetus was rotting inside her body, should have listened more seriously to the enslaved woman's claims. Yet the dictates of antiblackness and gendered chauvinism did not allow space for them to believe a chattel slave in the 1840s, even one with "unusually good sense."

Thus, when I write about the medical experiences of a bondwoman like Rhody, a woman who carried a dead fetus in her uterus for six years while white medical men charged to heal her broken body characterized her as dishonest and possibly infested with parasites, I hurt. Simultaneously, I am also dissatisfied because I am filled with questions and lamentations about how this enslaved woman was treated as both a medical curiosity and a liar. How did she continue to proactively mother her five children even as she believed deeply she was carrying a dead child in her womb? What physical sensations did Rhody experience after each doctor's visit when Dr. Jennings and his colleagues were attempting to locate the source of her physical pain? Did she flinch when they pressed their hands and medical instruments against her flesh, her stomach? Was she embarrassed when she informed them that she felt bones pass through her body and settle into her feces? Did the doctors sift through Rhody's excrement in front of her? Were her children, her black lover, if she had one, holding her hand when she died April 18, 1849? Further, in mourning their mother's death, were her children and other kin informed when doctors performed an autopsy on Rhody as a cadaver? Was her fetus either destroyed or preserved? Frustratingly, my questions do not have answers that can be retrieved from nineteenth-century medical journal articles. Black women's voices were silenced, and white men decided which words and actions from their enslaved patients would be recorded in the pages of their professional writings. They served as fragmented objects, reduced to the function and dysfunction of their reproductive organs, vestibules for receiving untested potions, and living anatomical figures for surgeons to learn the inner workings of women's reproductive bodies. Positioning my questions and letting them inform the way I read sources disrupts the silences, much like historian Michele Mitchell advised scholars of gender and African American history to do in her article "Silences Broken, Silences Kept."[4]

I am also interested in having a conversation about how the haptic dimensions of the archives affect scholars of slavery who write about black women's trauma. I employ the concept of "soul care" as a framework for examining how enslaved women sparked nineteenth-century discourses on ethics and the moral parameters of womanhood. Tracing the lives of black women in slavery spatially and temporally, I offer a new methodology of understanding the resistive and life-sustaining measures black women employed in the world they lived in and made. Soul care allows scholars to enter the archives with questions and perspectives that seek to expand the boundaries of what we can know and how we can uncover and interpret the experiences of black women as subjects and agents of history. In writing about the difficulty of researching and writing about the fragmented lives of enslaved women for scholars interested in understanding "archival silences" about black women's personhood, historian Marisa Fuentes asserts, "Epistemic violence originates from the knowledge produced about enslaved women by white men and women in this [eighteenth-century] society, and that knowledge is what survives in archival form."[5] So understanding the hapticity of an archive that can be accessed immediately on smartphone technology also brings into question how quickly researchers can access and be impacted emotionally and physiologically by our contact to slavery within the digital archives. Haptic technology has created another method for scholars to gather information and interact with the impact of modernity on the archives. Despite this relatively new feature for research, those conducting research are human beings who will be impacted by the violence of the archives, especially when both the sexual and medical lives of enslaved women are centralized.

In March 2015 at Michigan State University for the Cross-Generational Dialogues in Black Women's History symposium, Professor Kennetta Hammond Perry, a scholar of black Britain, spoke candidly about the need for black women historians to formulate a praxis of soul care as we, those who do the heavy labor of research, thinking, processing ideas, and writing the stories of the formerly enslaved, are confronted with archival sources that reveal all manner of violent, depressing, triggering, and hateful experiences that black women historical actors lived through so many years ago. I was moved by her call to action but also left with many questions about how to approach the archives and leave intact emotionally. A number of sociological studies have reported that the various stressors and discriminatory treatments that black women academics encounter have long-standing negative effects on our health. As a historian of slavery, I know that Nell Irvin Painter's assertion "that physical abuse and slavery go together" is true and the historical record yields voluminous accounts of enslaved women's physical and sexual abuse.[6] I am also aware that antebellum medical records about bondwomen detail medical treatments that were sometimes brutal, inhumane, and based on incorrect biological knowledge about black women's bodies and what they could endure physically. To be situated in slavery studies and medicine is to sit at the center of haptic studies. And yet, understanding the medical lives of black women in slavery through "the perception and manipulation of them as objects by doctors who used their sense of touch . . . helped to create another ethic of being in the world" for doctor, patient, and perhaps contemporary researcher.[7] What I am proposing is that when we enter the archives, particularly with the set of experiences that black women have in an American society that has exceptionalized them across centuries,[8] that we do not lay aside the cultural knowledge(s) we possess but come armed with them in our search to root out the fullness and complexities of slave women's lives through a rereading of the archival source.

Accessing a "haptic visuality" allows me the capacity to use my "eye like an organ of touch," much like antebellum doctors treated their women patients.[9] Writing about the senses, the haptic, is just as much about trying to give voice to tactile experiences and their relationship to both the nineteenth-century and twenty-first-century worlds. The researcher reads and absorbs information mined from dusty boxes, old folders, and databases that appear on flat computer screens, organizes it, and writes as if she is a resident in limbo between the historic then and the present now. Using hapticity as a methodological tool makes the pursuit of objectivity a more honest endeavor. It allows the researcher to bring all of her faculties into the process of generating scholarship.

When I began my dissertation research over ten years ago, I decided that I would devote considerable time to understanding the interior lives of the women who lived, toiled, and were experimented on by slave owner and pioneering gynecological surgeon James Marion Sims. The only archival source about the women besides Sims's memoir and medical journal article was a lone 1850 census record. What new information could it have generated for me that other historians had not located and written about since Sims's rise to prominence as the "Father of American Gynecology?" I tried looking at it with the assumption that had I been a slave woman who was sexually active, what might that mean on a faraway slave farm–cum–medical laboratory? I knew that women who were isolated from their friends, family, and permanent homes and who were ill might be even more vulnerable to sexual abuse because their medical conditions might have interfered with their ability to ward off attackers; perhaps they were also simply depressed. Armed with this hunch, I found that one of Sims's slave patients of childbearing age had given birth to a little girl identified as "mulatto" during his four-year experimental trial. The girl was the youngest child on the slave farm and listed as two years old. Here was evidence that I could apply the framework of haptic studies to the discipline of history before I knew that I could examine, interpret, and analyze the politics of touch and manipulation through the lenses of race, gender, sexuality, and medicine. Knowing that enslaved women were touched constantly without their consent by men who viewed them with contempt and lust and as the physical tools of labor, I imagined that at least one of Sims's patients might have borne, quite literally, the mark and product of interracial sex, a child. The slave, experimental patient, and nurse was assumed to be a stronger medical specimen who could withstand the literal abuse of her body by white men who wielded surgical blades to hopefully heal their reproductive bodies and their penises to ensure that reproduction of wealth occurred. These white men not only assumed that black women were not fragile bodies but also practiced how to treat black women as receptacles for whatever desires they imagined. Yet members of the black slave community always resisted these treatments and procedures of exploitation.[10]

In August 1819, Nanny, a Columbia, South Carolina, enslaved woman, lay in agony for sixty hours because she was unable to give birth naturally. Despite the presence of a slave midwife, her labor could not be induced. Afraid that Nanny and her child would die, the midwife called Dr. Charles Atkins to intervene in this obstetrical case. After Nanny was examined, she underwent emergency surgeries on her bladder, ruptured cervix, and vagina. She endured the surgeries over a two-day period. Nanny was a high-risk obstetric and gynecologic patient because she was carrying twins who had died in utero. Her doctor removed one stillborn child by "hand art" and the other, the second day, with his surgical blade. As risky as antebellum-era surgeries were, Nanny amazingly survived the procedures.[11]

The nineteenth century was a watershed era in American gynecologic medicine. White men entered a field that had been dominated by women for millennia, but these men also pioneered surgical advances that repaired obstetrical fistulae, removed diseased ovaries, and performed successful caesarean section operations. In the South, enslaved women were disproportionately represented in these early surgical experiments. Physicians worked on them in their homes, hospitals, and classrooms. As doctors wrote about black women's diseases and bodies, their colleagues, perhaps inadvertently, learned how to think about and treat black women from medical journal articles. Doctors created a metanarrative about race, ability, and gender that centered on black women. This metanarrative might have been peppered with technical jargon about medical procedures, but their writings unquestionably offered an early "technology" of race through medicine. The technology of race was certainly employed in medical journals and the pedagogical framework of medical training taught in hospitals because it, as historian Evelyn Brooks Higginbotham argues, "signif[ied] the elaboration and implementation of discourses (classificatory and evaluative) in order to maintain the survival and hegemony of one group over another."[12] The metanarrative was deeply nuanced not because of its foundation in the politics of race and medical knowledge, always a contentious issue in antebellum America, but rather because much of the metanarrative included enslaved people's voices. When doctors chose to include their voices in medical literature, their testimony revealed deep fissures in the ideology of white Southern paternalism and black people's acceptance of this so-called benevolence. In numerous medical case narratives, doctors would write about the soundness and strength that black people possessed despite their illnesses and the ease with which black patients managed pain. Yet, in the same narratives, contradictions appeared that revealed black patients' frailties and pains. In Nanny's case, enslaved men and women intervened on her behalf because they witnessed the wasting away of her physical strength and vitality because she "bred" so often.

The narrative of Nanny's medical case exposed the concerns of the enslaved men and women from her community. They informed Dr. Atkins of their feelings about Nanny's physical frailty due to her seven former pregnancies.[13] They declared Nanny should have never been allowed to "breed" because her body was "too delicate." The manipulation of Nanny's body by the father, perhaps fathers, of her children, the slave midwife, and her doctor meant that at no point in her life was her body ever hers to control and direct. The manipulation and handling of her body by so many others who were connected to her by the web of slavery rendered her too fragile to labor as a slave woman was thought to be able to on the lying-in bed. The application of haptic studies in slave medical history demands that we investigate the cartography of touch as sources reveal information to us. A fellow black woman slave, the midwife, was with Nanny during the bulk of her prelabor, surely wiping her brow, providing her with water, rubbing her body during contractions, and although there is no written evidence to substantiate my hunch that Nanny's pregnancy was a communal affair, I am certain that she probably received visitors from her neighbors and family. These visitors were probably the same slaves who informed Dr. Atkins of Nanny's fragility. In 1825, in one of the country's oldest articles about obstetrics and slave medicine, Dr. Charles Atkins wrote "Rupture of the Uterus and Vagina, Terminating in Recovery, with Remarks on These Accidents" in which he detailed how he used haptic methods to medically treat his slave patient. The one person stripped of any agency and voice in Atkins's article is Nanny. How did she respond to losing a baby? As a woman who bred a lot, how did her new infertility affect her sense of self as a woman, mother, and slave? How would Nanny's value be diminished as a slave whose womb was removed, whose economic value was reduced as a reproductive laborer, and who was marked as weak by the slave community. Medical science in 1825 believed a woman's constitution, temperament, and logic were tied to her uterus. Nanny's postsurgical body and existence were affected by each of these factors, practices, and ideologies. To minimize the impact of her tactile experiences in slavery and medicine is to deny the importance of understanding hapticity, a practice and way of being that slaves could neither ignore nor dismiss. They spoke of laying hands on each other in love and in defense of themselves and slept several to a bed; black women on large plantations were housed together in hospital rooms, and those who were nursing were forced to have their nipples suckled by both white and black babies who were not their own.

Thus to move from understanding the history of slavery and medicine as soul murder to a methodological framework of soul care, the researcher must employ haptic studies. We should consider how our senses—not only touch, but taste, sight, and sound—situate us and historical actors as bodies in political and economic contexts (such as labor), as well as in personal and sensory ones. Doing so provides scholars with additional methods to resituate historical objectivity and cultural experiences in our work and knowledge production. Further, the inclusion of haptic studies in the history of slavery and the history of medicine allows us to push against staid and one-dimensional ideologies that foreground historical objectivity as a philosophy and enterprise whereby the researcher's biases are excised. If objectivity is supposed to be about things in themselves, I am arguing that those "things," in this case, enslaved women's medical lives, are rooted in the inherent violence of the archives because of how they, as owned objects-subjects, were inserted into the archives. Once again, white medical men's placement and handling of black women within the historical record are a reflection of an inherent flaw in the archives that haptic studies can neither erase nor solve, but it assists us in naming the hierarchy as defective and complicating the pursuit of objectivity in slavery studies.

Notes

1. W. P. L. Jennings, "Curious Case of Fœtation." *Charleston Medical Journal and Review* 7, no. 2 (February1852): 29–31.

2. Adam Gopnik, "Feel Me: What the New Science of Touch Says about Ourselves," *New Yorker*, May 16, 2016, https://www.newyorker.com/magazine/2016/05/16/what-the-science-of-touch-says-about-us, accessed May 17, 2018.

3. See *Medical Bondage: Race, Gender and the Origins of American Gynecology* (Athens: University of Georgia Press, 2017) by Deirdre Cooper Owens to learn more about the early gynecological work of James Marion Sims, who

performed vaginal examinations on enslaved women who suffered from obstetrical fistula using pewter spoons initially. He later "perfected" the speculum, which he called the Sims speculum, from those early examinations of his enslaved experimental patients.

4. Michele Mitchell, "Silences Broken, Silences Kept: Gender and Sexuality in African-American History," *Gender and History* 11, no. 3 (November 1999): 433–44.

5. Marisa J. Fuentes, *Dispossessed Lives: Enslaved Women, Violence, and the Archive* (Philadelphia: University of Pennsylvania Press, 2016), 114.

6. *Soul Murder and Slavery*, Charles Edmondson Historical Lecture Series, 15 (Waco, TX: Baylor University Press, 1995), 5.

7. Kennetta Hammond Perry, talk given at Michigan State University for the Cross-Generational Dialogues in Black Women's History, March 2015.

8. For example, their children inherited their slave status; they were physically handled and mishandled while nude in public spaces; their virginity was often snatched from them as it was a cultural practice for Southern slaveholding white men to gain sexual experience from bondwomen they either supervised or owned through rape; and in the twentieth and twenty-first centuries, they have been made the mascots for sexually irresponsible "welfare queens" and demonized "baby mamas." Essentially, black women researchers in particular know through their lived experiences and socializations what racialized and gendered oppression looks like and feels like.

9. Abbie Garrington, "Touching Texts: The Haptic Sense in Modernist Literature," *Literature Compass* 7/9 (2010): 812.

10. More information about the enslaved mulatto child and Nanny's medical case appears in Cooper Owens, *Medical Bondage*.

11. "Atkins on the Rupture of the Uterus and Vagina, Terminating in Recovery, with Remarks on These Accidents," *Carolina Journal of Medicine, Science and Agriculture* 1, no. 3 (July 1825): 332–42.

12. Evelyn Brooks Higginbotham, "African-American Women's History and the Metalanguage of Race," *Signs* 17, no. 2 (Winter 1992): 252.

13. "Atkins on the Rupture," 332.

Part 2

✦

Abolitionism and
Black Intellectual History

INTRODUCTION

Kellie Carter-Jackson

In 1969, historian Benjamin Quarles published one of his most transformative works, *Black Abolitionists*. It was the first book to examine the history of the abolitionist movement through the lens, contributions, and ideas of Black leadership during the nineteenth century. He placed Black people at the center of the movement they created. Quarles gave Black Americans autonomy and agency. He put volume to their voices and added an incredible amount of value to their contributions intellectually, socially, politically, culturally, and even economically. Quarles set a precedent in the field of American abolitionist history for positioning African Americans as "expounders of the faith" rather than the beneficiaries or recipients of white favor. The absence of Black people in the telling of abolitionist history is not an abolitionist history, but a fantasy of white supremacy. In *Black Abolitionists*, Quarles informs readers that the neglect of Black actors in the movement validated myths Southerners concocted about happy and content slaves. He claimed, "To picture the Negro as civic-minded, as a reformer, might arouse interest in him as a human being and sympathy for him as a figure battling against the odds." In addition to uprooting the cardinal tenants of Southern ideology regarding Black inferiority, Quarles argues that while some white abolitionists would have "never consciously borrowed anything from the South," many valued the "ego-soothing role of exclusivity thrust upon them by the supporters of slavery."[1] For decades, scholars have been hard at work dismantling the myths of abolition.

What I appreciate about the following essays are the ways these three authors have deepened and enriched Quarles's original project and purpose to place Black thought at the center of Western political movements regarding emancipation and the dismantling of colonial thought. Vincent Carretta writes on "Black Intellectual History in the Period of Abolition before Abolition." Carretta examines how Black eighteenth-century authors anticipated the Black reformers that would succeed them in the calling for the abolition of slavery, moral reform, Black citizenship, and

Black labor more broadly. Carretta sees English-speaking authors of African descent at the vanguard of the abolitionist movement to end both the slave trade and the institution of slavery. Too often we have started the abolitionist movement with the nineteenth century and centered the popularity of Frederick Douglass as a stand-in for all Black intellectual thought. Carretta compels us to look much earlier and at the writings of both men and women. The theme of liberation was present throughout all of the eighteenth century among Black authors. Indeed, Phillis Wheatley was a pioneer in the ideological arguments later put forth by the radical writings of David Walker.[2] Her poetry caused people to question the revolutionary metaphor of "slavery" and consider the actual lived experiences of chattel slavery inflicted on Black bodies.

In Marlene L. Daut's chapter, "Anticonquest and the Development of Anticolonialism after the Haitian Constitution of 1805," she illustrates the intellectual history of Haiti as anticolonial from its origins. While the Haitian constitution went through several versions primarily from 1805 to 1816, three concepts remained a constant: Haiti was antislavery, Haiti was pro-Black, and Haiti was anticolonial. Daut makes a powerful argument that, in Afro-diaspora intellectual history, Haiti is the first state. As Black abolitionist Frederick Douglass rightly declared, "We should not forget that the freedom you and I enjoy today . . . is largely due to the brave stand taken by the black sons of Haiti . . . striking for their freedom, they struck for the freedom of every black man in the world."[3] Daut argues that anticolonialism was at the heart of Haitian nation building. Haitians were essentially concerned with protecting "black sovereignty in a white colonial world." Haiti saw conquest as fundamentally problematic and dehumanizing. With conquest came slavery; thus its first constitutions not only eradicated slavery but outlawed colonial rule.

Finally, Jeffrey R. Kerr-Ritchie's "The International Dimensions of West Indies Emancipation Day Speeches" examines antislavery activists and their speeches. By tracking the rhetoric and reception of Josiah Jones, Frederick Douglass, Henry W. Johnson, William Wells Brown, and white minister Henry Bleby, Kerr-Ritchie reveals their transnational and cross-border features. In addition, he challenges the limitations of a nationalist framework for understanding slavery, abolition, and postemancipation. Each abolitionist and speech seeks to convey a larger truth about the global connections of liberation struggles. Emancipation Day addresses were an opportunity to express current grievances and galvanize audiences about where progress was most needed all throughout the world. Kerr-Ritchie shows us men who are committed to memorializing emancipation victories while simultaneously striving for the complete abolition of slavery in the Western Hemisphere and beyond. Moreover, Kerr-Ritchie desires readers to think critically about the creation of an intellectual and political tradition that transcends local, state, and national borders.

There are several themes that draw these essays together. First, the centrality of Black voices in advocating for their own conceptions of freedom is critical. From Toussaint and Dessalines to Equiano and Phillis Wheatley to Douglass and Henry W. Johnson, these men and women served as prophets, eloquently communicating the will of Black people. From the framing of constitutions to the drafting of speeches and personal narratives, the ideas of Black men and women dictated the meaning and direction of emancipation. As Quarles he contended, "To the extent that American has a revolutionary tradition [the Black American] was its protagonist no less than its symbol."[4] Removing Black thinkers from the margins and putting them back to their rightful place at the center of abolitionist history is all but required for understanding the movement in its totality.

Second, the written word was fundamental to advancing Black intellectual activism. The written word operated as both a sword in defense of Black humanity and as a strategic weapon for condemning racist arguments and practices. There is a tendency to believe that abolition is a physical act, played out mainly through violence, collective rebellion, or war. However, Black people were intellectually invested in relaying the meaning of freedom first. Black thinkers engaged in the concept of abolitionism to define their humanity, protect their humanity, and prevent social, political, and economic systems from requiring oppression. Combatting the ideological stronghold of slavery through speeches and written documents was just as important as physical acts of resistance. In some instances, written words have impacted our understanding more than individual and collective acts. For example, the pervasive imprint of phrases such as "We the people," "Give me liberty or give me death," or "What does the Fourth of July mean to me?" is virtually known by all. These ideas have cemented our understanding of freedom and equality.

Third, no major action on the part of the abolitionist movement was accomplished without thinking through the possible outcome and consequences. Haiti constructed its constitutions repeatedly with an eye on the future. Daut explains how Haitian founders perceived the dangers of conquest and colonialism. The early Black writers of the eighteenth century understood how their words and advocacy might create opportunities for others to expand upon their activism. As Carretta argues, early Black leaders thought about abolition, before the time of abolition. Finally, Kerr-Ritchie explores how the international dimensions of antebellum

Emancipation Day speeches served as clarion calls and warnings to slaveholding societies. These abolitionist speakers reminded audiences of the past but also encouraged what could be possible for future generations if liberation was achieved.

Bishop Daniel A. Payne of the African Methodist Episcopal church once wrote, "I am opposed to slavery, not because it enslaves the black man, but because it enslaves man." What Daut, Carretta, and Kerr-Ritchie do for the field of abolitionist historiography is important not merely because their subjects are Black but because their subjects were striving for the protections of all people. With the abolitionist's contributions, for the first time, America was forced to face the rights of Black people and to some extent all oppressed peoples as a national priority. Abolitionists expanded how people understood human rights. Reforms in the realms of, but not limited to, labor, gender, criminality, capital, citizenship, empire, and nation all owe a debt to the efforts and tactics that abolitionists championed. In the long trajectory of Black freedom struggles, Black abolitionist leaders remain the standard by which scholars have examined the civil rights movement, the Black Power movement, and even Black Lives Matter. These essays reveal how we can understand the intersections of abolitionism and intellectual history as central to paving a better and bright future for all.

Notes

1. See Benjamin Quarles, *Black Abolitionists* (New York: Da Capo Press, 1969), viii–ix.

2. See Arlette Frund, "Phillis Wheatley, a Public Intellectual," in *Toward an Intellectual History of Black Women*, ed. Mia Bay, Farah J. Griffin, Martha Jones, and Barbara Savage (Chapel Hill: University of North Carolina, 2015), 35–52.

3. Frederick Douglass, speech on Haiti delivered at the World's Fair, January 2, 1893.

4. See Quarles, *Black Abolitionists*, 248–49.

Chapter 4

Black Intellectual History in the Period of Abolition before Abolition

Vincent Carretta

Recognition of the differences and similarities between eighteenth- and nineteenth-century works authored by Anglophone people of African descent and the contexts in which they were written compels us to expand the boundaries of black intellectual history. The genres of the as-told-to slave narrative and the slave narrative written directly by its author originated in the transatlantic eighteenth century. But failure to appreciate the ideological and economic disparities between the earlier and later periods leads to an underestimation of the achievement and significance of the works published before the abolition of the transatlantic slave trade by Britain and the United States in 1807 and 1808, respectively. Olaudah Equiano's *The Interesting Narrative of the Life of Olaudah Equiano, or Gustavus Vassa, the African. Written by Himself* (London, 1789), for example, is often approached anachronistically and teleologically as a literary and intellectual *type* in the development of the African American slave narrative genre. His promise is supposedly only fulfilled in the *antitype* of the slave narrative of Frederick Douglass (1818–95). The achievements of earlier authors of African descent are frequently evaluated by the extent to which they are deemed to have foreshadowed Douglass, rather than on their own merits or in their own historical and intellectual contexts.[1]

Eighteenth-century authors of African descent anticipated in many ways those who followed. Equiano (ca. 1745–97), for example, established many of the formal elements and marketing tactics that later authors of African descent would imitate: an engraved portrait of the author, the claim on the title page that the text was "Written by Himself," an epigraph, a description of the treatment of the enslaved, a petition

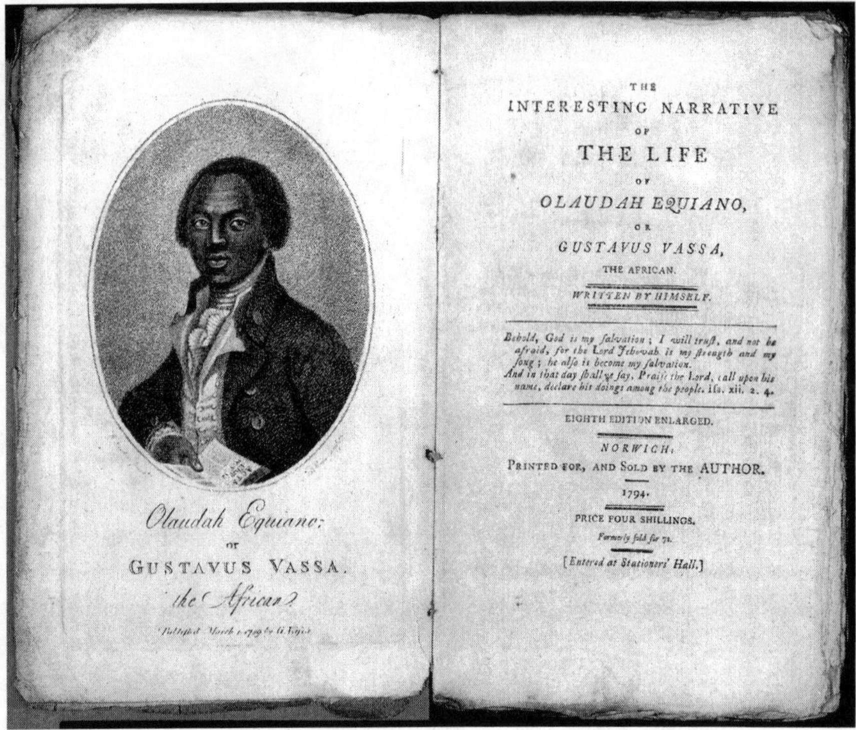
Olaudah Equiano;
or
GUSTAVUS VASSA.
the African.

THE
INTERESTING NARRATIVE
OF
THE LIFE
OF
OLAUDAH EQUIANO,
OR
GUSTAVUS VASSA,
THE AFRICAN.
WRITTEN BY HIMSELF.

Behold, God is my salvation; I will trust, and not be afraid, for the Lord Jehovah is my strength and my song; he also is become my salvation.
And in that day shall ye say, Praise the Lord, call upon his name, declare his doings among the people. Isa. xii. 2. 4.

EIGHTH EDITION ENLARGED.

NORWICH:
PRINTED FOR, AND SOLD BY THE AUTHOR.
1794.
PRICE FOUR SHILLINGS.
Formerly sold for 7s.
[*Entered at Stationers' Hall.*]

Fig. 1. Frontispiece and title page from *The Interesting Narrative of the Life of Olaudah Equiano* (London, 1789; 8th ed., Norwich, 1794) Library of Congress, Prints and Photographs Division.

(Equiano's subscription list), the inclusion of documents, testimonials by people of European descent, the addition of blurbs from reviews of the book, book tours.

But the strategies, tactics, and tone used by Equiano and his contemporaries of African descent before the abolition of the transatlantic slave trade differ significantly from those employed after 1807. Such differences in black intellectual history include the concepts of abolition, the definition of national identity, the question of citizenship, the importance of religion, the varieties of unfree labor, the relationship between phenotype and social status, and the role of Africa. For example, before 1807 the term *abolition*, rather than being synonymous with *emancipation*, usually referred to opposition to the transatlantic slave trade, a position that could be embraced by those who defended the enslavement of people of African descent as well as by those who denounced slavery.

Once the transatlantic slave trade came under sustained religious, moral, and economic attack during the last quarter of the century, supporters of slavery felt compelled to develop the racist defense that in the next century would become the now all-too-familiar justification of the institution. The traditional definition of *race* as *bloodline* was increasingly replaced by the notion of *race* as *species* that became dominant in the nineteenth century. This "modern" concept of race, which was secondary during the early colonial American period, became primary after 1800.[2]

Former eighteenth-century differences in degree between equally human masters and slaves became nineteenth-century differences in kind between allegedly superior people of European descent and supposedly inferior people of African descent. The post-1800 justification for chattel slavery was ethnic at its core. All slaves were now of African descent (though not all persons of African descent were slaves). And this type of slavery was hereditary, with no statute of limitations. The nineteenth-century model of the "peculiar institution" of slavery in the antebellum American South comprises cotton plantations worked by American-born enslaved people of African descent owned by people of European descent. The enslaved are essentially undifferentiated from one another except by occupation. The whole economic institution of slavery is defended by assertions of the racial inferiority of the enslaved based on spurious pseudoscientific claims of the polygenetic origins of humans.

The eighteenth century presents a far more varied picture. Throughout this period, slaves were imported directly to the colonies from Africa, especially to the sugar-growing plantations of the West Indies, where the very high mortality rate meant that the native slave population was not self-sustaining. By 1750, the majority of slaves in British North America, on the other hand, were native born, with the population growing by natural increase. Mainly because of disease, before the widespread use of quinine, Europeans were restricted to factories (trading posts) on the coast of Africa and were dependent on Africans for the maintenance of the slave trade.

Very few enslaved Africans could have been exported to the Americas without the complicity of their fellow Africans. Europeans were able to exploit this complicity because the concept of *Africa* was primarily geographic, rather than social, political, or religious to the extent that *Europe* had become by the eighteenth century. Nor were the notions of *nation* and *state* equivalent on the two continents. The indigenous peoples of Africa did not think of themselves as *African*: they were Ashanti, Fante, Yoruba, or any one of a number of other ethnic groups with differing languages, religions, customs, and political systems. Tending to see themselves as more dissimilar than alike, the various African peoples were willing to enslave and sell to Europeans those outside their own group because they did not identify with them.

Before the end of the legal transatlantic slave trade in 1807, Anglophone authors made much of the alleged differing suitability of the various African peoples for enslavement. Some African nations were seen as too warlike, for example. Only in the last quarter of the eighteenth century did some of the people removed from Africa as slaves begin to embrace a public social and political identity of *African*, calling themselves "Sons of Africa" in both Britain and America, for example.[3] In a sense, *Africa* did not exist as an idea, as well as a place, until after the antitransatlantic slave trade and antislavery movements began. Olaudah Equiano's *Interesting Narrative*, for example, traces the development of his expanding identity from Igbo, to "almost an Englishman," to the African-British man in his frontispiece portrait.[4]

Underlying Equiano's evolving identity is his belief in uniformitarianism, which he shared with the vast majority of his contemporaries. The idea that human nature is everywhere and at all times essentially the same is the logical extension of the orthodox monogenetic belief that all humans are direct descendants of Adam and Eve. Customs (or manners) change and vary. Human nature does not. In the face of the small but increasingly influential number of polygenists, who argued that God created various types of humans at different times, Equiano uses his description of "Eboe" to support orthodox Christianity.[5] He elaborates his analogy between Africans and Old Testament Jews to make his monogenetic point and to imply that Africans are fully prepared for Christian Revelation. Equiano does not compare Africans culturally to eighteenth-century Jews, isolated and treated as aliens by their Christian neighbors, because they had the opportunity to embrace Christianity but refused to do so.

Not even the most fervent eighteenth-century opponent of slavery contended that Africans were the cultural equals of Europeans. But like the ancient Hebrews, according to Equiano, Africans are as fully human as Europeans, although at different stages of social and economic development. Their putative inferiority is due only to their current situation. By using the analogy between Jews and Africans to invoke stadial theory, which held that human societies progressed from the stage of hunting and gathering (e.g., Native Americans), to herding (Scottish Highlanders), to agriculture (classical Greeks and Romans, Old Testament Hebrews), to commercial exchange (England), Equiano places Africans just one step below civilized Europeans. Thus, they are closer to becoming equivalent to modern Englishmen than even some Britons are. This argument becomes overt in the concluding paragraph of chapter 1 of the *Interesting Narrative*, where Equiano spells out the implications of expanding categories from Igbo to African to human:

> Let the polished and haughty European recollect that *his* ancestors were once, like the Africans, uncivilized, and even barbarous. Did Nature make *them* inferior to their sons? and should *they too* have been made slaves? Every rational mind answers, No. Let such reflections as these melt the pride of their superiority into sympathy for the wants and miseries of their sable brethren, and compel them to acknowledge, that understanding is not confined to feature or colour.[6]

Such beliefs in uniformitarianism, monogenesis, and stadial theory, which eighteenth-century authors of African descent could assume that most of their readers accepted, would be rejected by nineteenth-century apologists for slavery.

Before the last quarter of the eighteenth century, slavery was perceived primarily as an economic concern, not a moral problem, and the initial basis of African slavery was predominantly financial rather than racial. Slavery and Christianity were rarely seen as incompatible. References to slavery are widespread in the Old Testament, and nowhere in the New Testament is slavery explicitly prohibited. To those who believed that the afterlife was far more important than temporal existence, what mattered most was that pagan Africans be exposed to the truth of Christianity, and that they be humanely treated in whatever social condition they were placed. Thus, slavery could even be seen as a kind of fortunate fall, whereby the discomfort of the enslaved African was overcompensated by the opportunity to achieve eternal salvation. Jacobus Elisa Joannes Capitein (ca. 1717–47), a native African, defends this notion of a fortunate fall in his Latin dissertation.[7] One of the most celebrated and learned eighteenth-century blacks, Capitein had been brought from present-day Ghana, where the Dutch had a slave-trading factory at Elmina, to Holland. There he studied theology from 1726 to 1742, when he was ordained. He returned to Elmina as a missionary. Capitein justifies slavery as having biblical precedent in the past and as serving evangelical ends in the present and future. The fortunate fall into slavery is also the subject of one of Phillis Wheatley's earliest poems, the notorious "On Being Brought from Africa to America."

During most of the eighteenth century, slavery was generally accepted as one of the long-familiar statuses of the social and economic structure that formed the hierarchy of society. Talk of general emancipation—the abolition of the institution of race-based, chattel slavery—was rare. Manumissions of the few were not seen as challenging the validity of enslaving the many. The actions as well as the words of some eighteenth-century authors of African descent demonstrate their acceptance of the institution of slavery at some points in their lives. Olaudah Equiano, for example, was a slave driver in the 1770s, when he was a free man.

Social or economic status could supersede ethnicity and phenotype in determining the suitability of enslavement for someone during the period of the transatlantic slave trade. Throughout the eighteenth century, British subjects on both sides of the Atlantic recognized slavery as an inappropriate status for at least some Africans. Individual Africans could be deemed either too inherently noble, or too valuable as slave-trading partners, to be enslaved. In two separate historical cases during the first half of the eighteenth century, Africans who were thought to have been wrongfully or mistakenly enslaved were ransomed into freedom when their situations became publicly known. The lives of Job Ben Solomon, also known as Ayuba Suleiman Diallo (1701–73), and William Ansah Sessarakoo (flourished 1736–49) found their way into print, respectively, in the 1730s and 1740s.[8] Enslaved in different parts of Africa, Ben Solomon was taken to Maryland, and Sessarakoo to the West Indies. When their fates became known in London, the Royal African Company redeemed Ben Solomon and the British government bought Sessarakoo's freedom. Both men were brought to London, where they were fêted as aristocratic celebrities. Each was deemed worthy of having his portrait painted by an eminent artist. Ben Solomon, a Muslim, was considered too well educated to be enslaved. Sessarakoo was treated as too well bred to be a slave. Both were eventually repatriated to their respective homelands in Africa. There each resumed his previous participation in the British transatlantic slave trade. Solomon and Sessarakoo were recognized as being more valuable as economic partners than as slaves. Even after the American Revolution, Anglo-Americans tended to acknowledge the significance of social status. And claims of noble or royal birth by wrongly enslaved Africans on both sides of the Atlantic were at least plausible before the abolition of the transatlantic slave trade in 1808, no matter how improbable. But outside of fictional accounts those fortunate Africans were a precious few.

During the eighteenth century, many slaves knew from their own African experience that being black was not equivalent to being enslaved. Freedom for them was a memory of the recent past rather than a dream deferred to a distant future. Prior to the British occupation of Boston, Phillis Wheatley (ca. 1753–84) quite carefully balanced her public expressions of revolutionary and loyalist sentiments. In her poem "To the Right Honourable William, Earl of Dartmouth, His Majesty's Principal Secretary of State for North America, &c." Wheatley reappropriates the concept of *slavery* from its common metaphorical use in the colonial discourse of discontent, which described any perceived limitation on colonial rights and liberty as an attempt by England to "enslave" (white) Americans.[9] Wheatley appears to use *slavery* in this conventional sense in the poem. She invokes her authority (her ethos) to speak from experience and appeals to her readers' pathos to remind her readers of the reality of chattel slavery trivialized by the political metaphor:

> No more, *America*, in mournful strain
> Of wrongs, and grievance unredress'd complain,
> No longer shall thou dread the iron chain,
> Which wanton *Tyranny* with lawless hand
> Had made, and with it meant t'enslave the land.
> Should you, my lord, while you peruse my song,
> Wonder from whence my love of *Freedom* sprung,
> Whence flow these wishes for the common good,
> By feeling hearts alone best understood,
> I, young in life, by seeming cruel fate
> Was snatch'd from *Afric's* fancy'd happy seat[.]
> . . . .
> Such, such my case. And can I then but pray
> Others may never feel tyrannic sway? (lines 15–25 [emphases in original], 30–31)[10]

Wheatley revised the poem from manuscript to publication to move directly from metaphorical to actual slavery.[11] Most enslaved authors of African descent in Anglo-America during the nineteenth century, however, had never known freedom. Their enslavers sought to deracinate their African heritage. For someone like Mary Prince, childhood was at best a brief period of illusory innocence, a prelude to a life of hardship.[12]

Revolutionary rhetoric made many colonists, black as well as white, question for the first time the hypocrisy of owners of chattel slaves who protested against their own metaphorical enslavement. The African-born former slave Caesar Sarter asks the readers of the *Essex Journal and Merrimack Packet* on August 17, 1774,

> to attend to the request of a poor African, and consider these evil consequences, and gross heinousness of reducing to, and retaining in slavery a free people. Would you desire the preservation of your

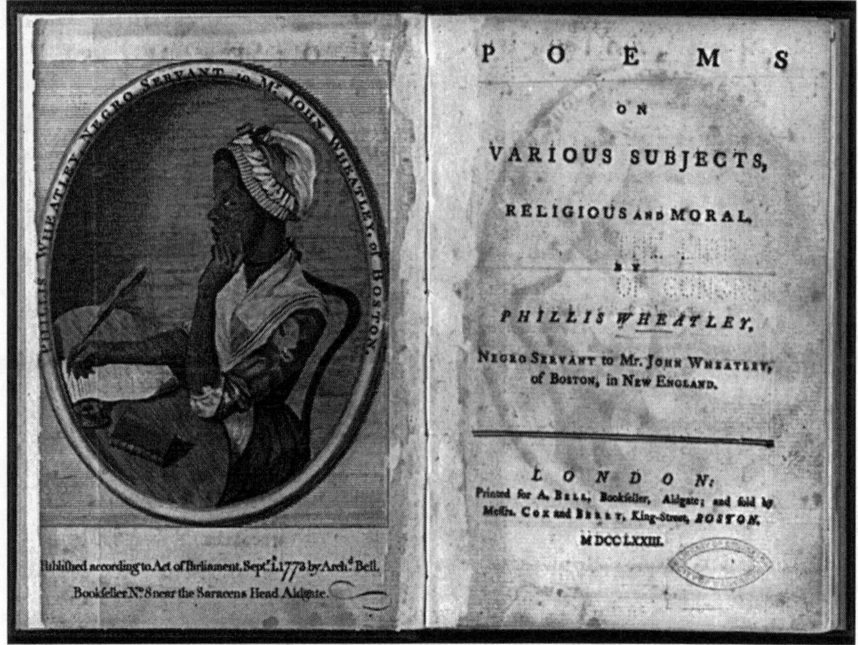

POEMS
ON
VARIOUS SUBJECTS,
RELIGIOUS AND MORAL.
BY
PHILLIS WHEATLEY,
NEGRO SERVANT to Mr. JOHN WHEATLEY,
of BOSTON, in NEW ENGLAND.

LONDON:
Printed for A. BELL, Bookseller, Aldgate; and sold by
Messrs. COX and BERRY, King-Street, BOSTON.
MDCCLXXIII.

Fig. 2. Frontispiece from Phillis Wheatley, *Poems on Various Subjects, Religious and Moral* (1773). Library of Congress, Prints and Photographs Division.

> own liberty? As the first step let the oppressed Africans be liberated; then, and not till then, may you with confidence and consistency of conduct, look to Heaven for a blessing on your endeavours to knock the shackles with which your task masters are hampering you, from your own feet.

During the same period, people of African origin and descent, such as Phillis Wheatley and Benjamin Banneker (1731–1806), asserted their claims to being African Americans in the new United States.[13]

A repeated theme in Wheatley's writings is the similitude of the political agency denied to white colonists, and that which they in turn denied to their black compatriots. Wheatley's own emancipation allowed her to join the conversation about slavery overtly by appropriating revolutionary rhetoric to openly equate contemporaneous slave owners with Old Testament villains, and by implication people of African descent with the Israelites, God's chosen people.[14] In the published letter that Wheatley sent to Samson Occom (1723–92) in February 1774, she assails "Modern Egyptians" by combining an argument based on natural rights—"in every human Breast, God has implanted a Principle, which we call Love of Freedom; it is impatient of Oppression, and pants for Deliverance"—with a prophetic voice to warn slave owners that divine punishment awaits "those whose Avarice impels them to countenance and help forward the Calamities of their Fellow Creatures" by disobeying "the glorious Dispensation of civil and religious Liberty." Wheatley's own liberation allowed her to use an ironic tone bordering on sarcasm to close her indictment of slave owners: "How well the Cry for Liberty, and the reverse Disposition for the Exercise of oppressive Power over others agree,—I humbly think it does not require the Penetration of a Philosopher to determine."[15] Wheatley was thus a pioneer in the development of the tradition of the African American jeremiad found in the writings of David Walker (1785–1830) and other nineteenth-century emancipationists.[16] She was an African American trailblazer in the development of what would come to be called liberation theology, the belief that God favored the oppressed. In her poems "To His Excellency General Washington," "On the Death of General Wooster," and *Liberty and Peace*, Wheatley expresses her hopes for the extension of revolutionary principles to include people like her. Similarly, Banneker's confident tone in his published letter to Thomas Jefferson reflects his apparent conviction that logic will compel Jefferson to acknowledge that the tenets of the Declaration of Independence apply to people of African, as well as European, descent in the new nation.

Developments between 1776 and 1808 seemed to justify optimism that the ideological grounds for the American Revolution would lead ineluctably to a general emancipation of the enslaved throughout the United States. The institution of slavery appeared to be eroding during the period. Manumissions became increasingly common, especially in the states around the Chesapeake; slavery was outlawed by either legislation or judicial decisions in some states in the North; states in the mid-Atlantic region enacted gradual emancipation laws. And the economic foundation of slavery in the South looked increasingly tenuous because the international market for tobacco, the principal crop produced by enslaved labor, was saturated. But hopes for an early end to slavery proved premature.

Peter Williams Jr. (1780?–1840), "A Descendant of Africa," was prescient in his oration celebrating the abolition of the American transatlantic slave trade in 1808. He warned his audience about the "number of opposers" who "from interest and prejudice" remained "carefully watching for every opportunity to injure the cause" of emancipation.[17] A resurgence of slavery followed the invention of the cotton gin, the consequent growth of the international market for the products of the slavery-based cotton industry, and the expansion of slavery into new territories in the West and Deep South. Slavery became so fundamental to the prosperity of the United States that its eradication seemed anything but inevitable.

A significant difference between the guarded optimism of late-eighteenth-century authors of African descent and subsequent authors can be seen by comparing the pronouns, substance, and tone of a paragraph in Banneker's 1792 letter to Thomas Jefferson to those in a paragraph in Douglass's 1852 address in Rochester, New York. In the former the first-person plural transitions from referring only to people of African descent to including Jefferson and others of European descent:

> Now Sir, if this is founded in truth, I apprehend you will embrace every opportunity to eradicate that train of absurd and false ideas and opinions which so generally prevails with respect to us; and that your sentiments are concurrent with mine, which are, that one universal Father has given being to us all; and that he hath not only made us all of one flesh, but that he hath also, without partiality, afforded us all the same sensations and endowed us all with the same faculties; and that however variable we may be in society or religion, however diversified in situation or color, we are all of the same family, and stand in the same relation to him.[18]

In Douglass's text, however, the conflict between the enslaved person of African descent referred to in the third person and the audience of European descent referred to in the second person, remains unresolved:

> What, to the American slave, is your 4th of July? I answer: a day that reveals to him, more than all other days in the year, the gross injustice and cruelty to which he is the constant victim. To him, your celebration is a sham . . . a thin veil to cover up crimes which would disgrace a nation of savages. There is not a nation on the earth guilty of practices, more shocking and bloody, than are the people of these United States, at this very hour.[19]

English-speaking authors of African descent were at the forefront of the eighteenth- and nineteenth-century abolitionist movements to eradicate first the transatlantic slave trade and subsequently the institution of slavery. Black intellectuals countered the economic and racist arguments of apologists for slavery with arguments based on ethical, historical, moral, political, and religious principles. The theme of liberation from either physical or spiritual captivity, and often from both, is found in virtually all the writings by authors of African descent during the eighteenth and antebellum nineteenth centuries. The range of representations of the theme reflects the various geographical, social, and temporal settings in which the different eighteenth-century Anglophone African authors produced their writings. Until the financially motivated development of the pseudoscientific justification for race-based slavery, the victory of black intellectuals in the debate over slavery appeared to be ineluctable. The promised land of general emancipation that seemed so close before 1808, however, soon became a dream deferred until more than a half century later.

Notes

1. See, e.g., A. Robert Lee, "Selves Subscribed: Early Afro-America and the Signifying of Phillis Wheatley, Jupiter Hammon, Olaudah Equiano, and David Walker," in *Making America/Making American Literature: Franklin to Cooper*, ed. A. Robert Lee and W. M. Verhoeven (Amsterdam: Rodolphi, 1996), 275–95. "Douglass's *Narrative* [is] a kind of template or grid for the fuller reading of the prior 'self-subscriptions' of Wheatley, Hammon, Equiano/Vassa, and Walker" (280).

2. See Betty Wood, *The Origins of American Slavery* (New York: Hill and Wang, 1997), 7.

3. James Sidbury, *Becoming African in America: Race and Nation in the Early Black Atlantic* (New York: Oxford University Press, 2007).

4. Olaudah Equiano, *The Interesting Narrative of the Life of Olaudah Equiano, or Gustavus Vassa, the African; Written by Himself* (London, 1789) in *Olaudah Equiano: The Interesting Narrative and Other Writings*, ed. Vincent Carretta (1995; New York: Penguin, 2020), 77.

5. The most significant polygenist at the time was Edward Long, whose atypical eighteenth-century arguments in his *History of Jamaica* (London, 1774) anticipate dominant nineteenth-century pseudoscientific racism.

6. Equiano, *Interesting Narrative*, 45.

7. Jacobus Elisa Joannes Capitein, *The Agony of Asar: A Thesis on Slavery by the Former Slave, Jacobus Elisa Joannes Capitein, 1717–1747*, trans. and ed. Grant Parker (Princeton, NJ: Markus Wiener Publishers, 2001).

8. Thomas Bluett, *Some Memoirs of the Life of Job, the Son of Solomon the High Priest of Boonda in Africa; Who Was a Slave about Two Years in Maryland; and Afterwards Being Brought to England, Was Set Free, and Sent to His Native Land in the Year 1734* (London, 1734); anonymous, *The Royal Africa; or, Memoirs of the Young Prince of Annamaboe* (London, 1749).

9. On the pervasive use of metaphorical slavery in colonial discourse, see Peter A. Dorsey, *Common Bondage: Slavery as Metaphor in Revolutionary America* (Knoxville: University of Tennessee Press, 2010).

10. Phillis Wheatley, *The Writings of Phillis Wheatley*, ed. Vincent Carretta (Oxford: Oxford University Press, 2019), 81–82.

11. Thirteen lines separate the metaphorical "enslave" and the account of the speaker's physical enslavement in the manuscript version of the poem.

12. *History of Mary Prince, A West Indian Slave. Related by Herself* (London, 1831).

13. Benjamin Banneker, *Copy of a Letter from Benjamin Banneker to the Secretary of State, with His Answer* (Philadelphia, 1792) in *Unchained Voices: An Anthology of Black Authors in the English-Speaking World of the 18th Century. Expanded Edition*, ed. Vincent Carretta (Lexington: University Press of Kentucky, 2004), 319.

14. Bruce Feiler, *America's Prophet: Moses and the American Story* (New York: William Morrow, 2010). The best-known comparison of American colonists with Old Testament Israelites is probably by Thomas Paine in *Common Sense* (Philadelphia, 1776).

15. Phillis Wheatley to Samson Occom, February 11, 1774, published March 11, 1774. Wheatley. *Writings*, 119–20.

16. Melvin L. Rogers, "David Walker and the Political Power of the Appeal." *Political Theory* 43, no. 2 (2015): 208–33, 223–24.

17. Peter Williams, *An Oration on the Abolition of the Slave Trade; Delivered in the African Church, in the City of New York, January 1, 1808* (New York: Samuel Wood) in *Early Negro Writing, 1760–1837*, ed. Dorothy Porter (Baltimore: Black Classic Press, 1995), 352.

18. Banneker, *Copy of a Letter*, 319.

19. Frederick Douglass, "What to the Slave Is the Fourth of July," *Oration, Delivered in Corinthian Hall, Rochester* (Rochester, 1852) in *Narrative of the Life of Frederick Douglass, an American Slave*, ed. Ira Dworkin (New York: Penguin, 2014), 132.

Chapter 5

✦

Anticonquest and the Development of Anticolonialism after the Haitian Constitution of 1805

Marlene L. Daut

Julia Gaffield's 2010 unearthing of an original printed version of the Haitian Declaration of Independence (dated January 1, 1804) in the National Archives of the United Kingdom brought mainstream attention in the United States to this founding document of Haitian sovereignty.[1] This was partially because of the declaration's challenge to American exceptionalism—Deborah Jenson writes, channeling David Armitage, "It was in Haiti . . . that the declaration of independence as a genre began its trajectory from a single nation's document to a 'global history' of 'imitations and analogues' "—and equally because of what Celucien Joseph has termed "the Haitian Turn," or the resurgence of interest in Haiti among North American scholars following on the heels of Michel-Rolph Trouillot's much referenced *Silencing the Past: Power and the Production of History* (1995).[2] Such a turn toward Haiti—part of larger efforts to combat historical tendencies to turn away from its war of independence—has sparked new questions about the process by which Haiti became sovereign in a colonial Atlantic world. "Why did the generals feel the need to issue two proclamations?" Gaffield and Armitage have asked in their introduction to Gaffield's collection of scholarly essays, *The Haitian Declaration of Independence* (2016). Their question refers to the fact that the first document proclaiming independence from France was actually issued on November 29, 1803, and was signed by only three men: Dessalines (the future emperor of Haiti), Henry Christophe (the future king of Haiti), and the Haitian revolutionary general, Augustin Clervaux. And "why," Gaffield and Armitage continue, "is January 1 celebrated as Independence Day and not November 29? What was the motivation in the writing and distribution of the January 1 document in place of the November 29 document?"[3]

One reason may have been that the generals wanted to change the name of the former colony. The November declaration announces that the "independence of St. Domingo is proclaimed," while the January 1 version announces that the island is now called Haiti and that the Haitian people have "sworn to posterity, in front of the entire universe, to renounce France forever, and to die rather than live under her domination."[4] Despite many still unanswered questions, Gaffield and Armitage insist that "we now know more about the 1804 Haitian declaration than we do about any other similar document, with the exception of the US Declaration of Independence."[5]

Acknowledging the extraordinary new world charted for African descended peoples in the Americas through the founding documents of Haitian independence has similarly inspired us to understand anew Haiti's role in the trajectory of African American intellectual history. In a recent article, Michael Drexler and Ed White have argued that the Saint-Domingue Constitution of 1801,[6] commissioned and signed by Governor-General Toussaint Louverture, "following its dissemination throughout the US in the fall of 1801, . . . became the most widely read piece of literature authored by an African American and may have remained so until the publication of the *Narrative of the Life of Frederick Douglass* in 1845."[7] What attracted US readers to this early constitution was undoubtedly its unequivocal third article: "There can no longer exist any slaves in this land, servitude is forever abolished here. All men are here born, live, and will die free and French."[8] The 1801 constitution, even while preserving Saint-Domingue's colonial status, "made universal freedom from slavery its radical foundation," as Philip Kaisary has written. It thus provided a stark contrast to the founding documents of the United States or any of the French revolutionary constitutions.[9]

Like the 1801 Saint-Domingue Constitution, and Haiti's multiple declarations of independence, Haiti's first constitution circulated heavily across the Atlantic world[10] and broke "entirely new ground in this period of colonial modernity."[11] The 1805 constitution, issued under the name of the Emperor Jean-Jacques Dessalines, for example, declared that "slavery is forever abolished" (art. 2) but went even a step further to outlaw color prejudice. The clause in the first part of article 14 bans the recognition of difference: "All distinctions of color among children of one and the same family, of whom the head of State is the father, needing necessarily to cease"; while the part after the clause declares, "Haitians will from now on be known only under the generic denomination of Black."

It is the latter part of the article that has been the subject of fascinating debate for scholars.[12] Despite the radical move of a nineteenth-century head of state attempting to legally ban racial prejudices (in the first part of the article),[13] researchers have been mainly interested in the relationship of the second part of article 14 to the two articles that preceded it. Article 12 has been considered quite infamous, historically speaking, because it forbade white property ownership: "No white man, whatever his nationality, will set foot on this territory with the title of master or proprietor and can never, even in the future, acquire any property." Article 13 undoes the seeming contradiction of article 12 vis-à-vis article 14's interdiction of color prejudice by describing which whites could own property despite article 12, for example, "white women," "Poles," and "Germans," who became Haitian through marriage. Sibylle Fischer writes that articles 13 and 14 together interrupt "any biologistic or racialist expectations" by allowing for white women, Germans, and Polish people to attain citizenship, rendering "'black' a mere implication of being Haitian and thus a political rather than a biological category."[14] Jean Casimir, for his part, suggests that "this new 'black'" demonstrated Haiti's essential diversity, as it "encompassed the various ethnic groups that had been involved in the struggle against the Western vision of mankind. Victory in adversity gave birth to this new character," Casimir continues, "which was a synthesis not only of Ibos, Aradas, and Hausas but also of French, Germans, and Poles."[15] Anthony Bogues adds, "By making all Haitians black the Constitution reversed the colonial hierarchical status of human being."[16]

As scholars of transatlantic slavery have increasingly come to recognize, Haitian independence challenged Enlightenment humanisms,[17] as well as hierarchies of race and color and the very meaning of freedom.[18] However, what has been much less acknowledged is that the foundational documents of Haitian sovereignty also challenged the logic and material practices of colonialism in the Atlantic world. This is not simply because these documents declared emancipation from slavery on the basis of universal equality but also because they provided a clear and direct language with which to challenge colonial discourse.

Although article 1 of the 1805 constitution prescribed that the country would henceforth be known "under the name of the Empire of Haiti," article 36 contests the traditional definition of "empire" by mandating, "The emperor will never form any enterprise with the goal of conquest nor of troubling the peace or the interior affairs of foreign colonies." Article 36 enacted into law the anticolonial ideals first expressed in the Haitian Declaration of Independence: "Let us guard against the spirit of proselytizing so that it does not destroy our efforts; let us leave in tranquil repose our neighbors," the declaration reads, "for we are not going to, as revolutionary destroyers, erect ourselves legislators of the Caribbean, by seeking our glory through troubling the tranquility of the other islands in our vicinity."[19] If we can say, therefore, that Haiti's founding documents ensured that the country would never again be ruled by colonizers, these documents also mandated that Haiti's rulers could never become colonizers either.[20]

In fact, I do not see the anticonquest stances articulated in Haiti's founding documents as incidental challenges to the colonial powers of the Atlantic world, nor do I regard them as mere relics of the fact that the words "imperial" and "empire" may not have had "the same political meanings in early nineteenth century Haiti as they did in imperial Europe of the period."[21] Instead, I view the anticonquest positioning of Dessalines's "empire" as the foundation for a postcolonial heuristic that both inaugurated and enabled anticolonial thought to become a normative political perspective among radical black intellectuals across the Americas.[22] In other words, I see in this article of the constitution much more than a pragmatic method of governing designed to preserve and protect black sovereignty in a white colonial world. Article 36, in its formulation, is the radical foundation of global anticolonial thought.[23]

Raphael Dalleo has recently made a compelling case that it was the US Occupation of Haiti (1915–34) that foretold the rise of anticolonial thought among such well-known Pan-Africanists as C. L. R. James, George Padmore, Marcus Garvey, Amy Jacques Garvey, Claude McKay, Eric Walrond, and Alejo Carpentier.[24] However, returning to the political and legal discourses of anticolonialism first articulated in early sovereign Haiti points to alternative genealogies. The early constitutions of Haiti left behind a distinct legacy of anti-imperialism that would be more concretely theorized by mid-late nineteenth-century Haitian intellectuals like Demesvar Delorme and Louis Joseph Janvier, who were perhaps two of the earliest black writers to connect US American imperialism to capitalism.[25] The development of this kind of radical anticolonialism, with its explicitly anticapitalist critique, is usually associated with later twentieth-century Pan-African thought.[26] Rather than ruminating on the causes and consequences of the endemic suppression of nineteenth-century Haitian thought in global black intellectual history,[27] in the pages that follow, I want instead to provide examples demonstrating how Haiti's own longstanding and well-known anticolonialism, often read as innocence in the global political sphere—which was merely illuminated by the occupation rather than developed in response to it—created the possibility for the chain of anticolonial philosophies to develop that we witness in later twentieth-century Afro-diasporic intellectual history. A comparative reading of the country's first constitutions (1805–16) positions early Haiti's global declaration of a politics of anticonquest as elemental to the development of later black American nineteenth- and early twentieth-century anticolonial movements.

The Constitution of Anticolonial Thought

In my prior work on Haitian intellectual history, I have observed that both the anticonquest stance evident in Henry Christophe's 1807 constitution and Baron de Vastey's later writings on the matter present a challenge to current genealogies of postcolonial inquiry.[28] In this section, I want to return to the origins of the notion itself that colonialism is *bad*. An underlying assumption of postcolonial studies today is that forcefully extending the rule of law from one nation to another (regardless of any perceived benefit to the country under occupation) is the essence of colonial racism. Yet the anticolonialism of early Haiti was certainly not shared by the only other independent nation of the American hemisphere at the time, the United States, nor was it an inevitable political position for Haitian leaders to have mandated as they sought to develop sovereign black political institutions in the Americas. This much was recognized by British parliamentarian Fowell Buxton who, on May 15, 1823, addressed the British House of Commons on the subject of the abolition of slavery by first referencing Haiti's existence as a slavery-free and independent state in the Caribbean:

> What does the negro, working under the lash on the mountains of Jamaica, see? He sees another island, on which every labourer is free; in which eight hundred thousand blacks, men, women, and children, exercise all the rights, and enjoy all the blessings—and they are innumerable and incalculable—which freedom gives. Hitherto, indeed, no attempt has been made, from that quarter. The late emperor Christophe, and the president Boyer, may have been moderate men; or they may have found at home sufficient employment. But, who will venture to secure us against the ambition of their successors?[29]

Buxton then explicitly referenced Haiti's politics of anticolonialism by way of drawing a contrast between Great Britain, Haiti, and the United States: "It would be singular enough, if the only emperor who did not feel a desire to meddle with the affairs of his neighbours should be the emperor of Hayti. Look at America," he continued. "She may send at her own leisure, and from the adjacent shore, an army to Jamaica, proclaiming freedom to all the slaves. And—what is worse still—she may do so in exact conformity to our own example; not only in the first American war, but in the recent contest of 1813."[30]

It was actually article 36 of the Empire of Haiti's 1805 constitution that laid the groundwork for the later antimeddling clause issued under Christophe that Buxton ostensibly references. But article 36 appears in Dessalines's constitution only after careful scaffolding of the meaning of black sovereignty itself, which was defined as much by what it was (antislavery and antiracist) as by what it was not (colonial). The constitution makes explicit Haiti's claim to sovereignty on the basis of these three positions—antislavery, antiracist, and anticolonial—first, by its proclamation of the essential equality of all human beings (the preamble and art. 3); second, through the granting of a new sovereign name, "the Empire of Haiti," rather than "the colony of Saint-Domingue" (art. 1); third, by the abolition of slavery (art. 2); fourth, by the constitution's delineation of who could become a citizen and therefore a Haitian (arts. 7–14); fifth, through the legal ban against color prejudice (arts. 3 and 14); sixth, through the establishment of a clearly defined territory (arts. 15 and 18); seventh, through the designation of a sovereign ruler (art. 20); and finally, through the unequivocal declaration that the emperor has no desire or intention to pursue any "conquests" (art. 36). This patient construction of sovereignty in Haiti, as antislavery, antiracist, and anticolonial, forms a fundamental part of Haitian intellectual history from the origins of the nation onward, but one whose contributions to wider Afro-diasporic intellectual traditions we have yet to fully examine.

Let us now consider more completely how the anticonquest stance of Dessalines's 1805 constitution—whereby the country continued to eschew the idea, initially pronounced in the Acte d'indépendance that Haitians would become "legislators of the Caribbean"—laid the foundation for anticolonialism to become an axiomatic *African American* proposition distinctly opposed to all forms of conquest and imperialism. Although article 36 may have initially been created in order to "pragmatically" reassure "the international community that [Haitians] would not instigate rebellion abroad,"[31] the examination of subsequent constitutions issued in early Haiti allows us to trace the longitudinal consequences of independent Haiti's instantiation of an anticolonial state. Seen in this light, Haiti's first constitutions not only helped to define conquest as *bad* in the nineteenth-century Atlantic world but paved the way for anticolonialism to become an explicit stance of Pan-Africanism. Linking article 36 of the 1805 constitution to the development of anticolonialism that undergirds the black radical tradition—in so much as the constitution outlawed both colonial rule and colonial racism—not only further disrupts the common misconception that "the black Atlantic is Anglophone"[32] but connects the anticolonial/anticonquest stance of Afro-diasporic intellectual history to the first state(s) of Haiti.

The Stability of Anticolonialism in Early Haitian Constitutions

If the Haitian Declaration of Independence was the work of "many hands,"[33] so too was the constitution of 1805. The constitution's preamble discloses that it was written by a combination of former enslaved and free(d) people of color, and subsequently "submitted" to be "sanctioned" by Dessalines, "his majesty, the Emperor." The constitution was signed by Dessalines on May 20, 1805, but under the emperor's signature also appeared that of Juste Chanlatte, his secretary-general.[34] In October 1806, Dessalines was assassinated and General Henry Christophe was named provisory president. Before the division of the country into north and south, this provisory government issued a new constitution, which similarly forbade slavery (art. 1) and banned conquest with nearly the same language as the constitution of 1805 (art. 2). Article 2 of the 1806 constitution inserts one small revision, however, as the new language emanates now from the state itself rather than the state's sovereign ruler, that is, "the Republic of Haiti," instead of the "Emperor of Haiti," "will never form any enterprise with the goal of conquest nor of troubling the peace or the interior affairs of foreign colonies." While the constitution of 1805 was signed by twenty-two men, beginning with Christophe himself, the 1806 constitution (adopted by Alexandre Pétion in 1807 after he became president of the country and not revised by his government until 1816)[35] was signed on December 27, 1806, by a daunting sixty-four men, including Pétion and Jean-Pierre Boyer, but not Christophe.[36] Unlike the 1805 constitution, the preamble to the 1806 revision makes it clear that despite the many signatories, this document is actually coming from the people of Haiti themselves. The preamble reads: "The people of Haiti proclaim, in the presence of the Supreme Being, the present Constitution."[37] As semantically nuanced as this revision may seem, the idea that all of the articles of this constitution were now manifestations of the will of the people, who were the republic, demonstrates the essential rather than incidental quality of the original article that banned slavery and conquest. The fact that the anticonquest article remained (while the article requiring the recognition of all Haitians as blacks did not, for example),[38] suggests that being anticolonial was considered a fundamental key not only to Haiti's early sovereignty but to its sovereign identity.

Dessalines's constitution had reversed many of the laws created by the group of men who authored the 1801 constitution: it enabled divorce (art. 15) and religious freedom (arts. 50–52). The 1806 constitution also allowed divorce, but while it did not completely reverse the religious freedoms established under Dessalines (art. 37), it did proclaim Catholicism to be the state religion (art. 35). In great contrast, the February 17, 1807, constitution issued under Christophe's rule after he established a separate state in the north of Haiti, immediately reversed both of these trends with respect to marriage and religion. Like the 1801 constitution issued under Louverture, the 1807 version reoutlawed divorce (art. 46) and declared that Catholicism was the only religion that could be professed in public, "though the practice of other religions would be tolerated" (art. 30).[39] Other omissions evident in the 1807 constitution include its lack of outlawing color prejudice and its silence on the question of whether or not all Haitians were to be considered black. Perhaps, more tellingly, neither Christophe's 1807 constitution nor the revised version issued in 1811 after he became king proscribed white property ownership, which on the contrary had remained forbidden in the 1806 version, as well as in the revision issued under Pétion in 1816 (arts. 38 and 39).[40]

Despite these crucial differences, one principle that continued, and indeed was extended in this later 1807 constitution, was the ban against conquest. The new article 36 contains an antiempire statement that addresses the charge that Haitians would want to transfer control of the Caribbean from the "whites to the blacks."[41] The 1807 constitution also addresses much more specifically the idea that Haitians might try to encourage rebellion elsewhere in the Caribbean: "The government of Haiti declares to all the powers of the region, which still have colonies in our vicinity, its unshakeable resolution to never trouble the regimes by which they are governed." Article 37 then returns to the more general anticonquest language of the 1805 and 1806 constitutions but turns the spirit of the idea into a material fact by using the present tense rather than the conditional and by attributing the desire for anticonquest to Haitians themselves rather than to the emperor or to the republic: "The people of Haiti," article 37 reads, "do not engage in conquest outside of their island, and limit themselves to preserving their own territory." Anticonquest was transformed from being the will of a ruler (1805), to the will of a republic (1806), to the fact of a people (1807).

The People of Haiti and the Fact of Empire

Early Haiti's anticolonial stance, which did not prohibit actively combating slavery, is also reflected in subsequent Haitian governmental interventions in the Americas. These interventions include Pétion's monetary support of Simón Bolívar's Latin American wars of independence, which established the sovereign and eventually the slavery-free states of Gran Colombia (Venezuela, Bolivia, Colombia, Ecuador, northern Peru, and Panama),[42] as well as Pétion's subsequent creation of the southern republic of Haiti as a "free soil" nation and therefore as an ostensible safe haven for all the enslaved of the world.[43] Later, in the mid-nineteenth century, the Haitian people took it upon themselves to provide aid to Santo Domingo, or the eastern side of the island, in their efforts to repel Spain, despite president Geffrard's declared position of neutrality,[44] while in 1870, the Puerto Rican radical Ramon Emeterio Betances, in the course of being exiled in Haiti, gave a speech at the Masonic Lodge of Port-au-Prince in which he directly implored Haitians to help Cubans not only end slavery but obtain independence from Spain:

> Where are the people, who more than any other, have the right to take into their own hands the defense of the oppressed? Your heart has already told you: they are in Haiti; it is you . . . you are Haitians, you are men of equality, you are the sons of those first great citizens who knew how to achieve, for their race, civil and political rights. You are therefore suited to understand better than any other people, this valiant Liberating Army [of Cuba], which is composed of all the races mixed together, and which fights to proclaim, by supporting Cuba against Spain, the honor of raising the same standard of liberty that you made triumphant in Haiti against the power of France.[45]

What these examples suggest is that nineteenth-century Haiti had not only "taught the world the danger of slavery and the value of liberty," to use the words of Frederick Douglass,[46] but had demonstrated to that same world that black sovereignty did not need to entail overseas expansion.

Various Haitian governments, as well as the Haitian people themselves, seemed to have understood the sliding scale difference between seeking to help liberate other enslaved Africans, or attempting to unify the island of Ayiti under one government, and desiring to colonize the other islands of the Caribbean through conquest.[47] Henry Christophe, whose government had criticized both Pétion's aid to Bolívar and his "free soil policy,"[48] appears to have made a very clear distinction between attempting to "interfere" in the governance of another colony or nation and attempting to free enslaved peoples. The October 10, 1817, issue of the *Gazette royale d'Hayti*, for example, righteously reports the Haitian military's capture of a Portuguese slave ship in Haitian waters and the Kingdom of Haiti's subsequent release of 145 of "our unfortunate brothers, victims of greed and the odious traffic in human flesh."[49]

Even if article 36 of the 1805 constitution may have partially been inserted "pragmatically" because of various international pressures, its ideological and philosophical importance appears to be much more longstanding. Except for a brief period of reunification with what is now the Dominican Republic under the presidency of Jean-Pierre Boyer (1822–44),[50] Haiti has never occupied any other territory than the one in which it now sits. Part of US African American outrage at the Wilson administration's occupation appears to have stemmed precisely from the fact that Haiti had not only never colonized any other nation but had never declared war against any other country. This made the occupation an indefensibly aggressive act on the part of the United States, as James Weldon Johnson reminded readers of the US magazine the *Nation* when he observed that Haiti had "never slaughtered an American citizen, it never molested an American woman, it never injured a dollar's worth of American property."[51] W. E. B. Du Bois, too, framed the US occupation as the "violation of a sister state," precisely because Haitians, despite his acknowledgement of their domestic political problems, could be characterized as internationally pacifistic. He wrote, "Here, then, is the outrage of uninvited American intervention, the shooting and disarming of peaceful Haytian citizens."[52]

In the end, even though the anticonquest ban did not appear again in Haiti after the overthrow of Boyer in 1843, when a new constitution was issued, we do find Haitian intellectuals throughout the nineteenth century such as Pierre Faubert, Demesvar Delorme, Louis Joseph Janvier, Frédéric Marcelin, and Anténor Firmin continuing to criticize imperialism and collaborating with anticolonial and antislavery activists from across the Americas, such as Betances and José Martí.[53] If we can clearly see how the existence of an independent Haiti in the nineteenth century ushered in "alternative practices and conceptions of freedom,"[54] with respect to slavery, I hope we can now begin to explore how yet another of those "alternative practices" brought to bear by Haitian independence was that it provided the grammar for a politics of anticolonialism to become a virtual universalism among radical intellectuals of the Americas.

Notes

1. See the *New York Times* article, "Haiti's Founding Document Found in London," April 10, 2010, https://www.nytimes.com/2010/04/01/world/americas/01document.html.

2. Deborah Jenson, "Dessalines's American Proclamations of Haitian Independence," *Journal of Haitian Studies* 15, no. 1 (2009): 11; Celucien Joseph, "The Haitian Turn: An Appraisal of Recent Literary and Historiographical Works on the Haitian Revolution," *Africology: The Journal of Pan-African Studies* 5, no. 6 (2012): 37.

3. Julia Gaffield and David Armitage, "Introduction: The Haitian Declaration of Independence in an Atlantic Context," in *The Haitian Declaration of Independence: Creation, Context, and Legacy*, ed. Julia Gaffield (Charlottesville: University of Virginia Press, 2016), 7, 11.

4. Acte d'indépendance, January 1, 1804, https://mjp.univ-perp.fr/constit/ht1804.htm. All translations mine unless otherwise noted. For an English translation of the 1803 version, see David Geggus, "The 29 November 1803 Declaration of Independence," https://haitidoi.com/2013/03/03/the-29-november-1803-declaration-of-independence-post-by-david-geggus/.

5. "Introduction: The Haitian Declaration of Independence," 7, 11.

6. In February 1801, Louverture called forth a constitutional assembly to create a constitution for Saint-Domingue. It was completed in May, and Louverture signed it in July 1801. Louis Joseph Janvier, *Les constitutions d'Haïti, 1801–1885* (Paris: C. Marpon et E. Flammarion, 1886), 2.

7. Michael J. Drexler and Ed White, "The Constitution of Toussaint: Another Origin of African American Literature," in *A Companion to African American Literature*, ed. Gene A. Jarrett (Hoboken, NJ: Wiley Blackwell, 2010), 59.

8. "Constitution de 3 Juillet 1801," http://mjp.univ-perp.fr/constit/ht1801.htm.

9. Philip Kaisary, "Hercules, the Hydra, and the 1801 Constitution of Toussaint Louverture," *Atlantic Studies* 12, no. 4 (2012): 399.

10. Jenson, "Dessalines's American Proclamations, 77.

11. Anthony Bogues, "The Dual Haitian Revolution and the Making of Freedom in Modernity," in *Human Rights from a Third World Perspective: Critique, History and International Law*, ed. José-Manuel Barreto (Newcastle upon Tyne, UK: Cambridge Scholars Publishing, 2013), 224.

12. "Constitution du 20 mai 1805," http://mjp.univ-perp.fr/constit/ht1805.htm.

13. See Marlene L. Daut, "Beyond 'American for Americans': Race and Empire in the Work of Demesvar Delorme," *J19* 6, no. 1 (Spring 2018): 189–97.

14. Sibylle Fischer, *Modernity Disavowed: Haiti and the Cultures of Slavery in the Age of Revolution* (Durham, NC: Duke University Press, 2004), 232.

15. Jean Casimir, "Prologue," in *The World of the Haitian Revolution*, ed. David Patrick Geggus and Norman Fiering (Bloomington: Indiana University Press, 2009), xv.

16. Bogues, "The Dual Haitian Revolution," 230.

17. Laurent Dubois, "An Enslaved Enlightenment: Rethinking the Intellectual History of the French Atlantic," *Social History* 31, no. 1 (February 2006): 1–14.

18. Marlene L. Daut, *Baron de Vastey and the Origins of Black Atlantic Humanism* (London: Palgrave Macmillan, 2017).

19. "Acte d'indépendance."

20. It is worth pointing out that the constitution was issued a few months after Dessalines and Christophe's failed siege of Santo Domingo, whereby the Haitian army tried to wrest control of the eastern side of the island from France. The goal of this siege was to reunite the island under one government as it had been under Toussaint Louverture. For the first half century of independence, Haitians tended to see the schism with the eastern side of the island as unnatural. See Chelsea Stieber, *Haiti's Paper War* (New York: New York University Press, 2020), 161; and Anne Eller, *We Dream Together: Dominican Independence, Haiti, and the Fight for Caribbean Freedom* (Durham, NC: Duke University Press, 2016).

21. Bogues, "The Dual Haitian Revolution," 221. It might be more accurate to say, however, that the words did not have the same meaning to Dessalines. Critiquing Dessalines's nomination as emperor, Baron de Vastey explained that this was an inappropriate title since it suggested "that he who possessed it also possessed great power over large territories and peoples." See Baron de Vastey, *Essai sur les causes de la révolution et des guerres civiles d'Hayti, faisant suite au Réflexions politiques sur quelques ouvrages et journaux français concernant Hayti* (Sans-Souci, Haïti: L'Imprimerie Royale, 1819), 47.

22. By arguing that anticolonialism is normative in comparative black American intellectual traditions, I do not mean to suggest that all Afro-diasporic intellectuals did oppose in the past or even now unequivocally reject colonialism. Rather, I mean to point out that anticolonialism has become essentially the default position of black intellectuals in the Americas and that for a considerable time procolonialism has been considered a divergence from the norm. Deviations from the norm characterized as extraordinary can be illustrated by responses to Zora Neale Hurston's defense of the US occupation of Haiti, which she referred to as a "white hope" in *Tell My Horse* (1938). For the way in which Hurston's stance was contrary to that of other black US Americans, including the official position of the NAACP, see Dorothea Fischer-Hornung, "An Island Occupied: The Interpretation of the U.S. Marine Occupation of Haiti in Zora Neale Hurston's *Tell My Horse* and Katherine Dunham's *Island Possessed*," in *Holding Their Own: Perspectives on the Multi-ethnic Literatures of the United States*, ed. Dorothea Fischer-Hornung and Heike Raphael Hernandez (Tübingen, Germany: Stauffenburg, 2000), 153–68.

23. To glimpse the normativity of anticolonial frameworks and ideologies in the Global South (including India and Africa) and across the Black Atlantic (primarily, the Americas and western Europe), recall the September 2017 controversy over an article published in the *Third World Quarterly*, which defended the historical practice of colonialism and indeed encouraged its revival. The journal editor's decision to publish the article over the objections of the peer reviewers, who did not recommend it for publication, led to the resignation of half the journal's editorial board. See, Colleen Flaherty, "Resignations at Third World Quarterly." https://www.insidehighered.com/news/2017/09/20/much-third-world-quarterlys-editorial-board-resigns-saying-controversial-article 20 September 2017.

24. Raphael Dalleo, *American Imperialism's Undead: The Occupation and the Rise of Caribbean Anticolonialism* (Charlottesville: University of Virginia Press, 2016).

25. For Delorme and Janvier's association of imperialism with capitalism, see Marlene L. Daut, "Caribbean 'Race Men': Louis Joseph Janvier,

Demesvar Delorme, and the Haitian Atlantic," *L'Esprit Créateur* 56, no. 1 (Spring 2016): 9–23.

26. Dalleo, *American Imperialism's Undead*, 3.

27. For an analysis of this nature, see Marlene L. Daut, "Beyond Trouillot: Unsettling Genealogies of Historical Thought," *Small Axe* (March 2021): 132–54.

28. Daut, *Baron de Vastey*, 22.

29. Henry Christophe became king of the northern part of Haiti in March 1811, but many foreign commentators mistakenly referred to him as an emperor.

30. "Abolition of Slavery,*" House of Commons Debates, May 15, 1823, vol. 9, cc257–360, https://api.parliament.uk/historic-hansard/commons/1823/may/15/abolition-of-slavery.

31. Julia Gaffield, *Haitian Connections in the Atlantic World: Recognition after Revolution* (Chapel Hill: University of North Carolina Press, 2015), 57, 73–74.

32. Jenson, "Before Malcolm X, Dessalines: A 'French' Tradition of Black Atlantic Radicalism," *International Journal of Francophone Studies* 10, no. 3 (2007): 330.

33. Gaffield and Armitage, "Introduction: The Haitian Declaration of Independence," 16.

34. The question of whether or not Dessalines can be considered the *author* of any of the numerous state documents issued under his name has sparked spirited debate among academics. See Jenson, "Dessalines's American Proclamations," 77; David Geggus, "Haiti's Declaration of Independence," in *The Haitian Declaration of Independence*, 27; and Chris Bongie, "The Cry of History: Juste Chanlatte and the Unsettling (Presence) of Race in Early Haitian Literature," *MLN* 130, no. 4 (September 2015): 809.

35. The provision against empire appears in article 5 of the 1816 constitution but disappears in the 1843 constitution that names Charles Hérard provisory president. See Janvier, *Les constitutions d'Haïti*, 112, 154.

36. After the death of Pétion in spring 1818, Jean-Pierre Boyer, also a former general, became president of the southern republic.

37. "Constitution du 27 décembre 1806," http://mjp.univ-perp.fr/constit/ht1806.htm.

38. The 1816 revision to the constitution did, however, reinsert this clause to some extent by mandating in article 39: "They will be recognized as Haitians, those whites who are a part of the military, those who are civil servants, and those who were admitted to the Republic at the time of the adoption of the Constitution of 27 December 1806; but no other [whites], after the publication of the present revision can claim the same right, nor can they be employed, nor can they enjoy the rights of citizenship, nor can they acquire any property within the republic."

39. "Constitution royale du 28 mars 1811," http://mjp.univ-perp.fr/constit/ht1811.htm.

40. Vastey was a huge critic of banning white property ownership, which was a part of every Haitian constitution except Christophe's until 1918 (Gaffield, *Haitian Connections*, 17). Vastey believed that a more reasonable law would have been, "no French person whatever his color can set foot on this territory for any reason at all until the French government has recognized the independence of Haiti." He justified this claim by arguing that "the declaration of independence

only effectively excluded the French [les français] from the territory of Haiti." Vastey, *Essai*, 318, 520.

41. Malouet, *Collection de mémoires sur les colonies et particulièrement sur Saint-Domingue* (Paris: Baudouin, 1802), 4:32; Vastey, *Notes à M. le Baron V. P. de Malouet* (Cap-Henry: Chez P. Roux, 1814), 7.

42. Anténor Firmin, *De l'egalité des races humaines: Anthropologie positive* (Paris: Librairie Cotillon, 1885), 586.

43. Ada Ferrer, "Haiti, Free Soil, and Antislavery in the Revolutionary Atlantic," *American Historical Review* 117, no. 1 (February 2012): 40–66.

44. Previously, in concert with Haitian claims that people of the island of Haiti belonged under one government, Faustin Soulouque I, who became emperor in April 1849, two years after being elected president of Haiti, went on a brief, but failed, campaign to once again reunify Dominicans and Haitians. Soulouque's efforts were opposed by many in the Dominican elite and were used to bolster anti-Haitian sentiment by claiming that Haitians had attempted to colonize the eastern side of the island. See Eller, *We Dream Together*, 52, 196.

45. Ramon Emeterio Betances, "AL.G.D.P.A.D.L.U," in *Betances*, ed. Luis Bonafoux (San Juan: Instituto de Cultura Puertorriqueña, 1970), 111.

46. "Speech of Frederick Douglass, Haitian Pavilion Dedication Ceremonies at Chicago World Fair, 1893," https://canada-haiti.ca/sites/default/files/Douglass%201893.pdf.

47. For debates about the meaning of early Haiti's actions in this regard, see Gaffield *Haitian Connections in the Atlantic World*, 50–58; Jenson, *Beyond the Slave Narrative: Politics, Sex, and Manuscripts in the Haitian Revolution* (Liverpool: Liverpool University Press, 2011), 176; and Bogues, "The Dual Haitian Revolution," 22.

48. Ferrer, "Haiti, Free Soil, and Antislavery in the Revolutionary Atlantic."

49. *La Gazette royale d'Hayti*, October 10, 1817, 3.

50. However, this reunification with the eastern side of Ayiti/Kiskeya was widely supported on both sides of the island in its era. See Anne Eller, *We Dream Together*, 5.

51. Johnson, "Self-Determining Haiti," *Nation*, August 28, 1920, https://www.thenation.com/article/self-determining-haiti/.

52. W. E. B. Du Bois, "Hayti," *Crisis* 10, no. 6 (October 1915): 291.

53. See Pierre Faubert's anti-imperial poem, "Aux Haïtiens" in *Ogé, ou le préjugé de couleur* (Paris: C. Maillet-Schmitz, 1856). An excerpt was translated and published by Jesse Fauset for the *Crisis* in September 1920. See reprint in Fauset, *The Chinaberry Tree: A Novel of American Life and Selected Writings*. (Boston: Northeastern University Press, 1995), 359. For Martí and Haiti, see Brenda Gayle Plummer, "Firmin and Martí at the Intersection of Pan-Americanism and Pan-Africanism," in *José Martí's "Our America": From National to Hemispheric Cultural Studies*, ed. Jeffrey Grant Belnap and Raul A. Fernandez (Durham, NC: Duke University Press, 1998), 210–27.

54. Bogues, "The Dual Haitian Revolution," 212.

Chapter 6

✦

The International Dimensions of West Indies Emancipation Day Speeches

Jeffrey R. Kerr-Ritchie

In the early dawn hours of August 4, 1842, residents of Chatham, Canada West (today's Ontario), were awakened by a twenty-one-gun salute. A company of one hundred black soldiers marched through the town where they met up with a large crowd of antislavery supporters consisting of local black and white men, women, and children. Josiah Jones delivered the keynote address. This farmer, Baptist, and militiaman had self-emancipated from slavery in Tennessee twenty-six years previously. Jones opened by thanking "many of our friends assembled together" to celebrate this "glorious day of liberty." He reminded them that the "British government had emptied their Coffers of Twenty millions of Pounds" (more than $2 billion today) to redeem "our foreign friends" from "their distressed condition." This act was unforgettable, and "our gratitude shall be manifested on every suitable occasion." We are known, explained the former American slave and now free man in Canada, "to be true British subjects and all of the most loyal kind." Southern slaves were "tigers," he said, who only needed to hear the roar of John Bull (Britain's national personification) to "burst in sunder their prison house, and sweep with the bosom of destruction, the enemies of liberty and of humanity."[1]

Josiah Jones's West Indies Emancipation Day speech was direct and succinct. He apologized for not being "better qualified to deliver a long speech," although what his address lacked in erudition and conventional classical references was more than made up for in exposition and memorable metaphor. Its most telling point was the connection between the ending of British colonial slavery and the defense of emancipation by "loyal subjects" who would defend their new liberties in Canada. The conceptualization of "loyalist" was twofold: American slaves who were offered freedom by the British armies if they would desert slaveholders, which was a function of the wartime-based liberties during both the American Revolution and the second Anglo-American War in 1812–1814, together with self-emancipators (like Jones) crossing into British Canada, which became free soil after the abolition of colonial slavery in 1833.[2] Moreover, Jones's conceptual linkage of subversive Southern slaves with British colonial abolition had historical precedent in 1776, 1812, and the 1830s, suggesting that Southern slaveholders were not entirely paranoid about the destabilizing impact of colonial abolition across borders.[3]

Much like Chatham, Rochester represented a borderland between slave and free soil. Resting on the southern shoreline of Lake Ontario, this small town in upstate New York emerged as an abolitionist hotbed by the mid-nineteenth century. This was partly due to the vigorous activities of Frederick Douglass. Former slave, self-emancipator, and famous abolitionist,[4] Douglass helped organize several West Indies Emancipation Day celebrations during the 1840s. In February 1848, the French monarchy was toppled. On April 27, the French National Assembly passed a colonial act with the first article: "Slavery is completely abolished in the French colonies and possessions."[5] Three months later, Douglass helped to organize the tenth anniversary of British colonial abolition. On August 1, 1848, a procession of abolitionists and their supporters formed at the Baptist Church on Ford Street, marched across the Genesee River, and walked to Washington Square in downtown Rochester. The parade was followed by keynotes speeches. "We live," marveled the thirty-year-old Douglass to the large crowd:

> in times which have no parallel in the history of the world. The grand commotion is universal and all-pervading. Kingdoms, realms, empires, and republics, roll to and fro like ships upon a stormy sea. The long pent-up energies of human rights and sympathies, are at last let loose on the world. The grand conflict of the angel Liberty with the monster Slavery, has at last come. The globe shakes with the contest.[6]

Among the first acts of the new regime, he reminded his listeners, was "the complete, unconditional emancipation of every slave throughout the French colonies. This act of justice and consistency went into the joys of freedom." "Commotion" was also evident in Austria, Russia, Ireland, and England, whose people "are lifting their heads and hearts in hopes of better days." Douglass's speech coupled American abolition with the 1848 revolutionary moment in this unfolding "grand conflict."[7] British colonial abolition, European revolutions, and the struggle against American slavery promised the springtime of the people.[8]

Sharing the Rochester platform with Douglass was Henry W. Johnson. Born free in upstate New York, he became a successful barber, property owner, and prominent abolitionist orator.[9] We assemble, Johnson told the Washington Square crowd, "under auspices more favorable" than in the past. Not only do we commemorate "Freedom's Jubilee, the birthday of liberty to 800,000 crushed and bleeding victims of oppression, in the British West India Isles; but also rejoice over the progress of liberty abroad—over the fall of thrones, and the destruction of tyranny in other lands." France "has demolished her throne and reared upon its ruins a new republic." Consequently, Johnson enthused, the new republic "struck off the fetters that bound the limbs of her colonial slaves. . . . Not a slave can clank his chains in that soil of liberty." France, once renowned for persecution, intolerance, and terror, was now the home of freedom upon which "the world must look with admiration."[10] Not only was this a momentous occasion weaving past (1834) and present (1848), but France too had now joined Britain (and Denmark in 1848) in freedom's progress.

One would expect Johnson to next argue that the same process would visit America's shores as a consequence of history's unfolding logic. Instead, he condemned the hypocrisy of the United States. Americans welcomed freedom in contrast to the old world, resulting in a successful revolution for the universal rights of man. But "this soil, once watered with the life-blood of the martyrs of freedom, is now saturated with the tears and stained blood of the slave." There "is not one spot," fumed Johnson, "upon which a colored man can rest his feet and declare that he is free." Compared to its free origins, was "not this inconsistency the most irreconcilable—guilt the most abandoned—hypocrisy the most unblushing," he inquired rhetorically? Moreover, toleration of these iniquities stood in marked contrast to American people's passion for freedom struggles elsewhere. The whole country, bemoaned the speaker, "was filled with melting tones of sympathy for the oppressed Greeks," during their recent struggle for liberty against the Turkish Empire. "One spontaneous burst of sympathy gushed forth from our great national fountain" when South American states "endeavored to throw off the yoke of Spanish oppression." The "tear of sympathy flowed from every American eye" when Poland "attempted to strike off the fetters of tyranny." American congressmen expressed "earnest sympathies for France," some of whom "but a short time since, were down upon their Southern plantations, flourishing their whips over the shrinking form of the bleeding slave." Today, concluded Johnson, "talk no more of American freedom, but cover with sack-cloth and ashes." The eagle "will not scream of liberty, but proclaim a deep and solemn requiem over the grave of American freedom."[11] Was Johnson trying to shame the United States into living up to its self-declared ideals? Or was he espousing profound regret at America's inability to make such a change because of its traditional toleration of racial iniquities?

These speeches at Rochester were different. Henry Johnson's was far less hopeful than Frederick Douglass's (and Josiah Jones's). If 1848 was springtime for the latter two, it was—like Gil Scott Heron's song—winter in America for the former. But both shared similarities. Unlike Jones's brevity, these were elaborately prepared addresses. The locally famous Johnson (as well as nationally/internationally renowned Douglass) worked hard on their speeches, presumably in the knowledge that their words would be printed and thus reach a broader audience. Most important, these addresses linked revolutions, national independence movements, and slave emancipation in the Americas and Europe. Slavery's abolition would constitute a radical transformation of American society on par with national liberation struggles in Europe. It would also add to the continued overthrow of slave societies, as was the case with the Haitian republic, the French colonies, and the Danish colonies. Even Johnson's pessimism did not uncouple national liberation from slave emancipation.[12] These connections were repeated three years later and nearly four thousand miles eastward across the Atlantic Ocean.

On August 1, 1851, around one thousand men and women crowded into the Hall of Commerce on Threadneedle Street, London. They included Christian and secular activists united against slavery and calling for its termination globally. The meeting was organized by several self-emancipators from American slavery including William Wells Brown, Benjamin Benson, Alexander Duval, and Francis S. Anderson.[13] Duval was born enslaved in Baltimore, escaped in 1849, and settled in New Bedford as a cooper. He relocated to England in 1851 after spying his owner seeking his re-enslavement. Duval's companion on the ship bound for Liverpool was Anderson, who had also self-emancipated. The meeting's objectives included celebrating West Indies Emancipation and welcoming the return of British abolitionist George Thompson from his successful antislavery tour of the United States.[14]

Two years prior, former slave, autobiographer, and abolitionist William Brown had relocated to England to both promote the cause of antislavery internationally as well as to earn a living from his intellectual and cultural pursuits.[15] Although comparatively shorter than the speeches delivered at Rochester in 1848, Brown's address in London brimmed with international connections. Many of those in attendance were refugees, he observed, who "were fugitives from their native land, not fugitives from justice." One of the aims of the London meeting was to commemorate West Indies emancipation, "an event sublime in its nature." If Britain bore responsibility for the establishment of slavery in the American colonies, reasoned Brown, then "as England abolished slavery in the West Indies, she would have done the same for the American States." Instead, "a people boasting of their liberty, their humanity, their Christianity, their love of justice . . . at the same time [kept] in slavery more than three millions of God's children, and shut[ ] out from them the light of the Gospel, by denying the Bible to the slave." This was republican slaveholding hypocrisy in contrast to monarchical liberty.[16] The unconstitutionality of the Fugitive Slave Act passed the previous year in 1850 represented another international connection. Its annulment of fugitive slaves' rights of trial by jury and writ of habeas corpus trampled ancient rights first established through traditional English law. George Thompson symbolized transatlantic abolitionism. Speaker Brown turned to the honoree and gushed: "Beg to thank you for your noble exertions on behalf of my oppressed people." The system those in attendance sought to end was the most tyrannical system of all oppressive systems. The slave trade was the "most inhuman of all trafficks" that would not cease so long as slavery existed "for where there was a market there would be merchandise." The "slavery of the United States of America was a system the most abandoned and the most tyrannical." The implication was clear: it had to be destroyed if all were to be free.[17]

Although social historians provided some sense of the size, racial identity, and provenance of the crowds addressed by Jones, Douglass, and Johnson, we lack precise understanding of what these assembled people thought of the speeches to which they were listening. This is not the case regarding William Brown's 1851 speech in London. The reporter's recording of audible responses to Brown's words several times in the published article through parenthetical insertions allows us to gauge those ideas that resonated most favorably with the crowd. His castigation of republican slavery's hypocrisy was met with a chorus of approbation "(Hear, hear)." The same enthusiasm met the speaker's condemnation of slaveholders' "keeping in slavery more than three millions of God's children." (It also reveals the Christian sentiments of many in the audience. His attack on the unconstitutionality of the 1850 Fugitive Slave Act, his praise for the "noble and heroic band" in Boston who opposed slavery, and his characterization of American slavery as the "most tyrannical" were all hailed with "(Hear)" and "(Hear, hear)." The most demonstrative expression occurred when Brown shook Thompson's hand "amidst the loud applause of the meeting."[18] We cannot gauge how many of the assembly responded. Nor can we be absolutely certain that these were not ex post facto editorial insertions. But they gave the reader of the *Liberator* article (as well as the historian) a sense of what was important to the 1851 London assembly. This public enthusiasm was to be replicated several years later toward a Methodist missionary from Barbados at a West Indies Day in New England.

English born in 1809, Henry Bleby entered the Wesleyan faith at about the same time that Methodism was providing a powerful rationalization for an emerging industrial capitalism to both capitalists and proletarians in England.[19] By 1831, the young evangelist was residing in the town of Lucea, Hanover Parish, Jamaica. Every second week, Rev. Bleby visited Savannah-la-Mar in Westmoreland Parish. Both parishes were central locations for the massive slave rebellion that broke out in December 1831. Although uninvolved, Rev. Bleby was targeted by "white ruffians" who tarred him and nearly burned him to death before his wife—who was also attacked—intervened and they escaped with their infant child. He eventually relocated to Barbados.[20]

The Wesleyan missionary decided to write a history of the Jamaican slave revolt called *Death Struggles of Slavery* published in 1853.[21] In twenty-eight chapters spanning more than three hundred pages, Bleby narrated the history of the revolt and the system's last days. Although it failed in its original objective, the rebellion "demonstrated to the imperial legislature, that among the negroes themselves the spirit of freedom had been so widely diffused, as to render it most perilous to postpone the settlement of the important question of emancipation to a later period."[22] The aim of the book was to inspire "our large-souled Transatlantic fellow-Christians" in Britain and the United States to "overthrow the system" in the "great and glorious republic."[23]

The book's objective clearly resonated with some transatlantic abolitionists because a few years later Bleby embarked from Bridgetown to Boston. Every August, the Massachusetts Anti-Slavery Society organized a West Indies Day at Abington. Twenty miles southeast of the beacon of US abolitionism, it served as one of most important locales for antebellum antislavery meetings. William Lloyd Garrison and Wendell Phillips of Boston, together with Frederick Douglass of Rochester and Charles L. Remond of Salem, regularly addressed crowds here. Charles Remond served as vice president for the July 31, 1858, celebration to which Rev. Bleby had been invited to deliver the keynote address.[24]

I have summarized this important speech elsewhere.[25] The clear connections between slavery and abolition in the Caribbean and the United

States, however, require particular emphasis. Rev. Bleby narrated the brutal and bloody details of a Jamaican slave revolt to an audience who would have been familiar with Nat Turner's brutal and bloody revolt in Virginia. Rev. Bleby's interview with Jamaican rebel leader Samuel Sharpe no doubt recalled Virginian Thomas R. Gray's famous interview with Nat Turner in his death cell in the best-selling book.[26] Rev. Bleby's report of Sharpe's dying words: "I would rather go out and die on that gallow, than live a slave," obviously met with the approbation of an American audience familiar with Virginia patriot Patrick Henry's famous declaration, "Give me liberty, or give me death!"[27] Rev. Bleby's description of midnight watches in chapels across the British West Indies in 1834 paralleled West Indies Emancipation Day meetings in North America. The "condition of the people is incomparably superior" to the days of slavery concluded the visiting speaker. Postemancipation Barbados was prosperous, while free colored leaders like Edward Jordan and Richard Hill were transforming Jamaican life. The implication was clear: emancipation in the United States would produce the same happy condition and was to be embraced.[28]

As was the case with William Brown's London audience, we can gather the crowd's reaction to Rev. Bleby's address due to parenthetical insertions in the printed newspaper report.[29] The crowd applauded Rev. Bleby's account of rebel slave leader Lieutenant Dehaney's "manly courage" while being executed. Rebel leader Sharpe's insistence that he would rather die free than live enslaved drew "loud applause," as did the missionaries' determination to stand up against intimidation from hostile planters. The speaker's joke that if emancipation ruined the planters, they got what they deserved drew great "laughter." Rev. Bleby's statement that colored people had not raised themselves from degradation in the United States was met by "(A voice—that is not true)." This presumably from a free colored member of the audience who felt compelled to challenge a public falsehood.[30]

Having examined the movements, political language, and crowd reactions pertaining to West Indies Emancipation Day in the 1840s and 1850s Black Atlantic, let us conclude with a summation of their international dimensions.

People moved across national borders with important consequences. Jones left Tennessee and relocated to Chatham where he defended liberty by deed and word. He also called for the overthrow of American slavery from a safe location. Johnson mixed his business pursuits and abolitionist activities with ice-skating. "Mr. Johnson, the colored barber, is the best skater in town," reported one local, and he "is going to Liberia," where "his skates won't do him any good."[31] Both Douglass and Brown gained their liberty in England while promoting antislavery and helping to build a wall around American slavery.[32] Rev. Bleby left Barbados to help his transatlantic fellow Christians overthrow American slavery. These cross-border movements are lost when abolitionists are examined exclusively within nation centric frameworks.[33]

Moreover, the struggle for American abolition was analogous to European revolutions. The United States had fought a successful revolution against British colonial rule. Now it needed to terminate slavery to complete that revolution. The outbreaks in Europe in 1848 mirrored emancipation struggles in the United States. American slaveholders embraced liberty overseas but could not support emancipation at home. This was more than American republican hypocrisy; it was also an ironic contrast to British monarchical liberties. Moreover, slave revolt in the colonial West Indies had important lessons for the struggle against American slavery. Emancipation worked in the Caribbean, Canada, and West Africa. In short, revolutions were connected in ways usually absent in narratives of slave abolition in the United States or national independence struggles in Europe.

Intellectual vitality was the third significant international dimension of these addresses. Jones's speechifying sought to summon the "tigers of the south." Douglass's ship of state metaphor—"Kingdoms, realms, empires, and republics, roll to and fro like ships upon a stormy sea"—probably rocked the audience. Brown's description of the slave trade market—"where there were carcasses there would be vultures"—is unforgettable.[34] These symbolic representations were powerful and left their mark on audiences. Memorable phraseology also resonated. "Every breeze from the western world brought upon its wings the groans and cries of the victims of this guilt," bewailed Brown. "I will not open," opined Johnson, "the black and bloody pages of my country's history, and look over that dark catalogue of crime, oppression, outrage and wrong, of which she has been guilty, from the earliest stages of her existence down to the present moment." This from the 1840s, not the 1960s! Douglass exalted that high "upon the whirlwind, Liberty rides as on a chariot of fire." The short, hatchet-like, sharp language used by Bleby mirrored the historical action of the slave revolt that it was describing.[35] These West Indies speeches remain an untapped well for ideas, language, metaphor, poetics, symbolism, and rhetoric.[36]

Press coverage of these Emancipation Day speeches was also international. All six addresses examined in this chapter were reported in the local and abolitionist press: Jones's in the *Chatham Journal*, Douglass's and Johnson's in the *North Star*, Brown's and Bleby's in the *Liberator*.

These printed speeches also reached readers beyond Canada, the northern United States, and England. The *Chatham Journal* report was reprinted in the *Liberator* as well as in the *Western Herald*. The *Liberator* was read in both Canada and England. The abolitionist journal *Voice of the Fugitive* based in Canada reported on fugitive escapes from Kentucky. Indeed, one reliable source claims that the *North Star* reached more than four thousand readers in the United States, Europe, and the West Indies.[37] There is little doubt that West Indies Emancipation Day events and speeches reached an even wider audience through word of mouth, discussion, and debate. Moreover, visiting agents to Britain and elsewhere sold copies of these newspapers to help earn a living. Former American slaves Josiah Henson, Henry Garnet, and James Pennington distributed Canada's *Voice of Freedom* edited by former Kentucky bondsman Henry Bibb to readers in England during the early 1850s.[38] Although sales were modest, these newspapers provided local readers (and listeners) with some sense of the international dimensions of slavery and emancipation.[39] These broader features get lost with a focus on the black press and its construction of an "impossible national community" of African Americans.[40]

West Indies Emancipation Day and its speeches also educated ordinary men, women, and children about the international dimensions of slavery and emancipation in two distinct ways. Large audiences listened to these speakers and picked up history, politics, stories, and so forth. They did so in public spaces. London's Hall of Commerce, Rochester's Washington Square, Abington's Island Grove, and so forth all served as universities without walls. The impact of the lessons can be gauged from the audible responses recorded by reporters. In addition, West Indies Emancipation Day speeches were often reproduced in newspapers like the *Chatham Journal*, *Liberator*, *North Star*, and *Voice of the Fugitive* and read by people who were not present at the commemorative event. Indeed, these press organs often brought local events to an international audience. Readers were educated through reading and rereading these speeches as well as retelling those features that were memorable. In other words, there was an oral and written intellectual tradition that brought the world of slavery, emancipation, and revolution into shared public spaces as well as into individual private homes. Concepts, debates, and comparisons crossed borders, making speakers, assemblies, and readers more internationally informed than they are usually presented in historical scholarship on black antebellum life.

Finally, there was the creation of intellectual and political traditions transcendent of local, regional, and national borders. Black abolitionists are usually presented as some sort of Northern vanguard in the reformation of American life beginning with the struggle for the termination of slavery together with or followed by the struggle for equal rights of citizenship. Northern abolitionists are invariably pitted against Southern slaveholders in the sectional crisis that led to the American Civil War. But these West Indies Emancipation Day speakers, speeches, crowds, and print culture point toward an alternative international framework of slavery, abolition, revolution, and postemancipation expectations. America was less of a shining beacon than a tyrannical Egypt. August First (West Indies Emancipation Day) was far more historically significant than July Fourth because it liberated people from bondage. Eighteen forty-eight was not simply a year of European revolutions but was linked to a global movement toward expanding human rights. Freedom succeeded over there and would over here. Modernity was impossible without the eradication of all forms of servitude. And emancipation was the universal hope of humankind.

Notes

1. "Dear Beloved Brethren," *Chatham Journal*, August 6, 1842. Thanks to the librarian at Chatham Kent County Public Library for emailing the newspaper issue. Jones's speech is also reproduced in C. Peter Ripley, ed., *The Black Abolitionist Papers*, vol. 2, *Canada 1830–1865* (Chapel Hill: University of North Carolina Press, 1985–92), 95–96, as well as the Black Abolitionist Archive at the University of Detroit Mercy at http://libraries.udmercy.edu/archives/special-collections/index.php?record_id=1757&collectionCode=baa.

2. Jeffrey R. Kerr-Ritchie, *Rebellious Passage: The* Creole *Revolt and America's Coastal Slave Trade* (New York: Cambridge University Press, 2019), chap. 1.

3. For American captives liberated from several US coastal slave ships in the British Caribbean during the 1830s, see Kerr-Ritchie, *Rebellious Passage*, chap. 3. Jones's linkage reflected his understanding of the cross-border dynamics of slavery and abolition and is overlooked if we simply focus on him as a "refugee" from American slavery. For some comments on the 1842 Chatham event that is mute on Jones, his speech, and his transnational perspective, see Patrick Rael, *Black Identity and Black Protest in the Antebellum North* (Chapel Hill: University of North Carolina Press, 2002), 62, 63, 68.

4. William L. Andrews and William S. McFeeley, eds., *Narrative of the Life of Frederick Douglass, an American Slave, Written by Himself* (New York: W. W. Norton, 2017).

5. Mike Rapport, *1848: Year of Revolution* (New York: Basic Books, 2008), 45–57; Robin Blackburn, *The Overthrow of Colonial Slavery, 1776–1848* (London: Verso, 1988), 494–96; "The Revolution in France," *Liberator*, March 31, 1848; Frank Moya Pons, *History of the Caribbean: Plantations, Trade, and War in the Atlantic World* (Princeton, NJ: Markus Wiener Publishers, 2007), 217–18; "The French Colonial Act of Emancipation (1848)," in Junius Rodriguez, ed., *Encyclopedia of Emancipation and Abolition in the Transatlantic World* (Armonk, NY: M. E. Sharpe, 2007), 3:707.

6. Frederick Douglass, "Frederick Douglass' Address," *North Star*, August 4, 1848, 48.

7. Douglass, "Frederick Douglass' Address."

8. Three weeks after his address, Douglass's newspaper reported: "News is brought of a revolution in St. Croix [Danish West Indies now US Virgin Islands], and the blacks have been successful in overthrowing the Government. There was fighting, and many murders committed." *North Star*, August 25, 1848. Most historians continue to discuss 1848 as the springtime of the people without reference to emancipation struggles in the Caribbean. Mike Rapport's *1848* provides an eminently readable survey of the European scene, but is mute on transatlantic developments.

9. Preston Pierce, "Liberian Dreams, West African Nightmare: The Life of Henry W. Johnson Part One," *Rochester History* 66 (Fall 2004): 4–11.

10. "Address of H. W. Johnson," *North Star*, August 21, 1848.

11. "Address of H. W. Johnson."

12. Jeffrey R. Kerr-Ritchie, "1848 *Volkerfruling* in the French and Danish Caribbean," unpublished paper, 46th Congrès des Historiens de la Caraibe," Fort de France, Martinique, May 12, 2014. For an examination of 1848 Rochester as an elite-organized event that is silent on West Indies Emancipation Day speeches, see Rael, *Black Identity*, 62–67.

13. I prefer the term "self-emancipator" to "fugitive slave" because it represents a more accurate understanding of the actions of slaves seeking freedom rather than their status as criminal entities. These people sought liberty in defiance of the law. Besides, it was the language of choice of some contemporaries. Henry Bibb, who departed Kentucky's slave soil for Canada West's free soil, referred to "thousands of self-emancipated ones now protected in the enjoyment of liberty on the Queen's soil." *Voice of the Fugitive*, July 30, 1851. He edited the *Voice of the Fugitive* before dying coincidentally on the twentieth anniversary of British colonial abolition in 1854.

14. "Celebration of West India Negro Emancipation and Welcome to George Thompson, Esq., M. P.," *Liberator*, September 5, 1851; Ripley, *Black Abolitionist Papers*, vol. 1 *The British Isles, 1830–1865*, 285.

15. William Wells Brown, *Narrative of William Wells Brown, A Fugitive Slave* (Boston: Anti-Slavery Society, 1847); Ezra Greenspan, *William Wells Brown: An African American Life* (New York: Norton, 2014); William Wells Brown, *The Anti-Slavery Harp: A Collection of Songs for Anti-Slavery Meetings* (Boston: Bela Marsh, 1848); R. J. M. Blackett, *Building an Antislavery Wall: Black Americans in the Atlantic Abolitionist Movement, 1830–1860* (Baton Rouge: Louisiana State University Press, 1983).

16. "Celebration of West India Negro Emancipation"; Ripley, *Black Abolitionist Papers*, 1:285.

17. "Celebration," *Liberator*, September 5, 1851; Blackett, *Building an Antislavery Wall*, 201. One could question Brown's judgment—was slavery in the antebellum United States worse than in Spanish Cuba or Brazil?—but not that he was making an international comparison.

18. "Celebration," *Liberator*, September 5, 1851.

19. E. P. Thompson, "The Transforming Power of the Cross," in *The Making of the English Working Class* (London: Pelican, 1980), chap. 11.

20. "Speech of Reverend Henry Bleby, Missionary from Barbados," *Liberator*, August 6, 1858. There is an engraving of Bleby in the British Methodist clergy collection in the Pitts Theology Library at Emory University and reproduced online at http://www.pitts.emory.edu/woodcuts/MSS023/00003873.jpg.

21. Henry Bleby, *Death Struggles of Slavery: Being a Narrative of Facts and Incidents, Which Occurred in a British Colony, during the Two Years Immediately preceding Negro Emancipation* (London: Adams, Hamilton, 1853), chap. 19. I believe this was the first published history of the slave rebellion and it was sympathetic.

22. Bleby, *Death Struggles*, 1.

23. Bleby, *Death Struggles*, 304.

24. "West India Emancipation: Celebration at Abington," *Liberator*, August 6, 1858.

25. Jeffrey R. Kerr-Ritchie, *Rites of August First: Emancipation Day in the Black Atlantic World* (Baton Rouge: Louisiana State University Press, 2007), 77–78.

26. Kenneth S. Greenberg, *The Confessions of Nat Turner and Related Documents* (New York: Bedford, 1996).

27. On his way to being hanged for plotting to assassinate the British cabinet in 1820, Cato Street conspirator James Ings repeatedly sang, "Oh! Give me death or liberty!" V. A. C. Gatrell, *The Hanging Tree: Execution and the English People 1770–1868* (Oxford: Oxford University Press, 1994), 305.

28. "Speech of Reverend Henry Bleby, Missionary from Barbados," *Liberator*, August 6, 1858.

29. James Brown Yerrington, printer of the *Liberator*, phonographically reported Reverend Bleby's 1858 speech.

30. "Speech of Reverend Henry Bleby, Missionary from Barbados," *Liberator*, August 6, 1858.

31. Preston Pierce, "Liberian Dreams, West African Nightmare: The Life of Henry W. Johnson Part One," *Rochester History* 66 (Fall 2004): 17–18.

32. Jamaican slave Henry Williams, his wife, and their children gained their freedom from Christian friends of his owner resident in England for two hundred pounds sterling. See Bleby, *Death Struggles of Slavery*, 73.

33. The most recent edition of Douglass's *Narrative* edited by Andrews and McFeely inexplicably leaves out Douglass's emancipation in England in the chronology (193).

34. "Dear Beloved Brethren," *Chatham Journal*, August 6, 1842 (Jones); "Frederick Douglass' Address," *North Star*, August 4, 1848 (Douglass); "Celebration of West India Negro Emancipation."

35. "Celebration of West India Negro Emancipation"; "Address of H. W. Johnson," *North Star*, August 21, 1848 (Johnson); "Frederick Douglass' Address," *North Star*, August 4, 1848 (Douglass); "Speech of Reverend Henry Bleby, Missionary from Barbados," *Liberator*, August 6, 1858 (Bleby).

36. Chapter 4 of Ernest's *Liberation Historiography* on orations is mute on Emancipation Day speeches, with the exception of Douglass's 1857 West Indies address evaluated as evidence of the speaker becoming a "more aggressive historian" of African Americans (249). Emancipation Day in chapter 2 of Rael's *Black Identity* is viewed as an elite-controlled public event designed to assert control of black communities devoid of any discussion of orations, speeches, and their

political language. Chapters 3 and 4 in Hall's *Faithful Account of the Race* on African American historical discourse are mute on Emancipation Day speeches. In contrast to these scholars, I believe that Emancipation Day speeches are deep mines of rich historical and political ideas and language that remain largely untapped. I also find it difficult to project a nationalist framework—African American, American—on these events and speeches since West Indies Day represented an international commemoration of abolition and ongoing struggles against slavery.

37. "The North Star," *Encyclopedia Britannica*, https://www.britannica.com/topic/The-North-Star-American-newspaper.

38. Kerr-Ritchie, *Rites of August First*, 206. This sentence's expansive geographical references are deliberate.

39. For a pioneering study of the transatlantic abolitionist movement focusing upon the transnational circulation of people, publications, and ideas, see Blackett, *Building an Antislavery Wall.*

40. Rael, *Black Identity*, 216. Benedict Anderson's *Imagined Communities: Reflections on the Origin and Spread of Nationalism* (London: Verso, 1983) has proved useful to scholarly constructions of early African American national identity. But press coverage of West India Day beckons toward a more transnational consciousness that must be one of three things: (1) not that important; (2) primarily African diasporic; or (3) primarily internationalist. I'll conclude by noting the irony that one of the most influential studies of modern nationalism was penned by one from "a cosmopolitan and comparative" milieu. Benedict Anderson, *A Life Beyond Boundaries* (London: Verso, 2016), 23.

Part 3

✦

Black Internationalism

INTRODUCTION

Michael O. West

"I cannot understand," the poet June Jordan observed in 1976, "how any of us can fail to perceive the necessarily international nature of our oppression and, hence, our need for international unity and planned rebellion."[1] Jordan was addressing fellow African Americans, against the backdrop of the nationalist paroxysm attendant on the bicentennial of the United States Declaration of Independence. Pointedly, she entitled her essay "Declaration of an Independence I Would Just as Soon Not Have." Seeking confirmation of her contrarian conclusion, the poet ended her essay with a plea to her audience: "Please verify."[2] Many readers, especially black women, did. Jordan summed up the consensus of her correspondents as follows: "Yes, they said, you are not alone!"[3]

Black rejection of US nationhood was hardly new. Already at the founding moment of the republic, many an enslaved scion of Africa had espied an independence they too would just as soon not have had. It was for this reason that, among African descendants actively involved in the military struggle surrounding the bid for US independence, pro-British "black loyalists" easily outnumbered pro-American "black patriots." The reason for siding with the white colonialists over the white nationalists was not far to seek. For all the nostrums about liberty and human rights in its manifesto—the Declaration of Independence—the dominant wing of the US nationalist movement offered black bondsmen and women little of concrete value. From the standpoint of the enslaved, the colonialists offered a much more attractive alternative, namely, freedom from human bondage in return for military service against the nationalists, albeit mainly in segregated, white-officered units like the Ethiopian Regiment.

Temporally, the Declaration of Independence stood betwixt two other foundational documents that made clear, implicitly or explicitly, that there would be little or no place for black folk, whether enslaved or nominally free, in the emerging US social contract. One of those other documents was, of course, the Constitution of 1787, which reaffirmed the institution of slavery in multiple ways. The other document foundational to US nationhood, this one no less crucial for its being an unofficial text (unlike the officially constituted Declaration of Independence and Constitution), was Thomas Paine's pamphlet *Common Sense*, the country's first bestseller. Writing in the months leading up to the Declaration of Independence, and anticipating it, Paine rejected all talk of compromise with the British colonialists (as many urged), insisting on independence, and independence alone, with the goal of creating a pan-European republic in North America. "Europe, and not England, is the parent country of America," Paine assured his intended white audience, before adding, "We claim brotherhood with every European Christian, and triumph in the generosity of the sentiment."[4] The offer of fraternity, secular and sacred, did not extend to those of African and Native American heritage, whose "parent countries" would have no part in the envisioned pan-European Christian commonwealth.

Exclusion from the nation's social contract, as enunciated in its foundational documents, the unofficial no less than the official ones, led African Americans to think beyond the nation-state. The result was an internationalist conception of the black liberation struggle in the United States, the subject to which June Jordan called attention in her independence-rebuffing essay on the occasion of the nation's two hundredth birthday, a document with echoes of Frederick Douglass's inquisitional demarche of 1852: "What, to the American slave, is your Fourth of July?"

Haiti played a seminal role in the emergence of the international conception of black freedom in the United States. Of the four chapters in this part, two center on Haiti, with the others focusing on Liberia and Guyana, respectively. Haiti was huge, its paradigm-shattering revolution disrupting not just the systems of slavery, colonialism, and white supremacy in the Atlantic world but also the global capitalist mode of production itself, which abruptly lost its single largest source of sugar and coffee and an important source of cotton. Capitalism's loss was struggling humanity's gain. For the enslaved and oppressed descendants of Africa in the Atlantic world especially, Haiti was heady, the seeming potential of its revolution for replication electrifying enslaved freedom fighters everywhere.[5] Indeed, the origins of the Pan-African project, the emergence of a self-consciously black internationalism, are inseparable from the making of Haiti.

Leslie M. Alexander has discovered a novel aspect of this story, which she tells in her contribution to this part of the collection. While Alexander's evidence is nationally specific, the queries that animate her research have international implications. How, she asks, "did Black people, particularly in the United States, view Haiti and Haitian independence during this era? What did a sovereign Haiti represent to them, and how did it influence the development of Black political consciousness during the nineteenth century?" To answer these questions, Alexander turns to an anonymous, self-proclaimed "Injured Man of Color," author of what she describes as "the first known commentary from a Black person in the United States publicly discussing Haitian independence." The commentary appeared in a pair of newspaper articles in 1804, just months after Haiti officially became independent on the first day of the same year.

Several things about the Injured Man command attention. One is the author's anonymity, which invites conjecture, including the speculation that the Injured Man may not have been a man at all. Surely a black woman writing in that vein, in that era, would have had even more compelling reasons than a black man to mask her identity, including her gender, behind a veil of anonymity. We need not speculate about the Injured Man's political injury, which was genuine and heartfelt. Very explicitly, the Injured Man set out to defend Haiti against racist calumny in the US press. The global disinformation campaign against the Haitian Revolution was already under way, a campaign that has been so brilliantly explicated by the Haitian scholar of the Haitian Revolution, Michel-Rolph Trouillot,[6] whom Alexander cites. Adopting a Haitian identity, seemingly a synonym for an international black one, the Injured Man's self-defined task was to "vindicate his countrymen of St. Domingo from the charges which have been repeatedly presented [against them] in the public papers." Thus did the Injured Man squarely assume a position in the black vindicationist tradition, exponents of which would wage a long (and ongoing) defense in support of the historical achievements and mental capacities of African-descended people globally.[7]

For nearly a century, from its inception in 1791 till the fall of the hemisphere's last major slave regime in Brazil in 1888, the Haitian Revolution continued to excite antislavery agitators all over the Americas. Yet Haiti's impact on the black (and larger emancipatory) imagination hardly ended with the demise of chattel slavery. In a rude affront to Haiti's sovereignty, the Haitian revolutionary tradition and, with them, black internationalist sensibilities, the United States invaded Haiti in 1915 and occupied it for the next two decades. The US occupation, beginning as it did in the midst of World War I (before the United States entered the war) and continuing well into the turbulent postwar years, elicited fierce resistance, ranging from armed struggle by Haitian peasants to international protest, political and cultural. All the major (and competing) transnational movements concerned with black liberation during the interwar years—among them the Universal Negro Improvement Association, the Pan-African Congress, the Communist International, and Negritude—were deeply involved in the struggle against US imperialism in Haiti. In turn, the legacy of the Haitian Revolution exercised a power hold on the antioccupation struggle.

Such is the backdrop to Brandon R. Byrd's contribution to this part. If Leslie M. Alexander's discovery is empirical in nature, then Byrd's is largely epistemic, with a focus on that towering figure in African American letters, W. E. B. Du Bois. Specifically, Byrd examines the impact of the US occupation of Haiti on the writing of *Black Reconstruction in America*, Du Bois's massive and majestic work on the postemancipation reckoning in the United States that appeared in 1935, the year after the occupation of Haiti ended. "Haiti and *Black Reconstruction* are inseparable," Byrd observes of his findings.

At its core, *Black Reconstruction* is a disquisition on the aborting of social democracy in the United States by a coalition of white plutocracy and white supremacy. The result was the apartheid regime nicknamed Jim Crow, which put paid to all notions of land reform—"forty acres and a mule"—and sent African Americans back toward slavery. By comparison, and despite its notoriously antidemocratic politics, the postrevolutionary Haitian state sowed the seeds of social democracy, without actually establishing social democracy,[8] by abolishing the plantation system and redistributing the land to the freedpeople. It was this contrast with the United States that led Du Bois to conclude, a conclusion that doubles as the title of Byrd's chapter, that the Haitian agrarian cultivators were "the happiest peasants in the world." On its own terms this is, transparently, an overblown claim. That, however, is not the yardstick by which it should be measured. Juxtaposed against the wretched conditions of the African American rural masses under the yoke of Jim Crow—the sharecropping, the debt peonage, the convict-lease system, the lynching, and, not least, the wanton sexual violence, mostly against women but also not sparing men and children—in many ways the status of the Haitian peasantry was indeed enviable.

Liberia, the subject of Jessica Millward's chapter, often appeared alongside Haiti in African American political discourse on both sides of the US Civil War. Millward seeks to "explore the relationship between colonization, family and black internationalism." The starting point indeed is colonization, or expatriation, an integral part of African American internationalist politics from the outset. Like black internationalism more broadly, emigration—the terminology originally given to the expatriation of free blacks from the United States—was a by-product of exclusion from the social contract. From the era of the US Revolutionary War, African American prospective emigrants set their sights on multiple destinations, among them Canada, Haiti, and Sierra Leone.

Then there was Liberia. Founded as a colony in 1821, Liberia officially became an independent nation-state in 1847, ruled by black emigrants largely from the United States, with a smattering from the Caribbean and elsewhere. Liberia introduced a new rancor into the emigration movement, with the objection centering on the colony's sponsor, the American Colonization Society (ACS). A white-run group, the ACS was an odd-bedfellow coalition, its ranks including certain self-professed friends of the blacks. However, these individuals played second fiddle to the supporters of slavery, who originally were the dominant force within the ACS, which they envisioned as a vehicle to rid the United States of free blacks, the better to make slavery more secure.

Unsurprisingly, the response was withering. "Colonization," often used as a code word for Liberia, came under sustained attack from members of the free black intelligentsia. The critics included David Walker, whose iconic pamphlet of 1829 listed "the colonizing plan" as one of four reasons (the others being slavery, ignorance, and the corruption of Christianity) for the "wretchedness" of black folk in the United States.[9] Walker's staunch ally Maria Stewart similarly condemned the ACS as false "friends to Africa."[10] In a subsequent and more sustained attack on Liberia, Martin Delany compared it unfavorably to Haiti. "We do not," Delany announced, "expect Liberia to be all that Hayti is."[11] (Ever the chameleon, Delany would later reverse himself and declare for Liberia.) Liberia, however, had its defenders. The latter included two of the most distinguished Pan-African intellectuals of the nineteenth century, the Caribbean-born Edward Wilmot Blyden and the US-born Alexander Crummell, both emigrants to Liberia, although Crummell would return to the United States after the Civil War. All the while, a political and moral dilemma remained at the root of the Liberian experiment. As Jessica Millward writes, "The world's second black-ruled republic," after Haiti, was also "a settler society marred by many of the same exclusionary, oppressive characteristics common to modern colonial regimes."

Russell Rickford's chapter is set in the postcolonial era. Rickford's task is to make legible the 1978 tragedy in Jonestown, Guyana, which resulted in hundreds of mostly African American deaths. Although removed in time and space from them, Rickford's story is thematically connected to the other three chapters in this part of the collection. The sole English-speaking country in South America, Guyana became a British colony during, and largely because of, the Haitian Revolution.[12] Among the destinations Martin Delany (at one point) thought ideal for African American expatriates was New Granada, the former Spanish viceroyalty that would have included at least parts of Guyana's Essequibo region, where the Jonestown settlement was located.[13] The fact that neighboring Venezuela, which was part of New Granada, claimed sovereignty over Guyana-administered Essequibo was all the more reason for the Guyanese government to seek to implicate the United States in this border dispute by inviting US citizens, albeit predominantly black and working-class ones, to establish the Jonestown settlement. From the Guyanese standpoint, Jonestown was insurance against Venezuelan incursion into Essequibo. There are other points of convergence between Rickford's chapter and the other three. The language used by the Jonestown sojourners and their narrators—missionaries, pilgrims, exodus, Promised Land—mirrors the religious discourse that surrounded both Liberia and Haiti. Some nineteenth-century African Americans even dreamed of supplanting Haiti's dominant faiths, Roman Catholicism and Vodou, with variants of Protestantism, which was also the creed of the Jonestown settlers.

For black people in the United States, much had changed in the more than century and a half that separated the Haitian Revolution and the founding of Liberia on the one hand and the establishment of the Jonestown settlement on the other. But there was also continuity, with the result that African Americans remained systematically excluded from the social contract and the social-mobility ladder. The horror of slavery had been followed by the hope of Reconstruction, which was soon supplanted by a second horror, that of Jim Crow. The post–World War II civil rights movement formally ended Jim Crow and desegregated public spaces, most crucially the voting booth, but did little to substantively improve the socioeconomic status of most African Americans.

This was deracialization without transformation, and it was not unique to the United States. Similar processes unfolded simultaneously in the ex-colonies, including in Africa and the greater Caribbean, where the phenomenon was called neocolonialism. The Black Power movement emerged as an antidote to neocolonialism. As a term, and to a large extent as a cultural style, Black Power originated in the United States. In its most progressive and revolutionary forms, though, Black Power was a global political phenomenon offering a critique of deracialization without transformation and suggesting alternative modes of human existence. In short, Black Power was a corrective to neocolonialism. It was precisely the worldwide character of neocolonialism that facilitated the equally wide spatial appeal of Black Power, just as the universality of colonialism and apartheid had given rise to the Garveyite Universal Negro Improvement Association and, before that, the prevalence and persistence of slavery in the Atlantic world had made the Haitian Revolution so mesmerizing to so many for so long.

Russell Rickford's Jonestown pilgrims, as he styles them and as he shows, were scions of Black Power, directly and indirectly. The pilgrims' rural-based "apostolic socialism" corresponded with an agrarian strain within Black Power, with Black Power's Christian-grounded Black theology and, in all likelihood, also with the US Southern rural backgrounds of many of the Jonestown sojourners or their parents. For all their Catholic-synchronizing Vodou beliefs, Brandon R. Byrd's Du Boisian–inflected Haitian "happy peasants" would not entirely have been out of place in Jonestown, nor would Jessica Millward's Protestant-confessing, Liberia-bound emigrants. In their different ways, all of them, along with Leslie M. Alexander's Injured Man, really "were attempting to repudiate empire itself," as Rickford writes of the Jonestown pilgrims. That, ultimately, is what black internationalism is about—ceaselessly endeavoring to resist, and replace, the systems of oppression that have deformed human existence in the modern world, at the center of which is the capitalist mode of production.

Notes

1. June Jordan, "Declaration of an Independence I Would Just as Soon Not Have," in *Civil Wars* (Boston: Beacon Books, 1981), 119. This piece first appeared in *Ms.* magazine under a different title.

2. Jordan, "Declaration of an Independence," 121.

3. Jordan, "Declaration of an Independence," 115.

4. Thomas Paine, *Common Sense and Other Political Writings* (Indianapolis: Bobbs-Merrill, 1953; first published 1776), 21.

5. The literature on the global impact of the Haitian Revolution continues to grow. A recent, and defining, addition is Julius Scott's dissertation, now finally published. See Julius S. Scott, *The Common Wind: Afro-American Currents in the Age of the Haitian Revolution* (London: Verso, 2018).

6. Michel-Rolph Trouillot, *Silencing the Past: Power and the Production of History* (Boston: Beacon Press, 1995).

7. The most systematic exploration of this tradition is St. Claire Drake, *Black Folk Here and There: An Essay in History and Anthropology*, 2 vols. (Los Angeles: Center for Afro-American Studies, University of California, 1987–90).

8. The state-society conflict in Haiti has also been brilliantly dissected by Michel-Rolph Trouillot. See his *Haiti, State against Nation: The Origins and Legacy of Duvalierism* (New York: Monthly Review Press, 1990).

9. *David Walker's Appeal to the Coloured Citizens of the World*, ed. Peter P. Hinks (University Park: Pennsylvania State University Press, 2000; first published 1829).

10. Marilyn Richardson, ed., *Maria W. Stewart, America's First Black Woman Political Writer: Essays and Speeches* (Bloomington: Indiana University Press, 1987), 61.

11. Martin R. Delany, *The Condition, Elevation, Emigration and Destiny of the Colored People of the United States* (Baltimore: Black Classic Press, 1993; first published 1852), 170–71.

12. Winston Mc Gowan, *A Survey of Guyanese History: A Collection of Historical Essays and Articles by a Guyanese Scholar* (Georgetown: Guyenterprise, 2018), 414–16.

13. Delany, *Condition*, 188–89.

Chapter 7

"A United and Valiant People"

Black Visions of Haiti at the Dawn of the Nineteenth Century

Leslie M. Alexander

In late November 1803, the epic struggle later known as the Haitian Revolution finally reached a definitive conclusion. Declaring unequivocal victory over their former enslavers, Jean-Jacques Dessalines, leader of the rebel army, along with generals Henry Christophe and Augustin Clervaux issued a proclamation heralding Saint Domingue's liberation from French colonial rule.[1] Weeks later, on January 1, 1804, Dessalines unveiled the Acte d'indépendance (Act of Independence), which formally announced the establishment of a free and autonomous Haiti and publicly proclaimed their sovereignty. In a speech delivered in Gonaïves, Dessalines called upon the Haitian people to pledge themselves to liberty at any cost: "Let us swear before the whole universe, to posterity, to ourselves to renounce France forever, and to die rather than live under its dominion. To fight until our last breath for the independence of our country." More than thirty-five generals signed the Act of Independence and pronounced Dessalines "Governor-General, for life, of Hayti," thereby renouncing European dominion and swearing to "blindly obey the Laws issued by [Dessalines's] authority, the only one we acknowledge."[2] With these powerful, inspiring acts, the Haitian people created the first sovereign Black nation in the Western Hemisphere.

The Haitian Act of Independence forever altered the meanings and conceptions of liberty in the Atlantic world. Admittedly, as historian Julia Gaffield notes, the Haitian Declaration of Independence was "not the first or even the second such pronouncement, either in the Americas or the Atlantic World more broadly defined."[3] Haiti was, however, the first and only country in the Americas where enslaved Africans threw off their shackles, fought for their freedom, eradicated slavery, defeated European powers, established their own nation, and pledged themselves to defend their freedom and independence until their "last breath." In so doing, they accomplished what scholar Michel-Rolph Trouillot described as the "unthinkable."[4] They radically upended the basic premise of white supremacy upon which slavery rested and asserted Black people's fundamental human right to liberty and self-governance. As Dessalines affirmed in his November 29, 1803, decree, "We have proclaimed our rights; we swear to never yield them to any power on earth: the frightful veil of prejudice is torn to pieces and is so forever. Woe be to whomsoever would dare again to put together its bloody tatters."[5] Inherent in Dessalines's declaration was both a promise and threat. Not only did he vow to expand the notion of liberty and natural rights to people of African descent, he also warned the enemies of Black freedom that the Haitian people were prepared to defend their rights with deadly force, even if it required sacrificing their lives. The Haitian Act of Independence thus transformed global conceptions of liberty and challenged existing assumptions about who possessed human rights and who did not.[6]

Haiti's Act of Independence received wide circulation throughout the Atlantic world, creating considerable consternation, and even panic, among white people in the slaveholding nations.[7] Yet while historians have begun to document how Haiti was perceived among whites, particularly white politicians in the western nations, scant attention has been given to other equally significant questions: how did Black people, particularly in the United States, view Haiti and Haitian independence during this era?[8] What did a sovereign Haiti represent to them, and how did it influence the development of Black political consciousness during the nineteenth century? This essay seeks to answer those questions by examining how US Black activists perceived Haiti in the earliest moments following Haitian independence. It focuses specifically on the year 1804 to chronicle Black people's earliest feelings about postindependence Haiti and to explore why they eventually came to view the Black republic as their "cradle of hope."[9] As this essay demonstrates, Black activists understood Haiti's symbolic significance as the only country in the world where a "united and valiant people" had courageously conquered slavery and established a free Black nation.[10] They were also aware that as people of African descent in the diaspora, they shared a common destiny with Haitians and believed that their own fate was entwined with Haiti's success or failure. Through a careful examination of newspaper editorials and street protests, this essay reconstructs the birth of Black political thought regarding Haiti and delves deeply into Black activists' ideas about Haitian independence as they sought to create an alternative vision of Black freedom in the Americas.

On May 25, 1804, just months after Jean-Jacques Dessalines presented the Haitian Act of Independence, an anonymous writer calling himself "An Injured Man of Color" published his views about Haiti's current affairs in the *Commercial Advertiser* newspaper in New York City.[11] The Injured Man was writing at a complicated historical moment. In February 1804, shortly after declaring Haiti's independence, Dessalines announced that all remaining white colonists must leave the island. Those who refused would be killed. Convinced that lingering French residents endangered the welfare of the new nation and its emancipated citizens, Dessalines pledged that the Haitian army would use all necessary means to "exterminate" their oppressors.[12] Perhaps doubting Dessalines's commitment, thousands of French colonists remained, and in the early months of 1804, Dessalines and his army tortured and slaughtered many who did not heed his warning.[13] Word spread rapidly across the Atlantic World that Dessalines and the Haitian army had unleashed a murderous rampage, killing thousands of innocent whites—a campaign that became known as "the horrors of St. Domingo." Marlene Daut and Julia Gaffield have demonstrated that the total dead from Dessalines's campaign was in fact only a few hundred white soldiers and colonists.[14]

For Dessalines, however, his mandate was an act of corrective justice. "Our vengeance," he explained, "could never equal the sum of injustices and atrocities of our enemies."[15] As a result, midway through the attacks, Dessalines issued a formal arrêté to justify his actions and to hopefully silence his detractors. Frustrated with those who criticized his deeds as an "indiscriminate destruction of the whites," Dessalines sought to set the record straight and expose "the true motives" that drove the government to enact such extreme measures. In Dessalines's view, French colonists could not be allowed to remain in Haiti because they threatened the country's domestic security. After all, he angrily noted, the French had "contributed either by their guilty writings or by their sanguinary accusations to the drowning, suffocating, assassinating, hanging, and shooting of more than sixty thousand of our Brethren under the inhuman government of Le Clerc and Rochambeau." Therefore, Dessalines argued, their enemies "ought to be classed with assassins, and delivered up to the sword of justice." He emphasized that all guilty parties would be punished because "nothing shall ever turn our vengeance from those murderers, who have bathed themselves with pleasure in the blood of the innocent children of Hayti."[16]

Despite Dessalines's searing reply, however, US newspaper reports immediately began condemning him as stories about the massacre spread across the Atlantic Ocean. On May 15, 1804, the *New York Gazette* printed a story from Captain Hodge, a US ship captain who had just returned from Port-au-Prince. Alarmed about the violence enacted against the French, and the inability of American merchants to freely conduct business in Haiti, Hodge anxiously wrote, "The French people at the Cape are in the most distressing situation . . . the whites are daily missing, supposed to be secretly murdered, and their property immediately confiscated and sold at auction." Worse, Hodge hysterically claimed that Haitians had resolved to indiscriminately abuse white people and reduce them to slavery. "No age or sex is spared from the outrage and inhumanity of the blacks," he declared. "Men, women and children are held in the most abject slavery, and daily expire from hardship and fatigue." Hodge further maintained that the ports were largely inaccessible and unsafe for merchants. "Americans who arrive at the Cape are obliged to be extremely circumspect," he worriedly explained. "For want of proper regulations, and from the ignorance and jealousy of the blacks, they are subjected to much hazard and inconvenience."[17]

Like Hodge, many white Americans nervously monitored Haiti's commercial activity since, for decades prior, US merchants had enjoyed a rather profitable trade relationship with Saint Domingue. The colony exported desirable cash crops, such as coffee, sugar, and cotton, and it relied upon the Americans and the English to import much needed manufactured goods. But what would happen now that Saint Domingue had become a free Black nation? Captain Hodge and many other American merchants predicted disaster. According to Hodge, Dessalines and his main general, Henry Christophe, had no authority or control over the country, which threatened the United States' economic standing. "The arrêtés and proclamations of Dessalines and Christophe are mere flummery," Hodge complained, "and seldom or never put in execution."[18]

Within days, the Injured Man of Color delivered an impassioned rebuttal. It is the first known commentary from a Black person in the United States publicly discussing Haitian independence and is therefore worthy of extensive analysis. Essentially nothing is known about the Injured Man, which raises a series of compelling questions: Who was the Injured Man of Color and why did he feel so passionately compelled to defend Haiti? Was he a person of Haitian descent himself, and why did he describe himself as injured? Although the answers to these questions remain mysteries, upon closer examination it is clear that, at a minimum, the Injured Man viewed himself and the entire Black race as *politically* injured—damaged by the cruel and inhumane systems that kept millions in bondage and denied human rights even to those who were legally free.

In response, he positioned himself as an early vindicationist, who sought to defend the Black race and to champion their fundamental right to freedom and justice. As he explained, "An inherent love for his brethren of color" compelled him to "vindicate his countrymen of St. Domingo from the charges which have been repeatedly presented in the public papers." Bemoaning the persistent "stings of injustice" that plagued Black people in the Americas, the Injured Man argued that racism and ignorance motivated the attacks against Dessalines and the Haitian government. Therefore, he resolved to eradicate the misconceptions and provide an accurate account of Haiti's historical and political dynamics.[19]

His resulting plea for Haiti utilized a clever and effective rhetorical strategy, one that future generations of Black activists routinely employed in the decades that followed. The Injured Man appealed to the revolutionary spirit in white America that persisted following their own successful revolution and drew a compelling parallel between the battle for US independence from Britain and the Haitian struggle against French rule. Conjuring up patriotic images of the triumphant victory against British tyranny, he asked his readers: "When you fought for your independence, when you resisted the arm of Britain, and gained the cause for which you struggled, were you not elated with your success? Were you not proud of your victory? Did not your souls spurn at the man who dared to call you rebels and traitors?" After reminding Americans of their enthusiastic victory, he asked them to reflect on the similarities between their situation and the Haitians' circumstances: "Is not the cause for which the Haytians fought the same in principle with yours? If your cause was just and honorable, was not theirs the same?" The Injured Man also encouraged his readers to consider the matter from the Haitians' perspective and to put aside their fears and anxieties. As he explained, the Haitians (like their American counterparts) were "actuated by principles of honor and justice, and not by a spirit of revenge." To the contrary, he argued, it was their oppressors who were motivated by misguided agendas: "It is evident that the Haytians have nothing in view but to be acknowledged and treated as men, and as people. Those who oppose them are guided by avarice, and the love of oppressing their fellow creatures."[20]

Drawing upon the Americans' rallying cry of "Liberty or Death," the Injured Man also highlighted the core contradiction between slavery and a human being's fundamental right to liberty. After all, he pointed out, the Americans might have *felt* enslaved by British rule, but the Haitians had been *actual* slaves. Chronicling the horrors of slavery and the injustice it wrought, the Injured Man painfully described how Africans had been "torn from their families and friends; dragged from their native country;

transported to a distant clime; sentenced to linger out a miserable life under the lash . . . of those to whom, in justice, they owed no allegiance; and doomed to fatten with their blood a soil from which they reap no advantage." Therefore, unlike the American rebels, the Haitians had an even more compelling reason to risk their lives to free themselves. "Were they not more oppressed," he asked, "and had they not even stronger stimulants to urge them on to independence?"[21]

In reply to those who criticized Dessalines's policy of removal and extermination, he maintained that the Haitian government's response was perfectly rational given the fear that the French would try to reimpose slavery. "It is, indeed, a hard case," he reflected, "for those who have once tasted the sweets of liberty, to be reduced again to a state of slavery." Although he claimed to oppose "the spilling of human blood," the Injured Man openly endorsed Dessalines's campaigns against the French colonists, arguing that since the French were particularly guilty of brutality and violence, the Haitians should justifiably protect themselves from future attacks. "The cruelties of the agents and officers of France is well known to the world," he reminded his readers. "Name the country into which they have been able to enter, where they have spared high or low, rich or poor, age or sex; where their footsteps have not been marked with blood; where terror has not been their forerunner, and desolation, misery, and death their perpetual attendant."[22] In many ways, the Injured Man's concerns about the French colonists' efforts to reconquer the island were legitimate, given that, as one historian noted, the French had "neither gone away or given up."[23]

The Injured Man's final appeal passionately defended Haiti's image. Chastising those who gave false, negative impressions of Haiti, he criticized their efforts to "infuse a spirit of distrust into the minds of the benevolent and philanthropic citizens of this country." He further affirmed his belief that most white Americans actually supported Haiti's fight for full independence and comforted his readers that the Haitians would respond in kind. "The Haytians will always view your efforts with gratitude," he assured them. "They know how to discriminate between their friends and their enemies; and as they have arrows stored in their quivers for the latter, so they possess the highest respect and gratitude for the former."[24] In so doing, he tried to convince his readers that they had nothing to fear from independent Haiti and that as long as they dealt fairly with the new nation, their economic security would be retained.

The Injured Man's closing section took a surprising turn away from his white American readership. He directed his comments to two specific groups of Haitians: those who were living in the United States after being forcibly relocated during the revolution and the "chiefs"—the military and political leaders in Haiti—upon whose shoulders the nation's fate rested. For the dislocated Haitians, the Injured Man issued a message of repatriation. Here he echoed Dessalines, who had pledged two months earlier to pay for the transportation of any person of Haitian descent living in the United States who wished to return home.[25] The Injured Man encouraged displaced Haitians to demonstrate their solidarity and patriotism and return to build a new nation. Haiti could undoubtedly fulfill its destiny, he maintained, if its exiled children pledged their commitment to advance the nation's mission. "Reflect on the precarious situation of your countrymen," he urged. "Embrace the offer of your Chiefs . . . to return to your home; reflect that your future destiny is concerned, and the safety of your friends, race and color, is at hazard; accept the opportunity . . . to reclaim your rights and maintain your country's cause." He also pleaded with them to demonstrate their bravery, and to fight to the death to protect their freedom and the independence of the entire Haitian nation. Affirming again the rallying cry of revolution that reverberated across the Atlantic world, he concluded, "Let this be the motto on your helmet and on your shield—JUSTICE, RELIGION, and LIBERTY OR DEATH."[26]

Lastly, the Injured Man addressed the chiefs, Haiti's political and military leaders. Departing slightly from the revolutionary language in his earlier pronouncements, he employed a classic nineteenth-century moral uplift strategy. Specifically, he counseled the chiefs to rely on morality and religion as the country's guiding principles and urged them to keep God's commandments. The Injured Man also entreated the chiefs to honor the Sabbath because they had a duty to demonstrate their gratitude for freedom. "Shew [*sic*] yourselves grateful to your Creator," he insisted. "Set an example to your neighbors . . . Remember and keep holy the Sabbath Day, that the Lord may bless your labors and that it may be well with you." Although his departing words endorsed adherence to white Christian morality, his overall message still represented a radical declaration of Black people's basic human right to freedom and their right to defend themselves against anyone who sought to deny their liberties.[27]

The Injured Man reaffirmed his commitment to Black freedom, Haitian independence, and the right to self-defense three weeks later, when another newspaper, the New York *Spectator*, published a supplement to his original article. Intended as an open letter to Jean-Jacques Dessalines, the Injured Man praised Dessalines's leadership and expressed gratitude for his efforts to deliver Haiti from the hands of "our cruel oppressors." More significantly, however, the Injured Man warned Dessalines against forming alliances with foreign nations and strongly urged him to use all necessary means to protect Haiti from future invasions: "In our present situation, let us not trust any foreign governance to guard our rights and liberties. Let us continue in our determination . . . to maintain our independence with our last breath against those who dare to attempt to dispossess us of the inestimable treasure—a treasure which the Author of our Being originally bestowed on mankind indiscriminately. Liberty is an inherent and inalienable right of man." The Injured Man continued by affirming his faith in Dessalines's abilities to defend their freedom, "secure our liberties and independence," and use his keen judgment to navigate the perilous circumstances that his country faced.[28]

Notably, in this particular section, the Injured Man ceased using the terms "you" and "your" and instead used "we," "us," and "our." It is particularly noticeable in the passage above, in which he states: "Let *us* continue in *our* determination . . . to maintain *our* independence with *our* last breath" (emphasis added). Perhaps this suggests that the Injured Man was, in fact, a person of Haitian descent. This is certainly possible, since in his previous article he repeatedly referred to Haitians as his "countrymen."[29] Perhaps, however, such language simply indicated that he shared a strong sense of racial solidarity with Haitians and wanted to pledge his commitment to their common cause. Regardless, his closing words to Dessalines emphasized the importance of unity and solidarity. "It is my unfeigned wish and confident expectation," he proclaimed, "that you will prove to your enemies and to the world, that an attempt to subvert your independence, and enslave your fellow citizens, will terminate in the disgrace and the ruin of your adversaries—and that a united and valiant people . . . are an unconquerable bulwark against an empire of treachery, violence, and unrelenting ambition." Thus, in an impassioned testament to human rights, and the spirit of those who were willing to fight to defend their freedom, the Injured Man of Color not only affirmed Haiti's right to independence but also issued a radical call for Black liberation throughout the diaspora.[30]

It is impossible to know whether Black people in the United States read the Injured Man's messages or whether they shared his sentiments. What we do know, however, is that hundreds of Black people in Philadelphia apparently admired the Haitians' bravery, courage, and willingness to take up arms to defend the cause of freedom. Less than one month after the Injured Man published his articles, as many as two hundred Black Philadelphians, reportedly all men, took to the streets in the form of a rebellion.[31] The editor of the *Columbian Centinel* newspaper described their actions as being "a la mode de Hayti," implying that the group endorsed using violent means to claim their right to liberty and equality.

They chose July 4, US Independence Day, as the moment to express their discontent, likely in a purposeful effort to expose the contradiction between Black enslavement and American freedom. Throughout the nineteenth century, Black activists protested July 4 in cities across the North, sometimes in an uprising, other times parading through the streets on July 5, which they claimed as a Black Independence Day. Their goal, of course, was to raise questions about the true meaning of freedom and liberty while slavery persisted throughout the Americas.[32]

On this particular occasion, protestors "created some alarm" in the city streets, boldly marching through town and attacking local residents.[33] On the first night, July 4, at about "half past eight," an unspecified number of Black men gathered on Small Street, where they "formed themselves into a company, and appointed a captain, lieutenant, and ensign." Shortly after 9:00 P.M., rebels allegedly attacked a man, and robbed him, before proceeding, military style, to Shippen Street near the corner of Fifth Street, where they threatened to kill an unnamed man and woman, as well as a "Mr. Kane and his family." One block later, near Sixth Street, they attacked a man with a brickbat, and then entered a house on Small Street and assaulted two other people. By then the group had reached about one hundred and roamed with streets with "clubs and swords." The following night, protesters assembled again, at about 10:00 p.m., this time numbering as many as two hundred. According to one account, the armed men "committed similar, if not greater excesses—damning the whites and saying they will shew them St. Domingo!"[34] In subsequent days, the rebels gathered multiple times, assembling "several nights successively," injuring numerous people and threatening to murder others, until the "ringleaders" were finally apprehended.[35]

As one historian noted, "Evoking 'St. Domingo' was shorthand for resistance, one that embraced violence as a principled step against slavery."[36] Even so, the group's ultimate goals remain unclear. What did they actually mean when they threatened to "shew the whites St. Domingo?" Were they simply continuing the tradition of demonstrating against the hypocrisy of American "freedom" in the midst of slavery? Or was it something more? Were they reflecting the Injured Man's point that Black people should have the same right as American patriots to use violence to secure their freedom? Were they mimicking and celebrating Jean-Jacques Dessalines's bold behavior by threating whites with violence? Or were they truly acting "a la mode de Hayti" and seeking to inspire an actual revolution?

Although the historical record fails to provide satisfying answers to these questions, there may be a small clue about the rebels' motivations buried in the language of one newspaper report. Notably, there are two distinct accounts of what the protestors allegedly shouted on the second night. According to the New York *Spectator*, they "damned the whites" and said they would "shew them St. Domingo!" but the *Columbian Centinel* reported a more nuanced version. In that account, which also appeared in several other newspapers, the protestors promised to "shew the whites '*St. Domingo play*.' "[37] The addition of the word "play" is significant for a few reasons. First, it suggests that the phrase may have been translated from, or been influenced by, French speakers. While the phrasing "shew the whites St. Domingo play" does not make much sense in English, the expression *jeux de St. Domingo* would have had rich meaning among French speakers in the early nineteenth century. As a colloquial expression, *jeux de St. Domingo* essentially meant that the rebels intended to protest "St. Domingo style," or the way they do in St. Domingo. Even more, the phrase carried the implication of a public spectacle—or public display of fighting—one that was reflected in their bold demonstration in the streets.[38] If, in fact, French speakers coined the phrase, it suggests that at least some of the rebels may have been Saint Domingue refugees who wanted to declare their solidarity with their Haitian brethren. While there is no evidence that Benjamin Lewis and Simon Fox, the two ringleaders taken into custody, spoke French, other rebels may have. As such, it is entirely possible that at least some of the rebels were Saint Domingue refugees who hoped to spark the fires of rebellion not just in Haiti but also in the United States. Regardless, the Philadelphia rebellion of 1804 demonstrates that at least some US Blacks celebrated and honored the Haitian Revolution—and independent Haiti—and used it as a model for their own local liberation struggles.

The year 1804 was a critical moment for Black activists across the Atlantic world. Jean-Jacques Dessalines's Declaration of Independence was a monumental event that inspired many champions of liberty to believe that they would soon witness the proliferation of abolition and emancipation across the Americas. Particularly in the United States, Haiti represented the culmination of Black activists' most treasured dreams—a strong, sovereign Black nation that would silence all those who claimed that Black people were not fit for freedom and self-rule. Unfortunately, however, in the aftermath of Haitian independence, Black activists witnessed a painful backlash as terrified whites fought back against the specter of Black freedom and sovereignty. Determined to punish the Haitians' bravado and to destroy its potential, the world's slaveholding nations imposed diplomatic and economic embargoes that crippled the burgeoning Black nation. They were especially critical of Dessalines's willingness to defend

Black freedom at any cost, and therefore commenced a propaganda campaign against Haiti that challenged the propriety of Black freedom and equality.

Certainly, these setbacks were devastating for Haitians, but they also had consequences for Black freedom fighters in other parts of the diaspora. Black activists in the United States, in particular, strongly believed that Haiti's image and destiny were deeply connected to their own struggle for freedom and equality. As a result, some, like the Injured Man of Color, responded by unleashing the power of the pen. His newspaper articles criticized the persistence of racism, angrily denounced negative stereotypes about Haiti circulating in the media, and defended the Haitians' right to struggle for the same freedoms that American rebels fought for in 1776. In so doing, he called upon white Americans to have compassion for the Haitian people and to recognize their common humanity. Others, such as the Philadelphia rebels, took their frustrations to the streets, and threatened to "shew the whites St. Domingo." Regardless of their differing strategies, these activists stood united in their passionate hope that Haiti would be successful and that its success would become their own.

Notes

This essay draws upon Leslie M. Alexander, *Fear of a Black Republic: Haiti and the Birth of Black Internationalism* (Urbana: University of Illinois Press, 2022).

1. Historians owe a debt of gratitude to historian Julia Gaffield, who discovered original versions of the Haitian Act of Independence. She also revealed that the act issued on January 1, 1804, was not the first or only version of the Haitian declaration. For a full analysis of the declaration(s), see Julia Gaffield, ed., *The Haitian Declaration of Independence: Creation, Context, and Legacy* (Charlottesville: University of Virginia Press, 2016). For an earlier discussion of Dessalines's role in creating the Act of Independence, see Deborah Jenson, "Dessalines's American Proclamations of Haitian Independence," *Journal of Haitian Studies* 15, no. 1 (2009): 72–102.

2. Gaffield, *Haitian Declaration of Independence*, 245–46. Julia Gaffield notes that, according to one source, Dessalines delivered an opening speech in Kreyòl but that the Act of Independence was actually read by one of his secretaries, Louis Félix Boisrond-Tonnerre, since Dessalines was not well-versed in French, and "certainly could not write" in French (11–12).

3. Gaffield, *Haitian Declaration of Independence*, 9.

4. Michel-Rolph Trouillot, *Silencing the Past: Power and the Production of History* (New York: Beacon Press, 1995), 82. For Trouillot's argument about the Haitian Revolution as an "unthinkable" event, see 70–107.

5. *Times* (London), February 6, 1804. A portion of this quote also appears in Gaffield, *The Haitian Declaration of Independence*, 5.

6. Beyond its challenge to the fundamental notion of liberty, historian Julia Gaffield argues that the Haitian Act of Independence "helped to initiate the feverish 'contagion of sovereignty' that swept the world, from Latin America to South

Asia, in the first half of the nineteenth century." Gaffield, *Haitian Declaration of Independence*, 5.

7. Ada Ferrer, *Freedom's Mirror: Cuba and Haiti in the Age of Revolution* (New York: Cambridge University Press, 2014), 189–90; Gaffield, *Haitian Declaration of Independence*, 9, 16.

8. In recent years, numerous studies have emerged that examine the relationship between Saint Domingue and the United States during the era of the Haitian Revolution. A few examples include Tim Matthewson, *A Proslavery Foreign Policy: Haitian-American Relations during the Early Republic* (Westport, CT: Praeger Publishers, 2003); Gordon Brown, *Toussaint's Clause: The Founding Fathers and the Haitian Revolution* (Jackson: University of Mississippi Press, 2005); Jose Saint-Louis, *The Haitian Revolution in the Shaping of American Democracy* (Coral Springs, FL: Llumina Press, 2008); Jeremy Popkin, *You Are All Free: The Haitian Revolution and the Abolition of Slavery* (New York: Cambridge University Press, 2010); Ashli White, *Encountering Revolution: Haiti and the Making of the Early Republic* (Baltimore: Johns Hopkins University Press, 2010); Julia Gaffield, *Haitian Connections: Recognition after Revolution in the Atlantic World* (Chapel Hill: University of North Carolina Press, 2015). A few studies have also begun to explore the question of how Black people in the United States and elsewhere in the diaspora viewed the Haitian Revolution; see Ada Ferrer, *Freedom's Mirror: Cuba and Haiti in the Age of Revolution* (New York: Cambridge University Press, 2014); James Alexander Dun, *Dangerous Neighbors: Making the Haitian Revolution in Early America* (Philadelphia: University of Pennsylvania Press, 2016); and Julius S. Scott, *The Common Wind: Afro-American Currents in the Age of the Haitian Revolution* (London: Verso Books, 2018). However, none have grappled extensively with nineteenth-century Black political consciousness in the United States after Haitian independence, except one: Gerald Horne, *Confronting Black Jacobins: The United States, The Haitian Revolution, and the Origins of the Dominican Republic* (New York: Monthly Review Press, 2015).

9. *Freedom's Journal*, October 24, 1828.

10. *Commercial Advertiser*, May 25, 1804.

11. *Commercial Advertiser*, May 25, 1804. This article was later reprinted in *Poulson's American Daily Advertiser*, May 30, 1804. Historian James Alexander Dun also briefly mentions this article in Dun, *Dangerous Neighbors*, 217–18.

12. Quoted in Jeremy Popkin, "Jean-Jacques Dessalines, Norbert Thoret, and the Violent Aftermath of the Haitian Declaration of Independence," in Gaffield, *Haitian Declaration of Independence*, 122.

13. Popkin, "Jean-Jacques Dessalines," 115–35; Ferrer, *Freedom's Mirror*, 194–95; Robin Blackburn, *The American Crucible: Slavery, Emancipation, and Human Rights* (London: Verso, 2011).

14. Julia Gaffield, "Haiti and the Atlantic World: Sources and Resources for Discussions about Haiti and Haitian History," March 18, 2013, https://haitidoi.com/2013/03/18/1804-census-gros-morne-haiti/; Marlene L. Daut, "All the Devils Are Here: How the visual history of the Haitian Revolution misrepresents Black suffering and death," October 14, 2020, https://www.laphamsquarterly.org/roundtable/all-devils-are-here. For more on the "horrors of St. Domingo," see Mary Hassal (Leonora Sansay), *Secret History, or, The Horrors of St. Domingo, in a series of letters, Written by a Lady at Cape François, to Colonel Burr, Late*

Vice-President of the United States, Principally during the Command of General Rochambeau (Philadelphia: Bradford and Innskeep, 1807).

15. Popkin, "Jean-Jacques Dessalines," 122.

16. *Philadelphia Gazette*, April 30, 1804; *Port Folio*, April 1810.

17. *New York Gazette*, May 15, 1804.

18. *New York Gazette*, May 15, 1804. For more on the United States' trade relationship with Haiti during this era, see Gaffield, *Haitian Connections*, 124–52.

19. *Commercial Advertiser*, May 25, 1804.

20. *Commercial Advertiser*, May 25, 1804.

21. *Commercial Advertiser*, May 25, 1804.

22. *Commercial Advertiser*, May 25, 1804.

23. Brown, *Toussaint's Clause*, 230.

24. *Commercial Advertiser*, May 25, 1804.

25. In a declaration issued on January 14, 1804, Dessalines offered to pay forty dollars to any American ship captain who was willing to bring Haitians in the United States back to Haiti. *Aurora General Advertiser*, March 29, 1804; *Christian Observer*, June 1804; Dun, *Dangerous Neighbors*, 214.

26. *Commercial Advertiser*, May 25, 1804. Emphasis is his.

27. *Commercial Advertiser*, May 25, 1804.

28. The Injured Man originally intended his open letter to Dessalines to serve as the conclusion to his first article, but his illness delayed its publication. *Spectator*, June 12, 1804.

29. *Commercial Advertiser*, May 25, 1804.

30. *Spectator*, June 12, 1804.

31. *Columbian Centinel*, July 18, 1804. Other newspapers reprinted the article, including the *Windham Herald* (July 26, 1804) and the Portland, Maine, *Gazette* (August 6, 1804).

32. For more on protest and parading culture among free Black Northerners in the antebellum era, see Sterling Stuckey, *Slave Culture: Nationalist Theory and the Foundations of Black America* (New York: Oxford University Press, 1987); Paul A. Gilje, *The Road to Mobocracy: Popular Disorder in New York City, 1763–1834* (Chapel Hill: University of North Carolina Press, 1987); Mitch Kachun, *Festivals of Freedom: Memory and Meaning in African American Emancipation Celebrations, 1808–1915* (Amherst: University of Massachusetts Press, 2003); and Leslie M. Alexander, *African or American?: Black Identity and Political Activism in New York City, 1784–1861* (Urbana: University of Illinois Press, 2008).

33. *Columbian Centinel*, July 18, 1804.

34. *Spectator*, July 14, 1804; Utica *Patriot*, July 23, 1804. Portions of this story also appear in Dun, *Dangerous Neighbors*, 237.

35. *Columbian Centinel*, July 18, 1804. Authorities took the ringleaders into custody but later released them. Gary Nash, "Reverberations of Haiti in the American North: Black Saint Dominguans in Philadelphia," *Pennsylvania History* 65 (1998): 73.

36. Dun, *Dangerous Neighbors*, 237.

37. *Columbian Centinel*, July 18, 1804, emphasis in the original.

38. *Dictionnaire de l'Académie Françoise* [1798]. Revu, corrigé et augumenté par l'académie elle-même. Cinquième edition. A Paris, Chez J. J. Smits et Ce., Imp.-Lib., rue de Tournon, N°. 1133, Faubourg Germain.

Chapter 8

"Give Our Love to All the Colored Folk"

African American Families and Black Internationalism in Nineteenth-Century Liberia

Jessica Millward

In 1833, General John H. Cocke of Virginia manumitted his bondman, Peyton Skipwith, after thirty-three years of enslavement. Cocke freed Skipwith, his wife Lydia, and their six children so that they "may go to Liberia and enjoy freedom."[1] The Skipwith family was like hundreds of other recently manumitted African Americans in the Chesapeake who were expressly "emancipated for the purpose of emigrating."[2] Undoubtedly Peyton Skipwith accepted Cocke's decision to liberate and then relocate with a spirit of both happiness and resignation; migrating to another country would allow him to secure his family's freedom, but leaving the United States meant leaving his mother in Virginia. It also meant leaving his brother and niece, who were both enslaved on Cocke's property in Alabama. Cocke used that particular plantation as a "training school" for the enslaved (and some free blacks) to receive the training he envisioned that was needed before their emigration. It is difficult to know whether Cocke ever planned on sending Skipwith's brother and niece, but it is clear from Peyton Skipwith's letters to Cocke that he and his family migrated with the expectation that their extended kin would join them in Liberia.

The Skipwith family has figured prominently in articles, monographs, and edited volumes. This essay uses the Skipwiths as a point of departure to explore the relationships among colonization, family, and black internationalism. Their letters back and forth across the Atlantic reveal much about the complicated nature of the forced relocation of enslaved people to Liberia.[3] Claude Clegg, John Grant, Marissa Stango, and Marie Tyler-McGraw have done much to expand how we understand family as a category of analysis when discussing Liberia.[4] However, far too little attention is given to the ways in which the concept of family influenced emigration patterns and by extension black internationalism.[5] Black internationalism, after all, tends to focus on the nation-state and the exportation of values. It is a given that religion-based organizations backed the colonization movement. What is less apparent is how African American notions of family were intertwined with black internationalism.

This essay explores the multifaceted ways that family and household functioned among enslaved and free blacks who migrated to Liberia from Maryland and Virginia during the nineteenth century.[6] The first section analyzes the role families played in the construction of the homeland. Next, the essay discusses the varied notions of "family" and, by extension, households. The household economy in Liberia was based on agriculture and depended on healthy family members to contribute to the work. Finally, the essay discusses the importance of family among enslaved and free blacks both in the United States and in Liberia.

Of Families, Homelands, and Relocation

According to John Cocke, Peyton Skipwith was a "good Christian man." The missionary impulse of colonization used African Americans like Skipwith to expand the Christian "family." Forced migration disguised as "recruitment" usually included the suggestion that free African Americans could leave with their family. Slaveholders often freed individuals with the promise that relocation meant that the family could be together. Irrespective of motivation, relocation called into question the notions of homelands and nations, and colonization called into question the relationship between homelands and households.

The Methodist Episcopal Church supported colonization more than any other Protestant denomination, with the belief that followers of Christianity "would pour their blessings over a suffering and degraded continent."[7] Letters from settlers and officials espoused the view that "every citizen of Liberia must consider himself as one of the builders of a great and cultivated nation, a Christian commonwealth, on the shores of a barbarous continent."[8] Therefore, in manumitting and resettling blacks, the Christian ethos dictated that Americans in Africa actualize the promises of Christian civilization and convert their African brethren in the process.[9]

One the best examples of the complexity of families and relocation occurred in 1854 when the American Colonization Society (ACS) began a campaign to resettle sixty-three enslaved men, women, and children belonging to the Herndon and Love families of Fauquier and Loudoun Counties, Virginia.[10] From August to December 1854, ACS supporters who considered themselves "very true friends of the black man" donated ten dollars each to support the manumission and forced resettlement of these individuals, at sixty dollars for each person on the voyage. The campaign raised enough money to send the original sixty-three individuals as well as a number of their free black kin. In total, seventy-two individuals relocated to Liberia.

The colonization movement preyed upon African American beliefs in family. Owners knew this and promised families freedom if they moved to Liberia. However, emigrants were aware that the actions of owners "concerned" with the fate of free blacks revealed determinism in how they thought blacks should best live their lives versus how African Americans might design their own fate. Still others had little choice. Janet Duitsman Cornelius recounts the fate of slaves owned by Mississippian Isaac Ross. Ross gave the slaves on his plantation the choice to migrate to Liberia or be sold; the profits made from their sale would be used to support a school he was building for migrants to Liberia.[11] Thus, the violence that undergirded slavery and race relations also took curious turns even within the "benevolent" aims of the ACS.

Manumitted blacks were hesitant to venture to Africa. Reports of the overseas voyage included accounts of persons falling ill with fever, malnutrition, and dehydration.[12] Accounts of the poor soil in northern Africa did not help recruitment efforts. In private letters, clearly not meant for circulation in public, Maryland State Colonization Society representative John Gill spoke of Monrovia as "the poorest you can name on the coast of Africa. Monrovia it is an unfertile, gravelly mountain nearly surrounded by a swamp as nauseous as death itself to a stranger."[13] Gill's assessment of life in Africa was mixed: "There are few that are doing well in the advancement of life but a great number are going back."[14] A still greater concern for emigrationists were the numerous bondspeople who chose to remain enslaved if manumission and resettlement meant separation from their family and kinship networks.[15]

The combination of unfavorable reports and a hesitancy to leave family and kin may have prevented a good number of black people from migrating to Liberia. Where were they safe and where could they go? The work of Elizabeth Pryor reveals a complex antebellum society where even in the North, African Americans were marked as "colored" and called "niggers."[16] The antiblack sentiment in the United States permeated beyond the plantation as suggested by Katherine McKittrick and into the very fabric of US imperialism.[17] Therefore it is important to underscore that free blacks often felt that they had very little viable options.

Sometimes, it was best to emigrate first and wonder later. White backlash was so strong in the wake of Nat Turner's rebellion that more than five hundred free and manumitted black Virginians sailed for Liberia in the year immediately following the uprising.[18] In Maryland, one man was encouraged to migrate because his free status was becoming a site of contention with local whites.[19]

Certainly, black people were also astute enough to manipulate white fears of a large free black class and lobby for resettlement on their own terms. Bondspeople were persistent in asking their owners to grant them freedom so that they could resettle in Africa.[20] Virginia bondman James Starkey sought support from the ACS to purchase his freedom.[21] He asked the ACS to fund the $400 he needed and used his life as security. Once he secured the funds for his own freedom and passage to Liberia, Starkey wrote to the ACS again, this time trying to raise funds to buy his wife and children.[22] Certainly, Starkey's experience complicates the notion that blacks were adamantly against resettlement. Whether or not Starkey trusted the benevolent motivations of the ACS is debatable. Whatever his opinion, Starkey used Liberia to his advantage. In his view, Liberia represented all things not possible in America.[23]

Households and Promises for a Better Life

For free and manumitted blacks, the familial unit was the chief form of social organization in Liberia. James Hall, an MSCS official, summarized the gendered nature of emigration in that "male heads of the family were bound to act for the good of that family."[24] The family mode of production was so predominant that single men and women were hired out to families and encouraged to build houses and cultivate the land at once. The family model was so critical in contributing to economic success that Hall suggested, "Men, and even women, with large families dependent on them, often do better than single men and women."[25]

Many advocates discouraged the resettlement of single black women.[26] Although women were given the same amount of land as men if they relocated, officials were greatly concerned about the safety of single black women. Occasionally older women, both white and black, accompanied unmarried black women as chaperones so that the young women were not travel to Liberia by themselves.[27] MSCS official Robert Gentry was concerned about a group of black women who wished to migrate alone.

He feared that "the Prospects of such young females should they remove to Liberia, I doubt would be good, provided they were to go out under the protection of respectable families."[28] He encouraged them to live with a family. Only under this condition did he project that these particular women would "do well."[29] In reality, African American women counted for about half of the population who emigrated. Women were encouraged to migrate with a group because it was assumed that men took care of women, thereby reinforcing the gender ideology of the time.[30] The need to "protect" black women also hints to gendered assumptions about who would succeed and who would not succeed in the colony. Certainly, Gentry's expectations of African American women's success were viewed only through the lens of having a male head of the household. Likewise, Gentry's own gender conventions about women and men's roles in the family are revealed in other letters, particularly when he discovered several women were willing to go without their husbands. Whereas Gentry and other officials were saddened that many black men relocated without their families, they were absolutely shocked that black women petitioned to go to Africa and have their husbands follow.[31]

ACS and MSCS officials equally feared disruptions and infidelity among black couples. In 1832, MSCS official John Henderson alerted the MSCS governing committee to what he feared would be a growing problem. He wrote of several men who wished to relocate, but "they have wives and children who are servants for a term of years and the persons owning them could not spare them at this time."[32] On the other hand, Henderson equally feared that some African Americans would use freedom as a means to escape a marriage.

Therefore, in manumitting and resettling blacks, Christian ethos dictated that Americans in Africa actualize the promises of Christian civilization and convert their African brethren in the process. Ultimately, this colonial project produced a social strata with light-skinned Liberians and some African Americans on top and dark-skinned African Americans on the bottom and with African Americans positioning themselves over indigenous Liberians.[33] In the process of forging the world's second black-ruled republic, they also constructed a settler society marred by many of the same exclusionary, oppressive characteristics common to modern colonial regimes.[34]

Mixed Legacies of Family in the Chesapeake and Liberia

Colonization produced a mixed familial legacy for African Americans on both sides of the Atlantic. In 1857, Mary Michie, a black Virginian, moved to Liberia. Upon her arrival in Monrovia, Michie, wrote to a friend back home: "I would not go back to America no how." Though she no longer considered Virginia her home, Michie was nonetheless tied to it. Her letters are replete with information about Afro-Virginians who settled in Liberia for the benefit of their kin back in America. She frequently signed her letters remembering those she and her family left behind: "Give our love to all the colored folks."[35] Michie, like scores of other emigrants to Liberia, understood that one's family ties transcended geographical boundaries.[36]

Certainly, it was not unusual for migrants to miss their family members. While waiting in New York to depart, Daniel Coker noted, "My dear family rests with great weight on my mind."[37] Relocation often meant separation from family and kin for the remainder of one's life. Coker reasoned that separation from his kin was not insurmountable. In his journal, Coker professed, "My soul cleaves to Africa in such a manner as to reconcile me to the idea of being separate from my dear friends and comforts of a Christian land." Likewise, other settlers wrote letters asking the receiver to inform all those still on the plantation that they missed them and thought about them often.[38]

The settlement experience also impacted family ties, simply because of the high mortality rates. The Skipwiths did not count on the level of disease, homesickness, and financial insecurity that they would face in their new home. Peyton's wife Lydia died within their first few years in Liberia. Peyton's daughter Matilda lost two of her four children to premature deaths. His son Nash noted that he worked during his life but sometimes had "but 1 dollar."[39]

Peyton himself suffered from depression throughout his life in Liberia. Peyton Skipwith died in 1849 after a health battle resulting in the loss of his eyesight. Nash wrote to General Cocke asking for black broadcloth so that he may bury his father. Nash noted that his financial woes were further compounded in that he supported his wife, their three children, and, since his father's death, Peyton Skipwith's wife. Nash Skipwith closed his letter with a repeated request to send the senior Skipwith's brother George.[40]

Peyton Skipwith died the same year that Liberia gained its independence, yet the shadow of US slavery touched him even in the new nation. During the thirteen-odd years that Peyton Skipwith lived in Liberia, he never forgot his family members who were left in slavery. In 1846, Skipwith wrote to Cocke, "You promised me in your letter that you was going to send my Brother George on to this place at the Expiration of three years & I would be happy indeed to see him and all the people that you have promised to send on."[41] For some immigrants, the prospect of being joined by friends and family afforded them the desire to make the best of their situation in Africa. Peyton Skipwith was "buoyed up" by the prospect that his owner General Cocke may free his brother George and his family and send him along to Liberia.[42] Skipwith died not having been reunited with his brother. However, his children did not let the desire to see family members die with their father. Peyton's children, Nash and Matilda, wrote several letters asking Cocke to make good on his promise.[43] There is no indication that these pleas were successful.

Conclusion

The contours of black internationalism elucidate the complexities of the nation-state. The lens of the families separated across the Atlantic calls into question how we understand "colonialism," as family was the tie that was hard to quantify within a local, much less global, setting. Emigrants either by themselves or with their families encountered high levels of disease, homesickness, and financial insecurity in their new home. Some colonists regretted their decision to emigrate and returned to the United States after a time, hoping to be reunited with their families. Some did well and managed to become independent householders and farmers in their new country. Some rose to positions of responsibility and power. When understanding the long complex arc of black internationalism, the notions of family cannot and should not be divorced from the African American experience.

Notes

1. General John Cocke to Peyton Skipwith, Manumission, 1833, Protestant Episcopal Church Records, Virginia Diocese Papers, Virginia Historical Society, Richmond, VA.

2. Manumission Ledger, 1832, Maryland State Colonization Society Papers, Maryland Historical Society, Baltimore.

3. Peyton Skipwith to Lucinda Nichols, June 27, 1846, and Peyton Skipwith to John Cocke, June 1846, Protestant Episcopal Church Records, Virginia Diocese Papers, Virginia Historical Society.

4. Claude Andrew Clegg, *The Price of Liberty: African Americans and the Making of Liberia* (Chapel Hill: University of North Carolina Press, 2004); John Wess Grant, "Stranded Families: Free Colored Responses to Liberian Colonization and the Formation of Black Families in Nineteenth-Century Richmond, Virginia," in *The United States and West Africa: Interactions and Relations*, ed. Alusine Jalloh and Toyin Falola (Cambridge: Harvard University Press, 2008), 61–74; Marie Tyler- McGraw, *An African Republic: Black and White Virginians*

in the Making of Liberia (Chapel Hill: University of North Carolina Press, 2007); Marie Elizabeth Stango, "Vine and Palm Tree: African American Families in Liberia, 1820–1860," (PhD diss., University of Michigan, 2016).

5. The recent exception being Brandon Mills's work on Pan-Africanism. Brandon Mills, "'The United States of Africa': Liberian Independence and the Contested Meaning of a Black Republic," *Journal of the Early Republic* 34, no. 1 (Spring 2014): 79–107.

6. The attribution that Virginia served as the "backbone" to the ACS's movement to relocate manumitted and freeborn blacks is found in "The Southern Leaders' Attitude toward Slavery," *Farmville (VA), Herald*, May 30, 1930, located in the Eggleston Family Papers, Virginia Historical Society; Eugene VanSickle, "The Missionary Presences and Influences in Maryland and in Liberia, 1834–1842" (MA thesis, West Virginia University), 38; Marie Tyler-McGraw, *An African Republic*, notes, "In the four decades before the Civil War, almost a third of the emigrants to Liberia came from Virginia, and the Chesapeake states of Maryland and Virginia together provided almost half of the emigrants and most of the Liberian leadership until the 1870s." Tyler-McGraw, *An African Repbulic*, 4.

7. Kurt Lee Kocher, "Religious and Educational Activities of the Maryland State Colonization Society, 1833–1843" (MA thesis, Towson State University, 1974), 28. Donald G. Matthew, *Slavery and Methodism: A Chapter in American Morality, 1780–1845* (Princeton, NJ: Princeton University Press, 1965); Mrs. Nelson to William McKenney, Pikesville, MD, May 18, June 12, and July 21, 1834, M.S.C.S. Letter Books, Vol. 2, Maryland Historical Society, Baltimore, Maryland.

8. "Things Which Every Emigrant to Liberia Ought to Know," *African Repository and Colonial Journal* 24, no. 4 (April 1848): 111.

9. Rev. Mr. Bacon to a Gentleman in Philadelphia, *African Intelligencer*, July 1820. Bacon writes, "There is work for us here; there is work for missionaries; for good men of all grades." Kocher suggests, "The emphasis on 'colored persons' as teachers was very likely due to the belief that he climate favored blacks more than whites." See Kocher, "Religious and Educational Activities."

10. B. Davis Nixon August 9, 1854, container 173, American Colonization Society Papers: Library of Congress, Washington, DC. See also Richard Boudin August 7, 1854, container, 173, American Colonization Society Papers, Library of Congress; and James P. Hosmer, August 25, 1854; container, 173, American Colonization Society Papers, Library of Congress. B. Davis Nixon August 9, 1854, container 173, American Colonization Society Papers, Library of Congress. Tyler-McGraw, *An African Republic*, 202. William McClain, Outgoing Letters, August 9, 1854, container 173, American Colonization Society Papers, Library of Congress. McClain notes, "Several of them can read, some can write, and one-third of them are professors of religion." The letter is reprinted in "Special Appeal for Funds-Liberal Responses from Our Friends," *African Repository and Colonial Journal* 30 (September 1854): 9; William McClain, Outgoing Letters, August 9, 1854, container 173, American Colonization Society Papers, Library of Congress.

11. Janet Duitsman Cornelius, *Slave Missions and the Black Church in the Antebellum South* (Columbia: University of South Carolina Press, 1999), 162.

12. J. Gill to the Maryland State Colonization Society, July 1832, Maryland State Colonization Society Papers, Maryland Historical Society.

13. J. Gill to the Maryland State Colonization Society.

14. J. Gill to the Maryland State Colonization Society.

15. Manumission Ledger, 1832, Maryland State Colonization Society Papers, Maryland Historical Society.

16. Elizabeth Stordeur Pryor, "The Etymology of Nigger: Resistance, Language, and the Politics of Freedom in the Antebellum North," *Journal of the Early Republic* 36, no. 2 (Summer 2016): 203–45.

17. Katherine McKittrick, "Plantation Futures," *Small Axe* 17, no. 3 (November 2013): 1–15

18. Douglas Egerton, "'Its Origin Is Not a Little Curious': A New Look at the American Colonization Society," *Journal of the Early Republic* 5, no. 4 (Winter 1985): 45.

19. A. Tatten to Maryland Colonization Society, June 1832, Maryland State Colonization Society Papers, Maryland Historical Society. Tatten writes, "This man is well known here, that I am very anxious for him to go . . . as this will remove more prejudice than anything I know of."

20. Manumission Ledgers, 1832–60, Maryland State Colonization Society Papers, Maryland Historical Society; John Blassingame, *Slave Testimony: Two Centuries of Letters, Speeches, Interviews and Autobiography* (Baton Rouge: Louisiana State University Press, 1977), 86; and Bruce Dorsey, "A Gendered History of the African Colonization Society in the Antebellum United States," *Journal of Social History* 34, no. 1 (Autumn 2000): 77–103.

21. James R. Starkey to Gerard Hallock, May 1850, in Blassingame, *Slave Testimony*, 86.

22. James R. Starkey to Gerard Hallock.

23. Margaret Coleman to Dr. James H. Minor, January 19, 1860. Liberian Letters Project, University of Virginia, http://xtf.lib.virginia.edu/xtf/view?docId=legacy_mss/uvaBook/tei/liberian_letters/L600119a.xml Date accessed October 10, 2021.

24. James Hall, "An Address to the Free People of Color of the State of Maryland," Baltimore, December 1858, American Pamphlets Collection, Library of Congress: Washington, DC.

25. James Hall, "An Address to the Free People." See also V. P. Franklin, "Education for Colonization: Attempts to Educate Free Blacks in the United States for Emigration to Africa," *Journal of Negro Education* 43, no. 1 (Winter 1974): 91–103. For discussions of subsistence-based farming and the modes of household production, see the classic texts Christopher Clark, *The Roots of Rural Capitalism: The Roots of Rural Capitalism: Western Massachusetts, 1780–1860* (Ithaca, NY: Cornell University Press, 1990); and Jeanne Boydston, *Home and Work: Housework, Wages, and the Ideology of Labor In the Early Republic*, reprint ed. (New York: Oxford University Press, 1994).

26. R. Anderson to William McKenney, November 26, 1834, Maryland State Colonization Society Letterbooks, vol. 2, Maryland State Colonization Society Papers, Maryland Historical Society.

27. R. Anderson to William McKenney; Kocher, "Religious and Educational Activities," 26; and Penelope Campbell, *Maryland in Africa: The Maryland State Colonization Society, 1831–1857* (Urbana: University of Illinois Press, 1971), 166–67.

28. R. Anderson to William McKenney.

29. R. Anderson to William McKenney.

30. Evelyn Brooks-Higginbotham, *Righteous Discontent: The Women's Movement in the Black Baptist Church, 1880–1920* (Cambridge, MA: Harvard University Press, 1993).

31. J. Henderson to Committee, November 14, 1832, Maryland State Colonization Society Papers, Maryland Historical Society.

32. J. Henderson to Committee.

33. Amos Beyan, *African American Settlements in West Africa: John Brown Russwurm and the American Civilizing Efforts* (New York: Palgrave Macmillan, 2005), 57.

34. Clegg, *The Price of Liberty*, 5.

35. Mary Michie to Dr. James Minor, February 4, 1857, Liberia Letters Project, University of Virginia, Charlottesville, VA, http://xtf.lib.virginia.edu/xtf/view?docId=legacy_mss/uvaBook/tei/liberian_letters/L570204.xml, accessed March 10, 2018.

36. McKittrick, "Plantation Futures," 1–15.

37. Daniel Coker, Journal of Daniel Coker. February 4, 1820.

38. John H. Faulcon to John H. Cocke, November 22, 1849, Virginia Diocese Papers, Virginia Historical Society. Faulcon asks for the receiver to give his love "to Mother, Sisters, Brother, aunts and uncles friends, also everybody on your plantation."

39. Nash Skipwith to John Cocke, November 2, 1849, Protestant Episcopal Church Records, Virginia Diocese Papers, Virginia Historical Society.

40. Nash Skipwith to John H. Cocke.

41. Peyton Skipwith to Lucinda Nichols, June 27, 1846, and Peyton Skipwith to John Cocke, June 1846, Protestant Episcopal Church Records, Virginia Diocese Papers, Virginia Historical Society.

42. Peyton Skipwith to Lucinda Nichols, June 27, 1846, and Peyton Skipwith to John Cocke, June 1846.

43. Matilda R. Lomax to John H. Cocke, November 23, 1849, Protestant Episcopal Church Records, Virginia Diocese Papers, Virginia Historical Society.

Chapter 9

✦

"The Happiest Peasants in the World"

W. E. B. Du Bois, Haiti, and Black Reconstruction

Brandon R. Byrd

In December 1909, Atlanta University professor W. E. B. Du Bois sent a letter to Albert Bushnell Hart, his former mentor at Harvard who had since become the president of the American Historical Association (AHA). "I regret very much to say," Du Bois began, "that I cannot afford the expense of coming north to the Annual meeting of the American Historical Association."[1] Du Bois had anticipated the chance to challenge the Dunning School, a group of historians including Columbia University's William Archibald Dunning, who had misrepresented Reconstruction as a tragic era of federal overreach and Black misgovernment.[2] Now, his funds running low, all he could do was thank Hart for extending him the generous invitation. "I highly appreciate and hate to miss," Du Bois lamented, "but as I say I will have to give it up."[3]

Du Bois was wrong. Thanks to financial support from Hart, he was soon bound for New York and the AHA annual meeting. There, with Dunning sitting a few feet away, Du Bois declared that the only "tragedy" of Reconstruction was that it ended. He, as one biographer later wrote, found "Reconstruction historiography standing on its head . . . [but] had left it upright."[4]

While his white contemporaries ignored Du Bois's feat, much has since been written about *Black Reconstruction in America*, the book that blossomed from his AHA paper. To scholars of Black radicalism,[5] *Black Reconstruction* is a triumph of Black Marxist scholarship, a book that, in the words of scholar Cedric Robinson, conceived of the Russian Revolution as the template for social change and proved that the "destruction of American slavery had been the consequence of a social revolution . . .

destroyed in its turn by the real force of racism acting on the American working class."[6] Historians of Reconstruction echo that analysis. For Eric Foner, *Black Reconstruction* remains "a monumental study" of the US South notable for its portrayal of "Reconstruction as an idealistic effort to construct a democratic, interracial political order from the ashes of slavery, as well as a phase in a prolonged struggle between capital and labor."[7]

Building on those interpretations, this chapter reconsiders the internationalist origins, evolution, and implications of *Black Reconstruction*. From the turn of the twentieth century to 1935, Du Bois moved from thinking about Reconstruction as an abandoned attempt to extend civil and political rights to former slaves or an era when African Americans proved their capacity for citizenship to writing about it as a new cornerstone of white imperialism and the missed opportunity for transformative land redistribution, economic restructuring, and true democracy. This change was no accident. While Du Bois had long-standing interest in Reconstruction, his most intense study of that period came not only in the wake of the Russian Revolution but also during the US occupation of Haiti (1915–34).[8] His characterizations of Reconstruction evolved alongside his growing assessment of the occupation as a glaring example of Western imperialism and a singular affront to Haiti, which he came to consider the portent of an international triumph of (Black) labor. Put simply, Haiti and *Black Reconstruction* are inseparable. Recognizing this connection advances our understanding of the transformative effect of Haiti's occupation on global Black thought—of the historical significance of thinking about and with Haiti's socioeconomic, political, and intellectual history, not just its symbolism. Indeed, it strengthens our appreciation of a foundational book that, as Trinidadian writer C. L. R. James would suggest, was an inspirational part of the radical Black internationalist canon.

In July 1910, Du Bois published his AHA speech in the *American Historical Review*. The question of Black suffrage was at its heart. "Reconstruction and Its Benefits" begins with the acknowledgment that white Americans saw "in negro suffrage the cause of the main evils of Reconstruction." Debunking that myth, Du Bois noted that Reconstruction-era "arguments for universal negro suffrage were strong and are still strong, and no one would question their strength were it not for the assumption that the experiment failed." Assessing a Reconstruction-era hearing of the US Congress, he highlighted the logical reasons for enfranchising Black men who had remained loyal to the US government at a time of mass treason among white Southerners. He then defended the results of Black enfranchisement. To the "chief charges against the negro governments . . .

Fig. 3. Portrait of W. E. B. Du Bois, ca. 1919. Library of Congress, Prints and Photographs Division.

extravagance, theft, and incompetency of officials," Du Bois reminded readers that Black Southerners were not responsible for corruption in the antebellum South or the Reconstruction-era North. Besides, he continued, Black politicians and voters had crafted state constitutions so strong that they remained intact even during the Jim Crow era.[9]

In Du Bois's estimation, the accurate interpretation of Reconstruction was thus clear. "Paint the 'carpet-bag' governments and negro rule as black as may be," he wrote, "the fact remains that . . . not only did their successors make few changes in the work which these legislatures and conventions had done, but they largely carried out their plans, followed their suggestions, and strengthened their institutions." The industrial "growth of the South was accomplished under laws which black men helped to frame thirty years ago," Du Bois concluded. There was no "greater accomplishment to negro suffrage."[10]

For Du Bois, there was an urgency to the vindication of Black suffrage during Reconstruction. In the same month that he published "Reconstruction and Its Benefits," Du Bois became the director of publicity and research for the National Association for the Advancement of Colored People (NAACP), the most prominent US civil rights organization of the twentieth century. In that position and as editor of the NAACP's official organ, the *Crisis*, Du Bois challenged the system of racial segregation that emerged after the federal abandonment of Reconstruction and championed liberal democracy by demanding the ballot and equal protection of political and civil rights regardless of race or religion. He became the most visible advocate of Black citizens stripped of the franchise, due process, and most other constitutional rights.[11]

Despite the necessary preoccupation with Black citizenship rights in the post-*Plessy* United States, there were germs of a more radical internationalism in "Reconstruction and Its Benefits." Hinting at an alternative to the racial and socioeconomic hierarchies of his day, Du Bois elaborated on an earlier article about the Freedmen's Bureau, the federal agency that helped freedpeople gain education and legal justice before its defunding by President Andrew Johnson and abandonment by Congress. The bureau, Du Bois insisted, "established for ten, twenty or forty years with *careful distribution of land and capital* and a system of education for the children, might have prevented such an extension of slavery" (emphasis mine) into the postemancipation era.[12] In fact, Du Bois continued, a recognition of formerly enslaved people as laborers deserving of economic justice might have laid the foundations for a different world than the one critiqued in the *Crisis*. He suggested but did not then elaborate on the possibility that land redistribution, socialism, workers' struggle, and Black liberation were intimately connected.

Along with World War I, the Russian Revolution, and Du Bois's better-known participation in the Pan-African movement, events in Haiti would encourage and shape the characteristics of Du Bois's internationalism. When the United States invaded Haiti in July 1915, Du Bois proposed a US commission to "co-operate with Hayti in establishing permanent peace and in assuring our stricken sister that the United States respects and will always respect her political integrity."[13] His recommendation that US elites work together to eliminate Haitian corruption, industrialize Haiti, and democratize its governance mirrored the principles of US progressivism and interventionism, the central tenets of Wilsonian foreign policy.[14] They also highlighted the importance of Haiti to Du Bois. Like generations of Black intellectuals before him, Du Bois expected that Haiti, the beacon of Black self-determination in the Western Hemisphere, could help or harm the Black image. He assumed, too, that African Americans could affirm their fitness for US citizenship by influencing US foreign policy and modernizing a Black nation.

This ambivalent reaction to the occupation was in complete harmony with "Black Reconstruction and Its Benefits" and the agenda of the NAACP.[15] Still, even before the Russian Revolution, Du Bois was rethinking the seeds planted in his *American Historical Review* article. In September 1915, Du Bois noted that Haiti was "a noble nation . . . that [gave] the world one of its greatest names—Toussaint L'Ouverture" and "made slaves free." He insisted that African Americans therefore could not "point scornful fingers at our brothers" or forget that "in one respect Hayti leads the world." Presaging a more critical analysis of the relationship among land redistribution, socialism, and the liberation of the [Black] worker, Du Bois contended that "out of a hell of slavery [Haiti] has succeeded in placing on their own little farms the happiest peasants in the world." It had, he concluded, achieved what "France, Germany, England [and] Russia" could not accomplish and succeeded where the United States had failed.[16]

Du Bois's analysis of land and emancipation in Haiti had the ring of truth, even if it was somewhat inaccurate.[17] According to the leading Haitian intellectual Jean Casimir, "The counter plantation is a specific social organization encompassing a variety of techniques invented by the workers . . . to oppose the owners and their metropolitan countries."[18] In postemancipation Haiti, this system sustained by the Haitian people, often in opposition to the reactionary policies of the Haitian state, centered on the *lakou*—the units of family land that Du Bois knew as the "little farms" of the "happiest peasants in the world." First developed during the Haitian Revolution, the *lakou* remains an important "model of social organization" in rural Haiti. As anthropologist Serge Larose writes, it is a residential unit in which extended families occupy individual housing units but share a collective yard space. Religion—the collective serving of the *lwas* and the veneration of shared ancestors—binds together its inhabitants. So does a commitment to economic autonomy and a resistance to modes of export-oriented, monocrop production upon which the plantation societies of the Americas were built.[19] Birthed in a desire to escape the violence and logic of the colonial plantation system, the *lakou* still challenges neocolonialism and racial capitalism, the modern and unequal global political economy built on the continued enslavement and exploitation of workers in the Global South.[20] It represents the enduring ideas of popular sovereignty possessed by the Haitian people. To Du Bois, Haitians' tradition of family landholding presaged a truly democratic world.[21]

Du Bois would theorize democracy in relationship to slavery in his subsequent writings about Reconstruction. In 1924, four years after the NAACP began in earnest its crusade against Haiti's occupation, Du Bois published *The Gift of Black Folk*. It opens with a set of questions. "Who made America?" Du Bois asked. "Who made this land that swings its empire from the Atlantic to the Sea of Peace and from Snow to Fire—this realm of New Freedom, with Opportunity and Ideal unlimited?" The answer, he continued, was Black people. Du Bois pointed out that Americans "usually assumed . . . that whatever the Negro has done for America has been passive and unintelligent, that he accompanied the explorers as a beast of burden and accomplished whatever he did by sheer accident." That was wrong, he proclaimed. "On the contrary, it was the rise and growth among the slaves of a determination to be free and an active part of American democracy that forced American democracy continually to look into the depths." It was, in short, African Americans "who raised a vision of democracy in America such as neither Americans nor Europeans conceived in the eighteenth century and such as they have not even accepted in the twentieth century." It was African Americans who made the United States, not as it was but as it should be.[22]

And Haiti made them, Du Bois continued, locating African Americans' notions of democracy within their experience of enslavement *and* their sense of belonging to a Black community that existed beyond the nation-state. To Du Bois, "The first influence of the Negro on American Democracy was naturally force to oppose force—revolt, murder, assassination coupled with running away." It was resistance in the spirit of the Haitian Revolution. Du Bois proclaimed that "black Haiti not only freed itself but helped to kindle liberty all through America" and inspire enslaved people who heard "news of the black revolt." Gabriel Prosser thought of Haiti when he tried to seize Richmond, and Denmark Vesey was "familiar with the Haitian revolution" when he "planned the total annihilation of the men, women, and children of Charleston." Du Bois's genealogy of revolutionaries extended from Toussaint Louverture to "the black, fugitive, soldier and freedman" who "after the Civil War helped to restore the Union, establish public schools, enfranchise the poor white and initiate democracy in America."[23]

In that vein, Du Bois asked another question: "What did the Emancipation of the slave really mean?" For Du Bois, the freedmen's struggles for suffrage, unionization, and freedom from the new class of industrial capitalists had a "peculiar" effect. "The Negro," Du Bois argued, "is making America and the world acknowledge democracy as feasible and desirable for all white folk, for only in this way do they see any possibility of defending their world-wide fear of yellow, brown and black folk." He had thrown into sharp relief the relationship between white democracy and Black enslavement. Looking back at Reconstruction, the final link in a chain that began with the Haitian Revolution, Du Bois thus wondered: "What do we mean by democracy? Do we mean democracy of the white races and the subjection of the colored races? Or do we mean the gradual working forward to a time when all men will have a voice in government and industry and will be intelligent enough to express the voice?" African Americans advanced the latter thesis, Du Bois concluded. Their self-emancipation was meant to be "one step toward the emancipation of all men" and a redefinition of democracy.[24]

In short, having earlier praised the counterplantation system, Du Bois now celebrated the Haitian Revolution for giving Black people and the world a radical praxis of democracy, an idea that Du Bois identified as central to the US occupation of Haiti *and* Reconstruction. Du Bois's thinking about this connection was on full display at a luncheon hosted by the Foreign Policy Association at New York's Hotel Astor in December 1929. Two months after the stock market crash that signaled the beginning of the Great Depression, Du Bois challenged the rationale for the US occupation of Haiti rather than accommodating it. Haiti, he pointed out, was not a land of peons like the Jim Crow South, where a "handful of [white] people" established "outward peace and quiet" by exerting violent and "absolute control of the great mass of [black] labor." Instead, it was a country where the "sovereign people," to quote Casimir, had "a growing sense of democracy" born from the institutions that sustained rural life. If not for the occupation, Haitians would have "pounded out by turmoil and uprising a free, popular and modern government," Du Bois insisted. They would have achieved an even more meaningful freedom informed by their "African Mores" and heightened sense of "what nationhood meant."[25]

Of course, Haitians' autonomy had, in fact, eroded at the point of US bayonets, which led Du Bois to a trenchant critique of racism, capitalism, imperialism, and militarism—of the structures that undermined democracy around the world. Du Bois told his audience that the United States had entered Haiti "ostensibly because there was not enough democracy, and thereupon we took away what little democracy there was there." It had dispersed the Haitian legislature. It had built "military roads so the marines can get from one end of Haiti quickly to kill peasants who ask questions." It had done "nothing about illiteracy at all" while prioritizing industrial training for Haitians. And why had the United States done these things, Du Bois asked? "Because if you can establish in Haiti the same kind of peonage you have in Cuba, you can have the same tremendous profits which you have out of Cuban sugar." You could preserve racial capitalism and a perverted idea of white democracy.[26] To Du Bois, the US occupation of Haiti affirmed how capitalists were trying to exploit African, Asian, and Caribbean laborers "by making the result of their labor give them bare support while it adds tremendous profits to the exploiting country." In his analysis, it also foreshadowed the dire results of trying "to use those profits as a fund by which democracy is nullified in so many of the so-called republican governments throughout the world." Du Bois warned his audience that "if you are going to keep the colored world in the position of exploitation in which it is today, then you are going to have war . . . between those white people who are fighting for the spoils that come from the exploitation of the colored folk." He explained that the first step to keeping "war out of the world" and expanding "democracy . . . not simply in Haiti but here in the United States" was to return to Haiti "the freedom which it so clearly won."[27]

Du Bois had found in Haiti the mirror to Reconstruction, the clearest illustration of that era's missed opportunities and the clue to its world-historical meaning. As Du Bois considered the history and occupation of Haiti, he concluded that Haiti was a model of postemancipation struggle rather than a failed Black state. He praised rural Haitians for carving out socioeconomic autonomy through the counterplantation system, arguing that this achievement instilled in them a powerful sense of popular democracy. In contrasting rural Haitians with US sharecroppers and tenant farmers, a disproportionate number of whom were Black, Du Bois found that Haitians were not just self-emancipated people but a subaltern population who laid out a vision of freedom and democracy for their peers in post-slavery societies and across the colonial world. Theirs was a radical dissent from capitalism and imperialism, racism and militarism. It was a bellwether of the Black freedom struggle across time and space—a legacy of the Haitian Revolution and a part of the ongoing projects of emancipation and anticolonialism in Africa, Asia, and the Caribbean.

With those ideas in mind, Du Bois set about writing *Black Reconstruction in America*, a book that he would call his "magnum opus."[28] For Du Bois, the struggles of Reconstruction stemmed from an antebellum period when "Black labor became the foundation stone not only of the Southern social structure, but of Northern manufacture and commerce, of the English factory system, of European commerce, of buying and selling on a world-wide scale."[29] Those struggles were symptoms of and another chapter in the intertwined history of slavery and capitalism. According to Du Bois, the dawning of an emancipation without equality accelerated "the transportation of capital from white to black countries where slavery prevailed, with the same tremendous and awful consequences upon the laboring classes of the world which we see about us today."[30] It not only sacrificed the landless "black worker" in the United States to "a new capitalism and a new enslavement of labor" but also threatened a similar fate for Haitians, who were now subjugated by the United States and the National City Bank of New York, which owned a 50 percent interest in the National Bank of Haiti and whose vice president had argued that the United States needed to occupy Haiti because the Haitian government was too weak to secure US investments there.[31] To Du Bois, the radical social revolution of Reconstruction had succumbed to the "Counter-Revolution of Property," the laying of "the cornerstone of that new imperialism which is subjecting the labor of yellow, brown and black peoples to the dictation of capitalism organized on a world basis."[32]

Consequently, the unfulfilled promise of Reconstruction was also the cause for internationalism, which, as practiced and understood by Du Bois, was a radical politics of transnational solidarity crafted in opposition to slavery, colonialism, and white imperialism.[33] The most quoted passage from *Black Reconstruction* remains Du Bois's searing lament that, during Reconstruction, the "slave went free; stood a brief moment in the sun; then moved back again toward slavery." Just as significant, however, is what comes next. In Du Bois's words, "The whole weight of America was thrown to color caste. The colored world went down before England, France, Germany, Russia, Italy and America. A new slavery arose. The upward moving of white labor was betrayed into wars for profit based on color caste. Democracy died save in the hearts of black folk."[34] The implications of this new world order were clear. The experience of racial domination transcended national boundaries. It was the time to forge transnational bonds and political solidarities among oppressed people, oppose racial capitalism, and redefine democracy, an idea that Du Bois now equated with the redistribution of wealth and the elimination of poverty.[35]

Indeed, it was the moment to bring global understandings of Black freedom to bear upon historical scholarship. Du Bois ends *Black Reconstruction* with an apocalyptic *and* internationalist vision. A "teacher sits in academic halls, learned in the tradition of its elms and its elders." He lies. While looking "into the upturned face of youth . . . he sneers at 'chinks' and 'niggers,'" assuring his white pupils that the United States had "at last virtually accepted the ideas of the South" about Reconstruction. Meanwhile the world burns. In "Africa, a black back runs red with the blood of the lash; in India, a brown girl is raped; in China, a coolie starves; in Alabama, seven darkies are more than lynched; while in London, the white limbs of a prostitute are hung with jewels and silk." Everywhere, "flames of jealous murder sweep the earth, while brains of little children smear the hills." This, Du Bois concluded, was the inevitable effect of the "Propaganda of History," the lies told about Black people and their postemancipation struggles.[36] This was the challenge of the activist-scholar, then and always.

Most white scholars ignored *Black Reconstruction*, a work that dismantled the racist propaganda that passed for "objective" scholarship. C. L. R. James did not. While speaking at the Institute of the Black World, the Trinidadian writer proclaimed that the first edition of *The Black Jacobins*, his Black Marxist study of the Haitian Revolution, tried to "show that black people were able to make historical progress . . . show how a revolution was made . . . produce the men who could lead a revolution and write new pages in the book of history." It was meant to encourage another uprising against slavery, this time in colonized Africa. For inspiration, James drew from *Black Reconstruction*, a book that, in James's words, showed that "the attempt of the black people in the Civil War to attempt democracy was the finest effort to achieve democracy that the world had ever seen . . . a tragedy that 'beggared the Greek' . . . [and] an upheaval of humanity, like the Reformation and the French Revolution, the two greatest events in the history of Western civilization." It made "clear to black people in what way they were involved in world history . . . [and] opened out the historical perspective in a manner that [James] didn't know."[37]

Few scholars have given serious consideration to James's claim that "Du Bois taught me to think in those terms" and see the world-historical importance of the Haitian Revolution.[38] Doing so opens up a range of questions and possibilities, however. What did James reveal in his comparative analysis of *The Black Jacobins* and *Black Reconstruction*? What did he, perhaps, omit? In reconsidering how and why James linked his magnum opus to Du Bois's, we might find that *Black Reconstruction* did more than influence James's revised edition of *The Black Jacobins* published in 1963.[39] Indeed, by extending in new directions the comparative analysis of the two texts, it might become apparent that Haiti was of similar importance to both men, a central catalyst in the revision of world history and subsequent reimagining of African revolution alike.

As Michael O. West and William G. Martin have shown, Haiti and the Haitian Revolution were cornerstones of the type of internationalism encouraged in *The Black Jacobins*.[40] The same also seems true of *Black Reconstruction*. Crafted in the same moment that Du Bois articulated growing concern with the intersections of global capitalism, imperialism, and white supremacy, *Black Reconstruction* offers less a critique of US history than a blueprint for what Du Bois called the "last great battle of the West."[41] Indeed, rather than recycling claims from his previous scholarship on Reconstruction, Du Bois presented new lessons applicable to colonized and oppressed people throughout the world. That was a remarkable shift, one that should animate scholars and inspire them to revisit *Black Reconstruction*. Assigned an unparalleled position in the historiography of Reconstruction and recognized for its Black Marxist analysis, Du Bois's magnum opus deserves to be where C. L. R. James placed it, alongside *The Black Jacobins*. As James recognized, *Black Reconstruction* was a part of the radical Black internationalist canon. It connected Haitians and African Americans, drawing the two together in a groundbreaking reassessment of slavery, emancipation, and the true meaning of democracy.

Notes

1. W. E. B. Du Bois, letter to the American Historical Association, December 6, 1909, in W. E. B. Du Bois Papers, Special Collections and University Archives, University of Massachusetts Amherst Libraries, Amherst, MA (hereafter Du Bois Papers).

2. John David Smith and J. Vincent Lowery, eds., *The Dunning School: Historians, Race and the Meaning of Reconstruction* (Lexington: University Press of Kentucky, 2013).

3. Du Bois, letter to the American Historical Association.

4. David Levering Lewis, *W. E. B. Du Bois: A Biography* (New York: Henry Holt, 2009): 250–52.

5. Bill V. Mullen, *Un-American: W. E. B. Du Bois and the Century of World Revolution* (Philadelphia: Temple University Press, 2015), 56–95.

6. Cedric Robinson, "A Critique of W. E. B. Du Bois' Black Reconstruction," *Black Scholar* 8, no. 7 (May 1977): 50.

7. Eric Foner, *Reconstruction: America's Unfinished Revolution, 1863–1877* (New York: Harper & Row, 1988), xix, 602–12.

8. Craig M. Stutman, "Reconstruction in the Mind of W. E. B. Du Bois: Myth, Memory, and the Meaning of American Democracy" (PhD diss., Temple University, 2008).

9. Du Bois, "Reconstruction and Its Benefits," *American Historical Review* 15, no. 4 (July 1910): 781, 788–92, 795, 799.

10. Du Bois, "Reconstruction and Its Benefits," 795, 799.
11. Lewis, *W. E. B. Du Bois*, 267–85.
12. Lewis, *W. E. B. Du Bois*, 267–85.
13. "Hayti," *Crisis* 10, no. 5 (September 1915): 232. On Du Bois and the US occupation of Haiti, see Brandon R. Byrd, *The Black Republic: African Americans and the Fate of Haiti* (Philadelphia: University of Pennsylvania Press, 2020), 196–238.
14. John Milton Cooper, Jr., *Woodrow Wilson: A Biography* (New York: Vintage Books, 2011).
15. Brandon R. Byrd, "'To Start Something to Help These People': African American Women and the Occupation of Haiti, 1915–1934," *Journal of Haitian Studies* 21, no. 2 (December 2015): 127–53; and Brenda Gayle Plummer, "The Afro-American Response to the U.S. Occupation of Haiti, 1915–1934," *Phylon* 43, no. 2 (2nd Quarter 1982).
16. "Hayti."
17. While beyond the scope of this chapter, rural Haitians have often had to struggle against Haitian elites whose visions of national development have sometimes prioritized the return of Haitians to plantation labor, the consolidation of land under the control of the Haitian state, or inducements of land and special economic privileges for US and European corporations and investors. See especially Michel-Rolph Trouillot, *Haiti: State against Nation: Origins and Legacy of Duvalierism* (New York: Monthly Review Press, 1990); Mimi Sheller, *Democracy after Slavery: Black Publics and Peasant Radicalism in Haiti and Jamaica* (Gainesville: University press of Florida, 2001); and Jean Casimir, *The Haitians: A Decolonial History*, trans. Laurent Dubois (Chapel Hill: University of North Carolina Press, 2020).
18. Jean Casimir, *The Caribbean: One and Divisible* (United Nations: Economic Commission for Latin America and the Caribbean, 1992), 79.
19. Serge Larose, "The Haitian Lakou, Land, Family and Ritual," in *Family and Kinship in Middle America and the Caribbean*, ed. Arnaud F. Marks and René A. Römer (Willemstadt/Curacao: Institute of Higher Studies in Curacao, 1975): 482–501.
20. Robinson, *Black Marxism: The Making of the Black Radical Tradition*, 2nd ed. (Chapel Hill: University of North Carolina Press, 2002); and Charisse Burden-Stelly, "Modern U.S. Racial Capitalism: Some Theoretical Insights," *Monthly Review* 72, no. 3 (July-August 2020).
21. Laurent Dubois, *Haiti: The Aftershocks of History* (New York: Metropolitan Books, 2010).
22. Du Bois, *The Gift of Black Folk: The Negroes in the Making of America* (Boston: Stratford, 1924), 33, 138, 136.
23. Du Bois, *The Gift of Black Folk*, 147, 153, 156, 184.
24. Du Bois, *The Gift of Black Folk*, 257–58.
25. Du Bois, "Haiti," transcript of radio broadcast, December 21, 1929, in the Du Bois Papers.
26. Du Bois, "Haiti."
27. Du Bois, "Haiti."
28. Letter from Du Bois to Ruth Anna Fisher, March 26, 1934, in the Du Bois Papers. On the publication history of *Black Reconstruction*, see Claire Parfait,

"Rewriting History: The Publication of W. E. B. Du Bois's "Black Reconstruction in America" (1935)," *Book History* 12 (2009): 266–94.

29. Du Bois, *Black Reconstruction in America: Toward a History of the Part Which Black Folk Played in the Attempt to Reconstruct Democracy in America, 1860–1880* (New Brunswick, NJ: Transaction Publishers, 2013), 3.

30. Du Bois, *Black Reconstruction in America*, 42.

31. Peter James Hudson, *Bankers and Empire: How Wall Street Colonized the Caribbean* (Chicago: University of Chicago Press, 2017).

32. Du Bois, *Black Reconstruction in America*, 563.

33. Here I find common ground with Moon-Ho Jung, who has argued that *Black Reconstruction* offered the possibility of global anti-imperial, anticolonial, antiracist, and anticapitalist struggle. See Jung, "*Black Reconstruction* and Empire," *South Atlantic Quarterly* 112, no. 3 (Summer 2013): 465–71. On Black internationalism, see especially Michael O. West, William G. Martin, and Fanon Che Wilkins, *From Toussaint to Tupac: The Black International since the Age of Revolutions* (Chapel Hill: University of North Carolina Press, 2009); and Keisha N. Blain and Tiffany M. Gill, eds., *To Turn the Whole World Over: Black Women and Internationalism* (Urbana: University of Illinois Press, 2019).

34. Du Bois, *Black Reconstruction in America*, 26.

35. R. David Sumpter, "W. E. B. Du Bois: Reflections on Democracy," *Journal of Thought* 36, no. 2 (Summer 2001): 25–31.

36. Sumpter, "W. E. B. Du Bois," 650.

37. C. L. R. James, "The Black Jacobins and Black Reconstruction: A Comparative Analysis (15 June 1971)," *Small Axe* 8 (September 2000): 83–98.

38. James, "The Black Jacobins."

39. Garry Bertholf, "Listening to Du Bois's *Black Reconstruction*: *After James*," *The Southern Literary Journal* 48, no. 1 (Fall 2015): 78–91.

40. West and Martin, "Haiti, I'm Sorry: The Haitian Revolution and the Forging of the Black International," in *From Toussaint to Tupac*, 72–106.

41. Du Bois, *Black Reconstruction*, 703.

Chapter 10

✦

"These People Are No Charles Mansons or Spaced-Out 'Moonies'"

Jonestown and African American Expatriation in the 1970s

Russell Rickford

In November 1978, more than nine hundred members of a religious colony embedded in the Guyanese jungle ingested a deadly, cyanide-laced cocktail. The colonists, roughly 80 percent of whom were African American,[1] were inhabitants of Jonestown, an agricultural settlement carved into the South American rainforest by followers of Reverend Jim Jones, pastor of Peoples Temple Church. The Jonestown tragedy was both a mass suicide and a massacre. Among the dead were scores of children along with others who had been coerced into swallowing the toxic drink. As authorities later discovered, however, some of the deceased had been more or less willing participants in the death pact, an exercise the community had rehearsed in grotesque "White Night" rituals. In the end it was an investigative visit by California congressman Leo Ryan, a tour gone horribly awry, that led Jones to predict an apocalyptic US raid and initiate the final suicide rite.[2]

In the aftermath of the incident, the eyes of the world turned to Guyana, and people everywhere tried to make sense of the carnage. As details about Jones and his flock emerged, US news outlets framed the affair with what soon became a stock set of interpretations. Tropes of madness and fanaticism predominated. Like many future writers, contemporary journalists relied on narratives of psychosis to explain why a large group of Americans had fled Northern California (home of Peoples Temple headquarters), journeyed to the hinterland of a poor, Third World country, and established a farming commune (an "agricultural mission," as Peoples Temple officials described it), only to perish in a ghastly act of self-destruction.[3]

For some commentators the deaths in Guyana underscored the pathologies of American society. Left-leaning observers saw the affair as the bitter fruit of capitalist decadence, as a result of the extreme alienation spawned by US racism and inequality, or as the outcome of a shadowy "mind-control" experiment administered by the CIA. Conservative figures saw the tragedy as evidence of the depravity of anticapitalist "totalitarianism."[4] African Americans of various ideological proclivities saw an act of genocide and a sign of profound identity crisis. "Black folks are still into the practice of following white religious leaders to the ends of the world," one African American activist lamented.[5]

What united many of these perspectives was a sense of impenetrability. Critics cast the actions of the Peoples Temple faithful as fundamentally incomprehensible. This was the case whether the commentators regarded Jonestown as a symptom of Western civilization's moral sickness; as the warped product of an obsolescent counterculture; as a tragic consequence of groupthink; or as an expression of America's post-Vietnam malaise. In these and other framings, the Jonestown holocaust marked a wholesale departure from reason.

The problem with such portrayals was that they mystified both the death *and* life of Jonestown. Seen as exemplars of the cultish and the bizarre, members of the community appeared totally aberrant. They were misfits and dupes—inert victims of Jones's charisma and messianic appeal. Their South American sojourn was an arcane and reckless adventure. It served as an object of endless psychoanalysis and as a tableau for the motifs of primitivism that the West has always projected onto the Caribbean.[6]

In a sense the intense reportage only further obscured the Jonestown affair. Discourses of insanity deprived the Peoples Temple congregants of agency and masked the range of motivations behind their efforts of alternative living. Why *did* the Jonestown missionaries choose life in a remote jungle settlement thousands of miles from home? The answers, of course, are diverse. Religious fervor played a part. The chance to start anew in a tropical paradise appealed to members of the parish's black majority, a large portion of which had faced poverty and addiction in California slums. But what cultural significance, if any, did Guyana hold? Did the rejection of the United States by the Peoples Temple faithful reflect larger patterns of political thought?

In this essay I argue that to better comprehend Jonestown one must place in a broader sociopolitical context the eclectic visions of its pilgrims. Even before the Guyana exodus of the mid-1970s, Peoples Temple was linked to a host of New Left and Black Power formations, from the American Indian Movement to the Republic of New Africa to the Free

Angela Davis campaign.[7] Jonestown becomes less unintelligible when one considers the contours of its politics rather than the spectacle of its demise. As one black leftist noted in 1978, referring to the African American victims of the jungle colony, "These people are no Charles Mansons or spaced-out 'Moonies.'"[8] In many respects, the Guyana settlement was a troubled iteration of a larger quest by Western anti-imperialists for meaningful participation in radical, Third World politics, an objective that galvanized many contemporary black internationalists. By attempting to transcend the revulsion that surrounds the memory of Jonestown, we may discover in the colony's utopian impulses the resonances of a vibrant politics of solidarity.

This is not to diminish the horror of the affair. My aim is not to "defend" any aspect of Jonestown. The community, it must be said, was plagued by exploitation, brutality, and paranoia long before the lethal vats of punch were prepared. Nor can the Guyana atrocity be separated from the megalomania of Jones himself. His tyranny robbed his followers of human dignity well before one-dimensional news reports could do so.[9]

My purpose here is simply to help make Jonestown more legible. By drawing evocative connections, I hope to find elements of coherence in the fragmentary strands of 1970s radicalism. Despite its catastrophic conclusion, the Peoples Temple agricultural mission began as a quest for the good life. Its themes of communion with the soil, applied socialism, and camaraderie with developing nations were embraced by other temporary or permanent US exiles, including the scores of black leftist and Pan-Africanist pioneers who ventured abroad in the 1960s and 1970s to help build new societies in the Global South.

It is significant that Jonestown's inhabitants regarded Guyana as the Promised Land (or Freedom Land) and discussed the republic in those terms.[10] The country appeared to provide the perfect setting for the practice of the congregation's ecumenical ideals. Its remoteness was an asset for a group that wished to escape Western materialism, while its rainforest provided refuge from the "asphalt jungle" of North America's deindustrialized slums. "Man," one Jonestown emigrant exclaimed upon leaving his old San Francisco neighborhood, "the Fillmore has seen the last of me!"[11]

Guyana's multiracial society complemented the interracial sensibilities of Jones and his flock, even as the nation's predominantly Afro-Guyanese governing party, the People's National Congress, parroted aspects of the "black is beautiful" rhetoric that also influenced the Peoples Temple worldview. Finally, the Caribbean country welcomed political refugees from the capitalist world, especially those who endorsed the government's policy of cooperative socialism. For at least some Jonestown residents, helping a nation of mostly South Asian and African descendants feed its people, develop its interior, and boost its agricultural output constituted nothing less than an act of black diasporic commitment. "Nobody wanted to return to Africa," one African American Jonestown resident later explained. "We just wanted to find out where we came from. Most of us didn't know anything about our heritage."[12]

I must pause here to acknowledge that writing about Jonestown can be an unsavory task. The odor of death continues to linger over the affair. Nor, for many reasons, does the subject lend itself to conventional methods of intellectual history. (Even the nature of the source base poses a challenge; members of the colony composed far more paeans to Jones than they prepared formal treatises or tracts.) It is clear, however, that the self-exile of the Peoples Temple pilgrims was no mere act of deranged fantasy, and that dismissing it as such only compounds the erasure of the full spectrum of 1970s radicalism. Utopianism, we must recall, is not simply a flight from normal existence. It is also an attempt to shatter conventional political boundaries. This essay highlights the more lucid ideological elements of one such effort.

One must tread carefully when attempting to ascribe political motives to a cloistered band of true believers. Still, the black parishioners of Jonestown did not exist outside of history. For all their complexity as individuals, they were subject to many of the social forces that shaped other African American sojourners in the Global South. More research must be done to situate People's Temple within the matrix of black political culture and thought. But the colony's links to other contemporary manifestations of African American internationalism are incontrovertible. Guyana was no random destination. The Jonestown faithful were not simply "going native" in the Amazonian wilderness. By placing themselves at the geographic periphery, far beyond the scope of bourgeois America, they were attempting to repudiate empire itself.

While the 1960s is often imagined as the age of radical quests, during the 1970s countless Americans pursued alternative political and cultural frameworks as a basis for transforming their lives.[13] Some were veterans of New Left movements looking to regroup from past campaigns or to launch the next phases of social struggle. Others were everyday seekers who had embraced the concept of cultural revolution and were striving to reorient themselves. Whatever their backgrounds may have been, a number of contemporary dissidents turned to the Third World or strengthened existing ties outside the United States, searching for a source of not just enlightenment but sustained political engagement.

Among them was a strain of hardcore black internationalists. Unlike some activists, these figures had not withdrawn into private life in the aftermath of 1960s mobilizations. Indeed, the 1970s furnished many globally conscious African Americans with the most profound political experiences of their lives.[14] Those who ventured abroad found new ways to express camaraderie with the people of developing nations. They participated in global solidarity campaigns, often while entering prolonged periods of exile from the United States. They regarded the United States not as a land of opportunity but as "the belly of the beast"—a global center of racism and imperialism. They hoped to explore the international dimensions of Black Power and feel "the Bandung spirit of African-Asian cooperation." They also wished to remake themselves, shedding "Coca-Cola values" and colonial mind-sets.[15]

Some of these sojourners joined the New York City–based Pan-African Skills Project (PASP). Formed by human rights activists in 1969, PASP recruited "skilled and committed" African Americans for "total service to progressive African nations."[16] By the early 1970s dozens of PASP volunteers had traveled to Tanzania to assist in nation-building projects overseen by the government of that East African country. Other black internationalists participated in the multiracial crusades of the Venceremos Brigade. The brigade arranged for groups of Americans to visit Cuba and perform agricultural work as a means of aiding the Cuban revolution and promoting transnational kinship.[17]

The PASP and the brigade embodied the central tenets of radical internationalism. Both organizations embraced the idea that living in a progressive foreign country for a period of weeks or months while engaged in collective labor was a valuable way for westerners to expand global consciousness and foster cultural exchange on the Left. By heading overseas, PASP and brigade volunteers were not just temporarily escaping what they considered an inhumane US society. They were also helping an emerging nation avoid economic domination by the West while supporting the revolutionary experiment unfolding within the host society. As they cut sugar cane or performed other arduous tasks, the recruits strove to reject artificial distinctions between manual and mental labor. They hoped to realize a vision of "people working together, not as competitors but as companions, building a society to meet the needs of all."[18]

The ethos of Third World solidarity also drew to Guyana a narrow stream of African Americans. A small expatriate community had formed in the country well before the founding of the Jonestown settlement in 1974. Although Tanzania remained perhaps the definitive site of transnational black endeavor, Guyana briefly emerged as the leading Pan-African outpost in the Western Hemisphere. An assortment of African American activists, artists, and intellectuals alighted in its capital city of Georgetown or ventured into its densely forested interior. Most were black nationalists and Pan-Africanists of a leftist inclination. They included the Harlem writer Julian Mayfield, the educator Ann F. Cook (later Tchaiko Kwayana), and artists Tom Feelings, Herman "Kofi" Bailey, and Otto Neals.[19]

The expats came to farm, to cultivate a revolutionary esthetic, or to work for the predominantly Afro-Guyanese government. "I wanted to visit a land whose people were black and whose functioning was in black hands," Neals later recalled.[20] Among the settlers were longtime New Yorkers, Malcolm X associates,[21] followers of heterodox religious faiths, and former members of Ghana's African American community who had been displaced by the 1966 ouster of Nkrumah. A few of the émigrés were also legal fugitives who had fled prison terms.[22] In a sense, however, *all* African American inhabitants of Guyana were refugees who arrived seeking not just sanctuary but a place in the sun. As Tom Feelings wrote in a 1971 letter to Mayfield, "The West is destructive to our human spirit."[23]

Guyana's image as a locus of Pan-African activity propelled the country into African American consciousness. In 1970 Guyanese organizer Eusi Kwayana, head of the African Society for Cultural Relations with Independent Africa (ASCRIA), hosted a Seminar of Pan-Africanist and Black Revolutionary Nationalists in Georgetown. The event, which occurred as many African Americans were striving to formalize and enact their internationalist ideals, produced an extraordinary assemblage of radicals. From the United States came veteran activists Mae Mallory and Jimmy Garrett, black nationalist intellectuals Ron Daniels and James Turner, Black Arts Movement luminaries Askia M. Touré and Barbara Ann Teer, and Courtland Cox, who went on to serve as secretary of the Sixth Pan-African Congress in 1974. Also present were Antiguan leftist Tim Hector and Jessica Huntley of London's Bogle L'Ouverture Publications.[24]

In the wake of the summit, several US militants helped ASCRIA launch the Pan-African Secretariat, which coordinated regional efforts to provide material aid for anticolonial struggles in Southern Africa. Some of these organizers returned to New York to distribute ASCRIA literature, publicize the activities of the secretariat, and otherwise assist Guyana in becoming "a model for African nations."[25] Meanwhile a number of the secretariat's African American officials moved to Guyana, responding to the nation's call for permanent settlers from the black diaspora to help populate and develop the country. They resided in the village of Buxton where they staffed ASCRIA's ideological institute and bolstered Guyana's image as a site of serious engagement with the revolutionary Third World.[26]

Other African Americans followed different paths to Guyana. Some came to join one of the black nationalist religious orders that operated on the country's social fringes. Others had escaped criminal charges back home and sought asylum under Guyana's generous sanctuary policy, which accorded to most black foreign nationals the status of political refugees.[27] Practically all the African American expats regarded the Caribbean nation as a bailiwick of righteous blackness. This was the case not only because Stokely Carmichael (later Kwame Ture) had visited the republic in 1970 or because Guyanese prime minister Forbes Burnham had endorsed the concept of "Black Power."[28] Quite simply, many African Americans embraced Guyana because, as attendees of the 1970 Pan-African seminar noted, the country seemed deeply committed to ensuring the "liberation of the black man wherever he might be."[29]

Guyana also offered a crucial testing ground for Third World socialism. Burnham strove to position his country as a stalwart member of the Community of Nonaligned Nations. He maintained warm relations with Cuba, China, North Korea, and Tanzania, and his government made financial contributions to armed liberation struggles in southern Africa.[30] In 1970 he proclaimed Guyana a "cooperative socialist republic." Producer cooperatives, especially agricultural ventures, were to enable the nation to combat capitalist exploitation and pursue economic self-reliance. Guyana thus supplied a base for concrete struggle at a time when many African American radicals feared that militant sloganeering had eclipsed revolutionary action in the United States.[31]

Emphasis on the primacy of revolutionary deeds led small groups of African American ideologues to visit Guyana and volunteer for nation-building projects in the nation's jungle interior. Pan-Africanist students from a handful of American universities and independent black institutions (including PASP and Washington, DC's Center for Black Education) journeyed to the Caribbean country to clear land and build roads, often while living in cooperative compounds and camps.[32] The labor was grueling. As one Brooklyn College organizer reported, "Trees will have to be cut, land plowed, cattle tended, and when all this is done there will be more trees, more cattle, and more land."[33] Yet volunteers could draw satisfaction from the knowledge that they were participating in a genuine quest for self-determination while helping a young nation develop its hinterland—the key to its economic autonomy and growth.

Indeed, Burnham invited African Americans to play a central role in populating Guyana's vast wilderness. "We have more land than we can deal with," the leader acknowledged in a 1973 interview.[34] Burnham's administration regularly helped foreign nationals establish agricultural cooperatives in the country, a strategy designed to increase national productivity. A variant of the US counterculture's back-to-the-land theme underlay practically all expatriate activity in Guyana. The agrarian ideal was especially powerful at a time when urban migration and debt had decimated the black land base in the rural American South. Over the course of the 1970s dozens of African Americans settled in the Guyanese rainforest, looking to raise crops, foster a communitarian spirit, and escape the unbridled consumerism of highly industrialized societies.[35]

Guyana's co-op movement furnished a tangible survival strategy in an age of stagflation and automation. It appeared to offer a practical answer to the scarcity and unemployment plaguing many African Americans back home. The cooperative model combined the ethos of participatory democracy and the promise of a planned economy. Few African Americans who toured Guyanese co-ops in the 1970s doubted the revolutionary power of the institutions. Thanks to Guyana's official embrace of the cooperative system, one black Brooklynite gushed in 1970, "There will be no rich quarters and poor quarters."[36]

African Americans in the United States had revived their own traditions of cooperative production during the 1960s.[37] The Poor People's Corporation, a self-help initiative based in Mississippi, shared its expertise in the creation and maintenance of co-ops during the 1970 Pan-African seminar in Georgetown.[38] Still, the aura of Third World autonomy endowed Guyana's cooperative agricultural ventures with special appeal. The country's early Amerindian and African inhabitants had practiced similarly collectivist farming techniques. Guyana's self-designation as a cooperative republic thus seemed to mark a return to practices of primitive communism that once had undergirded sustainable societies.[39]

Finally, cooperative ventures appeared to possess certain powers of moral regeneration. Conquering the Guyanese frontier required revolutionary discipline. It meant shedding bourgeois contempt for manual labor, an attitude associated with the cultural degradation of the colonial era. African Americans, some militants believed, could reeducate and revitalize themselves as they cultivated the soil, eliminating the inherited psychic frailties that were thought to cripple serious anti-imperialist struggle. "Do not apply to Guyana if you are in search of a soft life," organizers of the Pan-African Secretariat warned potential US recruits. "The country has a great future if enough people are prepared to rough it a little."[40]

Thus, while most westerners viewed the Caribbean as a sleepy tourist oasis, a coterie of devoted African Americans was helping consolidate

Guyana's reputation as a hub of Third World militancy. These expats rejected the idea that they had simply abandoned the racial battles that continued to rage in the United States. Indeed, they believed they had taken the fight to the next level. Like generations of African American internationalists before them, they insisted that the quest for black liberation could not be confined to the shores of America and that the rise of strong black nations would ensure the protection and empowerment of African descendants everywhere.

The pilgrims of Jonestown concurred. Traveling to Guyana in 1974 to establish an agricultural mission, the followers of Jim Jones arrived not in an obscure Third World outpost but in a place many left-leaning foreign nationals hailed as a social and cultural mecca. If the Jonestown parishioners were seen as eccentric, they were far from politically aberrant. The Peoples Temple worldview fit comfortably within a nexus of contemporary radical ideas. The lines of political affinity grow clearer as one peers beyond the idiosyncrasies of religious belief.

Like other expats, the people of Jonestown had been driven from their native country by poverty, social upheaval and alienation. They had seized the opportunity to escape a society they viewed as materially rich but spiritually destitute. They had embraced the possibilities of exile on a distant frontier. They shared with other internationalists the desire to restructure their lives and mold their own destiny in a progressive nation. They regarded themselves not simply as émigrés but as pioneers in a new world.[41]

And they viewed Guyana as a sanctuary. Here was a verdant, fertile land, a place drenched in sunshine and beauty. Guyana's lush rainforest contrasted with the slums many of the parishioners had once occupied. "When you look down the road you just know that you free from pollution & rascism (sic)," one colonist declared.[42] Another Jonestown resident described the community in deeply aspirational terms as "a place where there is no unemployment, no crime, no drugs, no social neglect, no substandard housing or inadequate nutrition."[43] The Peoples Temple faithful saw Guyana as "the Freedom Land" largely because they hoped to fashion within its secluded interior a society in which deprivation and social neglect were unthinkable. In the words of Jones himself, the objective was "to give some freedom to children, to get away from the asphalt jungles."[44]

Yet Guyana offered more than its fecundity and open terrain. It was also quite visibly a land of color. Government propaganda presented the nation as a harmonious "land of six peoples," despite the deep and long-standing strife that existed between Afro-Guyanese (descendants of enslaved people) and Indo-Guyanese (descendants of indentured servants from India).[45] The reality of Guyana as a crossroads for groups whose forebears hailed from South America, Asia, Africa, and Europe resonated with Peoples Temple, a church that celebrated interracial fellowship. From afar, the Caribbean nation almost seemed to embody the concept of the "beloved community," an integrationist ideal that pervaded civil rights discourse and the sermons of Jim Jones.[46]

At the same time, Guyana's heritage of slave rebellions and ethos of uncompromising blackness no doubt fascinated many Peoples Temple congregants.[47] In the wake of the Jonestown tragedy some commentators argued that the willingness of scores of black people to follow a white messiah into the wilderness signaled "the erosion of our racial instinct for self-determination, self-direction, and self-preservation."[48] Yet African American residents of Jonestown were hardly impervious to contemporary themes of black pride and self-assertion. The Peoples Temple settlement featured classes on black history and African geography, and its social activities—from drill teams to gospel and jazz concerts—celebrated black cultural vitality.[49] For some Jonestown inhabitants, the prospect of constructing a predominantly African American "model city" in an isolated section of a Caribbean country may well have evoked black nationalist dreams of incipient statehood.[50]

Jonestown, moreover, was steeped in the philosophy of Third World nation building. One of the settlement's goals, according to Jones, was "to help the Guyanese get on their feet." As a member of the community later reported, "Jim talked about self sufficiency, feeding ourselves and feeding the poor Guyanese."[51] This narrative was strategic; Jones hoped to curry favor with Burnham's government, which granted him a twenty-five-year lease and three thousand acres of wilderness on which to establish his colony.[52] The missionaries of Jonestown, however, were not immune to the allure of postcolonial striving. Some felt a genuine desire to assist in the economic and social development of Guyana, a land "of color." The Peoples Temple rank and file occasionally labored on the rural "self-help" projects initiated by the government. At least some of the faithful regarded such chores (including the grueling task of clearing forest) as part of the price one paid for the privilege of crafting a more egalitarian society.[53]

It was on the question of land and toil that the outlooks of Jonestown residents and those of other Guyana expats most visibly overlapped. Like many of their fellow émigrés, inhabitants of the Peoples Temple hailed the cooperative republic as a truly revolutionary concept. Communal farming offered a way to fulfill the church's gospel of "apostolic socialism."[54] It meant transforming one's self even as one strove to remold society. If the work was strenuous, it nevertheless beat the "comforts" of a highly technological yet soulless Western existence. As the denizens of Jonestown raised crops for their own consumption and for sale in Guyanese markets, some saw themselves as pursuing principles of Third World solidarity, self-reliance, and agrarian virtue that also galvanized other African American exiles, whether they toiled in the cooperative villages of Tanzania or in the sugarcane fields of Cuba. No single, ideological strain united such internationalists. Yet they all saw themselves as members of a vanguard (whether defined in primarily socioreligious or political terms) who were braving hardship in an underdeveloped country to ensure a more just, global future.

Of course, one must avoid overstressing commonality when examining the eclectic activities of contemporary African American internationalists. Although matters of faith drew other African American settlers to Guyana, few of the country's expats displayed the intense religiosity of the Jonestown congregants, who filtered their political convictions through a prism of ardent faith. Nor did the practices of the Peoples Temple colonists always align with those of other African American exiles. While most internationalists came to Guyana seeking radical fellowship, members of the secretive Jonestown mission spent most of their time sequestered in their jungle compound.[55] Ultimately the demented prescriptions of Jones, a demagogue who sought total submission from his followers, eclipsed the global perspectives that the Peoples Temple faithful shared with other expats.

Given the hideous outcome of the Jonestown experiment, it is tempting to regard the Guyana affair either as a historical anomaly or as yet another social nightmare of the 1970s, a decade that also witnessed the rise of the murderous Khmer Rouge of Cambodia. The purported credulity of the Peoples Temple missionaries—an idea embedded in the problematic expression "Don't drink the Kool-Aid"—continues to dominate the cultural memory of the settlement and its demise.[56] In retrospect, faith in Guyana as a new Jerusalem seems almost as misplaced as did belief in the messianic powers of Jones himself. Over the course of the decade, grim postcolonial realities shattered the country's progressive image and its mechanisms of cooperative socialism. Guyana descended into poverty and instability as the repressiveness and corruption of Burnham's regime intensified.[57] In truth, it was to a rapidly declining banana republic that the Peoples Temple faithful decamped in the mid-1970s.

Still, the denizens of Jonestown should not be dismissed as lunatics or sycophants. Their repudiation of the United States seems irrational only if we accept the premise that civilization has reached its apogee in the bosom of global capitalism. The pilgrims of Peoples Temple dreamed of realizing their human potential in a progressive foreign land free from hatred and racial strife. They were participants in an ongoing search for refuge and fulfillment that has long shaped African American life and politics.[58] They saw the United States as a hostile wilderness, and they removed to a remote jungle in search of peace, camaraderie, and a decent life. The simple logic of that decision may escape those who know nothing of the lives of the most marginal members of the black laboring classes.

The mass deaths at Jonestown never lose their power to disturb. Yet allusions to madness only further distort the story.[59] The Peoples Temple agricultural mission was not simply another Altamont—a latter-day symbol of the counterculture's demise. The Guyana settlement was also an expression of solidarity, radical hope, and black diasporic yearning. More research is needed to trace the strands of African American collectivism that span the 1960s and 1970s. How does Jonestown compare to the Move Organization in Philadelphia and to other contemporary models of black alternative and communal life? How does the colony relate to earlier crusades of black countercitizenship, from maroon societies to the exilic visions of Garveyism? How might it reflect larger trends of reverse migration, those pathways that emerged in the late twentieth century as African American urbanites, whose forerunners had traveled from field to factory, again strove to reimagine the social and geographic frontiers of freedom?

Like other contemporary black internationalists, the people of Jonestown never found paradise. Yet they did attempt to construct a prototype of cooperative life in the Guyanese jungle. However esoteric their experiment may seem today, the effort did not unfold in a political vacuum. Rather, it drew upon broad and generative ideological currents. If we wish to honor the victims of Jonestown, we must seek to understand the full scope of their social aspirations. We must remember, as well, that utopian visions are not futile dreams. They are blueprints for a better tomorrow. And in many ways the quest for dignity and autonomy beyond the tentacles of Western capitalism has never seemed more relevant than it does today.

Notes

The author wishes to thank Charisse Burden-Stelly for generous feedback on an earlier version of this essay.

1. Rebecca Moore, "Demographics and the Black Religious Culture of Peoples Temple," in *Peoples Temple and Black Religion in America*, ed. Rebecca Moore, Anthony Pinn, and Mary Sawyer (Bloomington: Indiana Press University, 2004), 57–80.

2. David Chidester, *Salvation and Suicide: Jim Jones, the Peoples Temple, and Jonestown* (Bloomington: Indiana University Press, 1988), 151–60.

3. See, e.g., Mike Davidow, "Jonestown, Guyana: An American Tragedy," *Labour Monthly*, August 1979, 363.

4. Jonestown clippings, box 139, *Daily Worker* and *Daily World* Photograph Collection, Tamiment Library and Wagner Research Center, New York University, New York; Michael Novak, "*Jonestown: Socialism* at Work," *Washington Star*, December 17, 1978.

5. "The Jonestown Massacre: An Act of Genocide," *Black News*, December 1978, 14–15, 34; "A View on Guyana Deaths," *New York Amsterdam News*, December 2, 1979.

6. See discussion of Jonestown and psychoanalysis in Domenico A. Nesci, *Revisiting Jonestown: An Interdisciplinary Study of Cults* (Lanham, MD: Lexington Books, 2018).

7. "U.S. Murders 900 in Guyana," *Burning Spear*, December 1978; February 28, 1978, Angela Y. Davis to President Jimmy Carter, and Dennis Banks to President Carter, n.d., box 2, folder 36, Peoples Temple Records, North Baker Research Library (hereafter NBRL), California Historical Society, San Francisco.

8. "U.S. Murders 900 in Guyana."

9. The cruelty and megalomania of Jones has been well chronicled. See, in general, Jeff Guinn, *The Road to Jonestown: Jim Jones and Peoples Temple* (New York: Simon & Schuster, 2017).

10. Guinn, *The Road to Jonestown*, 290–300; John R. Hall, *Gone from the Promised Land: Jonestown in American Cultural History* (New York: Routledge, 2004); August 25, 1977, Frances Buckley to Phyllis Houston, box 2, folder 44, Peoples Temple Records, NBRL, California Historical Society.

11. "All These Beautiful Black People Died in the Guyana Massacre," flyer, box 42, folder 32, John Henrik Clarke Papers, Schomburg Center for Research in Black Culture (hereafter Schomburg Center), New York City.

12. Catherine (Hyacinth) Thrash and Marian K. Towne, *The Onliest One Alive: Surviving Jonestown, Guyana* (Indianapolis: Marian K. Towne, 1995), 87.

13. See, in general, Dan Berger, ed., *The Hidden 1970s: Histories of Radicalism* (New Brunswick, NJ: Rutgers University Press, 2010).

14. See, e.g., Seth M. Markle, *A Motorcycle on Hell Run: Tanzania, Black Power, and the Uncertain Future of Pan-Africanism, 1964–1974* (East Lansing: Michigan State University Press, 2017); Ashley D. Farmer, *Remaking Black Power: How Black Women Transformed an Era* (Durham: University of North Carolina Press, 2019); and Brenda Gayle Plummer, *In Search of Power: African Americans in the Era of Decolonization, 1956–1974* (New York: Cambridge University Press, 2013).

15. Mamadou Lumumba and Shango Umoja, "Ripped Off in Guyana" *Third World*, March 30, 1973, 12; "Printed from the *Nationalist*, 1967, a Tanzania Newspaper," clipping, box 1, folder 4, Pan-African Skills Project Papers, Schomburg Center.

16. "PAS Policy Statement," November 1972, box 36, folder 4, Vincent Harding Papers, Manuscript, Archives, and Rare Book Library (hereafter MARBL), Emory University, Atlanta, GA.

17. "The Venceremos Brigade," 1975 pamphlet, box 44, folder 7, Records of the Washington Office on Africa, Special Collections, Yale Divinity Library, New Haven, CT.

18. "Cuba? Si!" Venceremos Brigade pamphlet, 1970, box 38, folder 5, Vincent Harding Papers, MARBL, Emory University.

19. Elton C. Fax, *Black Artists of the New Generation* (New York: Dodd Mead, 1977), 158.

20. Fax, *Black Artists of the New Generation*, 158.

21. "Special Guyana Section," *Black News*, October 1977, 8–9.

22. See, e.g., Herman Ferguson, *An Unlikely Warrior: Evolution of a Black Nationalist Revolutionary* (Holly Springs, NC: Ferguson-Swan Publications, 2011).

23. Tom Feelings, "A Letter from Tom Feelings to Julian Mayfield," *Black World*, August 1971, 31.

24. "Report of the Seminar of Pan-Africanists and Black Revolutionary Nationalists, February 24–26, 1970," box 5, folder "Guyana," Doris Adelaide Derby Papers, MARBL, Emory University; August 6, 2015, author interview with Eusi and Tchaiko Kwayana, San Diego, CA.

25. USA Office of Pan-African Secretariat to "Dear Brothers and Sisters," n.d., box 5, folder "Guyana," Doris Adelaide Derby Papers, MARBL, Emory University.

26. Ann F. Cook, "Guyana as Seen by an African American," *Muhammad Speaks*, February 6, 1970, 25, 28–29.

27. Carey Winfrey, "A Second Guyana Cult Is Focus of Dispute," *New York Times*, November 27, 1978, A12; Larry Watani Stiner and Scot Brown, "The US-Panther Conflict, Exile, and the Black Diaspora: The Plight of Larry Watani Stiner," *Journal of African American History* 92 (2007): 543; Marvin X, *Somethin' Proper* (Castro Valley, CA: Black Bird Press, 1998), 110.

28. "Pan-Africanist Leader Bro Carmichael in Guyana," *Liberation* (Guyana), May 1970, box 110, folder 10, James Forman Papers, Manuscript Division, Library of Congress, Washington, DC; "Black Power Legitimate Exercise—P.M.," *News from Guyana*, April 18, 1970, 2.

29. "Seminar of Pan-Africanists and Black Revolutionary Nationalists" Program, February 1970, Special Collections, MARBL, Emory University.

30. Charles Wartts, Jr., "Plot Festive Masks for Visiting Luminaries, to Hide Burnham's Policies," *Muhammad Speaks*, July 14, 1972, 25, 29.

31. For a discussion of contemporary fears about the rhetorical posturing of self-proclaimed black revolutionaries, see Russell Rickford, "'Kazi Is the Blackest of All': Pan-African Nationalism and the Making of the 'New Man,' 1969–1975," *Journal of African American History* 101 (2016): 97–125.

32. “Center for Black Education: One Year Later,” *Third World*, October 1970, 1–2; “Preliminary Programme in Outline,” April 1970, box 5, folder “Guyana,” Doris Adelaide Derby Papers, MARBL, Emory University.

33. May 15, 1970, Craig Bell to “Dear Brothers and Sisters,” box 5, folder “Guyana,” Doris Adelaide Derby Papers, MARBL, Emory University.

34. “Black News Exclusive: Interview with Prime Minister Forbes Burnham,” *Black News*, October 22, 1973, 6.

35. Ann F. Cook, “Guyana as Seen by an African American” (manuscript of an article written in 1970 and submitted to Muhammad Speaks but not published in its entirety), and “Guyana Welcomes African Americans and West Indians,” n.d., box 5, folder “Guyana,” Doris Adelaide Derby Papers, MARBL, Emory University; Adeyemi Bandele, “Reflections of a Year in the Guyanese Interior,” *Black News*, October 1977, 10–11. For more on black nationalism, Pan-Africanism, and agrarianism, see Russell Rickford, “ ‘We Can’t Grow Food on All This Concrete’: The Land Question, Agrarianism, and Black Nationalist Thought in the Late 1960s and 1970s,” *Journal of American History* 103 (2017): 956–80.

36. “Guyana Welcomes African Americans and West Indians,” *Black News*, July 23, 1970, 12.

37. See chap. 9, Jessica Gordon Nembhard, *Collective Courage: A History of African American Cooperative Economic Thought and Practice* (University Park: Pennsylvania State University Press, 2014); Gene Roberts, “Cooperatives Run by Negroes a Growing Trend in the South,” *New York Times*, November 21, 1965, 58.

38. “Seminar of Pan-Africanists and Black Revolutionary Nationalists” Program.

39. “Living in Co-operation,” 1974 pamphlet, box 16, Tom Feelings Papers, Schomburg Center; “Socialism to Be Built on Co-operatives,” *News from Guyana*, July 12, 1975, 2; Charles Wartts, Jr., “Historical Perspective on the Cooperatives in Guyana,” *Muhammad Speaks*, July 21, 1972, 21, 24; *Co-operative Republic: Guyana 1970: A Study of Aspects of Our Way of Life* (Georgetown, Guyana: Government of Guyana, 1970).

40. “Guyana Welcomes African Americans and West Indians,” n.d., box 5, folder “Guyana,” Doris Adelaide Derby Papers, MARBL, Emory University.

41. Letter to President Jimmy Carter, box 2, folder 36, Peoples Temple Records, NBRL, California Historical Society. For an exploration of the broader currents of anticolonial world making, see Adom Getachew, *Worldmaking after Empire: The Rise and Fall of Self-Determination* (Princeton, NJ: Princeton University Press, 2020).

42. Letter to Phyllis Houston, box 2, folder 44, Peoples Temple Records, NBRL, California Historical Society.

43. Laurie Efrein letter, box 3, folder 51, Peoples Temple Records, NBRL, California Historical Society.

44. Kit Nascimento, “The View from Guyana,” *First World*, 1979, 11.

45. “Guyana: Land of Hospitality and Natural Beauty,” pamphlet, n.d., Tourist Division, Guyana Development Corporation, box 5, folder “Guyana,” Doris Adelaide Derby Papers, MARBL, Emory University.

46. For social justice themes in the rhetoric and sermons of Jim Jones, see Moore, Pinn, and Sawyer, eds., *Peoples Temple and Black Religion in America*.

47. Rebecca Moore, "Jonestown in Literature: Caribbean Reflections on a Tragedy," *Literature and Theology* 23 (2009): 75; text of Eusi Kwayana article submitted to *Muhammad Speaks*, August 1969, box 5, folder "Guyana," Doris Adelaide Derby Papers, MARBL, Emory University.

48. "Black Reflections on the Jonestown Holocaust," *Institute of the Black World Monthly Report*, February 1979, box 42, folder 32, John Henrik Clarke Papers, Schomburg Center.

49. Thrash and Towne, *The Onliest One Alive*, 87; Hall, *Gone from the Promised Land*, 109.

50. Guyanese Pan-Africanist Eusi Kwayana described Jonestown as a "state within a state." Eusi Kwayana, "Guyanese Peoples View of the Jonestown Massacre," *Soulbook* (1980): 30–37.

51. Thrash and Towne, *The Onliest One Alive*, 87.

52. Nascimento, "View from Guyana," 11.

53. "Credit Guyana Gains to Self Help," *Chicago Defender*, October 9, 1971, 5; January 1, 1978, letter to Phyllis Houston, box 2, folder 44; and June 13, 1978, Gabriel Schack to President Jimmy Carter, box 3, folder 51, Peoples Temple Records, NBRL, California Historical Society.

54. Hugh B. Urban, *New Age, Neopagan, and New Religious Movements: Alternative Spirituality in Contemporary America* (Oakland: University of California Press, 2015), 251.

55. Ferguson, *An Unlikely Warrior*, 221; John Hamill, "B'klyn Group Stunned by Guyana Neighbors," *Daily News*, November 24, 1978, 8.

56. Chris Higgins, "Stop Saying 'Drink the Kool-Aid," *Atlantic*, November 8, 2018.

57. Eusi Kwayana, "Guyana Politics: Jaganism, Burnhamism and the People," *African World*, July 28, 1973, 12, 16; Jane Kramer, "Letter from Guyana," *New Yorker*, September 16, 1974, 100; Embert J. Hendrickson, "In Pursuit of the Cooperative Republic: Guyana in the 1970s," *World Today* 35 (1979): 214–22. Burnham's image as a progressive leader, which endured in some African American political circles, was irrevocably damaged by his government's involvement in the assassination of Pan-Africanist scholar-activist Walter Rodney in 1980. See Arnold Gibbons, *The Legacy of Walter Rodney in Guyana and the Caribbean* (Lanham, MD: University Press of America, 2011): 185–92.

58. See chap. 3, James T. Campbell, *Middle Passages: African American Journeys to Africa, 1787–2005* (New York: Penguin Books, 2006).

59. Cold War psychoanalysts often framed radical activism and expressions of anticapitalism as forms of insanity. See Tony Perucci, "The Red Mask of Sanity: Paul Robeson, HUAC, and the Sound of Cold War Performance," *Drama Review* 53 (2009): 18–48.

Part 4

✦

Black Protest, Politics, and Power

INTRODUCTION

N. D. B. Connolly

For the modern university at the end of the 1960s, Black Power, in the view of some, seemed to bring only bad news. As the psychologist Kenneth B. Clark lamented in 1969, "The dominant thing being publicized about the young Negro in college is his repudiation of what we consider some important values and goals." That Negro, by Clark's estimation, "is considering integration a dirty word."[1] America's preeminent black psychologist hardly stood alone in his concern. A collection of the nation's most decorated black intellectuals and political luminaries joined Clark and his host, Anne Reid, at Haverford College in late May 1969.[2] They were prompted—perhaps even panicked—by what they viewed as the apparent appeal of black separatism so soon on the heels of the Civil Rights and Voting Rights Acts, fair housing, and the promise of desegregation.

The principal battlefront remained education—the mind of "the Negro." Those gathered at Haverford that May, known as the Haverford Group, included Kenneth's chief collaborator, wife, and brilliant psychologist in her own right, Mamie Phipps Clark; the historian John Hope Franklin; sociologist St. Clair Drake; the novelist Ralph Ellison; literary critic and writer J. Saunders Redding; the first black man to belong to a presidential cabinet, Robert Clifton Weaver; and the first African American to hold a federal judgeship, William Hastie. They endeavored to put the genie of Black Power back in the bottle. They had hoped, indeed, to craft a "black integrationist manifesto" and reclaim from "separatists" the political and intellectual center of Afro-American letters.[3]

The accompanying essays in this part do not address the Haverford Group or its aims. Nevertheless, they illustrate brilliantly the durability and diversity of radical Black Power, visions of militant black self-determination of which Clark and his convening seemed so afraid. The accounts offered here by William Sturkey, Richard D. Benson II, Quito Swan, and Charisse Burden-Stelly capture distinct and overlapping elements of black liberation education. In tandem, they make the argument that black people exercised and developed their political consciousness en route to transforming their relationship to liberalism, to white supremacy, and to each other. In universities and Freedom Schools, Black Power educators and students built learning places and publications for articulating a high sense of self-regard within individual black persons. At the very same time, they preserved and disseminated a collective commitment to blackness as an aesthetic, political, and intellectual project. In Chicago, Mississippi, or even Papua New Guinea, we find the formerly "colored" and once colonized using liberation ideas and literacy to cultivate what historian Russell Rickford described elsewhere as "a people's intelligentsia."[4]

For the more established black intelligentsia, of course, the populist undertones of Black Power education were precisely the problem. In the view of the group gathered at Haverford in 1969, Black Power, particularly in the realm of education, had grown into something not so much beautiful as dangerous. Two Black Panthers had been killed at UCLA. Over a two-year period, more than two hundred college campuses had experienced some kind of student protest. Much of it had been directed at creating fresh curriculum, carving out physical space, sparking black faculty hiring, or setting other institutional agendas directed at meeting the needs of black students. But there had also been demands for an "all-Negro" dorm at the University of Chicago. Students at Cornell University executed an armed occupation of an administrative building. Schools as diverse as the University of Michigan and Antioch College seemed open to black studies institutes and departments that might openly exclude white students. The nation over, African American young people professed and exhibited sharp distrust of white liberalism, in general, and rejected, specifically, the qualified inclusion being offered in historically white centers of learning.[5] The students appeared to renounce precisely the kinds of "progress" to which members of the Haverford Group had dedicated their professional lives.

From their lofty positions as professors, opinion makers, and members of university boards of trustees (Robert Weaver was a university president!), Clark and company condemned the "fuzzy thinking," "clichés," and "suicidal rhetoric" of Black Power schooling and its adherents.[6] They mocked "Afrocentric" reading lists as largely unread and hastily compiled and ridiculed the average college-bred "revolutionary's" inexperience with "shooting guns."[7] The efforts at Haverford that May, however, would also fizzle and flame out quickly. Doomed in their efforts to squelch Black Power's intellectual influence, the Haverford Group never mustered more than a few meetings about their "integrationist manifesto."

How could a group so august and so well connected fail so miserably? The answer lies in the diversity and breadth of liberation schooling, Black Power schooling.

No one could deny that a desire for what one might call "Black Power education" propelled the black campus movement of the late 1960s and early 1970s.[8] Yet, as these essays attest, such a project could never be confined to college campuses or reduced to bibliographies, however thoroughly read or assembled. In spirit if not in name, Black Power education well precedes the arrival of "Black Power" as a slogan in 1966. Hear "Black Power," for instance, in 1938, as W. E. B. Du Bois addressed the graduating class of Fisk University: "The way to democracy lies through race loyalty."[9] "We may," he averred, "call this self-segregation . . . but the compulsion is from without and inevitable."[10] Hear it, too, in Zora Neale Hurston, in 1955, as she rejects the research of Kenneth and Mamie Clark in her defense of black education threatened, in her view, by the ruling in *Brown v. the Board of Education*. "It is a contradiction in terms to scream race pride and equality while at the same time spurning Negro teachers and self-association."[11] Black Power education extends, moreover, well beyond the personal concerns and political preoccupations of an African American intellectual elite based strictly in the United States. It animated, in some form or another, the efforts of Caribbean and African artists and writers to emancipate themselves from colonial education.[12] It also and simultaneously grew *from* and blossomed *into* political movements—local, national, and international.[13] And long after many of those movements suffered repression and demobilization, Black Power education remained preserved in the life habits and learning practices of those who would live on, read on, and write on. It persists among those writing *still*, with these essays and this volume serving as evidence. Black Power learnin' continues.

Affirming that Black Power owes much to black life in the Deep South, William Sturkey explores how, in the summer of 1964, Mississippi Freedom Schools gave students a chance to develop journalistic skills and literary spaces that Jim Crow had attempted to preempt and foreclose. Publishing *Freedom News*, students within Freedom Schools retreated into church basements and community centers, working themselves into a writing lather. They emerged offering clarion calls about the limits of *Brown* and the lie of school equalization and refuting establishment journalism that failed to capture the fullness of black political and educational disempowerment. "Most mainstream media outlets," Sturkey reminds, "acted as if the Civil Rights Movement did not exist." *Freedom News*, however, changed the broad understanding of what black intellectual and political self-determination looked like in Mississippi. Far from being some incidental student publication, *Freedom News* would be reprinted in the *Crisis* magazine, thus providing a national window into

Mississippi's Freedom Summer.[14] Moreover, by the late 1960s, many of the erstwhile reporters of the *Freedom News* would mature and, perhaps to the Haverford Group's chagrin, become full-blown campus and community activists, demanding—shouting—"Black Power."

Back "up North," at the very same time, educational self-determination, by Richard D. Benson II's telling, looked like Chicago's Communiversity—a project that braided into a single fabric religious leaders, community activists and organizers, students, and educators. An "alternative educational system" for black South Siders that was run mostly on Saturdays and in the evenings, Communiversity, Benson explains, drew on a combination of historical momentum, pedagogical creativity, and the geographic happenstance of Chicago as an epicenter for Afro-America. As in Mississippi's Freedom Summer, the often-surreptitious organizing of the late 1950s and early 1960s provided a critical foundation for later expressions of Black Power. Public school boycotts in 1963 and 1964, followed by antislum campaigns in 1965 and 1966, further fanned demands for "community control," demands members of the Communiversity would later help implement and institutionalize. It is this tight weave between different political struggles variously hatched or convening in Chicago—across geography, generations, and brick-and-mortar hubs of political awakening—that gave the Communiversity's version of liberation education exceptionally strong sinews. So endowed, the project proved able to survive the kinds of political or personal setbacks that sapped the strength of more rigid or centralized black political organizations in the city (such as the Illinois Chapter of the Black Panther Party). It also boasted, as something of a leaderless movement, a decentered structure that enabled African-centered teaching to coexist with strains of black Marxism. Such an ecumenical intellectual orientation—yet always on the Left—preempted the prospect of Communiversity collapsing from ideological infighting or blind orthodoxies. Benson impressively documents this holistic suppleness, explaining, in the process, why both scholarly and political outgrowths of liberation education in Chicago took hold and blossomed well into the 1980s.

Quito Swan takes readers into the Black Pacific with his look at anticolonial, Black Power education. In Swan's work we see how the black campus movement so loathed by the Haverford Group and liberals of their ilk actually had *global* reach. The University of Papua New Guinea (UPNG) had been established in 1966 to ensure both the preservation of "civilization" and a measure of continuity for the region's colonial rulers. Almost immediately, however, it got whipped up into efforts of anticolonial activists and black internationalists insistent on supporting the development of critical black epistemologies. The vantage point of being indigenous *and* black *and* tied into diasporic intellectual happenings, Swan explains, made the darker peoples of Oceania subject and witness to perhaps the most dramatic "pandemonium of colonialism" anywhere. The rapidity and sophistication of Black Power's institutionalization at UPNG can thus be explained, Swan illustrates, by recognizing a generations-long struggle against environmental racism, resource extraction, and cultural erasure. Through Melanesian collectives like the Niugini Black Power Group and a plethora of publications and artistic movements, Papuans' take on intellectual self-determination included challenging white cultural chauvinism in English, indigenous languages, and pidgin, while also drawing from solidarities with the Negritude, anti-apartheid, and US and British Black Power movements. Swan maintains that such remarkable linguistic and political fluency at UPNG made the university a hub for black political maturation and an indispensable site of Black Power internationalism in the Pacific World.

Regardless of where its discourses washed up, of course, Black Power, as a set of ideas, remained as contested as it was global. In light of capitalist and patriarchal traditions of black self-determination, Black Power's radical potential had to be fought for. Its redressing power had to evolve. In her essay on the tradition of radical blackness within Black Power, Burden-Stelly offers a concise and impressive survey of how Black Power fought off liberal, sexist, and capitalist cooptation through the thought work of Marxist, nationalist, and feminist intellectuals and activists across the twentieth century. The radical strain of Black Power, she explains, deepened Marxian preoccupations with exploitation, first on matters of race, then on race and gender. Thanks to countless imaginative and committed people working from within scores of communities and organizations, successive innovations on the black Left acknowledged a compounded or "superexploitation," never wandering far from progressive consideration of "Black [as] a Country."[15] Documenting seeds of radical black nationalism from the 1920s right through the 1970s, Burden-Stelly depicts Harry Haywood and W. E. B. Du Bois on a continuum that also includes Claudia Jones, the Combahee River Collective, and the Black Women's United Front. Within such a rich and variegated political ecosystem, Burden-Stelly compellingly illustrates that there was practically no way for commitments to self-determination *not* to become and remain the center of black politics. Black agency and effort helped make it so.

Black Power's deep pedagogical and intellectual roots, its stubborn anticapitalist strains, its international resonance, and, likely most of all, its evolutionary power, these, perhaps, helps us appreciate, if not wholly embrace, the frustration inspiring the Haverford discussions. For those like Kenneth Clark or Robert Weaver, the promise of the Civil Rights Act or "all deliberate speed"—integration and its accompanying equality—likely seemed maddingly close. And yet between the age of Jim Crow and the integrationist world unrealized stood a phalanx of students and activists, the insufficiently lettered and all of them blinded by their calls for Black Power. In the view of an elite few, these, as much as the lingering segregationists, were the folks who threatened to tear down everything. Indeed, in his first evening at the Haverford discussions, St. Clair Drake described what he called the "[H.] Rap Brown syndrome." I used to call it the "Sampson complex." This, by Drake's telling, represented the willingness of a strongman, eyeless, to crash the temple's pillars—the university's, the nation's—to his and all others' ruin, just to dispatch with one's enemies.[16]

In 1969, however, Black Power education did not portend calamity or a world collapsed. Nor was it merely an idea whose time had come. It had always been, in some form or another, baked into the aspirations and practices of black learning. It had to be counted among the bricks from which the temple of black freedom would be built. That the demand for greater access to liberation education on American college campuses happened within a decade of *Brown* should confirm for us what the Haverford Group likely knew and feared was true—that racial integration, for most, was never *really* the aim or even the means of black education. Freedom was.

Notes

1. Kenneth B. Clark, May 30, 1969, quoted in *The Haverford Discussions: A Black Integrationist Manifesto for Racial Justice*, ed. Michael Lackey (Charlottesville: University of Virginia Press, 2013), 5.

2. Anne Reid (neé Anna Margaret Cooke) was an Ivy League–educated drama instructor, former "Negro Fellow" of the Julius Rosenwald Fund (1948), and widow of Ira de Augustine Reid, a professor at Haverford who had passed away in 1968.

3. Books like Harold Cruse's *The Crisis of the Negro Intellectual* and Stokely Carmichael and Charles Hamilton's *Black Power: The Politics of Liberation in America.* Yet there had long been currents of black frustration with intellectual liberalism. See Lawrence P. Jackson, *The Indignant Generation (*Princeton, NJ: Princeton University Press, 2011).

4. Russell Rickford, *We Are an African People: Independent Education, Black Power, and the Radical Imagination* (Oxford: Oxford University Press, 2016), 5.

5. *The Staff Study of Campus Riots and Disorders of the Permanent Subcommittee on Investigations* (Washington: U.S. Government Printing Office, 1969),

cited in Study of Campus Unrest, 1969 in President's Commission on Campus Unrest, part 1 (January 1, 1970–December 31, 1970), 27, ProQuest History Vault.

6. Clark, *Haverford Discussions*, 11, 28, 38.

7. William Hastie, in particular sat on the board of trustees for Amherst College and Temple University, as well as belonged to a "visiting committee" at Harvard Law School.Clark, *Haverford Discussions*, 8. Much of time ridiculing Black Power reading lists was spent pointing out books, like Franz Fanon's *Wretched of the Earth*, that Haverford folks felt confident students had never read, or authors like Basil Davidson and Christopher Fyfe, whose whiteness seemed to slip past militant bibliographies of "Black Books by Black Scholars." Clark, *Haverford Discussions*, 32, 37.

8. Ibram H. Rogers, *The Black Campus Movement: Black Students and the Racial Reconstitution of Higher Education, 1965–1972* (New York: Palgrave Macmillan, 2012); Martha Biondi, *The Black Revolution on Campus* (Berkeley and Los Angeles, University of California Press, 2014); Noliwe M. Rooks, *White Money, Black Power: The Surprising History of African American Studies and the Crisis of Race in Higher Education* (Boston: Beacon Press, 2006).

9. W. E. B. Du Bois, "The Revelation of Saint Orgne the Damned," in *The Education of Black People: Ten Critiques, 1906–1960*, ed. Herbert Aptheker (New York: Monthly Review Press, 1973), 161.

10. Du Bois, "The Revelation of Saint Orgne the Damned," 159; Du Bois here serves to articulate a popular idea within communist and socialist circles during the late 1930s for self-determination for the "Black Belt," the majority-black counties crossing the states of the former Confederacy.

11. Letter to the *Orlando Sentinel*, August 11, 1955, reprinted in *The Age of Jim Crow*, ed. Jane Dailey (New York: W. W. Norton, 2009), 269.

12. See, for instance, Sylvia Wynter's discussion of the constant need to resemanticize and revalue blackness among the African-descended living in the West. David Scott, "The Re-Enchantment of Humanism: An Interview with Sylvia Wynter," *Small Axe* (September 8, 2000): 118–207, 173.

13. The historian Donna Murch, for example, offers compelling evidence of the Black Panther Party for Self Defense having originated, bibliographically, in Merritt College study groups and, institutionally, in the public-sector support given the California state university system. See Stefan M. Bradley, *Upending the Ivory Tower: Civil Rights, Black Power, and the Ivy League* (New York: New York University Press, 2018).

14. Departmental Reports of the NAACP, April 13, 1964, p. 24, in Secretary reports, including race riots, suspension of direct action demonstrations, voter registration, violence in Mississippi, Republican and Democratic national conventions, Civil Rights Act, police brutality and school integration, implementation of federal antipoverty programs, and economic boycotts, Papers of the NAACP, part 16: Supplement, Board of Directors File, 1956–65, ProQuest History Vault.

15. Nikhil Pal Singh, *Black Is a Country: Race and the Unfinished Struggle for Democracy* (Cambridge: Harvard University Press, 2005).

16. Clark, *Haverford Discussions*, 42.

Chapter 11

The Freedom News

Spaces of Intellectual Liberation during the Civil Rights Movement

William Sturkey

> *The Freedom News* will be published as often as possible throughout the summer. Everyone is welcome to write for the paper on any subject whatsoever.
>
> —Holly Springs, Mississippi *Freedom News*, July 10, 1964[1]

Hundreds of black Mississippi youths spent the summer of 1964 in church basements and community centers, slouched over desks and wrapped in deep thought as they pounded away on old typewriter keys. Ranging in age from five to nineteen years old, the young people sat in makeshift newspaper offices churning out a series of informal broadsheets carrying inspirational titles such as the *Freedom Carrier*, the *Freedom Star*, and the *Freedom Fighter*. Collectively referred to here as the "Freedom News," these newspapers were produced by young African Americans who were attending Freedom Schools—a series of independent schools that were operated as part of the 1964 Mississippi Freedom Summer.[2]

The Freedom News offered unique intellectual spaces for these inspired black youths. The papers themselves, written on typewriters and reproduced with mimeograph machines, became literary spaces where students published works that asserted their growing sense of community leadership and intellectual empowerment during the waning days of Jim Crow in Mississippi. Freedom School students filled these newspapers with

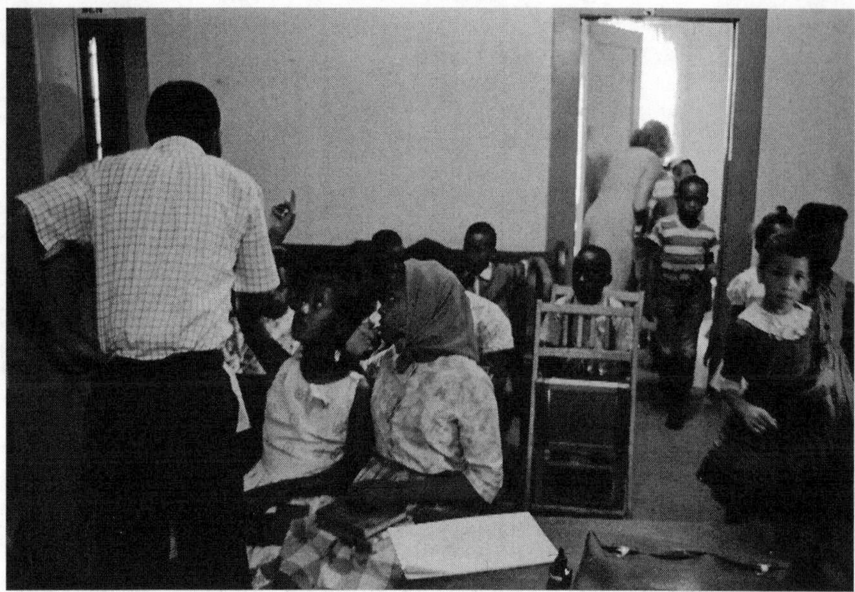

Fig. 4. Herbert Randall, Freedom School in session. Photograph. University of Southern Mississippi, Historical Manuscripts, Herbert Randall Freedom Summer Photographs, M351.

hundreds of essays, poems, editorials, and testimonies where they brazenly voiced resistance and affirmed their growing political consciousness. As a student named Bossie Mae Harring asserted in the *Drew Freedom Fighter*, "Someone has opened our eyes to freedom and we will walk in the light of freedom until we achieve the victory."[3] This essay examines the Freedom News to explore how black Mississippi youths created unique intellectual spaces to critique Jim Crow, demonstrate their growing leadership capabilities, and affirm their own intellectual empowerment.

Freedom Schools

The 1964 Mississippi Freedom Schools were conceived by civil rights activists in response to the poor public educational opportunities available to black Mississippians. A decade after the United States Supreme Court ruled racial school segregation unconstitutional with *Brown v. Board of Education*, Mississippi's public schools remained racially segregated due to rabid resistance from white segregationists. Despite the Supreme Court's ruling, many Mississippi officials believed they could maintain segregation for generations. To delay federally enforced integration, white Mississippi legislators in the late 1950s took superficial steps to try to demonstrate an effort to equalize black and white schools. Several school districts built or renovated school buildings for African Americans and in some cases provided additional equipment. But the majority of these efforts lacked real substance. As state NAACP president C. R. Darden advised branch leaders in 1959, "We will not be influenced or misled with Mississippi's so-called 'equalization' building program." "Don't be fascinated by the big buildings," Darden asserted in a later memo. "This is an outside show." These meager efforts never came close to closing the resource gap between black and white schools. And many school district officials did not even feign interest in improving black schools, simply diverting additional resources to white institutions.[4]

Ten years after *Brown*, black Mississippi schools received far fewer resources than their white counterparts. In 1963, an unpublished report by the Mississippi State Department of Education revealed stunning racial disparities in per-pupil expenditures across the state. For example, the Amite County School District spent an average amount of $70.45 on white students and only $2.24 on black ones. In Coffeeville, the average amount spent on white and black pupils was $68.95 and $6.55, respectively. In Tunica, the ratio was $172.80 to $5.99. In a state that struggled to educate most of its citizens, black students were tremendously disadvantaged. As late as 1964, thousands of African American students still attended school in dilapidated, overcrowded classrooms taught by undertrained and underpaid teachers.[5]

Black Mississippi schools were also censored. Because teachers were employed by the state, they were subject to termination for engaging in any semblance of civil rights activism. They were watched closely by an investigative unit called the Mississippi State Sovereignty Commission that was founded in 1956 to monitor civil rights activities in the state. The Sovereignty Commission hired investigators to report on the activities of noted civil rights activists and paid informants to infiltrate and spy on civil rights organizations. Any teacher, principal, or other school official found to have connections to movement activities could be dismissed. The state also surveilled textbooks and classrooms to prevent teachers from teaching the history of Reconstruction or discussing radical black leaders such as Frederick Douglass or W. E. B. Du Bois.[6]

In the fall of 1963, a coalition of civil rights organizers working in Mississippi began planning a massive campaign they initially called the Summer Project. Although this campaign focused primarily on voting rights, several movement veterans also noted the need for a program geared toward black youths. Civil rights activists, through years of experience working in the state, had become familiar with black Mississippians' lack of education. Freedom Schools were conceived as an educational supplement for young black students that would also help train future leaders. Organizers envisioned the schools as leadership training grounds, believing that Freedom Schools could create lifelong activists with the potential to "provide politically emerging communities with new, young leadership."[7]

The Freedom School curriculum was planned by a coalition of progressive educational leaders who gathered in New York City in March 1964. One of the most important themes that emerged from this "curriculum conference" was the adoption of Highlander Folk School founder Myles Horton's Highlander model of classroom instruction.[8] This Highlander model embraced the notion of classrooms as participatory democracies where students would have both the freedom and responsibility to contribute to their learning experience. Freedom Schools did not employ traditional pedagogical practices such as testing and compulsory attendance. Classes were optional. If students did not enjoy the lessons, they simply would not come. Therefore, the success of the schools depended on their ability to meet students' desires for self-expression and activism. Encouraging student participation was central to the basic Freedom School design. This approach helped encourage students to voice their views on their lives and futures, laying the groundwork for the essays that would be published in the Freedom News.[9]

Freedom Schools opened during the first full week of July 1964. Thousands of students turned out for classes. Due to spotty records, it is impossible to gauge precisely how many students attended Freedom Schools, but the most reliable estimates range between twenty-five hundred and three thousand pupils attending classes at more than forty schools across the state. Many students were immediately drawn into activism. Some helped door-to-door voter registration canvassing efforts. Others attended mass meetings and participated in marches, sit-ins, and other forms of protest. In several Freedom Schools, students rushed to produce newspapers.[10]

The Freedom News

Freedom School planners had long considered the idea of newspaper production. As one organizer suggested in the months before Freedom Summer, "A student newspaper emanating from the Freedom Schools will give students an opportunity to write, to run a press or mimeograph machine, to organize a complete project on their own."[11] Many instructors found students gravitating toward newspaper production. Bolstered by waves of material donations that arrived from across the country in support of Freedom Summer, teachers helped students begin producing school newspapers. They were written on donated typewriters and mass-produced using mimeograph machines. Dozens of young African Americans were excited to work on the newspapers. Just a week into the Summer Project, a Greenwood teacher reported, "The idea of the student newspaper is the hottest thing going."[12]

Within two weeks of the start of classes, statewide Freedom School coordinator Staughton Lynd noted the existence of twelve regularly published newspapers. The writers ranged in age from five to nineteen, with the majority of participants between eleven and thirteen years old. Some newspapers indicated writers' ages (included here when known). A few papers included authors' full names, but most provided only first names and abbreviated surnames due to the fear of potential reprisals from white supremacists. Freedom School newspapers often welcomed contributions without formal sign-ups or prerequisites. As an ad printed in the Meridian *Freedom Star* explained, "The FREEDOM STAR is your paper and any articles which you would like to submit for publication are welcome." A bulletin from the Holly Springs paper similarly encouraged, "If you want to write an article or if you have written something that you would like to have printed, speak to one of the Council of Federated Organizations (COFO) workers about it."[13]

In writing for the Freedom School newspapers, students were responding to a number of inequalities. Racial regulations in Jim Crow Mississippi affected newspaper coverage and printing practices. Most of the state's newspapers ignored news from black communities, only mentioning African Americans when they were arrested or killed. A few local papers sporadically covered black church activities or high school athletics, but these brief discussions were almost always relegated to the back pages. And on the rare occasions when individual African Americans were mentioned, newspaper writers made sure to adhere to the strict racial dialectal codes of their society, refusing to acknowledge black Mississippians with proper titles such as "Mr." or "Mrs." and often publicly referring to African American subjects as "nigger." As one newspaper editor wrote of African Americans in the Mississippi press, "In print he is never a man."[14]

Marginalization in the mainstream press was backed by rigid censorship as Mississippi white supremacist civic leaders attempted to exclude any racially progressive or radical perspectives. Especially after the passage of *Brown v. Board*, anyone who publicly advocated civil rights or racial equality was subject to social, political, and economic ostracism or physical attack, even if they were white. P. D. East, a white editor in Petal, Mississippi, was run out of town under the threat of death for questioning local segregationist tactics. Several years later, a Pascagoula editor named Ira Harkey experienced death threats, an advertiser boycott, and vandalism as retribution for his editorial advocating peaceful integration at the University of Mississippi in 1962.[15]

Black journalists experienced even more scrutiny. Decades of racial oppression had left Mississippi with only five African American newspapers by the mid-1950s, and only one of these, the Jackson-based *Eagle Eye*, publicly supported early movement activities. Arrington High, the brazen publisher of the *Eagle Eye*, experienced constant threats and was at one point incarcerated in a mental institution before being smuggled out of the state in a casket. Even as activism increased in Mississippi, most mainstream media outlets acted as if the civil rights movement did not exist, regularly blacking out portions of civil rights coverage on nationally syndicated television shows and ignoring local developments in the state's daily newspapers. By the early-1960s, there were several new pro-movement newsletters, but most of these were small broadsides produced by individuals or small groups.[16]

Publishing their newspapers within the context of such censorship, Freedom School students made significant contributions to movement coverage in the state. The wave of Freedom School newspapers produced in the summer of 1964 more than doubled the number of Mississippi's pro-movement newspapers. In several places, Freedom School newspapers were the first periodicals ever produced by the black community. The McComb *Freedom's Journal* and the *Benton County Freedom Train* were later taken over by adult activists and operated well beyond Freedom Summer as venues for community organizing and movement updates.[17]

Freedom School students engaged multiple audiences with their writings. The newspapers were usually distributed at churches, grocery stores, barbershops, and restaurants in local black communities, and many students produced works written for audiences that frequented those venues. These readers were members of tight-knit communities who would have been familiar to their young black neighbors. Freedom School students engaged with their fellow black citizens in a number of different ways.

The most basic engagement came through a series of movement updates in which students reported the latest news from the front lines of activism and encouraged the involvement of others. For example, the July 20 issue of the *Drew Freedom Fighter* opened with an update about a recent organizational meeting. The unnamed author of this movement update detailed some of the meeting's main points, described the crowd's overall mood, and reported the arrest of approximately twenty-five attendees.[18] A similar article in the July 16 issue of the Greenwood *Freedom Carrier* outlined the goals of that city's upcoming "Freedom Day" protest and offered information about how to participate. "All people who believe in freedom," the article's unnamed author asserted, "should join us for Freedom Day."[19]

Even more provocatively, some Freedom School students used the newspapers to publicly shame inactive community members or offer declarations designed to sway opinions and inspire activism. In an August 11 editorial, the editors of the McComb *Freedom's Journal* expressed their disappointment with inactive community members. "Many of the adults in McComb are a great disappointment to their race," the students wrote. "Some will not let their children attend Freedom School because they are afraid. They will not even Freedom Register" (agree to be included in a mock voter registration).[20]

In the Hattiesburg *Freedom Press*, a young girl named Stephanie B. wrote an article titled "Our Day of Canvassing" in which she described a conflict with a local black woman. After being told "you little children don't know what you are doing. You don't know what freedom is," Stephanie B. and several other Freedom School students reported that they debated the woman about the importance of joining the movement. Stephanie wrote that she and her peers replied, "Oh yes we do. . . . We know more than you know," before pointing out multiple ways in which the movement could potentially improve the older woman's life.[21]

In Ruleville, a student named Ora Boss criticized the teachers at her local high school for their lack of action. "The teachers at Ruleville Central High School do not take any part in the registration program when we try to talk to them," Ora wrote. "We will put forth every effort to change them because how can they teach us how to be first class citizens when they are not citizens themselves." In McComb, a sixteen-year-old student named Joyce Brown composed an emotional poem called "Houses of Liberty," in which she shamed the local black community for its inaction. "Because you've let fear conquer your soul," Brown chastised, "I must try to teach them to stand tall and be a man. When you, their parents, have cowered down and refused to make a stand."[22]

Other students offered testimonials of their own experiences that similarly critiqued Jim Crow by exposing its immorality. Benton County Freedom School student Mary Francie Harris composed an essay describing her family's difficult lives as cotton pickers. She wrote about how hard her father worked—from seven o'clock in the morning to six at night—for very little pay, describing the destitute conditions facing many Mississippi sharecropping families. But young Mary was optimistic that the movement was going to improve her family's lives. She connected the movement with better opportunities for her future, noting, "This year the people from all over the United States have come to help us. All we can say is we want freedom; everybody wants freedom. So, people, lift up your head and let your light shine. Let's begin to act like human beings."[23]

One of Mary's classmates, Archie B. Richard, wrote an essay describing his daily challenges as an African American in the Jim Crow South. "So many times we have to go to windows of cafes while Whites go inside," Archie wrote. "We go to stores and are there first, but then Whites come in and are waited on first. Or we may be walking alone minding our own business and whites come along and meddle, or maybe throw something or yell at you." "We have been treated badly so long by the Whites [*sic*]," noted Archie, "it's time someone made a change about this situation." Students whose lives had been clouded by racial segregation used the Freedom News to detail and critique the racial mores of their society.[24]

Freedom School students also used the spaces offered by the Freedom News to engage white powerbrokers. One girl named Lynette Y. addressed Mississippi Governor Paul B. Johnson, voicing her displeasure over Jim Crow segregation and the denial of voting rights at the state level. "I want to be able to vote when I am twenty-one," the young black girl told the governor of her state, adding, "And I want to be a first-class citizen."[25]

Some students wrote directly to President Lyndon B. Johnson, asking or even demanding for their freedom. They mailed these letters to the White House. Correspondence reprinted in the *Student Voice of True Light* demonstrated how a group of Hattiesburg Freedom School students appealed to President Johnson for better treatment. Donny E. said, "We want freedom . . . we do not want the policeman to beat up anyone else." Linda D. wrote, "Thank you for signing the Civil Rights Bill. We are so glad to know that someone is on our side." Dennis B. wrote, "I'm asking you for our freedom. Will you give us our freedom?" Student Anthony E., aware of the constant danger facing civil rights activists in Mississippi, asked President Johnson "to send more people down here to protect the people and Civil Rights workers in this state. Then there will be no more bombing and fighting."[26]

Freedom School students packed the discursive spaces offered by the Freedom News with bold declarations of freedom rooted in the fundamental language and concepts of American democracy. In the town of Palmer's Crossing, an ambitious group of students published their own

Declaration of Independence, noting, "In the course of human events, it has become necessary for the Negro people to break away from the customs which have made it very difficult for the Negro to get his God-given rights." The Palmer's Crossing students argued that African Americans should have access to basic civil rights including better job opportunities, schools, and roads. After listing a series of government abuses such as public segregation and voter discrimination, the students at the Palmer's Crossing Freedom School "hereby declare[d] Independence from the unjust laws of Mississippi which conflict with the United States Constitution."[27]

The rhetoric of American democracy informed student expression. A fifteen-year-old Hattiesburg student named Glenda B. similarly invoked the United States Declaration of Independence, asserting "right to 'life, liberty, and the pursuit of happiness.'" McComb student Georgia Patterson pointed out that "the Declaration of Independence says that all men are created equal. But we are not treated equally. So when will we be treated equally? The law was made July 4, 1776, and it [is] now all the same in 1964."[28]

Other students wrote essays about the meaning of freedom in the United States and the need for African Americans to achieve political equality. The letters addressed to the president made fairly basic assertions and requests, but their power rests in the temerity and imagination of the young authors. These young black Mississippians, who for years had been told that the finest opportunities of their society were not for them, came to envision themselves engaging with other Americans—ranging from the president of the United States to local community members—to demand equal access to the promises of American democracy.

Anxious to demonstrate their resolve and defend the morality of their evolving beliefs, Freedom School students created and used literary spaces in the Freedom News to promote their causes and reaffirm their actions. It is impossible to definitively explain how each writer envisioned his or her audience. The newspapers did not have formal subscription lists or track precise circulation figures. Surely, each writer or group of students held different expectations for their paper's audience and potential influence. And although some certainly did believe members of their local communities would read the newspaper articles and perhaps be persuaded into action, others probably had no hope that their words would ever reach or impact the individuals they were addressing, especially prominent political figures such as the governor or president. But regardless of audience, there was something powerful about the experience of expression and composition. As young people of color living amid a white supremacist racial order, they had spent much of their lives having racial parameters dictated to them. Freedom School newspapers helped provide a voice for many and allowed them to intellectually engage their society in multiple ways. Young people were involved in virtually every aspect of the civil rights movement, especially in school integration cases and in major demonstrations such as the 1963 Birmingham Children's Crusade. The Mississippi Freedom School newspapers provide a unique glimpse into the intellectual responses of young civil rights activists who used the opportunity to publicly address their own oppression and outline better hopes for the future.[29]

The Freedom School newspapers also demonstrate exceptional opportunities for intellectual liberation during the classical phase of the Southern civil rights movement, which is typically understood to have occurred between 1954 and 1968. Much of the literature of the later 1960s focuses on the emergence of the Black Power movement, a political and cultural phenomenon that historian Rod Bush argues emerged, in part, from "Black people's awareness that the civil rights movement did not address the key issues that would result in genuine empowerment." But the evidence provided in the writings of Freedom School students demonstrates a similar dynamic of empowerment more commonly associated with the Black Power movement. As William Van Deburg has argued, "In truth, the empowering spirit of blackness which came to characterize the late sixties movement was evident, in embryo, in the Freedom Schools and cultural enrichment programs which operated in Mississippi during the summers of 1964 and 1965." The newspapers produced by Freedom School students offer a unique vision of the process of empowerment available to young people during the nonviolent desegregation campaigns of the civil rights movement.[30]

Finally, the words of students who wrote for the Freedom News demonstrate an important but often overlooked component in the struggle for educational equality. As evidenced by the Freedom School newspapers, black students needed unrestricted intellectual spaces just as much as they needed better books, classrooms, and teachers. The Freedom News provided spaces of academic freedom for black youths who took brazen stands against racial injustice, engaged multiple audiences, critiqued older adults, and immersed themselves in the civil rights movement by asserting resolve to forever resist racial inequality.

Notes

1. "Important," *The Freedom News*, July 10, 1964, 2, box 6, folder 4, Staughton and Alice Lynd Papers (hereafter Lynd Papers), Kent State University Libraries Special Collections and Archives, Kent, OH.

2. Freedom Schools in Holly Springs and Palmer's Crossing each produced a newspaper named the *Freedom News*.

3. Bossie Mae Harring, "The Fight for Freedom," *Drew Freedom Fighter*, July 20, 1964, 1, box 1, folder 2, Tecklin Papers, State Historical Society of Wisconsin, Madison, WI (hereafter WHS).

4. C. R. Darden, "The President Speaks," memorandum, March 25, 1959, and C. R. Darden, "Dear Branch Officers," memorandum, September 8, 1959, both found in box 2, folder 29, Evers (Medgar and Myrlie) Papers, Mississippi Department of Archives and History (hereafter MDAH), Jackson, MS. For more on the Mississippi school equalization program, see Charles Bolton, *The Hardest Deal of All: The Battle over School Integration in Mississippi, 1870–1980* (Jackson: University Press of Mississippi, 2007), especially 117–66.

5. Statistics taken from Bolton, *The Hardest Deal of All*, 87.

6. See N. R. Burger, interview with R. Wayne Pyle, transcript, May 11, 1982, Hattiesburg, MS, Mississippi Oral History Program of the University of Southern Mississippi, Hattiesburg, MS; and John Dittmer, *Local People: The Struggle for Civil Rights in Mississippi* (Urbana: University of Illinois Press), especially 194–214; and Yashuhiro Katagiri, *The Mississippi State Sovereignty Commission: Civil Rights and States' Rights* (Jackson: University Press of Mississippi, 2001).

7. *Census of the Population: 1960, Volume I, Characteristics of the Population: Part 26, Mississippi* (Washington, DC: Government Printing Office, 1961), 26–118; Dittmer, *Local People*, esp. 194–214; and "Mississippi Freedom Schools," box 98, folder 8, Student Nonviolent Coordinating Committee Records (hereafter, SNCC Papers), 1959–72, Martin Luther King Jr. Center for Nonviolent Social Change, King Library and Archives (hereafter King Center), Atlanta.

8. For more on the Highlander influence on the Freedom School curriculum and pedagogy, see Jon Hale, "Early Pedagogical Influences on the Mississippi Freedom Schools: Myles Horton and Critical Education in the Deep South," *American Educational History Journal* 34, no. 2 (2007): 315–30.

9. Staughton Lynd, interview with William Sturkey, December 8, 2009, Niles, OH, recording in author's possession; "Participants at the COFO Curriculum Conference," "Curriculum Planning for Summer Project," and "Curriculum Planning for Summer Project" all found in box 5, folder 6, Records of the Mississippi Freedom Democratic Party, 1964–65, King Center; and Sandra Adickes, *Legacy of a Freedom School* (New York: Palgrave Macmillan, 2005), esp. 23–52.

10. "Freedom School Data," box 1, folder 4, Bowie Papers, WHS; and Arthur Reese, "Freedom Schools—Summer 1964," *Detroit Teacher*, December 1964, 4.

11. "Mississippi Freedom Schools," box 98, folder 8, SNCC Papers.

12. Judy Walborn, "Dear Staughton, Tom, and Sue," July 7, 1964, box 14, folder 17, Records of the Mississippi Freedom Democratic Party, 1964–65.

13. Untitled Correspondence from Staughton Lynd, n.d., box 6, folder 3, Lynd Papers; "Notice to Students of the Meridian Freedom School," Meridian *Freedom Star*, July 30, 1964, 4, box 4, folder 3, Mark Levy Collection, Queens

College Benjamin S. Rosenthal Library Special Collections, Flushing, NY; and "Important," *Freedom News*, July 10, 1964, 2, box 6, folder 4, Lynd Papers.

14. Ira B. Harkey, Jr., *The Smell of Burning Crosses: An Autobiography of a Mississippi Newspaper Man* (Jacksonville, FL: Harris-Wolfe, 1967), quoted on 47.

15. P. D. East, *The Magnolia Jungle: The Life, Times, and Education of a Southern Editor* (New York: Simon and Schuster, 1960); Harkey, Jr., *The Smell of Burning Crosses*; and David L. Bennett, "Ira B. Harkey, Jr., and the Pascagoula Chronicle," in *The Press and Race: Mississippi Journalists Confront the Movement*, ed. David R. Davies (Jackson: University Press of Mississippi, 2001).

16. "Arrington High as Told to Marc Crawford, *Jet* Exclusive: I Escaped Mississippi in a Casket," *Jet*, February 27, 1958, 11–13; Julius E. Thompson, *The Black Press in Mississippi, 1865–1985* (Gainesville: University Press of Florida, 1994); Julius Eric Thompson, "Mississippi," in Henry Lewis Suggs, ed., *The Black Press in the South* (Westport, CT: Greenwood Press, 1993), 177–210; and Julian Williams, "The Truth Shall Make You Free: The *Mississippi Free Press*, 1961–1963," *Journalism History* 32 (Summer 2006): 106–13. For more on the response of Mississippi's white media outlets to the civil rights movement, see Steven D. Classen, *Watching Jim Crow: The Struggles over Mississippi TV, 1955–1969* (Durham, NC: Duke University Press, 2004); and Susan Weill, *In a Madhouse's Din: Civil Rights Coverage by Mississippi's Daily Press, 1948–1968* (Westport, CT: Praeger, 2002).

17. Thompson, "Mississippi," especially 192. The *Benton County Freedom Train* lasted for at least four years after Freedom Summer.

18. Untitled article in *Drew Freedom Fighter*, July 20, 1964, 1, box 1, folder 2, Tecklin Papers, WHS.

19. "Freedom Day in Greenwood," *Freedom Carrier*, July 16, 1964, 1, box 101, folder 3, SNCC Papers.

20. "A Word from the Editors," McComb *Freedom's Journal*, August 11, 1964, 1, box 98, folder 9, SNCC Papers.

21. Stephanie B., "Our Day of Canvassing," *Freedom Press*, n.d., 1, box 2, folder 3, Ellin (Joseph and Nancy) Freedom Summer Collection (hereafter, Ellin Papers), University of Southern Mississippi, McCain Library and Archives, Hattiesburg, MS.

22. Ora Boss, "From the Ruleville Student Action Group," *Drew Freedom Fighter*, July 20, 1964, 1, box 1, folder 2, Tecklin Papers; and Joyce Brown, "The House of Liberty," *Freedom's Journal*, July 24, 1964, 3, box 98, folder 9, SNCC Papers.

23. Mary Francie Harris, "How We Live in Mississippi," *Benton County Freedom Train*, July 1, 1964, 1, box 1, folder 4, Bowie Papers.

24. Archie B. Richard, "The Negroes and Whites," *Benton County Freedom Train*, July 1, 1964, 2, box 1, folder 4, Bowie Papers.

25. Lynette Y., "Dear Gov. Johnson," *Freedom Press*, n.d., 1, box 2, folder 3, Ellin Papers.

26. Lynd, interview; and letters found in an undated edition of the *Student Voice of True Light*, 10–11, box 6, folder 3, Robert Beech Papers, 1963–72, WHS.

27. "Declaration of Independence," *Freedom News*, July 25, 1964, 7, box 1, folder 1, Adickes Papers, WHS.

28. Glenda B., "The Will to Be Free," Student Voice of True Light, 1, July 24, 1964, box 2, folder 3, Ellin Papers; and Georgia Patterson, "The Declaration of Independence," McComb *Freedom's Journal*, August 24, 1964, 5–6, box 98, folder 9, SNCC Papers.

29. For more on black youths in the civil rights movement, see Rebecca de Schweinitz, *If We Could Change the World: Young People and America's Long Struggle for Racial Equality* (Chapel Hill: University of North Carolina Press, 2011).

30. Rod Bush, *We Are Not What We Seem: Black Nationalism and Class Struggle in the American Century* (New York: New York University Press, 1999), 7; Russell Rickford, *We Are an African People: Independent Education, Black Power, and the Radical Imagination* (New York: Oxford University Press, 2016); and William L. Van Deburg, *New Day in Babylon: The Black Power Movement and American Culture, 1965–1975* (Chicago: University of Chicago Press, 1992), 49.

Chapter 12

A Learning Laboratory for Liberation

Black Power and the Communiversity of Chicago, 1969–78

Richard D. Benson II

The emergence of Black Power radicalism after 1966 changed the socio-political landscape of American society and marked the beginning of grassroots activism reflecting the sentiments of marginalized Black people. Ideologically and aesthetically, Black Power as a concept was viewed from a myriad of perspectives by society as whole. Most often, and as a consequence of the urban rebellions of the latter 1960s, Black Power as a violent force of corrosion was juxtaposed to the typically sociohistorically peaceful and passive activities of civil rights movement. This chapter investigates an often omitted historical legacy and site of the Black Power movement that embodied educational self-determinism, the Communiversity of Chicago. By providing counterhegemonic information and educational services, the Communiversity was a training ground that highlighted three critical elements of the Black Freedom movement: ideological rigor, educational praxis, and student-community relationship development/maintenance. Focusing on the Communiversity, this chapter centers the role of education in the movement as a tenet paramount to the liberation of Black people. Furthermore, it deconstructs the notion of Black Power movement organizations as solely erratic.

> The African American cultural identity has been and continues to be influenced by the U.S. social context, but it is essential to note that the African-American cultural orientation also represents an experiential context. Thus, while African Americans exist within the U.S. social context, they also exist within an African historical-cultural

> continuum that predates that social context and would continue to exist even if the nation-state and its social arrangements were to transform or demise.[1]

In February 1969 on Chicago's South Side, Black educators, students, college professors, activists, clergymen, and community organizers met for a month-long planning session to form an alternative Black education system in the city. This alternative education system would explicitly address the gross cultural, historical, and political deficiencies in the educational experiences of Black folks in Chicago. Black educators and student volunteers provided curriculum and instruction that critically intersected with Black life on a local, national, and transnational scale. From the February planning meetings, a Black congress was created that birthed the alternative *Black* independent "Communiversity."[2]

In many respects, the founding of the Communiversity reflects the pragmatic dimensions of a Black Power movement that by the late 1960s was emphasizing the need to resist capitalist cooptation and media manipulation while moving beyond slogans and fruitless activity. Black Power proponents grappled with the question of how the call for Black nationalist and internationalist solidarity to address white supremacy, capitalist exploitation, and imperialism should and could be articulated to everyday, working-class Black people. Masses of Black people—blue-collar workers, students, teachers, community organizers, and small business owners—wanted to improve their lives economically, culturally, and politically. To address these challenges, education advocates recognized that Black people must not only teach Black folks how to read, but they also had to teach Black people *what to read* to achieve liberation.[3] Therefore, Chicago of the late 1960s and early 1970s became an indigenous training site, a place in which Black sociopolitical resistance and the historical relationships that were connected to Chicago could be examined. To this end, the Communiversity came to epitomize an often overlooked and omitted perspective of the Black Power movement that displays an era that created educational processes, strategies, and critical study groups and provided intentional instruction for activists while creating institutions.

As a case study of an independent Black institution, this chapter argues that education and critical investigation were essential to achieving social, cultural, and historical liberation during the Black Power era. Historians of contemporary independent Black alternative institutions describe the intersections of political education and community organizing that fostered cultural pride in Black communities throughout the country.[4] The Communiversity, like other independent Black alternative educational institutions and think tanks of the late 1960s and 1970s, offered counterhegemonic instruction and curricula for students, educators, and activists to engage imbalanced power differentials for successful community control through educational and political enhancement. This chapter illustrates how the engagement of the Communiversity curriculum and instruction provided students with organizing models to frame and facilitate effective political participation.

Divided into four parts, this chapter explains the origins, development, and practices of the Communiversity in Chicago from the late 1960s through the late 1970s and concludes with the Communiversity's influence in and beyond Chicago. First, I briefly trace the origins of the Communiversity by describing the intersection of the national and local freedom struggles in Chicago roughly from 1963 to 1968. Second, I describe social and political events in Chicago that motivated student and youth organizing to bring about the Communiversity. This part also recounts efforts to establish the curriculum, pedagogy, personnel, mission, and programmatic structure of the Communiversity. Throughout this chapter, I identify the ideological threads that pervaded the work of the Communiversity as well as the key intellectual dynamics of the attempt to build and maintain a Black alternative educational system. Next, I focus on the national and international programs and political activities of the Communiversity. I conclude with a discussion of the Communiversity's contributions to the African Centered Movement in Chicago and the national and international Black freedom struggle.

Recognizing the significance of capturing this rich history, surviving members of the Communiversity gathered at the Northeastern Illinois University Jacob Carruthers Center for Inner City Studies on the South Side of Chicago in August 2011 to commemorate the legacy of the Communiversity. Dr. Harold Pates, founding member and instructor, called for the preservation of the legacy of the Communiversity as he recounted efforts to establish an alternative educational system. According to Pates, the institution arose amid "a national and international Black movement toward the development of Black universities across the country, that could and would address the students' enormous thirst for the scientific and historical truths."[5] Dr. Pates's statement reminds current historians of the urgent need to capture the movement's memories. In response to this call, this chapter on the Communiversity offers a nuanced history of Black sociopolitical and cultural life in Chicago during the Black Power era.

City of Fire: Background to the Communiversity

Chicago's second major wave of Black migration from the South came in the early 1940s, mainly from the states of Mississippi, Arkansas, and Alabama. Moving North to escape white terrorism, worker exploitation, and economic disenfranchisement, Black folks who migrated to the city established enclaves on the city's West and South Sides. The influx of Black Southerners moving to the North triggered discriminatory federal, state, and local housing policies and practices, which created restrictive covenants through blockbusting and redlining tactics among rental property owners, real estate agencies, and neighborhood associations. Despite the structural racism, Chicago's Black community thrived, and Black residents formed community strongholds such as the Black Belt of the South Side's "low-end" section, also known as Bronzeville.[6] Population increases also brought about massive public housing high-rises. According to historian Dionne Danns, "In 1964, Chicago's Black population was 930,000, while the city's White population decreased by 399,000 residents with the expansion of suburbs and transportation infrastructure."[7]

Restrictive covenants limiting financial and physical mobility for prospective Black homeowners, overcrowding, and the engineering of densely populated neighborhoods constrained Black life in the city. Paralleling this phenomenon was the overcrowding of the Chicago Public Schools system for Black elementary and high school students on the city's South and West Sides. While Black Chicagoans were reeling from a Northern version of discriminatory practices that excluded Black people from reaping economic benefits, neighborhood schools continued to suffer from white financial flight, a diminishing tax base, economic retrenchment at the municipal level, and overcrowding at the K-12 education levels. According to Danns:

> A 1957 Chicago National Association for the Advancement of Colored People (NAACP) report noted that due to de facto segregation, more than 90% of Chicago's students attended segregated schools. Many students were on double-shift assignments, where half came to school early and left early and the other half attended later and stayed in the afternoon. To combat overcrowding, Superintendent Benjamin Willis built or renovated 250 schools which led to the elimination of double-shift assignments by January 1963.[8]

Despite public outcry around overcrowding, Chicago's political power structure remained oblivious to the racist policies that engineered the conditions of the Black ghetto throughout the city. In fact, a vast majority of Chicago's white residents benefited in a diverse and vast array of the city's municipal sectors, which included politics, law, the labor force, jobs/careers city infrastructure maintenance, social services, job placement services, military veterans benefits, state and federal housing assistance, health care, and education. White backlash and fear of Black advancement throughout city neighborhoods and schools created Black ghettos and subhuman living conditions. Black teachers, students, and community activists continued to challenge the city's political establishment to improve the conditions of Black people.[9]

Spearheading the charge for civil and human rights advancement in Chicago during the mid-1960s was the Coordinating Council of Community Organizations (CCCO), the largest civil and human rights coalition in the country comprising over sixty national and Chicago-area organizations. Formed to challenge the Richard J. Daley mayoral administration,[10] the CCCO had working relationships with organizations such as the NAACP and the Student Nonviolent Coordinating Committee (SNCC). The CCCO organized the largest school protests in the nation with two respective boycotts of Chicago Public Schools in October 1963 and February 1964.[11] By 1965 Chicago had become a hotbed of political activity, with the Southern Christian Leadership Conference (SCLC) aiding the local Black community with a civil rights campaign aimed at attacking Northern racism and social inequities. Under the leadership of Martin Luther King Jr., the SCLC attempted to challenge the political machine of Richard J. Daley, which was deeply rooted in Irish Catholic nepotism, cronyism, and decades-long ethnic ties. Joining the Chicago Movement to put an end to slums in the summer of 1965, King decried the treatment of Black Chicagoans, stating, "The South is now a land of opportunity, while those who years ago, sang: *GOING TO CHICAGO, SORRY BUT I CAN'T TAKE YOU*, now sink into the depths of despair."[12]

College students and community youth created a major support base for SNCC, as the Friends of SNCC chapter in Chicago provided financial support for the organization that ushered in the energizing call for "Black Power" in 1966. Further heightening the political fervor of the Black Freedom movement in Chicago was the bold attempt of SNCC to implement the Black Project in Chicago under the direction of Monroe Sharp in early August 1966. Amid an increase of national and local militancy, Stokely Carmichael in a speech delivered to a Chicago audience on July 28, 1966, openly referred to Mayor Daley as a racist and chief custodian of Black exploitation in the city.[13]

By early 1968, the ideological current of the Black Power movement deeply influenced urban youth. Chicago held the world's attention as activists, intellectuals, and budding revolutionaries waited to see how the Black Freedom movement would fare against the city's political machine. As Black Power gained momentum in the city, Black students, parents, teachers, and community activists organized, held administrators accountable, and conducted and attended conferences to protest and mobilize efforts for Black youth in the city of Chicago.[14] These protests converged with the overt Black nationalist developments of the student movement on the high school and college levels where radicalized and restless Black students identified with the success of Fidel Castro and Che Guevara of the Cuban Revolution, the mounting global support for Ho Chi Minh and the Viet-Cong, and Malcolm X as martyr and symbol of the newly emerged era of Black Power.[15]

However, few events were more globally impactful than the assassination of Dr. Martin Luther King Jr. on April 4, 1968. This tragic event benchmarked the crucial uptick of student activism and campus takeovers by Black youth on college campuses around the country. In the inner cities of Washington, DC, Philadelphia, Cincinnati, Kansas City, Pittsburgh, and Detroit, Black folks took to the streets and rebelled against the white power structures of their municipalities. In Chicago, King's assassination led to Black people, both young and old, protesting in the streets of the city's West and South Sides. These actions were met with violent rejoinder from Mayor Richard J. Daley, who told the police to "shoot to kill . . . shoot to maim looters." Chicago officials now faced the threat of an even more racially and economically torn city.[16]

During Chicago's rebellion, nine people were killed, and over two hundred buildings were damaged. Black areas that could not afford further financial decline incurred major financial losses. Yet the uprisings in the "City of Big Shoulders" and other cities with dense Black populations signified a national charge by Black youth to reclaim their humanity. King's untimely death not only provoked Black youth to take to the streets in search of retribution; the historic tragedy also motivated many Black students to protest at their colleges and universities.

Black students at Cornell, Yale, Duke, and Howard took over administration buildings, locking administrators in their offices, and commandeered facilities to demand that Black students be recognized and treated with dignity. They demanded curricular changes, the hiring of additional Black faculty, and the establishment of Black studies programs on campuses nationwide. The mobilization of Black students served as a kind of political education, preparing young activists to launch further challenges to anti-Black racism and discrimination in higher education.[17]

Bolstering this challenge was the national call for a "Black university" issued by Black students, revolutionaries, and scholars who hoped to establish autonomous educational institutions. Debating the idea in the *Negro Digest* (later known as the *Black World*), theorists argued that the Black university must raise the sociopolitical consciousness of Black folks and meet the "real and total needs" of the Black community.[18] In 1970, the scholar Ronald Davis noted the need to involve the Black community in the cultivation of the Black intellectual experience. According to Davis:

> We were aware that we not only had to "catch" people and direct them to the community—we were also aware that we had to give them something to take there. This was our thinking about the "catch" action and Black Studies at the time. Most important of all, perhaps, was that feature of our thinking on Black Studies, which opposed its institutionalization. It was our belief that if such a program was institutionalized it would, at the same time, be de-radicalized and reduced to a purely academic experience. And we could see no good coming from an isolated, sterile dissection of the Black Experience. We refused to consider any program that would not have arms for action.[19]

In Chicago, the call for a Black university inspired such radical actions as the renaming of Crane Junior College (located on the city's West Side) to Malcolm X College, as well as the demand for Black studies at Northwestern University and Roosevelt University. The eruption of activism led Black students, scholars, activists, clergymen, schoolteachers, and community organizers to collectively found the "Communiversity" in February 1969.[20] This activity established an epicenter for Chicago Black nationalist collective action in the 1970s.

Breaking Ground: Founding the Communiversity

The Communiversity originated at a national conference for Black teachers in Chicago in April 1968. Approximately 1,000 participants including teachers, administrators, academics professionals, radicals, community activists, parents, and students from across the country gathered to discuss the critical issues at the nexus of Black life and Black education.[21] They wrestled, debated, dialogued, and produced solutions to Black educational deficiencies that plagued Black youth in the city. Moving beyond ideological differences, they agreed that "the solutions to these problems could and would only come from Black educators who re-commit and re-dedicate their lives to these ends."[22]

At this conference a structure was created, duties were delegated, and the National Association of Afro-American Educators (NAAAE) was formed to research and engineer a multitude of measures necessary to educate the Black community. The planning meetings of the NAAAE also birthed the development of strong local community involvement to support the goals of the national NAAAE structure. The Chicago faction, for example, was adamant about local Black community participation because "the Madison Avenue style of executive management and hierarchical omnipotence had to be ruptured."[23]

In Chicago, local Black communities met and organized a month-long series of planning meetings. Inspired by the effectiveness of the Chicago local communities in developing tacit Black education models, Loyola students Robert Starks, Standish Willis, and Earl Jones organized a Black student conference for students throughout the Midwest region. The conference took place in Reverend John R. Porter's church, the United Methodist Church in Englewood, a pillar in the Black community and the site of the SCLC's first Chicago chapter.[24]

The initial planning meetings for the Midwest Black student conference were at Porter's church. Among the many students, scholars, school administrators, and activists were the founding members Drs. Anderson Thompson, Harold Pates, and Bobby Wright along with student activists Robert Starks, Standish Willis, John Higginson, Ruwa Chiri, and Professor Bob Rhodes. During the planning stage, the meetings moved from Porter's church to the Northeastern Illinois University Center for Inner City Studies (CICS) located in the old "Lincoln Library" building at 700 East Oakwood Boulevard in the Bronzeville section of Chicago. College students from throughout the Chicago area joined high school students, community activists, clergymen, scholars, teachers, and university professors in planning meetings. These gatherings produced a Black congress, comprising participants such as Drs. Jacob Carruthers, Bobby Wright, Standish Willis, Sarudzayi Sevanhu, Leon Harris, Conrad Worrill, Yvonne Jones, Bernetta Bush, Cathy McAbee, Abdul Alkalimat (formerly Gerald McWhorter), Shirley Hawkins, Thelma Meyers, and Bobby Womack. The Black Communiversity evolved from the Black congress, and the CICS became the meeting site for classes of the newly formed independent Black educational institution.[25]

As an alternative site, the Communiversity was formed as a space for Black educational advancement for the intergenerational transmission of African-centered modalities through an African-centered lens. From its inception, the Communiversity's aims were to address educational, political, and social deficiencies in Black Chicago. Black educational praxis and institution building for members of the Communiversity were developed to counter psychological hegemony and the educational vestiges of white supremacy. By executing critical pedagogy, curriculum, and research methodologies, the Communiversity became a collective, defensive base against white educational and cultural oppression.

To this end, the Communiversity would (1) help Black people critically comprehend local, national, and international events that affected Black life, (2) help Black folks understand Euro-American colonialism, (3) aid the Black professional who stood between the white colonial world and the Black resistance movement, (4) help Black students to establish a frame of reference for the general struggle, (5) help Black parents and children who were victimized and exploited by the educational system, and (6) help Black community organizations in continuing their charge to help improve Black life locally, domestically, and internationally—by becoming fully acquainted with the difference between organization and movement.[26] Under such a framework, the Communiversity became a cornerstone of Black educational activity in Chicago as the Black Power movement transitioned into the 1970s.

The Communiversity: Curriculum and Instruction

In the late winter of 1969 at the CICS on Chicago's South Side, the Communiversity initiated its program as Saturday school for hundreds of participants, including parents, elementary and high school students, community organizers, college students, Black nationalists, Black leftists, cultural nationalists, university professors, and scholar-activists.[27] The Communiversity operated under and reflected four streams of social, political, and historical thought:

African and African American Cultural Nationalism
The African Researcher
The African Centered/Black Psychologist
Marxist-Leftist/Socialist & Communist Thought[28]

The Communiversity offered courses in contemporary African affairs, colonial culture, Black law, Black social theory and analysis, contemporary African affairs, cooperatives, African American history, Black nationalism, psychology of Black nationalism, Swahili, Chinese, French,

Black arts, Black literature, and teaching techniques. Curriculum and instruction were based on three pedagogical modalities: (1) lectures, (2) research/study workshops, and (3) project-based learning.[29]

Instructors such as radical Black psychologist Dr. Bobby E. Wright taught classes on Black psychology and the history of Black nationalism. Dr. Jacob Carruthers provided instruction on African history, hieroglyphs, and Kemetic philosophy through his founding of the Kemetic Institute. Dr. Anderson Thompson constructed his course offerings as research workshops that engaged in critical study of the white and Black Left and traced the historical genealogy of the Left from the First Communist International in 1864 to the 1970s in a course titled "Marxism-Leninism and the Black Struggle." Thompson also had students research the organizational and financial intersections of the Left with the overall Black Freedom movement. Thompson's research workshops included "ethnotheocratic" investigations of Chicago's governmental structure that he referred to as a city composed of "warring European tribal states" made up of Catholic and Jewish power wielders with the Irish, Polish, and German power wielders completing the Euro-American cabal that undergirded the power structure of the "Windy City."[30]

Professor Bob Rhodes, who initially led study groups at the University of Chicago as early as 1967, was an expert economist and devoted Black leftist who lectured to larger audiences during the Saturday sessions. As an authority on the Left, Rhodes's instruction sought to integrate the Marxist paradigm into Black life, and he taught exhaustively on Marx, Lenin, Soviet political philosophy, left politics, globalism, and political economy. "According to Stan Willis, once [the students] got into Bob's classes, they wouldn't go to any other classes; so we had to cancel all the classes that conflicted with Bob . . . People never heard it before. People really liked it."[31] Rhodes, a self-proclaimed "ideas man" of the overall movement and intellectual resource of the Communiversity along with Wright, Carruthers, and Thompson, provided significant leadership for establishing the cultural and intellectual foundations of the Communiversity.[32]

In addition to the lecture, instruction, and workshop learning strategies utilized by the teachers and facilitators, the Communiversity developed the *Communiviews* news organ to promote the organization's programs and ideological perspectives and provide alternative news regarding Black Chicago. The Communiversity also hosted several keynote lectures from notable scholars such as John Henrik Clarke, Max Roach, Harold Cruse, Yosef ben Jochannan, Chancellor Williams, and Asa Hilliard.[33] As classroom instructors, scholars, and community activists, Communiversity members were grounded in African-centered work that required

Communiversity Schedule (Spring 1970)

SUBJECT	TIME	ROOM	INSTRUCTIOR
BLACK HISTORY	10:30 – 12:00	EMERSON HALL	ROBERT RHODES
CONTEMPORARY AFRICAN AFFAIRS	11:00 – 12:00	402	RUWA CHIRI
BLACK SOCIAL THEORY & ANALYSIS	12:00 – 1:00	402	ABDUL ALKALIMAT
AFRICAN AMERICAN HISTORY	12:00 1:00	403	LORENZO MARTIN
COLONIAL CULTURE	1:00 – 2:00	402	ANDERSON THOMPSON
COLONIAL MIND	1:00 – 2:00	403	JOE HOWARD
MODERN COLONIAL SOCIETY	1:00 – 2:00	401	HAROLD RODGERS
TEACHER TRAINING INSTITUTE	1:00 – 2:00	EMERSON HALL	HAROLD PATES
BLACK NATIONALISM	2:00 – 3:30	402	BOBBY WRIGHT
RELEVANT BIOLOGY	2:00 – 3:30	401	(MAGA JACKSON & RETHA TAYLOR)
SWAHILI	2:00 – 3:30	403	NOAH NGOTHA
CHINESE	2:00 – 3:30	516	LIN CHAO

3:30 p.m. (Alternately held) DIRECTORS

BLACK BOOKS DISCUSSION -----------------HOYT FULLER, BEVERLY BALL

COMMUNITY FORM -------------------------BILL SPELLER, BOBBY WRIGHT

Fig. 5. Communiversity schedule of classes, spring 1970. Source: Abdul Alkalimat.

praxis for their activist goals to become a reality. Aligning theory to practice required pedagogical application that exceeded the confines of the Saturday classroom spaces held on Oakwood Boulevard; therefore, Communiversity participants needed to exemplify the meaning of field-based scholar activists in order to maximize their alternative Black educational experiences.

The Communiversity: Programming and Activities 1970–77

As the winds of change signaled a shift in the sociopolitical, and cultural consciousness for Black America, comprehensions of the Black Power movement evolved to intensify the budding relationships with the anti-imperialist and anticolonial struggles taking place on the African continent. Black Power consciousness morphed into an understanding and mantra of "We are an African people" that students and activists nationally adopted to support the eradication of African exploitation. In this international struggle, Black political power remained constant, and in the spirit of Malcolm X, the work to execute a Black united political party remained as a pressing agenda.[34]

To support these efforts, the Chicago Communiversity increased their participation on a local and transnational level by sending a delegation to Gary, Indiana, in March 1972 to participate in the National Black Political Convention along with ten thousand Black people from across the United States. In May 1973 as a Midwest regional site for the African Liberation Support Committee, the Communiversity and the Confederation of African Organizations spearheaded Chicago's first African Liberation Day parade and festivities. In June 1974, members of Communiversity leadership, Drs. Anderson Thompson and Bobby Wright along with Haki Madhubuti, became delegates and attended the Sixth Pan-African Congress in Dar es Salaam, Tanzania. To advance scholarship and practice in African-centered culture and epistemologies, in 1975 Dr. Jacob Carruthers took an academic leave to study at the University of Dakar with the renowned African historian, archeologist, physicist, and politician Dr. Cheikh Anta Diop. Upon the encouragement of Diop, Carruthers began intense study that evolved into an extensive research agenda into Medew Netcher (divine speech), also known as Egyptian hieroglyphs or the language of ancient Kemet. From this scholarly endeavor, Dr. Carruthers founded the Kemetic Institute in the fall of 1977 for the purpose of offering courses on ancient African languages, history, culture, and religion with a targeted interest in Kemet. Born out of the Communiversity, the Kemetic Institute provided curricular and pedagogical development for researchers and instructors at all levels of education.[35]

To bolster Communiversity programming, the think tank developed a significant relationship with the Organization of Black American Culture (OBAC). Established by Conrad Kent Rivers, Hoyt Fuller, and Abdul Alkalimat in 1967, the collective became a vanguard in the Black arts and literary movement of the Black Power era both in Chicago and on the national scene. Working in conjunction with the Communiversity to provide programming for Black Chicago, OBAC and the Communiversity developed the Black Forum Speakers Series, which highlighted the work of notable scholars that included C. L. R. James, Frantz Fanon, Albert Memmi, C. T. Vivian, Richard Wright, and Herman C. Gilbert. Every fourth Saturday of the month, the Communiversity and OBAC hosted the series with participation from notables such as Sterling Plumpp,

David L. Crowder, and George E. Kent.[36] The Black Forum Speakers Series at the Communiversity complemented the curricular advancements offered every Saturday by providing additional promotions to attract more members and provide exposure to the works of authors, playwrights, poets, activists, and professors throughout the Chicagoland area.

The advancement of the Communiversity curriculum by the mid-1970s was further influenced by the local happenings of Chicago and the nation. Communiversity teachers were leading forums, teacher trainings workshops, and lectures on Black studies and Pan-Africanism across the city. Still, the desire to conjoin Communiversity classroom study with international field study remained constant in the ideological developments of the independent Black institution. Thus, in July 1977, Drs. Carruthers and Thompson conducted the first Communiversity study tour on the African continent in the countries of the Sudan, Kenya, and Egypt. Concurrently, Dr. Anderson Thompson led study tours to Bahia el Salvador, Brazil, to further expose students to Pan-Africanism and culture in the Western Hemisphere and to deepen the curricular praxis of the Communiversity to that of the Pan-African diaspora.[37]

The Communiversity: Legacy and Contributions in the Black Freedom Struggle

By 1978, the Communiversity had spawned a number of organizations and projects as a result of Communiversity students and instructors advancing their careers as teachers, college professors, community activists, lawyers, ministers, and scholars. Communiversity's programming and influences led to the establishment of the Arusha-Konarki Institute, the Association of African American Educators, the Association of African Historians (AAH), and the National Committee on African Affairs. Organizations such as the AAH created the *Afrocentric World Review* and the *AAH Newsletter* as a base of continuous writing and scholarly advancements for the movement. By the late 1970s and into the 1980s, the Communiversity's momentum shifted, and two significant organizations were developed: the National Black United Front in 1980 and the National Black Independent Political Party.[38]

Communiversity notables such as Drs. Bobby E. Wright, Jacob Carruthers, and Anderson Thompson each became Black thought leaders whose scholarship directly influenced the development of the Communiversity. Dr. Wright developed his seminal scholarship *The Psychopathic Racial Personality* (1974) and *Mentacide: The Ultimate Threat to Black*

Survival (1979) during his time as a Communiversity instructor. Dr. Jacob Carruthers's development of the Kemetic Institute and his research on Kemetic language, history, and culture emerged from his immersion in the Communiversity throughout the 1970s. Drs. Carruthers and Thompson are often credited with cultivating the Chicago school of African-centered thought. In support of this notion, Dr. Carruthers authored numerous works that became foundational in Black studies and Kemetic studies. Dr. Carruthers's works include *Intellectual Warfare* (1999), *Essays in Egyptian Studies* (1984), and *The Irritated Genie* (1985). Dr. Anderson Thompson's work as a school administrator, professor, scholar, activist, and mentor throughout the Black freedom struggle provided tutelage in both scholarship and a covert style of leadership that sustained the life of the Communiversity that almost experienced a revitalization as an independent institution by 1980. Although this effort at a relaunch of the Communiversity was unsuccessful, Dr. Thompson along with Dr. Carruthers traveled to Los Angeles, California, in 1984 to become founding members of the Association for the Study of Classical African Civilizations (ASCAC). ASCAC hosted the organization's first national conference in 1985 in Chicago at Chicago State University. By the late 1980s, under the leadership of Thompson and Carruthers, ASCAC held its fourth annual conference in Aswan, Egypt, with over one thousand attendees representing the African diaspora.[39]

The Communiversity's legacy largely reflects the traditions of educational empowerment personified by enslaved Africans who risked life and limb to learn to read. The Communiversity legacy encapsulates the sweat equity newly freed Africans poured into the creation of Sabbath schools and community schools built throughout the American South. The revival of those traditions emerges throughout the early 1960s in the Freedom Schools of the SNCC and in the liberation school of Malcolm X's Organization of Afro-American Unity. However, the fight for cultural recovery through alternative education that emerged in the Black Power movement of the late 1960s is as distinct as the sociopolitical forces that created the Black Power movement. The national call for Black studies by high school and college Black students signaled a massive outpouring of both traditional and alternative Black independent educational institutions of which the Chicago Communiversity stands as a vanguard. The Communiversity became a vessel for the creation of ideology and Black organizational and institutional production, which can be found both in the history of the Black Power movement and in contemporary organizations that continue the legacy of research, teaching, and scholarship for the advancement of Black life in the maroon tradition.[40]

Notes

1. Mwalimu Shujaa, "Education and Schooling: You Can Have One without the Other," in *Too Much Schooling, Too Little Education: A Paradox of Black Life in White Societies* (Trenton, NJ: Africa World Press, 1994), 14–15.

2. Conrad Worrill, "Part 2: Chicago and the African Centered Movement," *South Shore Current*, June 2017, 7–9; William L. Van Deburg, *The New Day in Babylon: The Black Power Movement and American Culture, 1965–1975* (Chicago: University of Chicago Press, 1992), 76–78.

3. Dr. Abdul Alkalimat in discussion with the author March 2009; Dr. Alkalimat, who was one of the original instructors and organizers for the Communiversity and also for the OBAC, spoke extensively about his activities in organizing the second iteration of the Peoples College in Nashville, Tennessee, during the late 1960s/early 1970s. Dr. Alkalimat spoke of how the first Peoples College under the direction of Dr. Charles Johnson in the 1930s taught people how to read. However, the resurrected Peoples College of the Black Power era was teaching people *what to read*. In the context of radical Black education in Chicago with the establishment of the Communiversity, the statement is equally befitting.

4. The past decade has provided the emergence of Black Power studies, a subfield of history from which significant contributions have been made in the unpacking of a complex era of American history. From this scholarly awakening, a number of insightful manuscripts have been produced that have highlighted the nexus of the Black Freedom movement and the alternative education institutions that emerged. Contributing to this canon of works are Peniel E. Joseph, "Dashikis and Democracy: Black Studies, Student Activism, and the Black Power Movement," *Journal of African American History* 88, no. 2 (Spring 2003), 182–203; *Waiting till the Midnight Hour: A Narrative History of Black Power* (New York: Henry Holt, 2006); Richard D. Benson II, *Fighting for Our Place in the Sun: Malcolm X and the Radicalization of the Black Student Movement, 1960–1973* (New York: Peter Lang, 2015); Russell Rickford, *We Are an African People: Independent Education, Black Power, and the Radical Imagination* (Oxford: Oxford University Press, 2016); Kwasi Konadu, *Truth Crushed to the Earth Will Rise Again: The East Organization and the Principles and Practice of Black Nationalist Development* (Trenton, NJ: African World Press, 2012). Recent works that examine the relationships between the Black campus movement and the emergence of both Black studies departments and alternative community educational institutions and formations are Cecil Brown, *Dude, Where's My Black Studies Department?: The Disappearance of Black Americans from Our Universities* (Berkeley, CA: North Atlantic Books, 2007); Ibram H. Rogers, *The Black Campus Movement: Black Students and the Racial Reconstruction of Higher Education, 1965–1972* (New York: Palgrave Macmillan, 2012); Martha Biondi, *The Black Revolution on Campus* (Los Angeles: University of California Press, 2014), and Fabio Rojas, *From Black Power to Black Studies: How a Radical Social Movement Became an Academic Discipline* (Baltimore: Johns Hopkins University Press, 2007).

5. Harold Pates, "The Original Communiversity: Very Short History and Purpose—'Rebirth,'" unpublished paper, Dr. Conrad Worrill's private collection; "All African World University Presents: The Original Communiversity Research

Reunion Conference August 19th and 20th, 2011," reunion flier, in author's possession.

6. Dionne Danns, "Black Empowerment and Chicago School Reform Efforts in 1968," *Urban Education* 37, no. 5 (2002), 635–36; see also *The Warmth of Other Suns: The Epic Story of America's Great Migration* (New York: Vintage, 2011) by Isabel Wilkerson, with specific attention to Wilkerson's part 4 section on Chicago. For additional information on the two phases of the great migration to Chicago specifically, also see the works of historian Timuel Black, *Bridges of Memory: Chicago First Wave of Migration* (Evanston, IL: Northwestern University Press, 2005); *and Bridges of Memory: Chicago's Second Generation of Black Migration* (Evanston, IL: Northwestern University Press, 2008).

7. Danns, "Black Empowerment and Chicago School Reform Efforts in 1968."

8. Danns, "Black Empowerment and Chicago School Reform Efforts in 1968"; see also Preston H. Smith II, *Racial Democracy and the Black Metropolis: Housing Policy in Postwar Chicago* (Minneapolis: University of Minnesota Press, 2012).

9. Dionne Danns, "Racial Ideology and the Sanctity of the Neighborhood School in Chicago," *Urban Review* 40 (2008): 74.

10. Reverend Kwame John R. Porter, "The Greatest Black Generation," in *Rise of the Phoenix: Voices from Chicago's Black Struggle, 1960–1975*, ed. Useni Eugene Perkins (Chicago: Third World Press, 2017), 333.

11. Abdul Alkalimat and Doug Gills, *Harold Washington and the Crisis of Black Power in Chicago, Vol. 1: Mass Protest* (Chicago: Twenty First Century Books & Publications), 136.

12. "SCLC Starts Movement to End Slums," *Southern Christian Leadership Conference Newsletter*, January–February 1966, 6, Black History Collection/ James Bevel Collection, box 1, folder 11, University of Illinois at Chicago Archives.

13. "Black Power Issue: Notes and Comment Published by: Student Nonviolent Coordinating Committee," August issue, Black History Collection/James Bevel Collection, box 1, folder 11, University of Illinois at Chicago Archives.

14. Danns, "Black Empowerment," 637; also by Danns, see "Chicago High School Students' Movement for Quality Public Education," *Journal of African American History* 88, no. 2 (2003): 138–50.

15. S. E. Anderson, "Racial Consciousness and the Class Struggle, 1960–1976," *Black Scholar: Journal of Black Studies and Research* 8, no. 4 (1977): 35–43; Joseph, "Dashikis and Democracy"; Richard D. Benson II, "Black Student-Worker Revolution and Reparations: The National Association of Black Students, 1969–1972," *Phylon: The Clark Atlanta University of Race and Culture* 54, no. 1 (2017): 57–78.

16. Dave Potter and Bob Hunter, "Black Office Holders Rap Daley's Shoot, Kill Edict," *Chicago Daily Defender*, April 18, 1968, 3; Donald Mosby, "Black Cops, Lawyers 'Shocked' by Shoot to Kill Statement," *Chicago Daily Defender*, April 16, 1968, 3; Guest Editorial, *Milwaukee Star*, April 24, 1968.

17. Vincent Harding, "Black Students and the 'Impossible' Revolution," *Ebony*, August 1969, 141–48; Joseph, "Dashikis and Democracy."

18. Ronald Davis, "The Black University: In Peril before Birth," *Negro Digest/ Black World* 19 (1970): 12–19.

19. Davis, "The Black University," 17.

20. Charles G. Hurst "Malcolm X: A Community College with a New Perspective," *Negro Digest* 19 (1970), 30–36; Communiversity Research/Reunion Conference flier, August 19 (4 p.m.–9 p.m.) and 20 (9 a.m.–4 p.m.), 2011, in author's possession.

21. Rickford, *We Are an African People*, 58–59; Konadu, *Truth Crushed to the Earth Will Rise Again*, 54.

22. *Communiviews*, "An Alternative Independent System," May 1970, 1, Ansel Wong Papers, Black Cultural Archives, London, England.

23. "An Alternative Independent System: The Communiversity by the Staff, Students and Parents," *Negro Digest/Black World* 19 (1970): 25.

24. Pates, "The Original Communiversity"; Reverend Dr. Kwame John Hall Porter Interview with the History Makers, December 10, 2003; Robert Starks, "Remembering Robert Rhodes, Professor Emeritus of African American Studies," *Chicago Defender*, January 6, 2016.

25. *Communiviews*; Worrill, "Chicago and the African Centered Movement," "Fall 1977 Communiversity sessions information packet," Dr. Conrad Worrill private collection, 8; Pates, "The Original Communiversity."

26. *Communiviews*, 3.

27. "An Alternative Independent System: The Communiversity by the Staff, Students and Parents," *Negro Digest/Black World* 19 (1970): 28–29.

28. Robert Starks, "Remembering Robert Rhodes: Professor Emeritus of African American Studies," *Chicago Defender*, January 6, 2016.

29. Starks, "Remembering Robert Rhodes," 72. Throughout the 1970s, scheduling, courses, and instructors for the Communiversity were adjusted continuously to reflect the developments in scholarship, curriculum, and the availability of the instructors for Saturday classes. These adjustments were most visibly noted in the Communiversity September 1975 schedule of classes that offered karate, map and global skills, and a newly developed African forum series along with film showings on the second Friday of every month. The Communiversity's 1978 schedule of courses offered Arabic and French, basic photography, and a course on research and writing methods as complements to the existing battery of courses.

30. *Communiviews*, 3; "An Alternative Independent System: The Communiversity by the Staff, Students and Parents," *Negro Digest/Black World* 19 (1970), 28–29, 72.

31. Biondi, *The Black Revolution on Campus*, 112.

32. Biondi, *The Black Revolution on Campus*, 112; Starks, "Remembering Robert Rhodes."

33. Dr. Conrad Worrill in discussion with the author April 2017; Communiversity archives, Dr. Conrad Worrill private collection.

34. Robert Terrill, ed., *The Cambridge Companion to Malcolm X* (Cambridge: Cambridge University Press, 2010), 178–79; Stokely Carmichael (Kwame Ture), *Stokely Speaks; From Black Power to Pan-Africanism* (Chicago: Lawrence Hill Books, 2007), 113, 130, 183; Bob Brown (All African Peoples Revolutionary Party member, 1971–present) in discussion with the author, July 2018. Kwame Ture (Stokely Carmichael), who is famously credited with coining the term "Black Power," is also one of the first to use the phrase "We are an African people," which he first used February 17, 1968, in his speech delivered at the Free Huey

Rally in Oakland, California. Ture would later use the phrase throughout 1968, and the slogan was also later adopted by the organization founded by Ture, the All African Peoples Revolutionary Party. The slogan became a leading mantra of Pan-Africanism throughout the 1970s. Also see the speech delivered by Ture at Morehouse College in Atlanta and Federal City College in Washington, DC, in March and April 1970, respectively.

35. Worrill, "Chicago and the African Centered Movement," 8–9. For more information on the historical significance of the Sixth Pan-African Conference for Black activists in the 1970s, see Fanon Che Wilkins, "A Line of Steel: The Organization of the Sixth Pan-African Congress and the Struggle for International Black Power, 1969–1974," in *The Hidden 1970s: Histories of Radicalism*, ed. by Dan Berger (New Brunswick, NJ: Rutgers University Press, 2010).

36. Abdul Alkalimat aka Gerald McWhorter, "How OBAC Was Born: A Personal Memoir," in *Rise of the Phoenix: Voices From Chicago's Black Struggle, 1960–1975* (Chicago: Third World Press Foundation, 2017), 56–61; "Poet to Speak at OBAC Black Forum Series," *Chicago Daily Defender*, January 26, 1970, 11; "Black Literature Is Forum Topic," *Chicago Daily Defender*, March 28, 1970, 13; "Sociologist Speaks on 'Black Forum' Series," *Chicago Daily Defender*, February 24, 1970; Hoyt W. Fuller Collection, Atlanta University Center Robert W. Woodruff Library, box 17, folder 13; "Correspondence from Hoyt Fuller to Bernetta Bush 5/13/1970 re: Black Forum Series"; "Correspondence from Hoyt Fuller to Bernetta Bush 3/11/1970 re: Black Forum Series"; "Correspondence from Hoyt Fuller to Bernetta Bush 5/8/1970 re: Black Forum Series"; "Correspondence from Hoyt Fuller to Anderson Thompson 1/23/1970 re: Black Forum Series & Chicago Defender"; "Correspondence from Hoyt Fuller to Bernetta Bush 1/23/1970 re: Black Forum Series"; "Correspondence from Hoyt Fuller to Bernetta Bush 1/26/1970 re: Black Forum Series." Hoyt W. Fuller Collection, box 17, folder 13; William Barrow, "Status Quo Ante in Chicago: The Wall" (published draft) Hoyt W. Fuller Collection, box 23, folder 26.

37. Worrill, "Chicago and the African Centered Movement," 8–9.

38. Worrill, "Chicago and the African Centered Movement"; Dr. Conrad Worrill in discussion with the author, April 2017.

39. Worrill, "Chicago and the African Centered Movement"; Dr. Conrad Worrill in discussion with the author;"Good Night, Good Knight," *New African*, 426 (2004): 66.

40. For information on the establishment of Black schools in the postantebellum South, see the seminal work of James D. Anderson, *Education of Blacks in South, 1860–1935* (Chapel Hill: University of North Carolina Press, 1988); see also Vanessa Siddle Walker, *Their Highest Potential: An African American School Community in the Segregated South* (Chapel Hill: University of North Carolina Press, 1996). For an exhaustive review of SNCC's Freedom Schools, see Jon N. Hale, *The Freedom Schools: Student Activists in the Mississippi Civil Rights Movement* (New York: Columbia University Press, 2016). See also the foundational work of Clayborne Carson, *In Struggle: SNCC and the Black Awakening of the 1960s* (Cambridge, MA: Harvard University Press, 1995); and the biographical work of Diane Fujino on Japanese American Black freedom struggle activist Yuri Kochiyama, who joined the Organization of Afro-American Unity (OAAU) after Malcolm X's departure from the Nation of Islam. Chapter

5 of Fujino's book, "Meeting Malcolm X," provides detailed information of the OAAU Liberation School and the programs provided in the school's short tenure. For information on Black studies in the Black Power movement and on the independent Black institution building, see the following scholarship: Joseph, "Dashikis and Democracy" and *Waiting till the Midnight Hour*; Benson, *Fighting for Our Place in the Sun*; Rickford, *We Are an African People*; Konadu, *Truth Crushed to the Earth Will Rise Again*; Biondi, *The Black Revolution on Campus*; and Rojas, *From Black Power to Black Studies*.

Chapter 13

Toward a Black Pacific

Leo Hannett and Black Power in Papua New Guinea

Quito Swan

In 1970, in the morning hours of one of many "anticolonialist hate sessions," twelve students at the University of Papua New Guinea (UPNG) formed the Niugini Black Power Group (BGP). The BPG was composed of an emerging group of Black nationalist organizers who studied Africana cultural movements and liberation struggles. Through poetry, art, literature, debates, and demonstrations, the BPG went on to push for Black self-determination and political independence for Papua New Guinea, a colony of Australia located in the Melanesian region of Oceania. Engaging the ideas of Frantz Fanon, Negritude, Melanesian nationalism, and Pan-Africanism, the BPG engaged Black Power ideas within the context of Papua New Guinea, Oceania, and the freedom struggles of the Black world. For the organization's members, this meant a fight against ecological exploitation, police repression, Australian colonialism, Indonesian imperialism in West Papua, white power in Oceania, and imperial domination across the Global South.[1]

This chapter uses the BPG to highlight the global dynamics of Black Power in Oceania. It augments scholarship on Black intellectual history that has given limited attention to the Black Pacific, an understudied region of historical migration, exchange, and struggle on the part of African-descended people. Generally speaking, I would argue that the Black Pacific includes (1) the African Diaspora's literal and figurative engagements with the Pacific (including Asia and Oceania) and vice versa; (2) the experiences of indigenous communities of Oceania that were racialized as being Black or brown by European colonialism (namely, Melanesia, Polynesia, and Australia); and (3) the African-descended populations of the Pacific coast of the Americas who reached the region via the Atlantic slave trade and subsequent migration.

In terms of scholarship, Oceania is arguably the African diaspora's most marginalized region. The complicated notion of a Black Pacific raises significant questions for the mainstream orientation of the diaspora as an Atlantic world experience. Largely a narrative of involuntary migration stemming from the Atlantic slave trade (with a remerging focus on the Indian Ocean), diaspora studies has produced important themes such as slavery, resistance, Pan-Africanism, dispersal myths, identity, and Africa as homeland. But if we take the borders of Melanesia as a conceptual "starting place," what does the world look like?[2]

For example, Melanesia today encompasses approximately twelve million people across Vanuatu, Papua New Guinea, the Solomon Islands, West Papua, Fiji, and New Caledonia. Situated north and east of Australia, this chain of archipelagos witnessed a "pandemonium of colonialism" perhaps as dramatic as anywhere else on the planet.[3] By and large, Melanesian communities were not rapidly displaced from Africa via chattel enslavement. Rather, they reached Oceania through a slow process of voluntary migration by sea and land. Yet, as in the case of nineteenth-century blackbirding, Melanesian peoples did experience forms of slavery via forced migration to Australia, and most certainly colonialism. For these South Sea Islanders, home was not a distant Africa but the archipelagos of Oceania. What can these experiences teach us about the Black diaspora?[4]

The full interrogation of these ideas is far beyond the scope of this chapter, which is limited to Black Power and Black internationalism in Papua New Guinea in the era of decolonization. It is conversation with studies that are stretching our understandings of Black Power and Black internationalism in ways that address questions of gender, geography, and temporality.[5] A growing body of Africana scholarship has explored Black Power in Oceania, particularly through Australia's Black Panther Party, the Aborigines Advancement League, and New Zealand's Polynesian Panthers.[6] Less attention has been given to Black Power in Melanesia, much less Papua New Guinea.[7]

The largest country in Melanesia by land mass and population, Papua New Guinea secured political independence from Australia in 1975 under the direction of nationalist leader Michael Samore and the Pangu Party. Self-determination in the mineral-rich island represented the tangible potential of Black liberation in Oceania. This was partly because institutions such as UPNG and the Institute of Technology in Lae became beacons of Melanesian nationalism, Oceania political and cultural thought, and Black consciousness in the era of decolonization.

UPNG was formed in 1966 as part of colonial efforts to prepare a new "native" administration to maintain traditions of national dependency, gently steering the country along the path of neocolonialism after independence. However, within a few short years, the university became a vibrant hub of Black internationalism, so much so that European detractors denounced it as a "Mau Mau factory"—a reference to the militant uprisings of Kenya's Land and Freedom Army.[8] While this was a problematic assertion, UPNG did possess a politically active student body that defined itself as Black. It also hosted students from across Oceania who were involved in their own political movements. French colonial officials in Vanuatu expressed concern that subversive "leftist professors" were influencing New Hebridean students who studied at UPNG and Fiji's University of the South Pacific.[9] UPNG offered an intellectual base from which a host of thinkers could engage the politics of Oceania and explore Africana political thought and liberation struggles alongside students and faculty.

Starting in 1967, UPNG held annual Waigani seminars to address a range of social issues affecting Melanesia, including questions of economics, development, culture, education, history, land tenure, politics, Melanesian feminism, Pacific literature, and urbanization. While debate remains over the impact of the talks, scholars, students, and political leaders from across the Global South enthusiastically attended these seminars.[10] Through the mid-1970s, the list of attendees included leaders of Vanuatu's independence struggle, national leaders such as George Kalkoa, Donald Kalpokas, and Barak Sope, the radical Brazilian educational theorist Paulo Friere, Trinidadian intellectual Lloyd Best, Tanzanian educator Rapheal Kiyao, and Solomon Islander Francis Bugotu. Founders of the BPG, such as student activists Leo Hannett and John Kasaipwalova, also participated in the Waigani and similar forums.

In 1971, Hannett and Kasaipwalova discussed the BPG at a seminar on students and politics at the Institute of Technology in Lae. Hannett stated that some students and colonial administrators claimed that Black Power was dangerous and unnecessary in "Niugini (the Tok Pisin word for New Guinea)," where the population was majority Black. Hannett insisted, however, that the movement was as "relevant to Niugini as a betel nut," a reference to the popular cultural practice of chewing the nut for its mildly stimulating properties. The phrase "Black Power" gave the philosophy of self-determination political "bite," just as "ginger, pepper, and limestuff" did when chewing the betel.[11]

For Hannett, blackness represented more than phenotype and served as a reference to culture, social, and religious values. Citing Stokely

Carmichael and Charles Hamilton's *Black Power*, he argued that Niugini needed to "reclaim its history and identity from cultural terrorism." As such, the BPG sought more than Kwame Nkrumah's "political kingdom"—it also sought to cultivate national awareness and cultural identity.[12]

In 1971, Hannett was interviewed by Jean Gollan of *Lot's Wife*, the student newspaper of Australia's Monash University. For the activist from the autonomous northwestern province of Bougainville, the BPG was a "[Frantz] Fanon-inspired African Negritude" movement. Its main philosophy was to "redeem the identity of the Black man" and "make him proud of himself." Black Power was "essential to nation building," Hannett contended, because colonialism had forced Niuginians to condemn their indigenous ways of knowing.

Hannett argued that the first stage in the BPG's step-by-step program for liberation was to psychologically "grapple with the minds" of Niuginians who had been enslaved by a "colonial inferiority complex." Furthermore, the BPG was influenced by but not enslaved to the ideology of US Black Power and the philosophy of African Negritude. It had localized the concepts of Black struggle to reflect its own aspirations. Hannett felt that all Black people suffered from "the same sort of treatment from the ruling White races." As such, the BPG stood "in solidarity with all Black people," who, as an "exploited race," needed to exert themselves as a "world-wide ethnic group."[13] In a local context, this included embracing the ethnic, cultural, and regional differences of Papua New Guinea under the banner of Melanesian nationalism and forging political similarities with Polynesian political movements.

Gollan asked if the situation in Papua New Guinea would ever be like that of the United States, where violence seemed to be "the only way for the Negro to assert himself." Hannett could not predict such a thing. While Black Power did not aspire to be violent, he felt that as long as "the white man in his ethnocentric prejudice" refused to see Blacks as equal, then it was necessary for Black people to use whatever means necessary to liberate themselves. Still, Hannett stated, Black Power was not really directed toward white society at all. Rather, it was focused on building Black self-awareness and dignity and was not simply antiwhite. But, he argued, as Malcolm X said, "Black Power is a thing that the white man can't initiate or propagate and therefore won't tolerate for Black consumption."[14]

The Hannett interview was initially published in *Nilaidat* (Our voice), the fortnightly student newspaper of UPNG first produced in 1968. Its editor, Leo Morgan, promised that the publication would be attuned to the "cultural revolution" then transforming Papua New Guinea.[15] Members of the BPG frequently expressed their political activities in *Nilaidat*, even before the group had been formed. Hannett served as the paper's assistant editor. In 1971, the publication ran an ad about its forthcoming magazine, *Niugini Black Power*. The magazine was "to focus on the contemporary voices of the Black people in search of Niugini identity." It was to feature the works of Hannett, Kasaipwalova, Buluna, and others.[16]

Born in 1941, Hannett studied at Catholic seminaries in Rabaul and Madang.[17] At Madang he was introduced to and enthralled by the works of James Baldwin. In May 1968, he wrote an editorial in *Nilaidat* in the aftermath of Martin Luther King Jr.'s assassination. Hannett described King's political views, cited his 1963 "Letter from Birmingham Jail," and hailed him as "a martyr of the hypocrisy of American democracy." He found King's life, work, and death of relevance to Papua New Guinea: "Is it sufficient for me now to lie snugly on my bed of sanctimonious bombastic complacency and watch sadistically while the dignity of my neighbors is slowly sapped dry by inhuman living conditions, exploitation, and all sorts of injustice?" "We too in New Guinea have a dream," he asserted. It was to see their land grow into a nation where all were free and enjoying equal rights. This meant that tribalism, disunity, racism, and discrimination needed to be stamped out immediately.[18] Hannett's reverence for both Carmichael and King demonstrates the political flexibility of Black Power and Black internationalism in Papua New Guinea. This was critical, as Hannett's geopolitical "neighbors" included UPNG students from other ethnic groups in Papua New Guinea; Melanesian communities in West Papua, Oceania, Africa; and the broader Black diaspora.

Hannett served as the president of UPNG's Politics Club before forming the Niugini BPG. In 1968, the club organized a demonstration against a visit to Papua New Guinea by Johan Christiaan Holm Maree, the South African high commissioner to Australia. During Maree's visit to UPNG, students and faculty challenged him. According to *Nilaidat*, Hannett "struck the first spark" by asking questions about former African National Congress leader Inkosi Luthuli, who had been imprisoned by the apartheid state. Maree was also pressured by UPNG professor of creative writing Ulli Beier, whose questions set off a chain of "mass vocal outbursts and enthusiastic clapping" in the hall for the rest of the meeting.[19]

The club later continued the demonstrations, following Maree as he traveled to the airport to catch a departing flight. Led by Morgan, students hurried to the airport by all means available—the university bus, cars, motorbikes, an "exhausted" airport shuttle bus, and the back of a truck. They surrounded and rocked Maree's car at the airport, greeting him with boos and placards such as "Go Home Racialist," "Black Power," "Racialists Go to Hell," "No Apartheid," and "Leave Africa Alone." Maree eventually stepped out of the vehicle, and in "typical 007 style" took a photograph of the chanting, shouting, and fist-raising students, who were also singing African American freedom songs. Blocked from the tarmac by airport security, the students continued to protest as the plane departed. When the Australian minister for external territories Charles Barnes arrived at the airport, the demonstrators turned the heat on him as well.[20]

Nilaidat published a satirical play about the incident. Its characters included Mr. Big, Mr. Boer, Mr. Dusky, Mr. Colorless (likely Beier), and the Mob. Defended by Big, Boer was questioned by Dusky and Colorless: "Why does the government gaol writers, why does apartheid oppress and what about Black Power?"[21] This play demonstrated Black Power's use of political art at UPNG.

In contrast to *Nilaidat*, the Papua New Guinean newspaper *South Pacific Post* denounced the protest. It claimed that the students were practicing "apartheid in reverse" and that Black Power had no more moral justification than did "White Power." When it refused to print a letter written by a "Mr. Hide" in defense of the demonstration, *Nilaidat* promptly did so. Hide called for the *Post* to consider more deeply the global "connotations of apartheid, segregation and racial discrimination." While the protest was specifically against the South African policy of apartheid, racism was international. While the horrors of the 1960 Sharpeville massacre were publicly remembered, as an "Englishman" Hide remained shamed by the 1959 racial attacks on West Indians in London's Notting Hill neighborhood. But in refusing to understand the significance of Black Power, the *Post* was denying the universality of the issue. How could the paper ask what "Black Power" signs meant in a protest against apartheid? When a spokesman for nonviolence like King Jr. was gunned down in the streets, how could it not understand the hope that thousands of Blacks in America felt in the rally cry of Black Power?[22]

The pages of *Nilaidat* also reflect how UPNG students and the BGP were highly concerned about the violence of Indonesian imperialism in neighboring West Papua. Formerly colonized by the Dutch, West Papua was ceded to Indonesia through a fraudulent deal known as the Act of Free Choice. West Papuans declared their sovereignty through armed struggle via organizations such as the Revolutionary Provisional Government of West Papua New Guinea (RPG). While the Indonesian government claimed that it was historically and ethnically entitled to West Papua (called Irian Jaya by Indonesia), the RPG adamantly defended the country's sovereignty as the home of an Oceanic Melanesian people of Black African descent.[23] From Hollandia, Amsterdam, Dakar, Boroko, and New York, West Papuan activists garnered international support from Black organizations such as the NAACP. With the political and financial backing of Senegalese president Léopold Senghor, in 1975 the RPG established a coordinating office in Dakar. When pressed on the reason for this office, Senghor asserted that Papuans were Black and the concept of Negritude affirmed their right to "an independent state for the renaissance and development" of their civilization."[24]

In May 1969, *Nilaidat* published an extensive special edition on the political, geographic, historical, economic, and social implications of Indonesian imperialism in West Papua. It printed reports from the United Nations and accounts of the armed conflict from West Papuan spokespersons Marcus Kaisiepo and Nicolaas Jouwe. It detailed how, between 1965 and 1968, Indonesia's military bombarded West Papua with napalm, burned the houses of dissidents, and killed and tortured adults and children. Kaisiepo claimed that more than fifty thousand innocent men, women, and children had been killed in West Papua.[25]

Nilaidat found Indonesia's actions to be "depressingly reminiscent of Italy's enforced subjugation" of Ethiopia in 1936. It denounced Australia's backing of Indonesia. It covered the daylong forum held by the Politics Club, where students gathered supplies for children of West Papuan refugees who had fled into Papua New Guinea.[26]

About a month later, in May 1969, Hannett led a Politics Club march of more than five hundred students and other participants to protest Indonesia, Australia's support of its policies, and the UN's refusal to assertively address Indonesia's violation of basic human rights. Leading up to the march, Hannett penned an open letter to religious leaders in Papua New Guinea. The document, entitled "Lumine Gentium," stressed that churchgoers who did not express their moral support for West Papua were committing "clerical sin." They were "eclipsing the Sun of Justice from shining in the world through their lack of courage, complacency and ineptitude in bearing witness to Christian principles in season and out of season." The protestors marched to the Australian government house, where they sang songs such as "We Shall Overcome," and Hannett passed their petition on to the Australian administration.[27]

In response, a journalist accused Hannett of being a "front man for a white student," suggesting that Blacks were not capable of organizing the demonstration. Even a white UPNG student found this notion to be outrageous—Hannett was "nobody's stooge."[28] *Nilaidat* wrote a sharp rebuke of the "front man" accusation: "A native can't write anything intellectual, he must always have been influenced by whites. If he ever writes anything radical it must be communist-inspired or [American] Negro-inspired . . . if he ever writes anything thoughtful it must have been thought out by others."[29]

It was at this moment that Hannett and others first gave serious thought to forming the organization, which called for self-determination from Australian colonialism and an end to segregation, denounced a public order bill that restricted the public's rights to demonstrate while increasing police power, and decried the exploitation of Niugini's mineral resources in Bougainville by multinational companies.[30]

Bougainville was a major source of tension not only for the BPG but for the nation. In 1969, the building of a major copper mine displaced the Bougainville community of Rorovana. It was owned by Conzinc Riotinto Australia, an international company based in southern Africa. Twenty-five unarmed women wrestled with the riot squad police in protest and were beaten with batons and tear gassed in response. As Hannett was a spokesperson for Bougainville, the issue hit close to home.[31] Bougainville's struggle against environmental racism would linger through the era of decolonization. For example, in 1971 the BPG submitted a proposal to a UN visiting mission to Papua New Guinea. The document called for self-government, the people's control of all of Niugini's mineral resources, and, with its usual satire, a Black Niugini program to match Australia's "whites-only" immigration policies.[32]

Most strikingly, the BPG expressed its Melanesian nationalism through art and literature. Most of its leaders studied literature with UPNG professors Prithvindra Chakravarti and the aforementioned Ulli Beier. Beier, of German-Jewish descent, taught creative writing in UPNG's English Department. He had previously taught at Nigeria's University of Ibadan and used his extensive contacts with Africa-based writers and artists to design his courses. BPG members read Chinua Achebe, Wole Soyinke, Leopold Senghor, and the Negritude journal *Presence Africaine*. They produced plays, memoirs (such as Albert Maori Kiki's *Ten Thousand Years in a Lifetime*), novels, poetry, and short stories in English, indigenous languages, and pidgin.[33]

Through the publication of journals like *Kovave*, *Papua New Guinea Writing*, and *Papua Pocket Series*, these artists of the BPG became conduits of Melanesian transnationalism and Black consciousness in Oceania. This included Arthur Jawodimbari, who studied popular Black theater across the world. In 1974, he toured Japan, Ghana, Nigeria, and the United States. In Nigeria, he spent time with novelist and activist Obi Egbuna.

In Ghana, he sat with playwright Efua Sutherland. In Harlem, he visited Barbara Ann Teer's National Black Theatre. Based on these experiences Jawodimbari developed Papua New Guinea's National Theatre Company, which included artists such as Nora Vagi Brash, who participated in Nigeria's Black and African Festival of Arts and Culture (1977). The work of Brash and other women from Papua New Guinea was featured in the journal *Ondobondo*, cofounded by Chakravarti in 1982.[34]

Like Jawodimbari, John Kasaipwalova's work invoked Africana ideas of liberation and transnational diasporic themes. Kasaipwalova was also a member of the BPG, and his 1971 "Reluctant Flame" called for the fires of Niugini nationalism to take fuel from Black uprisings in South Africa and the United States. A self-described Black nationalist, he felt that the writer's challenge was to "capture and express the people's consciousness" and break the "colonial mentality" of Black people.[35]

In a 1970 interview in *New Guinea Writing*, popular poet Kumulau Tawali claimed that there was no need for Black Power in Papua New Guinea because the world had enough problems already. Totally disagreeing with the movement, he called for reconstruction of Papua New Guinean culture instead.[36]

This bewildered Kasaipwalova, as Tawali's widely cited poem "Bush Kanaka Speaks" lamented the white man's "lack of bones" and could have been considered Black Power literature. Kasaipwalova found the notion of cultural reconstruction to be a narcissistic dream based on the rhetoric of internationalism and that it implied that Papua New Guinean culture was static and fixed in time. But Black Power called for a radical approach that redefined values through a "continuous transformation of the present based on an understanding of the psychical and social environment that they found themselves in." To cry for the "milk of cultural reconstruction," argued Kasaipwalova, was to ask for "life from a corpse"; but Black people wanted life and to live and be free.[37]

The BPG's own vision of freedom spanned Oceania. It supported the political struggles of Aborigines in Australia. In 1972, Bobbi Sykes, an iconic figure in Australia's Black Power movement, wrote to Kasaipwalova during his tenure as the head of UPNG's Student Representative Council. She sought assistance from UPNG students in raising international interest about the Black struggle in Australia. Sykes visited UPNG under the invitation of the Student Representative Council.[38] Representing the Aboriginal Canberra Tent Embassy, she gave talks about "Australian apartheid" at the Institute of Technology.[39] In 1973, Australian Black Panther Cheryl Buchanan also visited UPNG to gain support for her organization's push for Aboriginal land rights.[40]

Papua New Guinea's Black arts movement attracted activists and artists from across the region. This included Fijian antinuclear and Pacific Women's Movement activists Vanessa Griffen and Claire Slatter. In 1974, both women undertook graduate studies in Papua New Guinea. Griffen toured with Jawodimbari's National Theatre Company.[41]

While Western media outlets like *Time* magazine framed Papua New Guinea as a Stone Age civilization, UPNG stood as a powerful example of Black modernity in Oceania. Papua New Guinea reflected the future—rather than just an ancient past—of the Black Pacific in terms of its discourses on race, Black internationalism, and sovereignty.[42] In the aftermath of independence, activists of the BPG went in many differing directions—some joined the government, some formed nationalist movements within Papua New Guinea, and others continued to produce their art. In this context, the activism of Hannett and the BPG demonstrated how Black Power in Papua New Guinea was a statement of Melanesian transnationalism. It was also a version of Black internationalism that appreciated the local, national, and regional concerns of Papua New Guinea and Oceania. Further studies could apply the same lens in examining the spread of Black internationalism and Black Power across the diaspora.

Notes

1. See Quito Swan, "Blinded by Bandung? Illumining West Papua, Senegal, and the Black Pacific," *Radical History Review* 131 (2018): 58–81.

2. Take, for example, Paul Gilroy's classic and still conceptually influential *Black Atlantic: Modernity and Double Consciousness* (Cambridge, MA: Harvard University Press, 1993); Franklin Knight and Ruth Iyob, *Dimensions of African and Other Diasporas* (Kingston: University of West Indies Press, 2014); Joseph Harris, ed., *Global Dimensions of the African Diaspora* (Washington, DC: Howard University Press, 1993); Walter Mignolo and Madina Tlostanova, "Theorizing from the Borders: Shifting to Geo- and Body-Politics of Knowledge," *European Journal of Social Theory* 9, no. 2 (2006): 205–21.

3. Walter Lini, *Beyond Pandemonium: From the New Hebrides to Vanuatu* (Port Vila: Asia Pacific Books, 1980); Serge Tcherkézoff, "A Long and Unfortunate Voyage towards the 'Invention' of the Melanesia/Polynesia Distinction, 1595–1832," *Journal of Pacific History* 38, no. 2 (2003): 175–96; Merze Tate, "Early European Discoveries in the Pacific," 1–2, 4, box 219-10, Merze Tate Papers, Moorland Spingarn Research Center, Howard University, Washington, DC.

4. Epeli Hau'ofa, *We Are the Ocean* (Mānoa: University of Hawai'i Press, 2008); Gerald Horne, *The White Pacific: Black Slavery in the South Seas* (Honolulu: University of Hawaii Press, 2007); Lea Lani Kinikini Kauvaka, "Berths and Anchorages: Pacific Cultural Studies from Oceania," *Contemporary Pacific* 28 (2016): 1.

5. Etsuko Taketani, *Black Pacific Narrative: Geographic Imaginings of Race and Empire between the World Wars* (Hanover, NH: Dartmouth College Press, 2014); John Maynard, *Origins of Australian Aboriginal Activism* (Canberra: Aboriginal Study Press, 2007); Monique Bedasse, *Jah Kingdom: Rastafarians, Tanzania, and Pan-Africanism in the Age of Decolonization* (Chapel Hill: University of North Carolina Press, 2017); Keisha Blain, *Set the World on Fire: Black Nationalist Women and the Global Struggle for Freedom* (Philadelphia: University of Pennsylvania Press, 2018); Ashley Farmer, *Remaking Black Power: How Black Women Transformed an Era* (Chapel Hill: University of North Carolina Press), 2017; Cheryl Higashida, *Black Internationalist Feminism: Women Writers of the Black Left, 1945–1995* (Champaign: University of Illinois Press, 2013); Taj Frazier, *The East Is Black: Cold War China in the Black Radical Imagination* (Durham, NC: Duke University Press, 2014).

6. Robbie Shilliam, *The Black Pacific: Anti-Colonial Struggles and Oceanic Connections* (New York: Bloomsbury Publishing, 2014); David Chappell, *The Kanak Awakening* (Honolulu: University of Hawaii Press, 2013).

7. Tracey Banivanua Mar, *Decolonisation and the Pacific: Indigenous Globalisation and the Ends of Empire* (Cambridge: Cambridge University Press, 2016).

8. Hank Nelson, *Papua New Guinea: Black Unity or Black Chaos?* (Middlesex: Penguin Books, 1972), 79.

9. Snythèse Mensuelle de mai 1974," box NH 026, New Hebrides Collection, National Archives of Vanuatu, Port Vila, Vanuatu.

10. Max Quanchi, "The Waigani Seminars and Other Talk-Fests; Looking Back—and Forward—in the Pacific Islands," Pacific Science Association Inter-Congress, March 2–6, 2009, Tahiti, French Polynesia.

11. Leo Hannett, "The Niugini Black Power Movement," in *Tertiary Students and the Politics of Papua New Guinea* (Lae: Papua New Guinea Institute of Technology, 1971), UPNG Library, Papua New Guinea Collection, Port Moresby, Papua New Guinea.

12. Hannett, "Niugini Black Power Movement."

13. Hannett, "Niugini Black Power," *Lot's Wife* 11, no. 4 (September 1971): 9.

14. Hannett, "Niugini Black Power."

15. Leo Morgan, *Nilaidat*, March 21, 1968, National Archives of Australia, Canberra.

16. "Niugini Black Power," *Nilaidat*, February 1971, 7.

17. Alexander Mamak, Richard Bedford, Leo Hannett, and Moses Havini, *Bougainvillean Nationalism: Aspects of Unity and Discord* (Christchurch, New Zealand: Bougainville Special Publications, 1974), vii.

18. Leo Hannett, "Dr. Martin Luther King," *Nilaidat*, May 9, 1968, Australia National Library, Canberra.

19. W. Hurrey, "The Demonstration," *Nilaidat*, July 8, 1968, 5–6.

20. Hurrey, "The Demonstration," 5–6.

21. "Papua New Guinea—76 Natural Nations?" Hurrey, "The Demonstration," 7.

22. "Reason Demonstrated," *Nilaidat*, July 8, 1968, 19–20.

23. Provisional Government of West Papua, "Indonesian Colonialism vs the People of West Papua New Guinea," 1, box 8313, West New Guinea, National

Association for the Advancement of Colored People (NAACP) Papers, Library of Congress, Washington, DC.

24. "African Papuans Being Slaughtered by Indonesian Government," NAACP Papers; "Nonaligned Nations, Liberation Fronts, Political Leaders, Meetings," July 7, 1976, Cable 1976DAKAR04287, National Archives, College Park, MD; *Le Monde*, March 30, 1976.

25. *Nilaidat*, May 22, 1969, 8.

26. *Nilaidat*, May 14, 1969, 20, UPNG Library, Papua New Guinea Collection, Port Moresby, Papua New Guinea.

27. *Nilaidat*, June 6, 199, 4; May 22, 1969, 1, 3, 8.

28. M. Maunsell Davis, "Student Hang-Ups and Student Action: Student Political Activity at the University of Papua and New Guinea," *Politics of Melanesia*, 297.

29. M. Buluna, "The Student in Niugini Politics," in *The Politics of Melanesia; Papers Delivered at the Fourth Waigani Seminar*, ed. Marion W. Ward (Canberra: Research School of Pacific Studies, Australian National University, 1970), 309.

30. Hannett, "Niugini Black Power Movement."

31. Tate, "Administration of Papua and New Guinea," box 219-8, Merz Tate Papers, Moorland Spingarn Research Center, Howard University, Washington DC; "Twenty-Five Women Fight with Police," *Post Courier*, August 4, 1969, 1.

32. Hannett, "Niugini Black Power," 9; Tate, "Administration of Papua and New Guinea," 271.

33. Kumulau Tawali, "Bush Kanaka Speaks," in *Modern Poetry from Papua New Guinea*, vol. 1, ed. Nigel Krauth and Elton Brash (Port Moresby: Papua Pocket Poets, 1972).

34. "Arthur Jawodimbari," *Papua New Guinea Writing* 13 (March 1974): 12.

35. *Post Courier*, January 28, 1970; interview with John Kasaipwalova, August 27, 1970, A452 1970/524, National Archives of Australia; Charles Cepulis, "Native Has Identity," *Post Courier*, January 27, 1970; John Kasaipwalova, *The Reluctant Flame* (Port Moresby: Papua Pocket Poets, 1971).

36. "An Interview with Kumalau Tawali," *New Guinea Writing* 2 (December 1970): 13.

37. John Kasaipwalova, "What Is Cultural Reconstruction???" *New Guinea Writing* 3 (March 1971): 14–16.

38. "Bobbi Sykes to UPNG Students Association" and "Bobbi Sykes," May 17, 1972, Roberta Sykes, vol. 1, ASIO, NAA.

39. "Aboriginal Seeks PNG Support," July 7, 1972, ASIO, NAA.

40. "Australians Should Cry in the Streets," interview with Peter Playpool and Ian MacIntosh, May 4, 1972, Roberta Sykes, vol. 1; "Cheryl Rose Buchanan, Visit to Papua New Guinea," May 29, 1973, Cheryl Buchanon, vol. 1, 25, ASIO, NAA.

41. Griffen and Slatter, 2014.

42. "Papua New Guinea: Out of the Stone Age," *Time*, December 17, 1973.

Chapter 14

Black Power in the Tradition of Radical Blackness

Charisse Burden-Stelly

For Gwendolyn Patton, a Student Nonviolent Coordinating Committee (SNCC) and anti–Vietnam War activist, Black Power was a strategy to develop and transform the Black community into "one that could exert its human potential to be an equal partner in the larger society."[1] Starting in the mid-1960s, a number of Black Power activists, inspired by insurgencies throughout the Third World; the radicalism of Mao Zedong, Frantz Fanon, and Che Guevara; and an older generation of Black Marxist-Leninists in the United States, held that such development and transformation required the overthrow of white supremacist capitalist imperialism.[2] The Black Women's United Front (BWUF), a Black Power federation of organizations and activists, dedicated itself to antiracism, anticapitalism, and anti-imperialism to effectively organize the Black masses generally, and Black working-class women particularly, for Black liberation, self-determination, and democratic rights.[3] Black Panther Party leaders Huey P. Newton and Eldridge Cleaver rejected Black capitalism because, as "the grease to ease the Black bourgeoisie into the power structure," it negated the fact that Black Power was quintessentially "people's power."[4] Relatedly, revolutionary nationalist James Boggs argued that the empowerment of Black "outcasts, castaways, and castoffs" required the establishment of "a material basis for communism, i.e., a society in which each has according to his needs and contributes according to his ability." He therefore defined Black Power as "the state power to destroy the existing system and replace it with a new one that [would] benefit not only Blacks but all the people in this country and throughout the world."[5] While Black Power is not reducible to these leftist, internationalist, and Marxist-Leninist articulations and political economic analyses,[6] this chapters seeks to expand the boundaries of

Black intellectual history by analyzing Black Power in the tradition of radical Blackness. It does so through an examination of twentieth-century Black writings and speeches centered on three themes—the inextricability of imperialism, white supremacy, and capitalist exploitation; triple exploitation as the ultimate form of superexploitation; and Blackness as a national question—that situate Black power praxis in a longer history of radical Black theory, critique, analysis, and activism.

The tradition of radical Blackness is defined as twentieth-century Black communist, socialist, leftist, and Marxist-Leninist challenges to the structural and material conditions of local, national, and global Blackness and efforts to imagine and bring into being liberating possibilities for all oppressed people. Internationalist in scope, it links the conditions of Black people to other colonized and racialized groups through anti-imperial, anticolonial, antiracist, and anticapitalist praxis. Gender analysis is constitutive of—not separate from or an addendum to—this tradition. Such interrogations play an essential, if not uneven, role in revealing multilayered forms of exploitation, challenging bourgeois values that reify capitalist hegemony, and centering the issues and concerns of the working class. To varying degrees, radical Black women and men alike have educed the gendered effects of oppression, domination, chauvinism, and exploitation. Such concerns were also integral to the ideological development of Black Power.[7] Historically, radical Black folk were by no means exempted from sexism, misogyny, misandry, and gender discrimination. Nonetheless, these contradictions were neither static nor all-encompassing, and freedom fighters of both sexes constantly grappled with their structural and interpersonal effects.

Harlem-based radical and one-time Garveyite Richard B. Moore's 1927 "Common Resolution on the Negro Question" epitomizes the tradition of radical Blackness. Moore linked the global histories of African descendants through the legacies of slavery, colonialism, imperialism, and apartheid and demanded an end to these forms of oppression and exploitation through organized political and economic power for Black people, unionization, cooperatives, and the coordination of liberation movements. He also insisted upon a direct challenge to "imperialist ideology: chauvinism, fascism, kukluxism, and race prejudice."[8] As the "Common Resolution on the Negro Question" demonstrates, the tradition of radical Blackness centers critical political economy analysis, attends to intraracial class conflict, emphasizes the importance of labor and workers, theorizes Blackness as a special condition of surplus value extraction, and strives for the eventual overthrow of capitalism. As such, it is indebted to, but departs from, Cedric Robinson's Black radical tradition.[9] Likewise, the tradition of radical Blackness is homologous with other radical political formations that challenged the racialized and gendered contours of US capitalist hegemony and European imposition, including the post-WWII "anticolonial front," proletarianized Pan-Africanism, Black left and internationalist feminisms, the "Bandung Spirit," and Third Worldism and tricontinentalism.[10]

In analyzing Black Power in the tradition of radical Blackness, the point is not to reproduce "long movement" analyses that elide periodization, regional difference, tactical particularity, and strategic objectives.[11] Rather, following Dayo Gore and John Munro, the chapter indicates that a radical Black critique of capitalist political economy was an essential component of twentieth-century Black freedom dreams that endured the violent anticommunist, antiradical, and antiblack repression that constituted US domestic and foreign policy after World War II.[12] While Gore and Munro use Black feminism and anticolonialism, respectively, to challenge arguments that "US anticommunism adjourned the left-oriented era of the Black freedom struggle's history,"[13] centering anticapitalism more directly challenges the intellectual McCarthyist tendency to marginalize and erase Marxist-Leninist thinkers, materialist analysis, and redistributive demands from Black liberation struggles. Concomitantly, such attention underscores the importance of critical political economy to understanding, specifying, and contextualizing Black folks' exploitation and oppression, on the one hand, and to challenging and eradicating these processes, on the other hand.

Imperialism, White Supremacy, and Capitalist Exploitation

A critique of imperialism, white supremacy, and capitalist exploitation as the tripartite of Black oppression features prominently in the tradition of radical Blackness and connects modes of Black anticapitalist thought throughout the twentieth century. In 1915, as the Great War menaced the world, W. E. B. Du Bois analyzed the conflict as a white supremacist pact between the ruling and working classes of the imperial nations to profit from the subjection of racialized peoples.[14] He argued that "democratic despotism" was activated by a shared vision of exploitation that demanded the expropriation of wealth "from the darker nations of the world—Asia and Africa, South and Central America, the West Indies and the islands of the South Seas." Moreover, he illuminated the relationship between the enslavement of African peoples, the conflation of Blackness and inferiority, the reduction of Africa to a space of pillage and plunder and imperialism as the conduit for all Europeans to "share the spoil of exploiting the 'chinks and niggers.'"[15] Du Bois continued this line of critique when European greed conscripted the world into another imperial war. He maintained in "The Realities in Africa: European Profit or Negro Development" (1943) that while Germany was the enemy in each of the World Wars, it was African self-determination that continued to be undermined by capitalist imperialism. These crises of Western civilization thus elucidated the endurance of white supremacist expropriation. Du Bois's writings in the aftermath of World War II, including "Imperialism, United Nations, and Colonial People" (1944), *Color and Democracy: Peace and the Colonies* (1945), "The Rape of Africa" (1956), and "Africa and World Peace" (1960), persisted in developing the inextricability of colonial domination, racialized oppression, capitalist exploitation, and imperialist warmongering.

The looming Great Depression brought about a similar analysis, this time offered by prominent Black communist James Ford in a 1929 report to the Second World Congress of the League against Imperialism.[16] He argued that the imminent capitalist crisis was especially serious for Negroes, who comprised a significant portion of the international working class and of the world's oppressed people. This was so because the imperialist stage of capitalist development that characterized the post–World World I era had consolidated Africa's partition and the "complete enslavement of its people," intensified the subjection of the Black working class in the United States to "white big business" and the "rising Negro bourgeoisie," and transformed the West Indies into a marketplace for American goods through militarism and occupation. Moreover, in Africa, the US South, and the Caribbean, Black workers were impressed into forced labor, laying railroads, building roads and bridges, working in mines, entrapped on plantations through peonage, subjected to convict leasing, and suffering intolerable working conditions and routinized violence. As such, liberation from the "imperialist oppression of the Negro peoples of the world" was wholly contingent upon "how they estimate[d] the present period of imperialism, the concrete task of organisation they set themselves to achieve these things and the unity they establish[ed] with the international working class in the struggle against imperialism."[17]

Ford's report, which rigorously analyzed capitalist political economy, connected the conditions of Black people globally, emphasized the importance of worker organization to world revolution, and demanded independence, self-determination, and full emancipation for oppressed people throughout the world, bears striking similarities to a speech given by the prominent Black Power activist and SNCC leader Stokely

Carmichael at the Organization of Latin American Solidarity conference in August 1967.[18] Just as Du Bois and Ford had identified the entanglement of imperialism, white supremacy, and capitalist exploitation based on their specific historical and material contexts, in "Black Power and the Third World" Carmichael interrogated the latter structures in the context of urban America in the late 1960s. He started his speech by asserting that US Blacks and racialized persons throughout the Americas had a common enemy: white Western imperialist society. He then expanded this analysis to include the entire Third World, which was the object of economic and cultural exploitation and therefore had the responsibility to overthrow the extant system.[19] The Black Power movement, according to Carmichael, was anti-imperial and anticolonial not least because the struggle of African Americans included the responsibility to "neutralize" US efforts to entrench white supremacy in the racialized world.[20] As such, the Black Power insurgency manifested in the heart of empire the liberation struggles in Africa, Asia, and Latin America.

Carmichael conceptualized Black oppression as a function of capitalist exploitation, the domination of the Black working class by the bourgeoisie, and white supremacist ideology. He explained that the Black masses lacked jobs, money, and decent housing and did not control resources, land, or institutions in their communities. As well, their "capital and cheap labor" were exploited from without, a relationship protected by racist laws and police forces. As such, the civil rights movement's bourgeois demands were inadequate to address the material conditions of the Black working class. While that movement was a beginning, he argued, it was the ghetto rebellions that expressed the reality of working-class Black folk, that levied a challenge to that reality, and that linked their struggle to the broader anti-imperialist, anticapitalist, and antiracist struggle. And it was Black Power that brought together the "revolutionary proletariat" to fight against and expose "racism and exploitation which permeate[d] all institutions in the United States."[21] Moreover, Carmichael held that "the United States has always found this justification [to enslave another human being] in proclaiming the superiority of whites and the inferiority of nonwhites . . . it therefore [became] just, in the mind of the white man, that we should be enslaved, exploited and oppressed."[22] Black Power, then, provided the means to combat capitalist imposition rationalized by white supremacist logic.

It is important to note that differences in ideology, time period, and historical conditions resulted in disagreements, variations, and contradictions in analyses of, and solutions to, the realities of imperialism, white supremacy, and capitalist exploitation. For example, Carmichael departed from Ford insofar as his economic and historical analyses were rooted in "color and culture" and his "interpretation of Marx" came from the racial foundations of capitalism.[23] In other words, he believed that racism and cultural imperialism were as important as economic exploitation and were fundamental fronts in the challenge to capitalism. Carmichael's contention that the United States avoided class struggle within its borders through imperialist expansion into the Third World, exploitation of the resources and labor of racialized people, and the sharing of those profits with the US white working class converged with Du Bois's arguments in "The African Roots of the War." However, while Du Bois's anti-imperialism centered on a critique of colonialism given his understanding that World War I was a competition between imperial powers for colonial possessions, Carmichael's Black Power anti-imperialism was preeminently concerned with the racial violence of the United States that compelled Black Americans to join with the Third World in armed struggle. Such divergences illuminate the multifaceted ways that the tradition of radical Blackness engaged white supremacist imperial capitalism as the preeminent source of Black abjection.

From Superexploitation to Triple Exploitation

Another major contention that structured the tradition of radical Blackness was that Black people were "superexploited." The conjuncture of imperialism, white supremacy, and capitalist exploitation, it was argued, produced an "especially oppressed people" subjected to "extra demands, *over and above those of white workers*."[24] As Black Communist and African Blood Brotherhood founder Otto Huiswoud explained, in the first half of the twentieth century persons racialized as Black experienced a combination of repression, violence, and surplus value extraction that reduced them to a servile class subjected to lynching, peonage, and segregation. As such, they were rendered social outcasts at the very bottom of capitalist society.[25] The transgenerational Black radical Harry Haywood argued that this "brutal caste system" exacerbated worker-based oppression and resulted in Black relegation to the worst forms of employment, the most dangerous and unhealthy work conditions, and paltry, unequal wages. Black folk were imprisoned in plantation systems in the South through sharecropping, tenancy, and land dispossession and were extremely marginalized in—if not excluded outright from—textile and other industries.[26] Additionally, Blacks were denied even the most basic civil rights and protection by law that would allow them to contest these conditions of exclusion and economic violence. *We Charge Genocide: The Historic Petition to the United Nations for Relief From a Crime of the United States Government Against the Negro People*, the Civil Rights Congress's seminal 1951 petition, thrust the peculiar suffering of US Blacks onto the international stage.[27] It meticulously documented the past and present subjection of Blacks to "institutionalized oppression" through "constant and invariable . . . discrimination in employment, low wages, enforced living in ghettos, denial of equality of accommodation and services as well equality in the courts." The petition further argued that their superexploitation was sustained by "genocidal terror," white supremacist law, and the drive of monopoly capitalists for superprofits.[28]

A particularly egregious manifestation of superexploitation was the inhumane living conditions in Black communities. This issue galvanized leftists including Grace Campbell and Hermina Huiswoud as early as 1928 and continued to be protested throughout the Black Power era by radical activists such as the influential Pan-Africanist Malcolm X. Under the leadership of Black communist and African Blood Brotherhood members Campbell and Huiswoud, the Harlem Tenant's League organized the Black working class in Harlem against exorbitant rent, deplorable living conditions, rat infestation, neglectful and rapacious landlords, and disproportionate evictions and "dispossess notices."[29] Since these issues persisted two decades later, William Patterson, the editor and visionary of *We Charge Genocide*, made sure to include in the report that "substandard housing . . . is a notorious breeder of disease and death . . . and an instrument of genocide when court decisions as well as consciously fostered economic policies, make it impossible for a people to leave such housing." Patterson and his comrades also noted that zoning laws, restrictive covenants, and violence forced Blacks into ugly, dirty, and disease-ridden ghettoes.[30] Continuing this line of attack in 1963, Malcolm X attested that the abysmal housing conditions characterizing overcrowded Black communities throughout the United States were a form of structural and racial violence. It was white liberals, he noted, that were the landlords who were "bilking," "robbing," and "exploiting" their poor Black tenants.[31] The Black Panther Party, whose formation had been deeply inspired by Malcolm X, condemned the racist denial of decent housing to Black folk in its October 1966 Ten-Point Program. The program also enumerated means of combatting superexploitation, including self-determination, full employment, "true" education, the end of police occupation in Black communities, and the cessation of mass incarceration.[32] In a similar vein, members of the Institute of the Black World—an organization founded in 1969 that combined Black Power, Black Marxist, and Black nationalist thought—declared in March 1972 that inadequate housing, along with high unemployment, prison overcrowding, inflation, and "business protectionism" were features of a collapsing imperial system reliant upon the extreme dispossession to which Black people had long been subjected.[33] Thus, Black Power radicals, like others in the tradition of radical Blackness, understood that superexploitation linked African Americans to the other oppressed peoples of the world through white supremacist capitalist imperialism.

Perhaps the most sophisticated argument about superexploitation came through the advancement of "triple exploitation" as a means of analyzing Black women's structural location. The BWUF's 1975 proclamation that the triple exploitation of Black women demanded the smashing of monopoly capitalism and a move toward socialist revolution was made possible by intellectual developments in 1936.[34] That year, the lifelong leftist Louise Thompson employed triple exploitation to explain that Black women's oppressive relationship to the mode of production was based on their race, gender, and subordination in the labor market. Black militants Marvel Cooke and Ella Baker published an article in which they studied superexploitation as it related to Black domestic workers. Cooke and Baker explained that the conjuncture of racialized womanhood and structural poverty—deeply intensified by the Great Depression—forced domestic workers to pauperize their labor for the abysmal wage of less than thirty cents an hour. Here labor exploitation was gendered insofar as domestic work was conventional "women's work" and racialized insofar as Blackness fitted this group of women for low-wage, unprotected, contingent labor. Moreover, the convergence of race, class, and gender in the superexploitation of Black domestics was manifested in the formation of white women as a "new employer class [of] [l]ower middle-class housewi[ves], who, having dreamed of the luxury of a maid, found opportunity staring [them] in the face in the form of Negro women pressed to the wall by poverty, starvation, and discrimination."[35] Patterson, Cooke, and Baker proved that the contours of exploitation could only be understood when race, gender, labor, and material conditions were taken into account.[36]

In 1940, radical Black activist-intellectual Esther V. Cooper took on triple exploitation from a different angle. In her master's thesis she argued that, given the triple exploitation of Black domestics, their organization and unionization was essential to socialist revolution. Excluding them from trade unions and the organized labor movement not only marginalized a key demographic of the proletarian struggle but also reified Black women's superexploitation by excluding them from labor protections afforded to other classes of workers. The argument that they were "unorganizable" was based on false and anti-Black assumptions that continued the social stigma and vulnerability of this class of workers.[37] For eminent Black communist Claudia Jones,[38] Black women's superexploitation was revealed through their unique relationship to the mode of production, the labor market, and the social relations that reduced them to the status of absolute "other." In the 1949 article, "An End to the Neglect of the Problems of the Negro Woman!" Jones concluded that the empowerment of Black women should be prioritized given their special form of subjection.[39] She forcibly argued that Black women's responsibility as partial or sole breadwinners, treatment in the labor market, and active participation in the social, political, and economic life of the Black community—in other words, their experience of superexploitation and their tireless efforts to eradicate its conditions—rendered them "the real active forces—the organizers and the workers."[40]

The importance of triple exploitation as a means of understanding the gendered nature of superexploitation is also evident in a 1949 unpublished essay by Du Bois entitled, "The American Negro Woman." In it, he argues that the Black woman's role as worker, head of household, and leader in cultural development has been essential to the progression of American culture and provides the key to resolving the central problem of the "woman question"—economic dependence.[41] By outlining the importance of Black women to the proletarian struggle and to the potential resolution of working-class exploitation, "The American Negro Woman" refined Du Bois's earlier stances on Black women that emphasized their spiritual strength and idealized Black womanhood.[42] This refashioning took its cue from the writings of radical Black women that postulated the leading role of Black women's activism in combatting the structures in which their trilateral debasement inhered. Such interventions convey the extent to which leftist gender inquiries were essential to understanding superexploitation and were constitutive of the tradition of radical Blackness.

The intellectual ground cleared by leftist gender inquiries in the previous three decades was sown by leftist Black women's organizations like the Third World Women's Alliance (TWWA)—transformed from the Black Women's Alliance in 1968—and the Combahee River Collective (CRC_1), founded in 1974, and by radical Black men. Echoing Cooper, Maxine Williams and Frances Beal pointed out that Black women continued to be overrepresented in nonunionized and service-based occupations, which transmuted them into a supply of surplus and cheap labor that was remunerated terribly, denied workforce advancement, restricted to the most exploitative forms of labor, and excluded from or subordinated in unions.[43] Like Patterson, Jones, and Jackson, Williams and Beal used the triple exploitation of Black women to expound the specificities of superexploitation. Along with being "economically exploited as a worker, being used as a source of cheap labor because she is a female, and being treated even worse because she is Black," Williams explained the "double exploitation" of Black women working in someone else's private household and then having to take care of their own. Beal added that Black women were forced to work in white peoples' kitchens because Black men were often excluded from the labor market, and these material demands resulted in "turmoil" in Black family structures and the disruption of Black relationships.[44] Moreover, Black women had the burden of caring for white folks' children before tending to their own, a structural reality that lent to the ideological denigration of Black women, who were misconstrued as the arbiters of Black family "dysfunction."

In a 1968 essay entitled, "Black Women and Birth Control," Julius Lester offered a Black male perspective on the ways that the imposition of motherhood gendered Black women's superexploitation. He argued that Black militant rejection of birth control and romanticization of Black motherhood enslaved Black women to their bodies, chained them to their physiology, foreclosed their possibility of being a "total revolutionary," and relegated them to an often-impoverished domestic sphere. Moreover, reducing Black women's role in liberation to reproduction eliminated half of the Black community's revolutionary potential. "There is power in numbers," he wrote, "but that power is greatly diminished if a lot of those numbers have to sit at home and change diapers instead of being on the front lines, where most of them would rather be."[45] Such conviction aligned with that of the TWWA, which centered issues of birth control, abortion, and forced sterilization to insist that Black women must have control over their own bodies. These thinkers maintained that revolutionaries should empower those who had been historically forced into motherhood and reproduction to decide whether or not they wanted children. Thus, in a number of ways, thinkers like Beal, Williams, and Lester showed how gender provided a deeper understanding of superexploitation by revealing the divergent social effects of Black men's and women's different relationships to the mode of production.[46]

For its part, the CRC_1 added heterosexism to racism, class oppression, sexism, and elitism as essential components of superexploitation. It saw as its intellectual and historical task the development of a praxis that challenged the interlocking systems of domination that particularly plagued women of color and that built upon the historical struggle of

Black women against the antagonisms of "white-male rule." Moreover, the CRC_1 coined the term "identity politics" to denote a "repugnant, dangerous, threatening, and therefore revolutionary" set of discursive and political practices that clarified the multiple forms of exploitation that precluded liberation. Like their anticapitalist foremothers, this group of militants believed that socialism was imperative to the eradication of superexploitation because "work must be organized for the collective benefit of those who do the work and create the products, and not for the profit of bosses. Material resources must be equally distributed among those who create these resources." However, such a revolution must be predicated upon leftist Black gender inquiry to ensure that "the specific class position of Black women" was accounted for.[47]

Blackness as a National Question

Throughout the twentieth century, conceptualizing Blackness as a national question was another effective way to connect the condition of Black people in the United States to other oppressed groups throughout the world. It was also a means of analyzing the unique effects of specific cycles of capitalist accumulation on Black people.[48] While Black Power theories of this sort sometimes amounted to narrowly nationalist enunciations of the "ethnic paradigm,"[49] radical and anticapitalist iterations inhered in internationalist, proletarian solidarity that brought analyses of superexploitation and critiques of imperialism, white supremacy, and capitalist exploitation into a single focus. In both its rural and urban applications, this approach expressed the Black community in the United States as a nation within a nation, a domestic colony, and/or an internal neocolony. Blackness as a national question was predicated on three central points: that Blacks were an oppressed national minority in the South of the United States, and later, in the urban ghettoes of the North; that the Black masses possessed the capacity to organize and liberate themselves; and that as a national question, the Black struggle in the United States was one iteration of international anticapitalist revolution. In 1924, for example, Otto Huiswoud argued that insofar as over 80 percent of Blacks lived in the South, it was essentially "a country all by itself" that was indispensable to the world proletarian insurgency. The Black nation therefore required special attention, namely, support for all forms of Black protest that challenged capitalism and imperialism, the organization of Black workers, and work among Blacks by Blacks.[50] Perhaps the best-known development of Blackness as a national question was the

Communist International's 1928 Black Belt nation thesis, spearheaded by Harry Haywood.[51] The Black Belt nation thesis posited that the "Black Belt" of the United States, encompassing "the old cotton country" that traversed twelve Southern states from the south of Maryland to the Mississippi Delta and that contained roughly five million Blacks—over 60 percent of the Black population[52]—was a nation with the right to secede from the United States if it so desired. Concomitantly, African American striving for liberation amounted to a national struggle for self-government and self-determination. Haywood added that a revolutionary nationalist movement led by a Black peasant-proletariat alliance was the most effective approach to fighting monopoly capitalism and statist and financial imperialism.[53]

In 1935, Du Bois offered a related analysis that moved beyond the South. He maintained that Blacks were a nation within a nation given the entrenchment of their economic, political, social, and educational dispossession at the hands of whites who had little interest in ensuring the survival or future of Black folk if it entailed freedom, self-assertion, and equality. As such, Black empowerment required "a group movement among Negroes, particularly along economic lines, involving increased racial separation and voluntary segregation."[54] Similarly, in making a case for Blacks as a separate nation, Jones aptly noted in 1946 that Black dispossession was not a phenomenon confined to the South; it was also the reality of the "Seventh Sons" warehoused in Northern industrial slums. She explained, "We kn[o]w that the semi-slavery of the Southern sharecroppers; the inferior status of the Negro people in industry, North and South . . . the Jim Crow practices of New York and Chicago, as well as Birmingham and Tampa . . . all can be traced back step by step to the continued existence of an oppressed Negro nation within our border."[55] Jones's 1949 position on triple exploitation was also relevant to Blackness as a national question insofar as she contended that race, as a national form of oppression, was the primary mode through which superexploitation was experienced, and therefore the Negro question was prior to the woman question.[56]

By the time Black Power became the predominant articulation of Black militancy in the late 1960s, the majority of the Black population had become an urbanized proletariat.[57] As such, the analysis of Blackness as a national question focused on the ways that imperial capitalism, in its embedded liberal form,[58] had turned Black folk into a domestic colony and an internal neocolony. Between 1966 and 1969, Black Power activists including Carmichael, Harold Cruse, and Robert L. Allen argued that, much like the situation in countries colonized by European imperial powers, ownership resided outside of the Black community; a few elites collaborated and identified with the oppressor for their own personal gain; and resources, particularly in the form of labor, were extracted from the Black community.[59] Further, capitalism produced the dependent and colonial status of Black people by restricting them to destitute areas in the rural Black belt, "shantytowns" throughout the South and "slums" in the industrialized West and North in which they owned and controlled virtually nothing.[60] Hence, in political and economic terms, Black people were "a colony within the United States" not so different from "outside" colonies in Africa, Asia, and the Caribbean, and Black Power was "the struggle to free these colonies from external domination" through rebellions that disrupted the flow of goods and services.[61] Likewise, in 1975 the BWUF asserted that the "National Oppression" of Black people called for a struggle for "Self-Determination" and "Democratic Rights," a struggle that would ultimately lead toward a socialist society where the working masses produced and controlled the wealth in a given society.[62] This echoed Carmichael's premise that the economic base of the United States had to be "shaken" if domestic colonies were to be liberated.[63]

Moreover, akin to Jones, in 1970 Williams and Beal of the TWWA reasoned that Black women saw their oppression as a national question as opposed to one that was primarily determined by gender. This was largely due to white women's myopia, racism, and ignorance of their darker sisters' plight.[64] This did not, however, mean that racism was the *only* structure of oppression. Beal asserted that miseducated Black male chauvinists who accepted the bourgeois narrative of Black women as emasculator and matriarch were counterrevolutionary. Such distortion obscured the fact that it was the capitalist system that "emasculated, lynched, and brutalized" Black men and that Black women were in fact "slave[s] of a slave," who suffered "the depth of degradation, [being] socially manipulated, physically raped, used to undermine [their] own household[s], and powerless to reverse this syndrome."[65] Black male chauvinism thus exacerbated the national character of Black oppression for triply exploited Black women.

Conclusion

Analyzing Black Power in the tradition of radical Blackness illuminates that a commitment to anticapitalism was congenital to struggles for Black liberation throughout the twentieth century. Diverse activist-intellectuals including W. E. B. Du Bois, James Ford, Louise Thompson Patterson,

Claudia Jones, Harry Haywood, Stokely Carmichael, Frances Beale, and Maxine Williams challenged the entanglements of imperialism, white supremacy, and capitalist exploitation. Organizations ranging from the left-wing interracial Civil Rights Congress to the radical Black feminist CRC_1 interrogated the superexploitation of Black people in its political, economic, gendered, and sexualized manifestations. In addition, a multitude of radical Black individuals and organizations analyzed Blackness as a national question based on their specific historical contexts and relationships to the capitalist mode of production. Even as the tradition of radical Blackness included diverse ideologies, strategies, tactics, and approaches, all efforts were aimed at answering the vexing question of how to "get free."

Notes

1. Gwendolyn Patton, "Born Freedom Fighter," in *Hands on the Freedom Plow: Personal Accounts by Women in SNCC*, ed. Faith S. Holsaert et al. (Urbana: University of Illinois Press, 2010), 581.

2. See, e.g., Robin D. G. Kelly and Betsy Esch, "Black Like Mao: Red China and Black Revolution," *Souls* 4 (1999): 6–41; Mark T. Berger, "After the Third World? Destiny and the Fate of Third Worldism," *Third World Quarterly* 25 (2004): 9–39; Sarah Seidman, "Tricontinental Routes of Solidarity: Stokely Carmichael in Cuba," *Journal of Transnational America* 4 (2012): 1–25; Besenia Rodriguez, "'Long Live Third World Unity! Long Live Intercommunalism: Huey P. Newton's Revolutionary Intercommunalism," *Souls* 8 (2006): 119–41; Gerald Horne, *Black Revolutionary: William Patterson and the Globalization of the African American Freedom Struggle* (Champaign: University of Illinois Press, 2013), 189–206; and Keith Gilyard, *Louise Thompson Patterson: A Life of Struggle* (Durham, NC: Duke University Press, 2017), 182–194.

3. Black Women's United Front, *Build the Black Women's United Front! Abolition of Every Possibility of Oppression and Exploitation!*, pamphlet, Newark, NJ, 1975, self-published, Widener Library, Harvard University.

4. Philip Foner, ed., *The Black Panthers Speak* (Chicago: Haymarket Books, 1970), 66, 105–6.

5. James Boggs, *Black Manifesto for a Black Revolutionary Party* (Philadelphia: Pacesetters Publishing House, 1969), 9–11, 17–28.

6. For a comprehensive discussion of Black Power as a form of capitalism, see Laura Warren Hill and Julia Rabig, *The Business of Black Power: Community Development, Capitalism, and Corporate Responsibility in Postwar American* (Rochester, NY: University of Rochester Press, 2012). For a critique of this Black Power as Black capitalism, see Robert L. Allen, *Black Awakening in Capitalist America: An Analytic History* (New York: Anchor Books, 1969).

7. Stephen Ward, "The Third World Women's Alliance: Black Feminist Radicalism and Black Power Politics," in *The Black Power Movement: Rethinking the Civil Rights-Black Power Era*, ed. Peniel E. Joseph (New York: Routledge, 2006), 120.

8. Richard B. Moore, "Statement at the Congress of the League against Imperialism and for National Independence," in *Richard B. Moore, Caribbean Militant in Harlem: Collected Writings, 1920–1972*, ed. Richard B. Turner et al. (Bloomington: Indiana University Press, 1992), 144–46.

9. Charisse Burden-Stelly, "Cold War Culturalism and African Diaspora Theory: Some Theoretical Sketches," *Souls* 19 (2017): 213–37; and Cedric Robinson, *Black Marxism: The Making of the Black Radical Tradition* (Chapel Hill: University of North Carolina Press, 2000), xxx–xxxii.

10. See, e.g., John Munro, *The Anticolonial Front: The African American freedom Struggle and Global Decolonisation, 1945–1960* (Cambridge: Cambridge University Press, 2017); Hakim Adi and Markia Sherwood, *The Pan-African Congress of 1945 Revisited* (London: New Beacon Books, 1995); Erik S. McDuffie, *Sojourning for Freedom: Black Women, American Communism, and the Making of Black Left Feminism* (Durham, NC: Duke University Press, 2011); Cheryl Higashida, *Black Internationalist Feminism: Women Writers of the Black Left, 1945–1995* (Champaign: University of Illinois Press, 2011; Richard Wright, *The Color Curtain: A Report on the Bandung Conference* (Jackson: University of Mississippi Press, 1995); and Anne Garland Mahler, *From the Tricontinental to the Global South: Race, Radicalism, and Transnational Solidarity* (Durham, NC: Duke University Press, 2018).

11. For an explication, historiography, and critique of "the long movement," see Sundiata Cha-Jua and Clarence Lang, "The 'Long Movement' as Vampire: Temporal and Spatial Fallacies in Recent Black Freedom Studies," *Journal of African American History* 92 (2007): 265–88. Also see Cedric Johnson and Mel Rothenberg, "Black Politics in the Age of Obama," *Platypus Review* 57 (2013), http://platypus1917.org/2013/06/01/black-politics-in-age-of-obama/; and Adolph Reed, "The Post-1965 Trajectory of Race, Class, and Urban Politics in the United States Reconsidered," *Labor Studies Journal* 41 (2016): 18–19.

12. Munro, *The Anticolonial Front*, 5–9; Dayo F. Gore, *Radicalism at the Crossroads: African American Women Activists in the Cold War* (New York: New York University Press, 2011), 7–12.

13. Munro, *The Anticolonial Front*, 5.

14. W. E. B. Du Bois, "The African Roots of War," *Atlantic Monthly*, May 1915, 707–14.

15. Du Bois, "The African Roots of War," 709.

16. James Ford, "The Negro Question: Report to the IInd World Congress of the League Against Imperialism," *Negro Worker*, August 1929, 1–14.

17. Ford, "The Negro Question," 2

18. Stokely Carmichael, "Black Power and the Third World," *Third World Information Service*, August 1967, 1–8. Also see Julius Lester, "'Black Revolution Is Real': Stokely Carmichael in Cuba," *Movement*, September 1967.

19. Carmichael, "Black Power and the Third World," 1.

20. Carmichael, "Black Power and the Third World," 8.

21. Carmichael, "Black Power and the Third World," 2.

22. Carmichael, "Black Power and the Third World," 5.

23. Carmichael, "Black Power and the Third World," 6.

24. James S. Allen, *Negro Liberation* (New York: International Publishers, 1938), 27. Emphasis in original.

25. Otto Huiswoud, "World Aspects of the Negro Question," *Communist*, 1930.
26. Harry Haywood, *Negro Liberation* (Chicago: Liberator Press, 1976), 46–48.
27. William Patterson, ed., *We Charge Genocide: The Historic Petition to the United Nations for Relief from a Crime of the United States Government against the Negro People* (New York: Civil Rights Congress, 1951). On the Civil Rights Congress, see Gerald Horne, *Communist Front? The Civil Rights Congress, 1946–1956* (Cranbury, NJ: Associated University Presses, 1988).
28. Horne, *Communist Front?*, 134.
29. Mark Solomon, *The Cry Was Unity: Communists and African Americas, 1917–1938* (Jackson: University of Mississippi Press, 1998), 61, 99.
30. Patterson, *We Charge Genocide*, 129.
31. Malcolm X, "Housing Conditions in Black Communities," *Malcolm X: The Best of the Speeches*, Stardust Records, August 7, 2007.
32. "What We Want, What We Believe," *Black Panther*, November 23, 1967, 1.
33. Institute of the black World, *IBW Monthly Report*, March 1972. For a thorough history of the Institute of the Black World, see Derrick E. White, *The Challenge of Blackness: The Institute of the Black World and Political Activism in the 1970s* (Tallahassee: University of Florida Press, 2011).
34. Black Women's United Front, "Congress of Afrikan People on the Woman Question," Detroit, January 25, 1975, 5.
35. Ella Baker and Marvel Cooke, "The Bronx Slave Market," *Crisis* 42 (November 1935). There is a similar discussion in Mary Anderson, "The Plight of Negro Domestic Labor," *Journal of Negro Education* 5 (1936): 66–72.
36. Louise Thompson Patterson, "Toward a Brighter Dawn," *Woman Today*, April 1936; Baker and Cooke, "The Bronx Slave Market.".
37. Erik McDuffie, "Esther V. Cooper's 'The Negro Woman Domestic Worker in Relation to Trade Unionism': Black Left Feminism and the Popular Front," *American Communist History* 7 (2008): 205.
38. See Buzz Johnson, *"I Think of My Mother": Notes on the Life and Times of Claudia Jones* (London: Karia Press, 1985); Marika Sherwood, *Claudia Jones: A Life in Exile* (London: Lawrence & Wishart, 1999); and Carole Boyce Davies, ed., *Claudia Jones: Beyond Containment* (Boulder, CO: Lynne Rienner, 2011).
39. Claudia Jones, "An End to the Neglect of the Problems of the Negro Woman!" in *Let Nobody Turn Us Around, Second Edition*, edited by Manning Marable (Lanham, MD: Rowan & Littlefield, 2009), 316.
40. Jones, "An End to the Neglect," 320.
41. W. E. B. Du Bois, "The American Negro Woman" (unpublished), ca. 1949, W. E. B. Du Bois Papers (MS 312), Special Collections and University Archives University of Massachusetts Amherst Libraries (hereafter Du Bois Papers).
42. For these earlier positions see e.g., W. E. B. Du Bois, "Morals and Manners among Negro Women," ca. 1913, Du Bois Papers; and Du Bois, *The Gift of Black Folk: The Negroes in the Making of America* (Garden City Park: Square One Publishers, 2009), 119–26.
43. Frances Beal, "Double Jeopardy: To Be Black and Female," in *Black Women's Manifesto*, ed. Third World Women's Alliance (New York: Third World Women's Alliance, 1970), 24.
44. Beal, "Double Jeopardy," 19.
45. Julius Lester, *Revolutionary Notes* (New York: Grove Press), 140–43.

46. Maxine Williams, "Black Women and the Struggle for Liberation," in *Black Women's Manifesto*, ed. Third World Women's Alliance (New York: Third World Women's Alliance, 1970), 14–15; Beal, "Double Jeopardy," 19–20.

47. Combahee River Collective, "The Combahee River Collective Statement," in *Homegirls: A Black Feminist Anthology*, ed. Barbara Smith (New Brunswick: Rutgers University Press, 1983), 264–69. Also see Keenaga Yahmatta-Taylor, *How We Get Free: Black Feminism and the Combahee River Collective* (Chicago: Haymarket Books, 2017).

48. On cycles of accumulation, see Robert Brenner, *The Economics of Global Turbulence* (New York: Verso, 2006). Also see Giovanni Arrighi and Beverly Silver, "Capitalism and World (Dis)order," *Review of International Studies* 27 (2001): 257–79.

49. On the ethnic paradigm, see Dean E. Robinson, *Black Nationalism in American Politics and Thought* (Cambridge: Cambridge University Press, 2001), 104–17. For critiques of Black Power as an ethnic paradigm, see Cedric Johnson, *Revolutionaries to Race Leaders: Black Power and the Making of African American Politics* (Minneapolis: University of Minnesota Press, 2007), 3–41; and Adolph L. Reed, Jr., "Black Particularity Reconsidered," *Telos* 39 (1979): 71–93.

50. Otto Huiswoud and Claude McKay, "Speeches to the Fourth World Congress of the Comintern on the Negro Question," *Bulletin of the IV Congress of the Communist International*, December 22, 1922, 17–23.

51. Harry Haywood, *Black Bolshevik: Autobiography of an African-American Communist* (Chicago: Liberator Press, 1978), 222–35. It is important to note that other Black communists, including James Ford, Otto Hall, Lovett Fort-Whiteman, and, later, Doxey Wilkerson, opposed the idea of a separate Black nation, instead arguing that the Blackness was a racial question that could not be resolved through nationalism, insofar as Black in the United States demanded full equality.

52. Allen, *Negro Liberation*, 13–14; Haywood, *Negro Liberation*, 11–13.

53. Harry Haywood, *Black Bolshevik* (Chicago: Liberator Press, 1978), 229–30.

54. W. E. B. Du Bois, "Keeping Blacks and Whites Apart," February 9, 1935, Du Bois Papers. This draft was published as "A Negro Nation within a Nation" in *Current History* in June 1935.

55. Claudia Jones, "On the Right to Self-Determination for the Negro People in the Black Belt," in *Claudia Jones: Beyond Containment*, ed. Carole Boyce Davies (Boulder, CO: Lynne Rienner, 2011), 62.

56. Jones, "On the Right to Self-Determination," 324.

57. Lloyd Hogan, *Principles of Black Political Economy* (Boston: Routledge & Kegan Paul, 1984), 115–62.

58. On embedded liberalism, see, e.g., Jens Steffek, *Embedded Liberalism and Its Critics: Justifying Global Governance in the American Century* (New York: Palgrave, 2006), 35–55.

59. Kwame Turè and Charles V. Hamilton, *Black Power: The Politics of Liberation* (New York: Vintage Books, 1992), 26–41; Harold Cruse, *Rebellion or Revolution* (New York: William Morrow, 1968), 76–77; Allen, *Black* (New York: Anchor Books, 1969), 1–20.

60. Carmichael, "Black Power and the Third World," 3–4.

61. Carmichael, "Black Power and the Third World," 4.
62. Black Women's United Front, "Congress of Afrikan People on the Woman Question," 4.
63. Stokely Carmichael, "Power and Racism," in *Stokely Speaks: From Black Power to Pan-Africanism* (Chicago: Lawrence Hill Books, 1971 [1965].
64. Williams, "Black Women," 15.
65. Beal, "Double Jeopardy," 22.

Part 5

✦

The Digital as Intellectual: Poetics and Possibilities

INTRODUCTION

Marisa Parham

In an essay titled "The Future of Time," Toni Morrison laments that futurism had become less bold over the course of the twentieth century, as Americans became more invested in recasting or recuperating the past than in conceptualizing new futures. Morrison's comments are especially striking given their context, first delivered as a speech accepting the twenty-fifth Jefferson Medal for the Humanities, awarded by President Clinton in 1996. The speech was thematically similar to her recent Nobel acceptance speech, which reminded listeners that the narratives that best express the realities of most lives persist unacknowledged by such honors.[1] In the Jefferson Medal speech, Morrison turns this perspective into a meditation on how technological innovation produces similar exclusions, as the triumphalism of progress rationalizes violent histories, thus emptying out time as a "course of time [that] seems to be narrowing to a vanishing point beyond which humanity neither exists nor wants to" dystopia.[2] By framing her meditation on technology in terms familiar to followers of other late twentieth-century debates around memory, history, and the kinds of data that underwrite social claims, Morrison was able to illustrate the dangers inherent in triumphant narratives about technological progress and to align those concerns with larger conversations regarding the kinds of worlds that might be made out of multiple and interlocking histories of violence.[3] She delivered her speech at a moment when the United States was financially, ideologically, and culturally enthralled with the "dot com boom" of the late 1990s, and she wanted her audience to notice that "where advance, progress and change have been signatory features," we find so many spaces "where confidence in an enduring future is at its slightest."[4] From this perspective, innovation is fundamentally disappointing, from apps that reify extant structures of inequality, to the Roomba self-driving vacuums developed by the same company and on the same platforms used for military drones and tactical pack dog robots. There are few contemporary digital or digital-industrial technologies that have not trickled down from larger market capitalist or military enterprises. Further, as Safiya Noble notes, "dominant and frequently technologically deterministic perspectives . . . ignore interlocking, structural, and globalized sites of oppression."[5] Because they ratify a future in which most people would never want to live, progress and innovation can accelerate social regression, supporting what Morrison describes as a "diminished, already withered desire for a future."

So what *does* it mean that so many of our most engaging technological imaginations of the future are so beholden to the most brutal aspects of our historical past? At the very least it means, when taking an intellectual history perspective on the digital humanities, that no discussion of a technological modernity, of digital labor, of the potentialities of speculative media, or of the ecological and the technological valences of human interactivity—the kinds of work made possible by software, media, and critical digital studies—can ignore the constitutive presence of structurally disenfranchised peoples or the artifact and energy of their various engagements with digital technologies. From this perspective, Black cultural strategies of heterogeneous growth and resistance can be described as precipitates of Black encounters with the digitizing functions—our breaking and constant remaking—of New World *dispositifs*. From Harriet Jacobs's orchestrations of virtual space, place, and word in her long game for freedom, to Ida B. Wells's tabulations of racial violence, and on to Adrian Piper's computational imaginings and Mendi+Keith Obadike's trailblazing work in data-based digital installation art, the diverse scions of Black diasporas in the Americas have always been digital, both generating *and* finding ourselves embedded within digital experiences, Black digitalities. In "Sample | Signal | Strobe," I frame diasporic digitality in relation to other Black technologies of cultural generation, transmission, and regeneration, what Paul D. Miller describes as "an involution engine."[6] Black life is both metaphor for and symptom of digital experience, as "transfer, migration, metonymy: the break and the remix persist as both witness and feature of the multiple and continual experiences of forced migration endemic to Afro-diasporic life in the Americas—the Middle Passage, the auction block, the Great Migration—'the digital.'"[7]

In other words, as Morrison highlights and as Simone Brown and other scholars have demonstrated, it is critically important to know how to contextualize digital technologies because they constitute, and are constituted by, the same social and economic machineries that have historically undergirded the numerous systems of surveillance, automation, and incarceration that continue to malign Black lives.[8] To live is both to navigate and to resist the social and technological forces that might otherwise break us, to feel the beat as it enters our bodies but also to transform it in its passage through our own kinds of knowing. In describing his own sense of why African Americans might find ways to flourish in an even more heavily technologized future, Ralph Ellison turns to the figure of John Henry as an example of what it means to master or overcome technology in the service of cherishing the value of one's own life. "What we have counterpoised against the necessary rage for progress in American life," Ellison contends, "will have been proved to be at least as valuable as all our triumphs of technology."[9] In her essay in this part, Jessica Marie Johnson puts it another way, "Digital technology has not made black resistance possible. It has made legible percussive black resistance that has been circulating, sailing, flying, throbbing, and absconding for generations."

Digital humanities emerge out of this complex mix of emergent possibility and nascent regressivity. What often gets referred to as "digital humanities" includes a broad range of perspectives on how to bring new or experimental technologies into the study of the humanities, and in so doing making space for new kinds of questions and connections. The term also refers to the work of scholars to describe and interpret the impact of digital technologies on social life and cultural production, with an emphasis on humanistically framed inquiries into technologies themselves.[10] In the essays in the following part, each writer introduces a different scholarly approach, an intellectual diversity that captures the digital humanities as simultaneously naming method, instrument, and critical orientation and that also bespeaks the particular possibilities of the commitments of Black digital humanities to enlarged critical and creative scholarly frames. Each piece also intervenes in the structural logics out of which its tools and methods have arisen. As noted by Moya Bailey and others, this sense of boundary between what can be given or taken from any technological formation is critical.[11] Nevertheless, the essays in this part offer tools for surfacing extant yet obscured knowledges, whether that be Alexis Pauline Gumbs's emphasis on futurity, Jessica Marie Johnson's narrative of how she has used digital tools to add curational approaches to her work as a historian, or Christy Hyman's use of digital tools to surface futures for knowledges otherwise submerged in the Great Dismal Swamp. At every turn, Gumbs, Hyman, and Johnson show us new ways of remembering how Black diasporic subjects have sought freedom as well as how to identify new and broader ways to be free, which is a comprehensively different and always newly difficult project—a process of *x*.

In "The Black Possible: Scenes from an Intellectual History of the Postdigital Future," Alexis Pauline Gumbs asks readers to think of themselves as scientists and "to be reflexive about the implications of your own (Black, intellectual) practices." She asks that we "be on the lookout for what comes up for you in all these layers of Black intellectual tech." In ways reminiscent of scientist Ashley Baccus-Clark and Hyphen Labs' work with prototype manufacturing and virtual reality in their *NeuroSpeculative AfroFeminism* project, Gumbs's piece implements a creative-process methodology she describes as "speculative documentary," which asks readers to engage a series of meditations on a small sampling of imaginable futures rooted in the intersection between Black digitality and the kinds of inquiry centered in Black intellectual traditions, "crossing something intergenerational, temporal and cosmic."[12] In the third vignette of "The Black Possible," Gumbs offers an image that enacts such multiple crossings by actively slipping meaning across grammatical signifiers:

> that's why they made the quilts and ranked the pieces and kissed them and stitched them. they knew how to circle the cloth that had soaked up your sweat and salt into a map back to the ocean. they knew who was first and who would last and they stitched, all the while singing songs that let the threads too know their names. they were physical metaphysicians. they wanted you to be warm enough to remember.

Here, Gumbs offers a complex image in which hard labor, sweat and salt, is transformed into care. In asking her reader to remember, she evokes histories of Black resistance and marronage, including the navigational arts that brought the natural world and its pathways—trail, map, constellation—into African American material cultures: routes encoded in story, song, hair, and cloth. Opening the segment in media res, as if it were a conversation already in progress, Gumbs's "that's why" bolsters the sense that whoever is being addressed is the recipient of an oracular power and has arrived in the present by following a map to the future granted by a shared or community past.

In "To Render a Landscape of Trauma: Deep Mapping a Historical Landscape of Domination—the Great Dismal Swamp," Christy Hyman describes her ongoing work with digitally mapping the escape routes of enslaved people in what we now call Virginia and North Carolina. "Deep mapping" is characterized by critical geographic practices that emphasize the meaning and constitution of place rather than coordinate-identified space. But while deep mapping is usually used to denote processes by which scholars can identify and subsequently elucidate the meaning of such accretion, in Hyman's projects we see how it can be used to broaden the sources out of which we sift historical material data. "To Render a Landscape" describes Hyman's long-term multimodal digital research toward constructing *The Oak of Jerusalem: Flight, Refuge, and Reconnaissance in the Great Dismal Swamp Region of North Carolina*, a large-scale digital humanities project that centers on what Hyman frames as the various kinds of "navigational literacy" enslaved people used to transform the untamable and uninhabitable space of the swamp into a *place*, a refuge she sets in stark contrast to plantations' hypermanaged and thus more drastically uninhabitable carceral space.

Hyman uses georeferencing to rectify historical documents with contemporary digital and satellite maps, which enables her to demonstrate transformations in landscape over time. Rectification is a process by which historical maps, for instance, the nineteenth-century materials Hyman works with, are squared with more technically precise data made available by the World Geodetic System, which is the physical data system that drives spatial mapping and positioning systems, for instance, the geographic information system used by Hyman to baseline historical maps, and the satellite-based positioning system many devices use to provide spatial data and orientation to objects moving across the Earth's surface and atmosphere (i.e., GPS). Digital spatial humanities projects, like Angel David Nieves's work with the digital reconstruction of townships in South Africa and Hyman's work with Moses Grundy's nineteenth-century narrative of his enslavement, put highly mechanized state data into play with close-reading strategies that demonstrate how to assay spatial data out of the narratives and knowledge worlds of otherwise marginalized persons.

In other words, historical maps and spaces are not just rectified through the application of modern spatial technologies; they are also *made right* through the inclusion of the epistemes, stories, and values of Black people. In her commitment to examining hybridized deep mapping techniques, Hyman is also able to remap spatial information from other kinds of sources, for instance, the narratives and storytelling of enslaved people, people who were able to use their status as cogs in slavery's machine to produce active knowledge bases about their physical environments. As Hyman notes, "The affordances of thinking spatially allow us to reappraise geographical concepts of space while attempting to understand how enslaved people came to understand the spaces around them. Spatial approaches to understanding the phenomenon of enslaved flight can reveal the challenges of that process at a scale previously unseen."

By enabling radical perspectival shifts, scaling is one of the most important intellectual opportunities that digital humanities scholarship makes available. Digital technologies greatly facilitate movement from the smallest and most localized to the most zoomed-out perspectives or positions. One might think here of a camera that allows you to magnify a grain of sand so that you can see it as a singular world. With the scope's eye locked on that grain, now imagine zooming out, scaling out: handful of sand, sandy beach, coastline, landmass, planet, and so on. Zoom in now to trace that grain of sand back to the origin that it fossilizes, to borrow a visual cue from Alexis Pauline Gumbs's meditation on sand in *M Archive*.[13] If we hold this notion of scale in resonance with Samuel Delaney, *Stars in My Pocket Like Grains of Sand*, we can understand that, as both object and metaphor, a grain of sand is an entire world or nothing at all. The North Star rectifies, and *knowing* to look enacts an eminently deep time way of understanding where you are, how to move from the scalar to the local: the place of your living, the space of your own possible resistance. With the idea of perspective itself put into new perspective, Hyman's research demonstrates how enslaved persons could produce their own digitally scaled epistemes—active, networked, and transformable—just by attending to the stars.

Citing Katherine McKittrick, Pier Gabrielle Foreman, and others, and with a visual style that shows a strong kinship with the poet Kamau Braithwaite's typographic experiments, Jessica Marie Johnson's "'All the Stars Are Closer'" carries us on an exploration of "black digital practice as the practice of creating constellations of being that surface histories of terror at the heart of the machine of the New World and map new routes to galaxies beyond black death." Building on Moya Bailey and Alexis Gumbs's 2010 observation that, even then, there were over one hundred blogs committed to "black feminism in cyberspace," Johnson contextualizes her development of the immensely influential digital project, *African Diaspora PhD* (*#ADPhD*), which began as a blog, a place for Johnson to curate, share, and archive different objects and insights that come to her as a historian of African enslavement in the Americas. But, as Johnson elaborates, it soon became clear that she needed the digital space she was building to do more, to flourish as a fugitive place where she could reframe her scholarly investigations and share them "with the people I know needed it—my community, the women in my life, diasporic kinfolk far and wide. Narrative history itself—facts, figures, text, images—seemed to hold the key, but not as narrated by slaveowners." Here Johnson highlights both the critical importance of building the kinds of gathering places made possible by digital technologies and how doing so enables Black communities to engage their intellectual concerns from perspectives outside of white supremacist mandates about value, meaning, and implication. Even though digital technologies technically enable the development of cross-spatial, distributed networks, this ease does not erase the difficulty of such work. In other words, much as easily looking up information on a contemporary search engine like Google is not the same as research, the curation of content and the cultivation of meaningful digital communities requires juggling multiple kinds of scholarly and emotional labor, as Johnson explains.

Digital experience, particularly in the course of perusing blogs and engaging social media, hinges on making oneself subject to constant dissonance between times, spaces, and materialities, the rhizomatic rabbit hole of the hyperlink, an unexpected encounter of trauma on a social media timeline. In "Stars," Johnson connects digitality to experiences of archival research:

> In slavery's archive, time and space cross. There is as much to know and not know, as there is to unknow 'entering the lists,' as Katherine McKittrick described the experience of encountering diasporic horrors in the archive. There is much to know, not know, and know *only for an instant* by culling what we can from lists of names. And yet, what lies in the margins somewhere between the list of names and the edge of the paper, between the sign and the list itself, in the silence, the null value, the empty record is also part of the work.

Here Johnson frames archival research in terms that resonate with characterizations of Black life in digital spaces, describing ephemeral experiences wherein meaning is made in the gap between the known and that which can only be unknown by the living—even as the prospect of livable futures depends on understanding painful pasts. "The null value, the empty record" is the place of lives passed unrecorded in ways that would carry their names into the future.

As Johnson wants us to see, a null value is not absence, as what gets called absence is usually a problem of recognition and tabulation—the problem of who matters and how that mattering is registered. It might be useful here to return briefly to the cartographic, in this case the story of Null Island. Null Island is the name given to the cartographic point that serves as the degree zero for global geographic systems (0° north 0° east)—where the equator and the prime meridian cross in the Gulf of Guinea. "Null Island" is shorthand for the default or reset number assigned to unlocatable or incorrect spatial coordinates entered into digital spatial systems that use the World Geodetic System. Like the number zero or an empty set, Null Island is critical to spatial orientation but is also mainly only comprehensible through deduction. It is, in other words, absolutely concrete—zero is a number—and invisible; there is no island at Null Island, even though it is the site around which all other spaces become legible and thus mappable.

Much as places like Elmina and Goree Island are often taken as degree zero for Black Atlantic enslavement, the historical forces that led to the establishment of Null Island as the degree zero for modern cartographic practice share history with those places. Located in the Gulf of Guinea, the nonplace that we call Null Island also historically sites the technological degree zero for westward exploration and the vast machineries of displacement and exploitation that would follow. Holding this image, we might return here to Morrison's melancholic image for technological progress unmitigated by an ethical orientation toward history's lessons, the vanishing point. A vanishing point is a perspectival trick of the eye, for instance, when parallel rails seem to converge and disappear in a far distance. The image hints at the simultaneously wondrous and sinister, an image for how rationalizing progress as the value of progress decimates opportunities for livable futures, even as it also gestures toward distant promises. We might hear in this Gumbs's description of the digitally inflected method that informs her work in speculative documentary, which she describes as "a form of future listening that challenges us in the present to imagine the implications of our present moment from the perspective of the futures that are made possible and impossible by our current thinking." As the essays in the following section remind us, this is no less true of Black digital humanities, and it is why digital scholarship that draws on Black intellectual histories will be of increasing importance in the coming decades.

Notes

1. Toni Morrison, "The Nobel Lecture in Literature," in *What Moves at the Margin: Selected Nonfiction*, ed. Carolyn C. Denard (Jackson: University Press of Mississippi, 2008).

2. This part extends remarks made in the course of *Black Haunts in the Anthropocene*, in the context of matters of care and technology, as refracted through Morrison, Bruno Latour, and Bethany Nowivskie. Marisa Parham, "Common Sympathy → for the Children," *Black Haunts in the Anthropocene* (October 2014), https://blackhaunts.mp285.com/common-sympathy.

3. "The Future of Time" also marks Morrison's participation in that era's scholarly debates around matters of memory, history, and politics—from Francis Fukuyama's "The End of History" and the Historikerstreit debate in Germany, through the various kinds of historical and political debates sparked by her own epigraph to 1987's *Beloved*, which brought the transatlantic slave trade into conversations that until that point had been mainly focused on how best to historicize

and memorialize the Holocaust. For a useful review of Toni Morrison's *Beloved* and the question of data numerical loss, also see Naomi Mandel, "'I Made the Ink': Identity, Complicity, 60 Million, and More," *MFS Modern Fiction Studies* 48, no. 3 (September 1, 2002): 581–613.

4. Morrison, "The Future of Time: Literature and Diminished Expectations," in *What Moves at the Margin*, 171.

5. Safiya Noble, "A Future for Intersectional Black Feminist Technology Studies." *S&F Online* 13.3–14.1 (2016), http://sfonline.barnard.edu/traversing-technologies/safiya-umoja-noble-a-future-for-intersectional-black-feminist-technology-studies/.

6. Paul D. Miller aka DJ Spooky That Subliminal Kid, *Rhythm Science* (Boston: MIT Press, 2004).

7. Marisa Parham, "Sample | Signal | Strobe: Haunting, Social Media, and Black Digitality," in *Debates in Digital Humanities 2019*, ed. Matthew Gold and Lauren Klein (Minneapolis: University of Minnesota Press, 2019).

8. Simone Browne, *Dark Matters: On the Surveillance of Blackness* (Durham, NC: Duke University Press, 2015).

9. Ralph Ellison, "Some Questions and Some Answers," in *The Collected Essays of Ralph Ellison*, ed. John F. Callahan (New York: Modern Library, 2003), 299.

10. When taken as an institutional formation, the digital humanities provide frameworks for centering scholarship historically marginalized in mainstream academic disciplines. Such projects include large-scale archival initiatives like the Colored Conventions Project and Documenting the Now, which are committed to the recovery and analysis of Black people's commentary about their own lives; institutional configurations like the African American History, Culture, and Digital Humanities initiative at University of Maryland (AADHum), and explicitly computational investigations collected under the auspices of the Data for Black Lives group.

11. For a succinct primer on this matter, see Moya Z. Bailey "All the Digital Humanists Are White, All the Nerds Are Men, but Some of Us Are Brave," *Journal of Digital Humanities*, March 9, 2012.

12. Ashley Baccus-Clark, Hyphen Labs team, *NeuroSpeculative AfroFeminism*, http://www.hyphen-labs.com/nsaf.html.

13. Alexis Pauline Gumbs, "From the Lab Notebooks of the Last* Experiments," in *M Archive: After the End of the World* (Durham, NC: Duke University Press, 2018).

Chapter 15

The Black Possible

Scenes from an Intellectual History of the Postdigital Future

Alexis Pauline Gumbs

Black digital realities are technologies for representing intellectual patterns and practices in thought, and they have shaped the way we think and what we can imagine. As Jessica Marie Johnson and Mark Anthony Neal explain in their introduction to "Black Code Studies," a special issue of the *Black Scholar: Journal of Black Studies and Research*, insurgent Black digital reality "seeps up and through tools, structures, analog and digital architecture we were never meant to survive much less occupy."[1] Renina Jarmon describes Black digital engagement online as one of the "vital, unstable and rigorous worlds within worlds online."[2] How might this fugitive yet mediated digital engagement show up in a future impacted by new technologies and patterns of breakdown?

To the extent that Black intellectual history, and especially Black feminist intellectual history, like that practiced by Farah Jasmine Griffin, Mia Bay, Martha Jones, and Barbara Savage, is engaged in the process of charting precedents, unearthing submerged narratives, and adding previously imagined futures to our set of resources for imagining even more futures from here,[3] this experimental chapter drawn from the archival scene process of my book *M Archive: After the End of the World* offers examples of what I call "speculative documentary," a form of future listening that challenges us in the present to imagine the implications of our present moment from the perspective of the futures that are made possible and impossible by our current thinking.[4]

The urgency of this speculative process comes out of the dynamics that David Scott explores in "The Archeology of Black Memory," how part if not most of the Black archival process is looking at "what has been obscured, what has been forgotten, what has been disappeared from view."[5] That may be what is Blackest about any Black archive: the institutionally systematically unknown, unknowable, actively hidden from sight by those who are threatened by it and those of us who wish to protect it.

At the same time, Black queer feminist archivists practice in the tradition of Barbara and Beverly Smith's 1978 proclamation that "there is no reason to assume that we or our movements will survive long enough to become safely historical, we must document ourselves now."[6] In the tension between insisting on our presence and acknowledging our always already absence lives this speculation, to document what cannot be documented, yes, because of who and what has not survived physically and in memory, but also because it has not happened yet. The implications have not fully unfurled. Speculative documentary, an afrofuturistic astral projection into the future, seeks to reflect back on this moment, offering us access to what we cannot know now either.

The process of creating a speculative archive is informed as much by failure (to know) as it is by faith (in the unknowable). This particular archival experiment comes from an intergenerational engagement with M. Jacqui Alexander's *Pedagogies of Crossing*, a crucial Black transnational feminist text that, among other interventions, questions the knowability of Black sexuality in the postcolonial Caribbean, the status of spiritual work by women of color as the predominant mode of work happening in the world, the role of memory in the unresolved feminist desires of the women of color hailed by *This Bridge Called My Back*, the particular knowledge making produced by protesting the silences of the university and the epistemological impact of the Middle Passage as an energy shift that has put the species in a perpetual state of crossing something.[7] In this work I am crossing something intergenerational, temporal, and cosmic. And I am joined by many. I would characterize this speculative archival practice as afrofuturistic with attention to Alondra Nelson's crucial role in the circulation of the term, not only through her work to archive the scientific futurism of the Black Panther Party and genetic time travel desires of the population genetics movement but also through her use of email to make Black futurists visible to each other.[8] I feel this work is kindred (at least cousin if not sibling) to the work of Black Quantum Futurism, practiced by Rasheedah Phillips and Camae Ayewa in Pittsburgh, Pennsylvania, which uses time travel, poetics, and sound to prioritize Black presence and to politicize time as a form of wealth and poverty imposed on Black people.[9]

The experiment offered here deploys scenes with a specific focus on Black thought and the digital, offering nine scenes enmeshed in paradigms

Fig. 6. after brightest star. Courtesy of the author.

and problems after the current stage of the digital and after the human. We could say then that this is one of the ceremonies that Jamaican theorist Sylvia Wynter says must be found after humanism. In the legacy of Wynter's challenge to the humanities and sciences to question the limitations of the stories so-called humans naturalize about what it means to be human, which is itself in the legacy of Aime Cesaire's proposition of a "science of the word," the experimentalism of this work is in the way it reveals our current moment and the ways we theorize it as experiments with consequences.

So as a reader you are a scientist, invited to be reflexive about the implications of your own (Black, intellectual) practices. Be on the lookout for what comes up for you in all these layers of Black intellectual tech. In my view the scenes offered here challenge current concepts of justice, failed engagements with the US juridical system, limits of ethnography, and contemporary understandings of music, meteorology, math, and poetry. These scenes speak with and challenge contemporary theorizations of subjugated technologies like quilting and prison tattooing and think on the Black queer possibilities of earth sciences, cave diving, and probing the core of the earth or listening to flamboyant speakers and/or Black women. These scenes challenge the ways Black power and freedom thinks of the US presidency, the online petition, and media representations of street protests in the age of social media. They imagine the connections between nationalism and neuroscience; the social ramifications of trigonometry, fingerprinting, teleportation; and the relevance or irrelevance of physical movement.

Imagine that your current actions, your current mode of thinking, the forms of Black thought you identify with and critique are influential ingredients in this future imaginability. What do these future scenes say about what you are thinking now and how and if it will cross over? Yes, no, maybe, something else?

yes

i.

some people said it was the strings of the kora, how they trained their hands to know the right moment. some people said it was no harp it was heartbeats stopping. the ethnographers of the poetry of math presented research that explained the correlations between the intervals of death, the number of bullets discharged, the numerology of the names of the jurors, the weather in the area on the day of the shooting, the estimated number of total heartbeats of the shot. you could only divide them by seven and three, which meant you could not divide them without reaching a crossroads or an ocean. so that was how they knew where to go.[10]

ii.

the prison tattoo artists were ahead of the game. they knew without anyone having to spell it out that the body was the home that mattered. that matter was the muscle of home, no matter that this too, this very flesh, could be repossessed. well it did matter, and how much more important than the inked science of permanence, the reverence for becoming gods with the most beautiful talent for rebirthmarks.

so the people spelled out their names. the names of their crews. the names of their dead. they sketched the remembered symbols that fell out of their knocked-around heads. they drew out the lines in the faces they would never see again. they built room on their skin. and when even their skin was stolen they remembered the maps and went within.[11]

iii.

that's why they made the quilts and ranked the pieces and kissed them and stitched them. they knew how to circle the cloth that had soaked up your sweat and salt into a map back to the ocean. they knew who was first and who would last and they stitched, all the while singing songs that let the threads too know their names. they were physical metaphysicians. they wanted you to be warm enough to remember.[12]

no

iv.

they never proved it, but we know. some of the hand-waving women had always known. some of the metaphysicians had been trying to say. no one took them literally. until the earth broke apart.

and then. with the probe technology, with the accurate diagrams. with the skilled cave divers going deep into the fault lines. and with the simultaneous release of the human heart project and the lateral lobe mapping, it became impossible to ignore.

the cracks where the earthquakes expressed themselves were exactly the same contours of the fissures in our minds and the breaks. all the breaks. in our hearts.[13]

v.

the combination of digital knowability and pretend participation means that they agreed to it. the backroom deals didn't need back rooms anymore. just distractions on twitter and petitions with broken links. when they got in the streets it was for photo ops. they mobilized to make the obvious visible, while the subtle deadly patterns kept moving.

there were the things they knew the president signed. and the things they never heard about. but they agreed to all of it, so thorough was their grief. so afraid were they of what they already understood. so nostalgic were they for a past they only thought was simpler because of the reductive way in which it had been taught. they were bought by the blankness they wanted in front of their eyes. they were anxious to ignore the beating in their hearts and the war drums everywhere.

there were the things they knew about themselves. and the things they refused to know. and they wouldn't grow. to take responsibility for their species, even one reflection at a time was too much. so they worked as if they were the fourth apprentices and not the master artists of their lives. they shaded and shadowed, at best they emphasized. at worst this is the paint by numbers they were always supposed to make anyway.
and so look. look what the world looks like now.[14]

vi.

the question for the neuronationalists was how to wash out the trauma without wiping away the skills we had built around all that hurt, all that longing, all that loss. and when they figured that out. well you had no chance. but we still had to live with the consequences.

so they went in like the eternal sunshine movie, like our brains were video game landscapes, and they hunted. they could chart the steady erosions of certain regions of our minds where we thought of you and what you had done. well not directly. the easiest thing was to find the places where the skills we had built to survive what you had done made hatch marks on our lobes. ruts, you might say. the depth of our resistance, the evidence of your erstwhile irrevocable presence.

during the time when we win no matter what. this is your last survival. how winning how we win still hurts from you.[15]

maybe

vii.

they attended to their fingertips. ridges and pulse. they channeled all their memory into their hands as if they knew what would happen to their brains and were determined to be able to make the world they needed from muscle memory. they believed in their reaching hands at least, that when the day came when they could not recognize themselves, at least some of their tired legs would lead them home and their open hands (their pulsing fingers) would be welcomed back again.[16]

viii.

in the end it was triangulation. they specified how different they were from each other until they could extrapolate and find god.

in the end it was a false triangle. they tried to chart god and kept getting back to themselves. they tried to chart each other and kept getting back to themselves. they tried to chart themselves, but how could that be objective?

in the end it was the Pythagorean theorem inverted. not this squared plus that squared equals the long side of hell squared. aka the way squared subtracts where you thought you started squared from where you'll never go squared. turns out it's not a square at all. it's a circle. if you put a triangle in the middle the edges either won't touch or will exceed the given space.

actually, it was not a circle, it was a sphere. it was not just a sphere, it was a globe. it was not just a globe, it was a planet with its own destiny. wasn't it? and the triangle didn't fit and the pyramids were pointing somewhere with the queens and treasures dead inside.

from here? i don't know. from here? i just don't know.[17]

ix.

most of us got there naked, burnt, raw with rashes, scarred. we had put down everything that didn't hold blood and some parts of us that did.

we had brushed against the jagged histories that forced us to travel our different ways out.

television had taught us that teleportation would be all lights and a man in a unitard with a booth. that we would arrive wearing the same thing, with our organs and facial expressions intact. maybe one day.

our teleportation was slow and it completely rearranged us. we never put ourselves back together the same way again. it was a daily practice, slowly changing our sound from the inside, chanting and singing and listening deeper, moving in response to older harmonies than the reactive ones around.

do you know how long it takes to train hairs that would stand on end at any touch to become pores open with thanksgiving? it is slower than the speed of light but takes at least one candle every day. once upon a time the core of the earth made the magma solid, built crust around itself where dreams could safely plant and grow. we are of that lineage.

but in addition to the everyday, for each of us there was the one day. the one day we decided (or found out in the midst) that we were ready to drop every form of armor and be as vulnerable as the first teleportation, the day we were born. we believed our lungs could breathe a totally different substance. we believed our muscles would adapt to whatever measure of gravity or salt we faced. we believed that even if we were wrong in our beliefs we were right to believe them. it was the only thing to do.

and now we are here. as who we are. ready to scream again.[18]

Notes

1. Jessica Marie Johnson and Mark Anthony Neal, "Introduction: Wild Seed in the Machine," in "Black Code Studies," special issue, *Black Scholar: Journal of Black Studies and Research* 47, no. 3 (2017): 1–2.

2. "Renina Jarmon on the Power of Black Girls on and off the Internet," interview by Sydney Gore, February 19, 2017, https://nylon.com/articles/renina-jarmon-interview.

3. See the introduction to *Toward an Intellectual History of Black Women*, ed. Mia Bay, Farah J. Griffin, Martha S. Jones, and Barbara Savage (Chapel Hill: University of North Carolina Press, 2015), 1–2. This is one example of the work of Black scholars to remedy gaps in intellectual history in order to offer precedents and connections to visionary work from recent (2004) and distant (1773) examples of Black women's thought.

4. Alexis Pauline Gumbs, *M Archive: After the End of the World* (Durham, NC: Duke University Press, 2018).

5. David Scott. "The Archeology of Black Memory: An Interview with Robert A. Hill," *Small Axe* 5 (March 1999): 102.

6. Barbara Smith and Beverly Smith, "I Am Not Meant to Be Alone and without You Who Understand," in *Conditions Four* (1979): 62.

7. M. Jacqui Alexander, *Pedagogies of Crossing: Meditations on Feminism, Sexual Politics, Memory, and the Sacred* (Durham, NC: Duke University Press, 2006).

8. Heidi Knoblauch, "Special Interview with Alondra Nelson on Criminalization and Public Health," *Just Publics @365*, November 26, 2013, https://justpublics365.commons.gc.cuny.edu/11/2013/special-interview-alondra-nelson-criminalization-public-health/.

9. Black Quantum Futurism, "What Is Black Quantum Futurism?," https://www.blackquantumfuturism.com/about.

10. 21 times 21 times 21 and more. Alexander, "Pedagogies of the Sacred," in *Pedagogies of Crossing*, 288.

11. Where is home? Alexander, "Remembering," in *Pedagogies of Crossing*, 269.

12. The Sacred is inconceivable without an aesthetic. Alexander, "Pedagogies of the Sacred," in *Pedagogies of Crossing*, 323.

13. Are there not fissures of class, skin color, shades of yellow and brown, within our respective nation/communities? Alexander, "Remembering," in *Pedagogies of Crossing*, 273.

14. Have you lost your mind to align yourself with this Proposal? Alexander, "Anatomy of a Mobilization," in *Pedagogies of Crossing*,150.

15. What is the threat that certain memory poses? Alexander, "Pedagogies of the Sacred," in *Pedagogies of Crossing*, 294.

16. With what keys are these codes activated? Alexander, "Pedagogies of the Sacred," in *Pedagogies of Crossing*, 295.

17. What is the degree of relationality between one's social location and the subject of one's theory? Alexander, "Anatomy of a Mobilization," in *Pedagogies of Crossing*, 167.

18. how we came to be there and got to be who we were. Alexander, "Remembering," in *Pedagogies of Crossing*, 262.

Chapter 16

✦

To Render a Landscape of Trauma

Deep Mapping a Historical Landscape of Domination—the Great Dismal Swamp

Christy Hyman

As a historical geographer of slavery focusing on concretizing the phenomenon of enslaved flight in the Great Dismal Swamp, I found that incorporating space and place into my investigation strengthened my understanding of self-liberation in geographies of domination during the antebellum years. Geographies of domination are places where marginalized agents are denied the possibility of personal autonomy because of sanctioned limitations on movement, social mobility, and judicial protections.[1] For enslaved people forced to work in the Great Dismal Swamp during the antebellum period, the relation they had to the swamp landscape enables us to understand more closely the incidence of enslaved flight from the plantation.

This essay is a critical reflection on the processes involved in digitally curating my story map, *Oak of Jerusalem: Flight, Refuge, and Reconnaissance in the Great Dismal Swamp Region of North Carolina*. The *Oak of Jerusalem* is a digital narrative of place that brings together the geospatial dimensions influencing the incidence of enslaved people escaping bondage near the Great Dismal Swamp. Using the testimony of Moses Grandy, a formerly enslaved canal laborer in the swamp, the story map provides users with the human impact of natural resource and enslaved labor exploitation in the swamp while illustrating Grandy's reminiscences. Grandy's reminiscences anchor this spatial narrative, while archival content, visual culture, and maps situate his account in an antebellum context. The digital media curated in the *Oak of Jerusalem* articulate legal, economic, and social aspects of Southern slave society that enslaved

Fig. 7. The Great Dismal Swamp. Photograph. Courtesy of the author.

people confronted in their journey toward freedom. Ultimately, the *Oak of Jerusalem* illuminates the challenges and spatial realities that enslaved people seeking refuge in the Great Dismal Swamp contended with, bringing into fuller view the degree of resistance exemplified through their efforts at self-liberation in a geography of domination. The affordances of thinking spatially allow us to reappraise geographical concepts of space while attempting to understand how enslaved people came to understand the spaces around them. Spatial approaches to understanding the phenomenon of enslaved flight can reveal the challenges of that process at a scale previously unseen.

Spatiality refers to processes involved in understanding the way space is conceived, located, or experienced. In illuminating the ways enslaved people interacted with the Great Dismal Swamp environment we are able to understand how enslaved people perceived the spaces around them and appropriated those spaces into sites of refuge and reconnaissance.

Creating this digital narrative of enslaved people's efforts toward self-liberation is in the spirit of recovery, which "rests at the heart of studies in Afro-descendant history as a scholarly tradition that seeks to restore the humanity of Black people lost and stolen through systemic global racialization."[2] In recovering the ways enslaved people understood the geography around them, we restore to the historical record knowledge networks enslaved people possessed in pursuing freedom and community within the Great Dismal Swamp.

To illustrate the story of enslaved movement in the Great Dismal Swamp, I began digitally mapping the life of enslaved canal laborer Moses Grandy. These mappings were spatial stories that I gathered from close reading his narrative of enslavement. Born in 1786 on a farm owned by slaveholder William Grandy in Camden County, North Carolina, Moses Grandy learned as a child how painful life was for an enslaved person. On his early life Grandy informs:

> I was the youngest. I remember well my mother often hid us all in the woods, to prevent master selling us. When we wanted water, she sought for it in any hole or puddle formed by falling trees or otherwise: it was often full of tadpoles and insects: she strained it, and gave it round to each of us in the hollow of her hand. For food, she gathered berries in the woods, got potatoes, raw corn. After a time the master would send word to her to come in, promising, he would not sell us. But at length persons came who agreed to give the prices he set on us. His wife, with much to be done, prevailed on him not to sell me; but he sold my brother, who was a little boy. My mother, frantic with grief, resisted their taking her child away: she was beaten and held down.[3]

Here Grandy discloses his mother's determination to keep her children with her against the profit-driven designs of slaveholder William Grandy who, as this quote shows, could not be safely relied upon to keep his word. This reminiscence also exemplifies how enslaved people, particularly enslaved women, found ways to adapt to the swamp's ruggedness by nourishing themselves with nature's bounty found within.

It was from the testimony of Moses Grandy's narrative that I was able to search for materials related to the places he referenced in order to begin collecting material for *The Oak of Jerusalem*. Like so many scholars before me, Grandy's narrative provided an eyewitness account of enslavement in the Great Dismal Swamp region. A number of historians such as John Blassingame, Wilma King, Calvin Schermerhorn, David Cecelski, Heather Andrea Williams, Daina Ramey Berry, Marcus Nevius, and Manisha Sinha have cited Grandy's narrative in their scholarly investigations; however, *The Oak of Jerusalem* focuses primarily on the way Grandy's narrative reveals how enslaved people responded to the physical geography of the Great Dismal Swamp.

The collection of materials that I gathered from the spatial moments and remembrances from Moses Grandy's narrative developed into a digital narrative implemented through a story map. Story maps achieve a dual purpose through showing and telling spatial dimensions of narrative accounts. This mode of storytelling is rooted in the ethos of deep mapping, which allows for a "new creative space . . . well-suited to a fresh conceptualization of humanities GIS [geographic information system]."[4]

Indeed, digital stories engage audiences across various media in multimodal ways; they encourage innovative forms of visual culture and code while taking advantage of the immersive possibilities of web-based forms. Digital narratives such as story maps combine digital media with storytelling practices and poetics to produce complex vistas of moments in time.[5]

Such an interface for telling the stories that have been obscured from history is restorative. The functionality of combining various types of media allows creators to use text, material culture, and moving image to convey these narratives. In recovering the histories of Afro-descended people, this amalgam of content provides a thoroughness of context that can be missed within the traditional strictures of historical storytelling, which often privilege linear chronicling in storytelling modes.

Historians of slavery are well aware of how the archive erases the lives of Afro-descendant people in service to the provenance of materials that serve to advance the motivation of hegemonic actors in history. Highlighting the wilderness landscapes within the Great Dismal Swamp illustrates the physical obstacles involved in enslaved movement across geographies of domination. Enslaved people were wedded to the land in uncanny ways. The land was something they were forced to contend with as they performed the heavy agricultural, pastoral, and manual labor required to drain the land and create transportation channels for commerce in the eastern region of North Carolina. Enslaved people were forced to dig the Dismal Swamp canal and other ditching systems throughout the marshland found near there and surrounding counties while also building roads with passageways that led to prosperity for those who held power over them.[6]

As chattel, enslaved people were commodified as property in the eyes of society and the law. Because of this dehumanized existence, the movements of enslaved people are taken for granted in the historical record. I often come across local histories of canal and bridge building in the antebellum era in locales across North Carolina and Virginia and no mention is made of the slave labor that made these channels of transport possible. This erasure perpetuates the dehumanized, devalued labor performed by enslaved people within the historical record. Cultural geographer Katherine McKittrick has analyzed the considerations within disciplinary encounters between black studies and geography and has observed the prevalent notion of black people as "ungeographic." McKittrick goes on to explain how "discourses erase and de-spatialize [enslaved people's] sense of place," and thus her work seeks to conceptualize black geographies from that tenuous position of alterity. The Great Dismal Swamp is a historic geography of domination where many of the struggles enslaved people experienced are unmarked and thus silenced. The Oak of Jerusalem intervenes with that silence by situating the phenomena of enslaved flight in dialogue with Grandy's narrative.

The process of curating media assets for my story map/digital narrative allowed me to discover the importance of cross-disciplinary exploration in locating evidence and sources related to Afro-descendant experiences. I made decisions stemming from determining just how much evidence I could marshal for an informed historical interpretation of making meaning from nontextual products. Nontextual products are images that invoke meaning and tell a story through visual engagement with the user. This process allowed me to push the boundaries of how imagery helped to construct signifying elements of meaning within stories that highlighted the inherent struggle of enslaved people's experiences. I found myself shuttling meaning from one context to another in attempting to recreate the world that Moses Grandy made. Within digital narratives such as story maps one can amass a variety of media containing meaning-making strands of the past that provide a fuller view of marginalized histories.

In the *Oak of Jerusalem* I wanted to highlight Moses Grandy's experience as an enslaved person forced to work in the Great Dismal Swamp, while providing the context for how and why it came to be that enslaved people were brought there.[7] As a result, I chose to place Grandy's experiences at the forefront but also integrated the hegemonic actors involved in not only the buying, selling, and renting of enslaved chattel for work in the Great Dismal Swamp but also the preconditions those actors created for extraction of the natural environment within the swamp. This meant including how agents of the hegemony dispossessed from their ancestral lands American Indians who had lived in the Great Dismal Swamp region for thousands of years before colonial encroachment.

As I continued in framing the digital narrative, I developed a sort of crisis of authorial agency. There were many elements of Grandy's story that I wanted to integrate, but the task proved challenging due to the nonlinear, often synaptic flow of Grandy's narrative. Also, the devastating nature of narratives involving trauma affect the story-framing process as I wanted users to bear witness to the injustice and outrages Grandy experienced but did not want to deter users from continuing their exploration of the story map due to the emotional fatigue from that witnessing. Grandy's narrative highlights a lived experience that is rife with innumerable trauma including witnessing torture, being cheated out of his purchased freedom twice, repeated physical abuse, disease, and the loss of his family members who were sold away. Grandy at one point considered jumping into the Chesapeake but ultimately decided against it.[8] The environs within the Great Dismal Swamp carried the invisible markers of enslaved swamp laborers' suffering—they are *traumascapes*, and the Great Dismal Swamp was the site of enslaved people's shared suffering. This shared trauma created powerful bonds between those determined to survive the ravages of the traumascape and the slavery regime itself. It was through these connections and resonances that enslaved people could recognize how the power and knowledge of the Great Dismal Swamp landscape could be appropriated for their own uses.

As a geographic area of historical confinement for enslaved people, the swamp held significant meaning as a site of contestation between enslavement and self-liberation. Writer Maria Tumarkin defines traumascapes as a "distinctive category of places transformed physically and psychically by suffering, where the scar tissues remain embedded in the landscape."[9] The death of Moses Grandy's brother is an example of how a traumascape functions: in this case the site where his brother's energy stores were depleted in their entirety until the winter's cold put an end to his suffering.

Traumascapes play a vital role in enabling mourning and shaping the meaning and interpretation of the traumatic events inscribed in them.[10] The site where Grandy's brother took his dying breaths may have been sought and remembered by those who cared for him, but the historical record lends no tangible signifier to its location or relevance. Nonetheless, this trauma and many others existed as very real and very personal degradations occurring to the enslaved people within the Great Dismal Swamp landscape. Through Grandy's dynamic memory, the retelling of his brother's death and other phantasmagoric scenes of suffering helps to explain the shadowy foundations of how the Great Dismal Swamp functioned as a quasi-dystopian landscape. Ultimately the swamp embodied the promise of freedom as a site of possible refuge but also the horrors of the slavery regime itself.[11] It was important for *The Oak of Jerusalem* to reflect the complex dimensions of enslaved people's connection to the Great Dismal Swamp landscape.

Apart from the historical interpretation I wished to convey in *The Oak of Jerusalem*, I also wanted to highlight how conceptions of visual culture interplayed with nineteenth-century understandings of slavery and landscape. In this I found that displaying artwork depicting scenes from the Great Dismal Swamp as well as paintings rendering images of enslaved people engaged in the flight process illuminated how artists viewed the spheres of life for those relegated to unfreedom in the swamp. The following section highlights the forms of media that helped to illustrate the Great Dismal Swamp landscape. I begin with a commentary on material culture to illustrate how *The Oak of Jerusalem* aims to inform users on the available modes of dress for enslaved people and how such clothing implements affected the process of flight from the plantation.

Material Culture

In Moses Grandy's narrative we learn about his brother's death within the first few pages—without a doubt, this was one of the most significant elements of trauma that Grandy wanted his readers to witness. As I ruminated on the sorrow I felt after reading the account, I knew I needed to immerse myself in the swamp environment to feel its physical essence. As I planned the trip, I remembered that I saved a garment made of osnaburg fabric that I had to wear during my time as a historic interpreter at the Somerset Place state historic site in Creswell, North Carolina (where I had to dress as an enslaved woman in third-person interpretation). I decided that I would bring the garment to the Great Dismal Swamp to photograph the garment and use the image for the story map as a visual reminder of the Grandy's brothers' memory.

After all it was the osnaburg nightshirt that his brother wore when he died of exposure in the swamp. That coarse yet thin fabric had not been enough to keep him warm—the elements of winter's cold air and his steadily weakening body from the previous abuses inflicted on him by the slaveholder Kemp assured that death would soon remove him from slavery's grip.

Osnaburg is part of a family of poor-quality textiles—made from coarse inexpensive linen with the main object being durability, a sturdiness appropriate for the unending toil of the forced agricultural, pastoral, and manual labor performed by enslaved people. Working enslaved women wore osnaburg dresses "reefed up" with a cord drawn tightly around their bodies, along the hips in order to work unencumbered by long dress hems. Booker T. Washington, who was formerly enslaved, recalled his experience wearing the fabric, describing osnaburg as feeling like "a hundred pin points in contact with the flesh."[12] His older brother eased Booker's discomfort by "breaking in" the shirt for some days before transferring the garment to him.

While enslaved people were forced to inhabit spaces devoid of ornamentation in the slave dwellings and forced to wear the dense osnaburg fabric that marked their status as slaves, the slaveholding class was "developing forms of art that conjured a refined image . . . rooted in the totality of plantation life."[13] The following section discusses artistic conceptions of the Great Dismal Swamp landscape. These renderings reveal what scholar Simon Gikandi has called the antebellum culture of taste as it relates to slave society.

Artistic Depictions

Some of the visual imagery in the *Oak of Jerusalem* include assorted artist renditions of the Great Dismal Swamp landscape that offer the viewer historical aesthetic conceptions of place specific to the swamp. *The Lake of the Dismal Swamp* by Currier and Ives is a bright and pristine look at Lake Drummond in spring. The image is idyllic, yet it fails to provide the atmosphere of the Great Dismal Swamp in spring, which, depending on the intensity of the wind, meant being assailed by biting flies while there. Despite the vividness of the painting, the desolate nature is still undeniable and helps the viewer to understand how many parts of the Great Dismal Swamp were sites completely unsettled, thereby creating opportunities for enslaved people to appropriate these spaces as possible sites of refuge and reconnaissance. *View, Dismal Swamp, North Carolina* by Régis François Gignoux imparts a more haunting feel to the landscape, suggesting a depiction of fall, with shades of red predominating the painting.

The most startling images of artwork featured within the *Oak of Jerusalem*, however, are those where artists depict enslaved people engaged in the process of flight, such as Thomas Moran's *Slave Hunt in the Great Dismal Swamp* and Eastman Johnson's *A Ride for Liberty—Fugitive Slaves*. In Johnson's painting we have an enslaved family fleeing by horse, with the child in front and wife behind, nervously looking back.

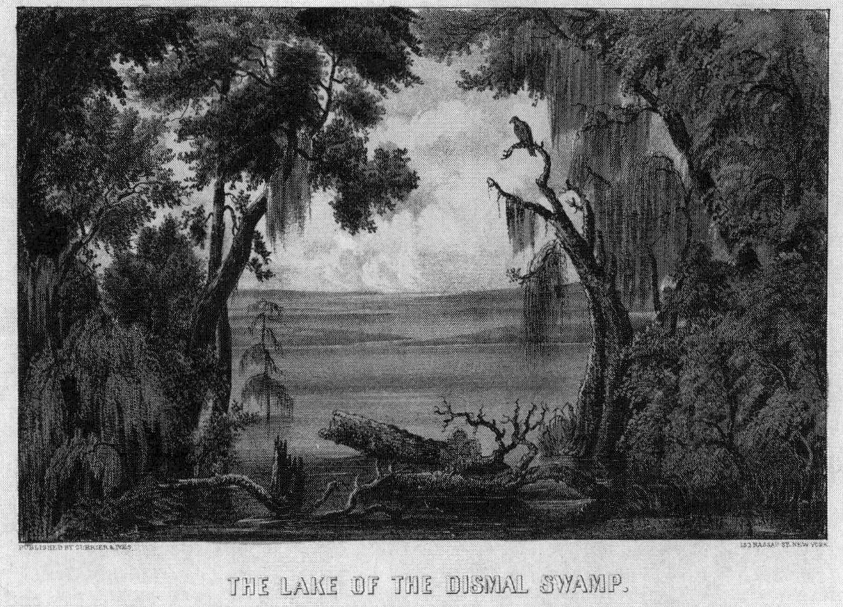

Fig. 8. Nathaniel Currier and James Merrit Ives, *The Lake of the Dismal Swamp*, ca. 1857–72. Lithograph with hand coloring. Fine Arts Museums of San Francisco, gift of Joseph Martin Jr., 1994.120.20.

Fig. 9. Régis François Gignoux, *View, Dismal Swamp, North Carolina*, 1850. Oil on canvas. Museum of Fine Arts, Boston, bequest of Henry Herbert Edes, 23.184.

Fig. 10. Eastman Johnson, *A Ride for Liberty—the Fugitive Slaves* (recto), ca. 1862. Brooklyn Museum, gift of Gwendolyn O. L. Conkling, 40.59a–b.

In these renderings, slaves are painted in a state of urgency, with cautious facial expressions meant to display their awareness and determination to elude the gangs of slave catchers whose job it was to track them down with teams of dogs. Enslaved people moved cautiously through the swamp environment and knew when to be still, when to watch, listen, and feel. Fleeing the plantation overland meant one step closer to freedom, but the noise of their footsteps could cause alarm to nearby birds and other animals. Enslaved people engaged in flight within the Great Dismal Swamp during the antebellum years demonstrated the courage to move through, the courage to move through geographies of domination. This courage was driven by the realization that life at the plantation was so adverse that the possible benefits of running away to the swamp outweighed the risks.

Addressing the realities of enslaved people's struggles within the Great Dismal Swamp reveals the peril and promise that led to their calculations for liberating themselves and their families out of bondage. Reconstructing Moses Grandy's world—whether through locating the footpaths and waterways that cut through the forest floor or identifying the trees overhead that would conceal—enslaved freedom seekers made plain the ever-present trauma underpinning the institution of slavery. This trauma created the committed yearning for enslaved people to flee, as well as rewired the material and psychic resonances of the swamp wilderness. Deep mapping these spaces, charting enslaved people's movements within them, honors those who had the knowledge of landscape to escape and envision a life closer to freedom.[14]

Notes

1. Katherine McKittrick, *Demonic Grounds: Black Women and the Cartographies of Struggle* (Minneapolis: University of Minnesota Press, 2006), x.

2. Kim Gallon, "Making a Case for the Black Digital Humanities," in *Debates in the Digital Humanities*, ed. Matthew K. Gold and Lauren F. Klein (Minneapolis: University of Minnesota Press, 2016), 42–49.

3. Moses Grandy, *Narrative of the Life of Moses Grandy: Late a Slave in the United States of America* (London: Gilpin, 1843), https://docsouth.unc.edu/fpn/grandy/grandy.html.

4. David J. Bodenhamer, John Corrigan, and Trevor M. Harris, *The Spatial Humanities: GIS and the Future of Humanities Scholarship* (Bloomington: Indiana University Press, 2010). GIS, or geographical information systems, integrate information from a common spatial location, regardless of format, while analyzing and/or visualizing spatiotemporal relationships.

5. Institute for Digital Research in the Humanities, "Digital Storytelling and the Humanities," Seventh Annual University of Kansas Digital Humanities Forum, September 28–29, 2017, Lawrence, Kansas, https://idrh.ku.edu/dhforum2017, accessed February 20, 2018.

6. A petition to Perquimans County court reads, "I shall counter to exempt to my Negro slaves working on the roads of Old Neck that they may be allowed to me in consideration keeping the road from Red House to Hertford." William Jones, 1829. Stewart E. Dunaway, *Perquimans County, North Carolina, Road Records* (North Carolina: Stewart E. Dunaway, 2015), 287. On marronage in the Great Dismal Swamp, the existing scholarship on enslaved people within the Great Dismal Swamp is scattered across the disciplines of anthropology, cultural studies, and history. Hugo Prosper Leaming's *Hidden Americans: Maroons of Virginia and North Carolina* was published in 1995 and brought attention to Great Dismal Swamp maroons using cultural and oral traditions to examine the presence of maroon communities. Anthropologist Daniel O. Sayers conducted the Great Dismal Swamp Landscape Study from 2003 to 2013 and published *A Desolate Place for a Defiant People* in 2014, using his findings from the study to identify possible sites of marronage within the Great Dismal Swamp landscape. Sayers's work is essential to understanding the locations of "diasporic exiles" that some enslaved people managed to find and sustain a life within. David O. Cecelski's *The Watermen's Song: Slavery and Freedom in Maritime North Carolina* is a comprehensive study of maritime functions in the antebellum South. Cecelski focuses on what he refers to as African American maritime culture along the shoreline of North Carolina and discusses the traditions created by prominent African American seamen. Charles Royster's "The Fabulous History of the Great Dismal Swamp" is a study that centers the motivations of eighteenth-century colonial elites trying to maximize gains through resource extraction of the Great

Dismal Swamp. Royster's work focuses on wealthy planters; thus African Americans appear more as objects than agents in the text. Calvin Schermerhorn centers enslaved people's efforts within the upper South to hold onto familial connections while confronting the harsh realities of the slave market. Schermerhorn's work *Money over Mastery, Family over Freedom* contributes significantly to studies of slavery by showing enslaved people's aims to choose family bonds in spite of the limitations the slave markets put on their attempts at freedom. *Slavery's Exiles: The Story of American Maroons* by Sylviane Diouf offers a chapter on the Great Dismal Swamp that highlights the legal codes circumscribing enslaved people's lives as well as an important overall framework for studying marronage by distinguishing between borderland and hinterland flight and surveying the incidences of marronage across America.

7. My story map can be accessed at https://www.arcgis.com/apps/Cascade/index.html?appid=f3a23e246cba476b8ece52fb1463ce5d.

8. After purchasing his freedom, Moses Grandy traveled back to Virginia to arrange to purchase his enslaved son. The slaveholder refused to take Grandy's payment, demanding a larger sum. Because Grandy and other enslaved people freed in Southern states were considered "spoiled" by freedom and because there were laws against freed slaves reentering Virginia, he could only remain in the Commonwealth for less than ten days. As the deadline approached for him to leave Virginia, Grandy sees a party of white men and fears they will commandeer him back into slavery: "I thought they were officers coming to take me; and such was my horror of slavery, that I twice ran to the ship's waist, to jump overboard into the strong ebb-tide then running, to drown myself, but a strong impression on my mind restrained me each time." Moses Grandy, *Narrative of the Life of Moses Grandy*, 45.

9. Maria Tumarkin, *Traumascapes: The Power and Fate of Places Transformed by Tragedy* (Carlton, VC: Melbourne University Publishing, 2005), 13–15.

10. I first heard the term "traumascape" while viewing a lecture given by scholar Angel David Nieves presented within the Five College Digital Humanities Speaker Series at Amherst College. During the lecture Nieves discussed his own project "Soweto 76" and the challenges of interpreting community histories alongside the attendant traumascapes inherent in the Soweto community memory. Angel D. Nieves, "Digital Humanities as Restorative Social Justice," February 2015, YouTube video, 1:14:18 https://www.youtube.com/watch?v=E_XvlNLr_OU.

11. On a very cold winter's day in 1795 (or thereabouts) in Camden County, North Carolina, Moses Grandy's older brother was forced to search for a yoke of steers that had wandered into the woods. This was his second attempt at searching for them, and Kemp, the slaveholder, has flogged him once for not recovering the animals. As the night approached, the enslaved child grew discouraged and felt sure he would be flogged once more if he returned without the steers. The cold became unbearable for the boy, and the thin osnaburg nightshirt he wore wasn't enough insulation from the chill of the air. Exposure was becoming imminent as the winter's cold air slowly began to overtake him. The enslaved boy decided to rest on a bed of leaves—the search for the steers had come to an end as well as this young slave's life. Moses Grandy, *Narrative of the Life of Moses Grandy*, 9.

12. Shane White and Graham White, "Slave Clothing and African-American Culture in the Eighteenth and Nineteenth Centuries," *Past and Present* 148 (August 1995): 154.

13. Simon Gikandi, *Slavery and the Culture of Taste* (Princeton, NJ: Princeton University Press, 2014).

14. Stephanie M. H. Camp demonstrated that enslaved freedom seekers demonstrated their "mobility in the face of restraint" as they ventured toward sites and spaces closer to freedom. Stephanie M. H. Camp, *Closer to Freedom: Enslaved Women and Everyday Resistance in the Plantation South* (Chapel Hill: University of North Carolina Press, 2004), 7.

Chapter 17

"All the Stars Are Closer"

Fugitives in the Machine and Black Resistance in a Digital Age

Jessica Marie Johnson

> This may be the night that my dreams might let me know
> All the stars are closer.
>
> —SZA, "All the Stars," *Black Panther: The Album* (2018)

> Our boats are open, and we sail them for everyone.
>
> —Édouard Glissant

In 2015, Black Dominican poet Gabriel Ramirez stepped on stage and performed these words before participants, fans, and attendees of the National Poetry Slam: "I am Black and full of stars/I am not the absence of light/I am who allows light to exist."[1] Twenty-six years earlier, Martinican poet, writer, and theorist Édouard Glissant grappled with the constituent elements of African diaspora, the poetics of Relation. Describing the terror of "these lowest depths," "these deeps" traversed by the slave ship and punctuated by the bodies of Africans thrown overboard, Glissant claimed the dead beneath the sea as "underwater signposts" that "mark the course between the Gold Coast and the Leeward Islands." Almost two decades apart, both Ramirez and Glissant chart a course for African-descended history, politics, and identity that challenges the cartography of the known world. Neither speak of land or the ceremonies of possession (planting a flag, enclosing space) that attend nation-making and empire building, particularly in the West. Instead, in a New World where blackness has been categorized as nonbeing, unthought, spectacle of death, impossible, non- or inhuman, Ramirez, Glissant, and others look above, below, and beyond terrestrial longitude/latitude for where entire galaxies of life and humanity remain possible.[2] "I am not ugly," Ramirez continues. "I am who allows you to be beautiful/Now isn't that the blackest thing you've ever heard God say?" Glissant likewise gathers his people and confronts the West's refusal to map the terrain of black being by populating Relation with a constellation of selves: "We know ourselves as part and as crowd, in an unknown that does not terrify. We cry our cry of poetry. Our boats are open, and we sail them for everyone."

This essay explores black digital practice as the practice of creating constellations of being that surface histories of terror at the heart of the machine of the New World and map new routes to galaxies beyond black death. Digital technology has not made black resistance possible. It has made legible percussive black resistance that has been circulating, sailing, flying, throbbing, and absconding for generations. From listservs to online journaling, from blogging to social media, from hashtags to podcasts, black digital practice has made public (and searchable) a rich archive of black diasporic dissent that has been and continues to be created by trans, queer, and cis fugitives in the machine. As digital humanities and black resistance against oppression continue to encounter each other, black digital practice serves as ground zero for insurgent digital humanistic thought. Black digital practice curates narrative history, disrupts political claims of legitimacy, and witnesses multiple registers of violence—from the gendered racial terror of police violence against Black, Latinx, and Afrxlatinx women, children, and men to the exploitative representations of black life as pathology popular in entertainment culture and mainstream news media. Digital space swims with black stars giving light to injustice and guiding user-travelers to new arrangements of humanity.[3] In this essay, I speak as a participant and observer of these networks and elaborate on the digital project African Diaspora, Ph.D. as rooted and rooting in these same atmospheric and submarine streams.

Constellations of Black Media

The Internet I emerged from was populated by queer and trans* radical women of color, activists, artists, and more. Alexis Pauline Gumbs describes many of them in her 2011 essay "Seek the Roots: An Immersive and Interactive Archive of Feminist Practice." This is Gumbs, writing a kind of introduction to the digital revolution fomented by radical womyn of color bloggers online (I flow with her):

> There is a queer ecology to the
> practice of digging for and growing
> from *r*
> *o*
> *o*
> *t*
> *s*
> that are never write "mini-series
> large" (a la Alex Haley), but are rather
> g r o u n
> d e d
> in unmarked graves, circumscribed
> by death, burn-out, thinkers, farmers,
> grassroots green thumbs,
> are queer
> ecologists.[4]

I am a black feminist media maker whose chosen archive of study consists of flayed limbs and ephemeral freedoms. The groups and activists described by Gumbs have never stopped speaking, believing, and creating, online and on the ground, in a society that is feminist, insurgent, and alive to centering community.[5] This lived and everyday attention to making robust links from individual to individual, between communities, and across the messiness of conflict, trauma, difference, and outside threats knits the participants together into new ways of being. Our digital practice, in other words, created new worlds or, as Ashleigh Wade has described, new genres of being human.[6] We didn't even know that was what we were doing. To us, black and radical womyn of color, the feminist labor of building community was work we'd first acquired around our kitchen tables, in femme of color spaces that were also crossroads for politics, healing, cleansing, and care. As a young digital denizen and a researcher invested in the study of Atlantic slavery and comparative African diaspora, I turned to digital media as a space for transmuting histories that could challenge *all* forms of violence and oppression, cover global experience, and utilize practices honed by transformative justice. In 2008, I created African Diaspora, Ph.D. to be part of this conversation.

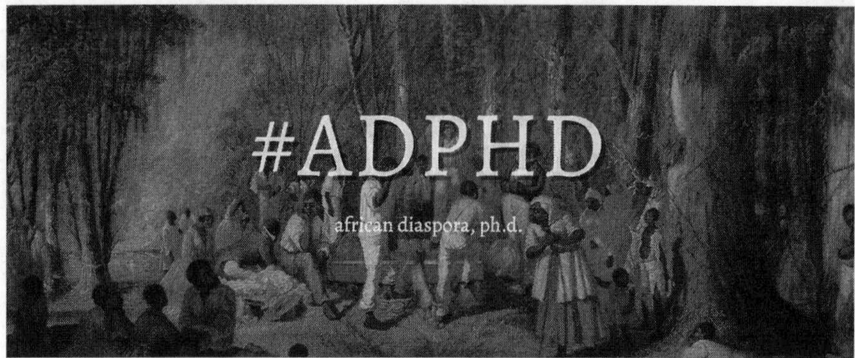

Fig. 11. African Diaspora, PhD. Screenshot. March 12, 2018. Courtesy of the author.

Now . . .

a conversation about periodization and the archive of slavery
is also an act of time travel—
an act that inevitably generates
s
p
i
n
o
f
f histories of intimate violence, of torment, but also of resistance, politics, and self-fashioning that is ephemeral, transchronic, and transspatial.

In the black diasporic subterranean that is slavery's archive, fluidity, dispersal, and mobility exist alongside astronomical levels of violence that is structural, personal, and intimate.[7] Threat of force and carcerality on macro- and micro-levels structures nearly every interaction. Chattel slavery functioned as the operating system for the New World; the slave ship surfed the command line. My excavation of enslaved and free black diasporic lives became a triumphant shout and a funeral dirge, attuned to loss and hauntings, echoes and heartbreaks, absences and silences. I welcomed the defiant joy and devastation of loss as part of the ritual of knowing who we are. The only question that remained was how to share this experience with the people I knew needed it—my community, the women in my life, diasporic kinfolk far and wide. Narrative history itself—facts, figures, text, images—seemed to hold the key, but not as narrated by slave owners. In the "subterranean caverns" of the archive, I sought to share, instead, "the wellsprings of dreams" nurtured "during the seasons when hope can't be found."[8]

In slavery's archive, time and space cross. There is as much to know and not know as there is to unknow "entering the lists," as Katherine McKittrick described the experience of encountering diasporic horrors in the archive.[9] There is much to know, not know, and know *onlyforaninstant* by culling what we can from lists of names. And yet, what lies in the margins somewhere between the list of names and the edge of the paper, between the sign and the list itself, in the silence, the null value, the empty record is also part of the work. In the margin and the null value, ephemerality meets the black quantum future, or as Rasheedah Phillips theorizes, "Recurrence meets (or diverges from) non-recurrence."

> "In a linear sequence, we are most
> concerned with finality and final judgment,
> what a situation will lead or fit into. This
> linear sequence of time flowing towards the future and
> not the past, has a built-in asymmetry, in that
> D
> could never effect
> C,
> B,
> or A.

—and this is black diasporic too."[10] Like Phillips, for McKittrick, time and space become blackened signifiers for lost time and missing space. In her critical read of diaspora keywords in the reference section of the library, McKittrick deliberately
reorders
the
list,
f r a g m
e n t s
encyclopedic texts, and mystifiesbibliographicclassification to reveal
powers shaping how we consume, produce, and organize knowledge.

Power to reorder the list can be exerted on, in, and through the media we make. Digital technology offers African diasporic creators tools and opportunities to interact, enter, visualize, dream, and fragment Western narrative, canon, and linear form in ways that capture the richness of our

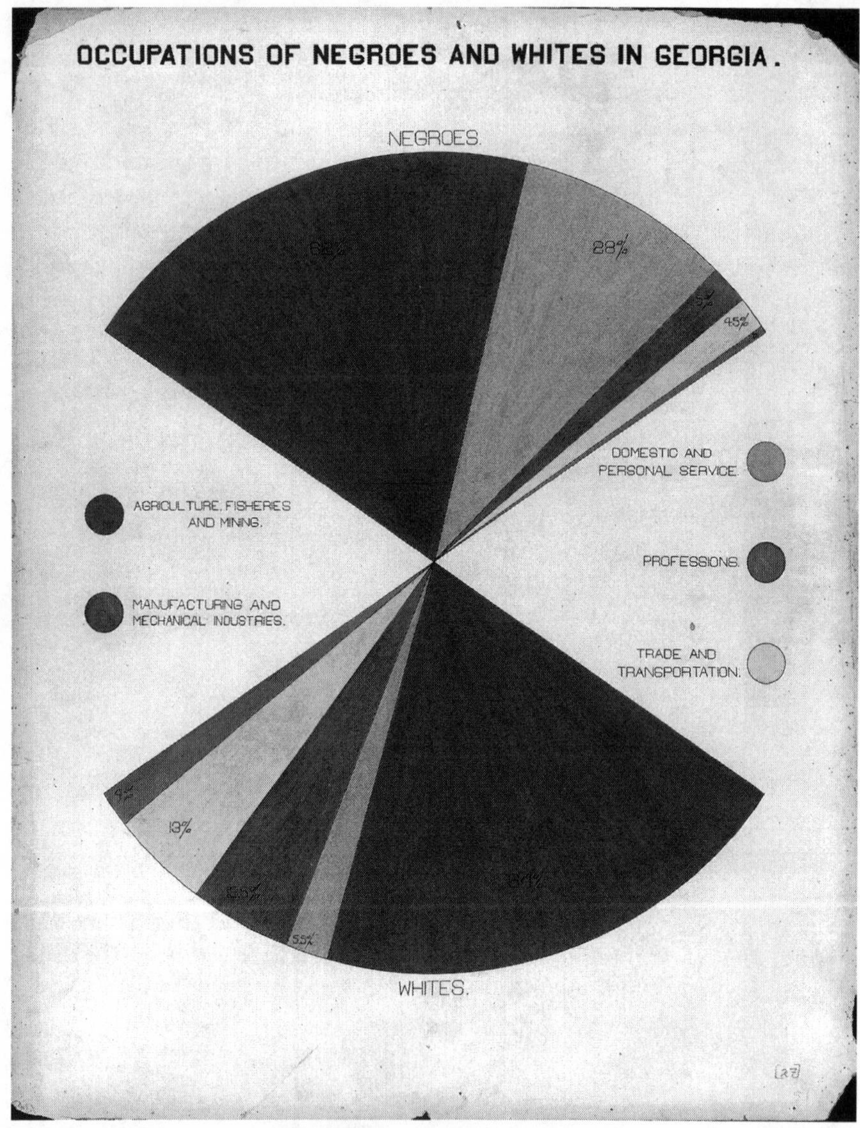

Fig. 12. W. E. B. Du Bois's "[The Georgia Negro] Occupations of Negroes and Whites in Georgia," 1900. Library of Congress, Prints and Photographs Division.

experiences, range of our intellectual production, and measure of violence enacted on us. For historians of slavery, particularly those of African descent, use of technology, computation, and, most recently, digital tools is not new. Researchers of African descent have taken up statistics, numerals, decimal points, and percentages to capture the experience of enslavement and dispel misconceptions of black life for some time. In the United States, early Southern historians like U. B. Phillips argued that firsthand accounts of life in the South from the hands and minds of slave owners provided data that could be used to interpret the making of the United States. Collections of documents, including registers of slaves culled from plantation records and slave ship manifests, constructed an archive that rewrote the history of the United States and included the accomplishments of Southern leaders. These histories, however, also often failed to disrupt the primacy of slave owners' narratives of themselves or incorporate black or white abolitionist texts. The resultant narratives of Southern life lent the period of bondage a moonlight and magnolias glow.

The first generation of black scholars after emancipation chose to confront the lists as social scientists invested in black labor histories. These "segregated scholars" refused to shy away from tools that might illuminate the experiences of bondspeople, taking up statistics, computation, and graphical representation (i.e., dataviz) as part of their intellectual production. They were "self-conscious, self-selected, and sometimes contentious colleagues committed to empirical research to address labor and economic inequalities."[11] From the 1919s into the 1930s, long before word processors and digital blogs, research teams at the Association for the Study of Negro Life and History (now Association for the Study of African American Life and History) led by Carter G. Woodson published hundreds of pages and volumes of information on enslaved people. In that same tradition, in the 2010s, Lanae Spruce and Ravon Ruffin have led the National Museum of African American History in disseminating and curating African American and African diasporic history on social and digital media with a special focus on the humanity of people of African descent and hidden history (#HiddenHistory). Black digital practice is central to reordering the lists that beget African American and African diaspora history.

An #ADPhD Universe

In creating African Diaspora, Ph.D.,[12] I sought to generate similar time-space transgressions. Established in 2008, African Diaspora, Ph.D. (#ADPhD) can be categorized in several ways—as a blog, digital project, online bibliography, DIY digital archive, and radical media. I created #ADPhD using WordPress.com, a free blogging platform started in 2005. At the time, blogging platforms ranged widely, from social forums such as LiveJournal, to minimalist blogging technology like TypePad, to more robust blogging platforms like Blogger (purchased by Google in 2003 and phased out in 2010) and WordPress. These platforms, hosted on remote servers, could be used without cost, although functionality was limited. For instance, for security purposes, neither the free Blogger nor WordPress options allowed users to manipulate the HTML or code of their individual blogs. In addition, these services offered only subdomains, leaving ownership and control of the blog ultimately in the hands of the owners of the service. That said, both Blogger and WordPress, as free services, created the space for organizers, activists, journalists, and researchers to make media under their own creative control and power. These free blogging spaces also laid the foundation for black feminist and radical womyn of color media making and online community formation.[13]

African Diaspora, Ph.D. was created out of these networks and part of this conversation. Key inspiration for African Diaspora, Ph.D. was the blog, project, and website BrokenBeautiful Press. Founded by Alexis Pauline Gumbs in 2006, BrokenBeautiful Press functioned as part distro (or poetry/zine distribution site), part publishing venue, part rallying cry, and part metaphysical digital geography for black feminist and radical womyn of color thought work. BrokenBeautiful Press existed in a broader network of blogs engaging in similar work. In 2010, Moya Bailey and Gumbs counted upward of one hundred blogs committed to "black feminism in cyberspace."[14] This constellation of media makers created Radical Womyn of Color blogrings, collectives like the SPEAK! Women of Color Media Collective, and edited online publications, generating a significant body of work on queer, disabled, undocumented, economically marginalized, African-descended, and Global South feminisms.[15] The rich diversity of this work, and its community members' attention to refusing binaries or singular visions of feminism while demanding feminist thought and politics engaging transformative reimaginings of the world, laid the foundation for the online feminism conversations occurring in 2018.

African Diaspora, Ph.D. generated content along these themes, but with a focus on Atlantic slavery and the Atlantic African diaspora history. The first posts created for the blog included essays on Saidiya Hartman's *Lose Your Mother: A Journey along the Atlantic Slave Route* and Katherine McKittrick's *Demonic Grounds: Black Women and the Cartographies of Struggle* and announced an online resource, "Research Guide in Atlantic Africa Diaspora History."[16] Subsequent posts highlighted new academic books and articles in the field but also drew attention to innovations in digital history occurring at different levels. The launch of *Africa Past and Present*, a podcast produced at Michigan State University by Peter Alegi and Peter Limb, was announced in February of 2008. A demo of the

Trans-Atlantic Slave Trade Database, a project led by David Eltis, was announced that February as well. From 2008 to 2012, the archive created by posts and comments at #ADPhD witnessed the increased attention paid to histories of slavery and diaspora and the use of digital tools to explore those histories. Each resource highlighted on the blog fell within the scope and parameters of #ADPhD interest—items by academics or established researchers, items related to the history of African-descended life and culture between 1441 and 1888, and items geographically situated in the Americas, Atlantic Africa, or Europe.

The year 2012 marked a significant restructuring of the blog and expansion of #ADPhD as a project. Although it remained on a free WordPress .com platform, I purchased the domain africandiasporaphd.com to take symbolic ownership over #ADPhD content and digital space. The same year, I created a Facebook page and Twitter, Pinterest, and Tumblr accounts, connecting each through strategic social media automation using IFTTT (If This Then That) and twitterfeed (now dlvr.it) feeds. These services operated through the use of "triggers"; as blog posts were created on African Diaspora, Ph.D., IFTTT and twitterfeed reposted parallel elements of the post (post content, featured images, hyperlinks) to its sibling social networks. Expanding the project also included expanding personnel. Howard University professor and historian of slavery and memory in Brazil Ana Lucia Araujo joined #ADPhD in 2012 as a Facebook administrator. Wayne State University professor and historian of African American history and politics Kidada Williams joined as a Tumblr administrator the same year. Araujo's expertise in histories of slavery and memory in Brazil and facility with French, Spanish, and Portuguese played a significant role in my desire to bring her onto the project. Williams's expertise in histories of Reconstruction and African Americans' postemancipation struggles for rights and dignity likewise played a significant role in her appointment. Even further, and perhaps more relevant, however, was the role both played as visible, dynamic, and social media–literate scholars with demonstrated histories of speaking back in public and online to issues of racial justice and violence, inclusive of gendered racial violence, violence against queer people of African descent, reparations, and prison abolition. Araujo and Williams demonstrated commitment to history as fighting gendered racial violence and other legacies of bondage captured the mission behind #ADPhD.

These early changes made to #ADPhD also index changes in my life as a scholar and researcher. In 2012, I graduated from my doctoral program, having navigated an anemic job market and as the second woman of African descent to complete the PhD in history at my institution. African

Diaspora, Ph.D.'s reconstitution occurred as I completed graduate training in the study of slavery and African diaspora. The affective labor of engaging archives of slavery and exploring published work in a field of study I hoped to become proficient in—and a profession I planned to enter—shaped the name of the project and, for better or worse, its trajectory. At the same time, community accountability, transformative justice, radical womyn of color, and black feminist thought continued to shape my engagement in digital spaces, shifting the scope, visibility, and possibility of the blog.[17] For instance, I did not intend to request university or corporate funding for #ADPhD, out of concern about the ways university sponsorship might influence editorial control. Digital humanities or digital history models for creating rich research content while maintaining autonomous authorship and centering issues of social justice, in 2012, remained few and far between. Inspiration included then well-established digital black studies and cultural projects like *New Black Man* operated by Mark Anthony Neal (Duke University), the film and visual culture blog *Shadow and Act*, and H-AfroAm, the eBlackStudies listserv curated by Abdul Alkalimat. And yet I was not the only one grappling with these issues in the wake of digital humanities' growing relevance and feminism's taut relationship with the Ivory Tower. The emergence of several other digital projects, concurrent but disconnected from my own, suggests issues of inclusion, justice, and dismantling the ivory tower would occupy a new generation of scholars for years to come.[18]

What's So Radical about an Oracle?

The digital landscape changed dramatically after 2012. In April 2012, the TV series *Scandal* debuted with Kerry Washington as a black female leading lady in an affair with the president of the United States. As a character, Olivia Pope was likened to Sally Hemings by some, but black queer and femme-identified social media users followed each episode online, live-tweeting and thereby debating and curating the terms of how to engage a high-profile woman of color as the world watched. Obama inaugurated his second term in office, bringing with it and continuing complicated conversations about what having a "First Black Family" would mean for a progressive coalition of poor, young, queer, nonwhite voters in the United States. Most impactful, however, particularly for people of color, would be the murder of Trayvon Martin on February 26, 2012.[19] The rapid circulation of images of Martin, alive and smiling, by family members, organizers, and everyday people on social media challenged his shooter George Zimmerman's representation of Martin as a "suspicious" figure in a dark hoodie. The social media outcry led to a Change.org petition and rallies around the country under the theme of "Million Hoodie March." Zimmerman's acquittal in 2013 prompted Alicia Garza to post, in a Facebook note, "Black people. I love you. I love us. Our lives matter. Black Lives Matter." With Patrisse Cullors and Opal Tometi, the phrase Black Lives Matter became a hashtag (#BlackLives-Matter) and a movement.[20] The next August, Mike Brown would be shot in Ferguson, Missouri, his body left for over four hours in the street.

In 2013, after giving a talk about African Diaspora, Ph.D. at an elite Midwest university, one of the attendees asked me: "What is radical about ADPHD?" Asked about radicalism in the wake of one devastating death and before the tide rolled in on yet another, I offer this question here, not with an answer, but as an oracle. In a world turned upside through alternative facts, black digital practice and truncated memory of people in power appear to occupy rocky but seemingly approximate terrain. To put it another way, even as Garza, Cullors, and Tometi created discursive space to challenge police violence against black people, and the acceptance of black death by media, martial, and legal authorities, Garza was also forced to write a "herstory" of #BlackLivesMatter that centered the black women, particularly the queer black women who created it. Historical erasure, like death, happened in an instant. Digital media, in this case, the *Feminist Wire*, created space to speak back to both black death and erasure of (queer) black women's theoretical framings. The *Feminist Wire*, however, did not inaugurate dissent. These strivings for black lives to matter—all black lives and livelihoods, queer, trans, and genders yet to be created inclusive—predate the digital, stretch back to those "scarcely corroded balls and chains" of sinking women, children, and men, climb up and beyond to the stars.

Four years after #ADPhD expanded, newly appointed secretary of housing and urban development (HUD) Dr. Ben Carson stood before HUD to express his enthusiasm for his new duties. On March 6, 2016, in his first remarks as secretary of HUD, Carson stated:

> That's what America is about, a land of dreams and
> opportunity. There were other
> i
> m
> m
> i
> g
> r
> a
> n
> t
> s
> who came here in the bottom of slave ships . . .

—these lowest depths, these deeps—

Carson's remarks transposing enslaved chattel into (voluntary) immigrants were the most recent in a series of remarks issued by the new administration indexing a fake history of slavery. Black diasporic historians and historical production in the digital realm disrupts fake history's dangerously reductive readings of black life and culture. As Ben Carson's words reverberated across the Internet, the African American Intellectual History Society's award-winning blog *Black Perspectives* hosted a forum on the very experience Carson so casually reconstructed. From March 6 to 11, 2018, in an online roundtable, scholars discussed Sowande' Mustakeem's award-winning book, *Slavery at Sea: Terror, Sex, and Sickness in the Middle Passage*. Rejecting Carson's premise that enslaved Africans' experiences in any way resembled those of European immigrants, *Slavery at Sea* deconstructed the world of the Middle Passage, demystifying it as a space with actors, actions, and history, even as those actions and that history revealed the horrific process of manufacturing human beings into slaves. On writing her book, Sowande' Mustakeem, like Foreman, noted:

> **As I moved throughout New York City, Rhode Island, Liverpool, London, Jamaica, and South Carolina,**
>
> *among*
> *a*
> *host*
> *of other*
> *former ports*
>
> **within the terrain of at least 25 archives, I let the sources and their ghosts lead me.**[21]

Like Glissant, led by the dead beneath the sea, or Spruce and Ruffin seeking hidden histories, Foreman and Mustakeem describe historical practice as being led by ghosts, acknowledging and following texts with heavy pasts into spiritual presents. Their narration of their research process does not cleave to the logic of the biopolitical, the terrestrial, or the university. Their praxis moves beyond to what Yomaira Figueroa has described as "worlds otherwise."[22] It demands mourning and witnessing, then offers a call and challenge. Having found fugitives in the machine of bondage, diving deep in archives where Africans and people of African descent were not meant to appear as more than alienated produce, the methodologies Foreman and Mustakeem employ move them as researchers beyond the landlocked imperial archive, past the binary between natural and supernatural, sacred and profane, and into some outer space where black life despite death resides. Instead of fake history, these interventions ~~fake~~ make history and bring news of where to find the ghosts of slavery.

In 2016, the African American Intellectual Historical Society, at its second annual conference, hosted a digital humanities workshop with Alexis Pauline Gumbs and Julia Sangodore Roxanne Wallace. Greeting participants with music and poetry, Gumbs and Wallace asked guests to "activate the oracle," to unseat their relationship to the digital from the hyperdrive of the job market, tenure, and excessive evaluative structures of the Ivory Tower. As the work of activating the oracle suggests, black digital humanities must take up the challenge of remaking the world with stardust more sacred than these landlocked, machine-enhanced pursuits. The challenge for digital humanities and black intellectual history will not be how well we plant our flag in what is understood to be radical at any time or place. It will be in continuing to reconcile living, flesh and blood communities of color with tools for making black lives matter. It will be immersing ourselves in histories of violence and the poetics of movement making and world-building, embracing ephemerality and species-wide coalition as the ingredients of a necessary future. In the wake of Hurricane Katrina and speaking to grassroots organizing along the Gulf Coast and Mississippi Delta, black scholar and theoretician Clyde Woods noted freedom dreams do not exist solely on the surface of political, social, or civic life. To tap into the depths of black resistance against racial terror requires a willingness to "explore the subterranean caverns that shelter the wellsprings of dreams during the seasons when hope can't be found."[23] Black digital practice must be both a dream of new skies and a desire to swim toward new worlds.

Notes

1. Button Poetry, *Gabriel Ramirez—"On Realizing I Am Black" (NPS 2015)*, accessed April 28, 2018, https://www.youtube.com/watch?v=YEQHRs_8F08. See also https://buttonpoetry.com/gabriel-ramirez-on-realizing-i-am-black-100k-views/.

2. Compare discussions of stars and seas in Octavia Butler, M. Jacqui Alexander, and Omise'eke Tinsley, to name a few.

3. Sylvia Wynter, "Unsettling the Coloniality of Being/Power/Truth/Freedom: Towards the Human, after Man, Its Overrepresentation—an Argument," *CR: The New Centennial Review* 3 (2003): 257–337; Sylvia Wynter, "1492: A New World View," in *Race, Discourse, and the Origin of the Americas: A New World View*, ed. Vera Lawrence Hyatt and Rex Nettleford (Washington, DC: Smithsonian Institution Press, 1995), 5–57.

4. Alexis Pauline Gumbs, "Seek the Roots: An Immersive and Interactive Archive of Black Feminist Practice," *Feminist Collections* 32, no. 1 (2011): 17–20.

5. Jessica Marie Johnson and Kismet Nuñez, "Alter Egos and Infinite Literacies, Part III: How to Build a Real Gyrl in 3 Easy Steps," *Black Scholar: Journal of Black Studies and Research* 45, no .4 (2015): 47–61.

6. Ashleigh Greene Wade, "'New Genres of Being Human': World Making through Viral Blackness," *Black Scholar: Journal of Black Studies and Research* 47, no. 3 (July 3, 2017): 33–44.

7. Marisa J. Fuentes. *Dispossessed Lives: Enslaved Women, Violence, and the Archive* (Philadelphia: University of Pennsylvania Press, 2016); Lisa Ze Winters, *The Mulatta Concubine: Terror, Intimacy, Freedom, and Desire in the Black Transatlantic* (Athens: University of Georgia Press, 2016); Treva B. Lindsey and Jessica Marie Johnson, "Searching for Climax: Black Erotic Lives in Slavery and Freedom," *Meridians: Feminism, Race, Transnationalism* 12 (2014): 169–95.

8. Clyde Woods, "Katrina's World: Blues, Bourbon, and the Return to the Source," *American Quarterly* 61, no. 3 (September 23, 2009): 427–53.

9. Katherine McKittrick, "I Entered the Lists . . . Diaspora Catalogues: The List, the Unbearable Territory, and Tormented Chronologies—Three Narratives and a Weltanschauung," *Xcp: Cross Cultural Poetics* 17 (2007): 7–29.

10. Rasheedah Phillips, "Constructing a Theory and Practice of Black Quantum Futurism. Part 1," in *Black Quantum Futurism: Theory & Practice, Vol. 1*, ed. Rasheedah Phillips (Philadelphia: House of Future Sciences Books, 2015).

11. Francille Rusan Wilson, *The Segregated Scholars: Black Social Scientists and the Creation of Black Labor Studies, 1890–1959* (Charlottesville: University of Virginia Press, 2006), 2.

12. http://africandiasporaphd.com.

13. Susana Loza, "Hashtag Feminism, #SolidarityIsForWhiteWomen, and the Other #FemFuture," *Ada: A Journal of Gender, New Media, and Technology* (blog), July 7, 2014, http://adanewmedia.org/2014/07/issue5-loza/. See also Johnson and Nuñez, "Alter Egos and Infinite Literacies.

14. Moya Bailey and Alexis Pauline Gumbs, "We Are the Ones We've Been Waiting For," *Ms.*, 2010; "Get These Women of Color to the AMC!," Allied Media Projects, May 9, 2008, https://alliedmedia.org/news/2008/05/09/get-these-women-color-amc.

15. Mandy Van Deven and Julie Kubala, eds., "Polyphonic Feminisms: Acting in Concert." http://sfonline.barnard.edu/polyphonic/index.htm.

16. In 2007, the guide was hosted on University of Maryland's servers. It is archived and available for download here: https://github.com/jmjafrx/adphd/tree/master/atlanticafricaresearch.

17. Even as that landscape also changed in powerful ways. For a historical reflection on these changes, see Jessica Marie Johnson, "#FemFuture, History and Loving Each Other Harder," *Diaspora Hypertext, the Blog*, posted April 12, 2013, http://dh.jmjafrx.com/2013/04/12/femfuture-history-loving-each-other-harder/.

18. A sampling of work—#transformDH starts in 2011, Mobile Homecoming project is rolling in 2012, Dismantling the Ivory Tower Network Gathering at AMC in 2013, Crunk Feminists founded in 2010, Feminist Wire founded in 2011, The Public Archive in 2010, AAIHS in 2014.

19. "Trayvon Martin: 15 Facts You Need to Know about Case of Teen Shot in Sanford, Florida—TheGrio," March 19, 2012, https://thegrio.com/2012/03/19/trayvon-martin-15-facts-you-need-to-know-about-teen-shot-in-sanford-florida/. For those of us online for some time, Trayvon's death felt very much part of the aftermath of Troy Davis being executed, despite multiple appeals and media attention to his case, on September 21, 2011.

20. Alicia Garza, "A Herstory of the #BlackLivesMatter Movement by Alicia Garza," *Feminist Wire* (blog), October 7, 2014, http://www.thefeministwire.com/2014/10/blacklivesmatter-2/; Elizabeth Day, "#BlackLivesMatter: The Birth of a New Civil Rights Movement," *Observer*, July 19, 2015, sec. US news, http://www.theguardian.com/world/2015/jul/19/blacklivesmatter-birth-civil-rights-movement.

21. Sowande' Mustakeem, "Ghosts of the Atlantic: An Author's Response—AAIHS," *African American Intellectual History Society Blog* (blog), March 11, 2017, http://www.aaihs.org/ghosts-of-the-atlantic-an-authors-response/.

22. Yomaira Figueroa, *Decolonial Diasporas: Radical Mappings of Afro-Atlantic Literature* (Evanston, IL: Northwestern University Press, 2020).

23. Woods, "Katrina's World."

CONTRIBUTORS

LESLIE M. ALEXANDER is an associate professor of History and African American Studies at Arizona State University. She is the author of *African or American?: Black Identity and Political Activism in New York City, 1784–1861*; and *Fear of a Black Republic: African Americans, Haiti, and the Birth of Black Internationalism*. She is also coeditor of *We Shall Independent Be: African American Place Making and the Struggle to Claim Space in the United States and the Encyclopedia of African American History*. Alexander is the recipient of numerous awards, including the Ford Foundation Senior Fellowship.

DAVARIAN L. BALDWIN is the Paul E. Raether Distinguished Professor of American Studies and Founding Director of the Smart Cities Research Lab at Trinity College in Hartford. He is the author of *In the Shadow of the Ivory Tower: How Universities Are Plundering Our Cities* and *Chicago's New Negroes: Modernity, the Great Migration, and Black Urban Life* and coeditor of *Escape From New York: The New Negro Renaissance beyond Harlem*.

RICHARD D. BENSON II is an associate professor in the Education Department at Spelman College. He is the author of *Fighting for our Place in the Sun: Malcolm X and the Radicalization of the Black Student Movement 1960-1973*.

ALEXIS BRODERICK is an assistant professor of history at the University of New Hampshire.

CHARISSE BURDEN-STELLY is an assistant professor of Africana studies and political science at Carleton College and the Visiting Scholar with the Race and Capitalism Project at the University of Chicago. She is the coauthor of *W. E. B. Du Bois: A Life in American History*.

BRANDON R. BYRD is an associate professor of History at Vanderbilt University. He is the author of *The Black Republic: African Americans and the Fate of Haiti*.

VINCENT CARRETTA is professor emeritus of English at the University of Maryland, College Park. In addition to numerous articles and reviews, he has published two books on verbal and visual Anglophone political satire, as well as authoritative editions of the works of eighteenth-century transatlantic authors of African descent. His books include *Equiano, the African: Biography of a Self-Made Man*; *The Life and Letters of Philip Quaque, the First African Anglican Missionary*, coedited with Ty M. Reese; and *Phillis*

Wheatley: Biography of a Genius in Bondage. The Modern Language Association of America awarded his *The Writings of Phillis Wheatley* an Honorable Mention for its Prize for a Scholarly Edition.

KELLIE CARTER JACKSON is the Knafel Assistant Professor of the Humanities in the Department of Africana Studies at Wellesley College. She is author of *Force and Freedom: Black Abolitionists and the Politics of Violence*, which was awarded, among other honors, the James H. Broussard Best First Book Prize. She is the coeditor of *Reconsidering Roots: Race, Politics, and Memory*.

N. D. B CONNOLLY is an associate professor of history at Johns Hopkins University, where he occupies the Herbert Baxter Adams Chair and directs the program in Racism, Immigration, and Citizenship. His book *A World More Concrete: Real Estate and the Remaking of Jim Crow South Florida* (2014) received awards from the Urban History Association, the Southern Historical Association, and the Organization of American Historians, among other organizations.

DEIRDRE COOPER OWENS is the Charles and Linda Wilson Professor in the History of Medicine and director of the Humanities in Medicine program at the University of Nebraska–Lincoln. Her book *Medical Bondage: Race, Gender and the Origins of American Gynecology* (2018) won the Organization of American Historians Darlene Clark Hine Book award.

MARLENE L. DAUT is a professor at the University of Virginia. She is the author of *Tropics of Haiti: Race and the Literary History of the Haitian Revolution in the Atlantic World* and *Baron de Vastey and the Origins of Black Atlantic Humanism* and the coeditor of *Haitian Revolutionary Fictions: An Anthology*.

SHANNON C. EAVES is an assistant professor of African American history at the College of Charleston.

THAVOLIA GLYMPH is a professor of history and law at Duke University. She is the author of *Out of the House of Bondage: The Transformation of the Plantation Household* and *The Women's Fight: The Civil War's Battles for Home, Freedom, and Nation*.

ALEXIS PAULINE GUMBS is the cofounder of Mobile Homecoming Trust in Durham, North Carolina, and a 2020–2021 National Humanities Fellow. She is the author of *Undrowned: Black Feminist Lessons from Marine Mammals*; *Dub: Finding Ceremony*; *M Archive: After the End of the World*; and *Spill: Scenes of Black Feminist Fugitivity* and coeditor of the anthology *Revolutionary Mothering: Love on the Front Lines*.

CHRISTY HYMAN is a PhD student in the program of Geography at the University of Nebraska–Lincoln.

JESSICA MARIE JOHNSON is an assistant professor of history at Johns Hopkins University. She is the author of *Wicked Flesh: Black Women, Intimacy, and Freedom in the Atlantic World* and coauthor of *Debates in DH: Computational Humanities.*

JEFFREY R. KERR-RITCHIE is a professor of history and director of Graduate Studies at Howard University. He has authored *Freedpeople in the Tobacco South, Virginia, 1860–1900*; *Rites of August First: Emancipation in the Black Atlantic World*; *Freedom's Seekers: Essays on Comparative Emancipation*; and *Rebellious Passage: The Creole Revolt and America's Coastal Slave Trade.*

JESSICA MILLWARD is an associate professor in the Department of History and Core Faculty member of African American studies at the University of California, Irvine. She is the author of *Finding Charity's Folk: Enslaved and Free Black Women in Maryland* as well as numerous essays and articles.

MARISA PARHAM is a professor of English at the University of Maryland, director for the African American Digital Humanities initiative, and associate director for the Maryland Institute for Technology in the Humanities.

RUSSELL RICKFORD is an associate professor of history at Cornell University. He is the author of *We Are an African People: Independent Education, Black Power, and the Radical Imagination*, which received the Liberty Legacy Foundation Award from the Organization of American Historians.

WILLIAM STURKEY is an associate professor of history at the University of North Carolina at Chapel Hill. He is the author of *Hattiesburg: An American City in Black and White* and the coeditor of *To Write in the Light of Freedom: The Newspapers of the 1964 Mississippi Freedom Schools.*

QUITO SWAN is a professor of African American and African Diaspora Studies at Indiana University, Bloomington. He is the author of *Pauulu's Diaspora: Black Internationalism and Environmental Justice, which* won the 2021 Pauli Murray Book Prize from the African American Intellectual History Association and the 2021 National Endowment for the Humanities Fellowship Book Award Prize, and *Black Power in Bermuda: The Struggle for Decolonization.*

MICHAEL O. WEST is a professor of African American studies, history, and African studies at Pennsylvania State University. He is the author of *The Rise of an African Middle Class: Colonial Zimbabwe, 1898–1965* and scores of journal articles and book chapters. He is also the coeditor of *Out of One, Many Africas: Reconstructing the Study and Meaning of Africa* and *From Toussaint to Tupac: The Black International since the Age of Revolution.*